EGYPT BEFORE
THE PHARAOHS

EGYPT BEFORE

MICHAEL·A·HOFFMAN

THE PHARAOHS

The Prehistoric Foundations

of Egyptian Civilization

DORSET PRESS • NEW YORK

Grateful acknowledgment is made to the following for permission to reprint previously published material:

Cambridge University Press: Excerpt from *Celebrations of Death* by Peter Metcalf and W. R. Huntington, 1979.

Egypt Exploration Society: Excerpts from *Rock Drawings of Southern Upper Egypt* by Dr. H. A. Winkler (Egypt Exploration Society, 1938), vols. 1 and 2. Excerpts from "Walter Brian Emery," *The Journal of Egyptian Archaeology,* 57, pp. 190–201. By courtesy of the Egypt Exploration Society, London.

Chris B. Giepen: Extracts from *Petrie's Naqada Excavation* by Elise Baumgartel (Quatritch: 1970).

Harper & Row, Publishers, Inc.: Excerpt from *The Archaeologist at Work* by Robert F. Heizer, ed., Harper and Brothers, 1959, pp. 108–10.

Dr. William P. McHugh, G.A.I. Consultants, Inc.: Excerpt from dissertation titled *Cultural Adaptation in the Southeastern Libyan Desert*, written at the University of Wisconsin, 1971.

Oxford University Press: Excerpts from *Cemeteries of Armant I*, by Sir Robert Mond and Oliver H. Myers (2 vols., 1937), pp. vii, viii, 49, 267, and 268. By permission of Oxford University Press.

Penguin Books Ltd.: Excerpts from *Archaic Egypt* by Walter B. Emery, pp. 21, 101–102, 105, 192, 235, 243, 246. Copyright © 1961 by the Estate of Walter B. Emery. Reprinted by permission of Penguin Books Ltd.

Royal Anthropological Institute of Great Britain and Ireland: Excerpts from "Recent Excavations in the Fayum" by Gertrude Caton-Thompson, MAN (old series), XXVIII, 1928, pp. 109–11.

Southern Methodist University Press: Excerpts from *Prehistory of Nubia* by Fred Wendorf, pp. 315, 954, 959, and four tables redrawn here by Michael Hoffman. Copyright 1968 by Southern Methodist University Press. Reprinted by permission of the publisher.

University of California Press: Excerpt from *Ancient Egyptian Literature, Vol. 1: The Old and Middle Kingdoms* by M. Lichtheim, 1973, pp. 20, 66, 87, 90, and 228. Reprinted by permission of the University of California Press.

University of Chicago Press: Excerpt from *First Report of the Prehistoric Survey Expedition*, OIC, no. 3, 1928, by K. S. Sanford and W. J. Arkell, pp. 28–30, 36, 52. By permission of Oriental Institute, University of Chicago.

This edition published by Dorset Press a division of Marboro Books Corporation, by arrangement with Alfred A. Knopf, Inc.

1990 Dorset Press

ISBN 0-88029-457-4
(formerly ISBN 0-394-41049-1)

Printed in the United States of America

M 9 8 7 6 5 4 3 2 1

To my father,

DONALD B. HOFFMAN

ILLUSTRATIONS

TABLES

ILLUSTRATIONS

Unless otherwise noted, all photographs and illustrations are by Michael A. Hoffman.

PREFACE

THERE ARE two ancient Egypts—the Egypt of the pharaohs and the Egypt of prehistory. Knowledge of the first has become commonplace in our society thanks to the massive pyramids of legendary autocrats like Khufu and the rich, golden treasures of the boy-king Tutankhamon. The historical epoch is both shorter and easier to understand. Its kings and their monuments stand like familiar signposts pointing the way to the past. On the other hand, prehistory is like a patchwork quilt with great segments omitted by the seamstress and its fabric ravaged by countless eons of neglect.

Even time itself, that familiar organizer of our thoughts and lives, loses its secure, linear shape when it crosses the borders of history. Five hundred years before the birth of Christ the Greek philosopher Heraclitus wrote, "There is nothing permanent except change"—a view compatible with that of the prehistorian who, though he admires the secure chronology and linear progression of historical time, turns ultimately to the nonlinear approach of Heraclitus, comprehending our dimmest past as a shifting balance of opposites, a complex system of interrelationships between man and his environment.

Ironically, despite the 150-year existence of the science of Egyptology and widespread public interest in the spectacular discoveries, scholarly writings, and occasionally heated feuds of archaeologists, no comprehensive account of Egyptian prehistory has appeared to date. In contrast to the relatively coherent and well-ordered succession of thirty-two historical dynasties stretching from the unification of the Egyptian state around 3100 B.C. to Cleopatra's unfortunate encounter with the asp in 31 B.C., Egypt's prehistoric past is generally portrayed as a series of disjointed segments whose story is an unimportant prelude to the age of the pharaohs. Today, with new archaeological information accumulating rapidly in technical journals, monographs, and museum storerooms, out-of-date interpretations and downright misconceptions still dominate both the popular and professional views of Egyptian prehistory.

This state of affairs not only deprives the world of the complete record of one of its earliest ancient civilizations, but obscures new discoveries that illuminate some of the most important cultural processes of the human career—the origins of civilization and the state, the beginnings of agriculture and animal domestication, the perfection of a rich hunting, fishing, and gathering technology and the evolution of a system of values and beliefs that nourished the roots of ancient Egyptian culture thousands of years before the first pharaoh ascended his throne.

"No attempt has ever been made," wrote the great Egyptologist James Henry Breasted in 1906, "to collect and present all the sources of Egyptian history in a modern language" (Breasted 1906, I: vii). Although Breasted himself accomplished that task with his six-volume *Records of Ancient Egypt* and a more popular account, *A History of Ancient Egypt*, no analogous summaries have ever been written for Egyptian prehistory. Despite important discoveries and mountains of information produced by numerous international expeditions to rescue the archaeological treasures of Nubia from the floodwaters of the new Aswan High Dam, no general account of the prehistory of Egypt is yet available. Following the lead of Breasted, it is my aim to collect much of the archaeological information on the prehistory of Egypt—information scattered through hundreds of articles, monographs, and books—and to integrate the minutiae into a general account of the prehistoric development of ancient Egyptian culture from the earliest stirrings of humanity nearly a million years ago in the Lower Palaeolithic to the final political struggles which catapulted Egypt into the arena of history about 3100 B.C.

If we consider that Breasted was able to offer a general account of ancient Egyptian history seventy years ago, it may seem paradoxical that it has taken so long to attempt the same task for prehistory—the eons of humanity's past that stretch back beyond the dawn of literacy. The first general treatment of Egyptian prehistory was published by Sir William Flinders Petrie in 1920. Although *Prehistoric Egypt* and an accompanying book of plates did present fresh insights into the later periods of Egypt's prehistoric past, it totally ignored the Palaeolithic era (in Egypt about 700,000–5500 B.C.) and concentrated on Petrie's own finds. The next summary, Elise Baumgartel's *The Cultures of Prehistoric Egypt* published between 1947 and 1960, suffered from the same myopia that had plagued Petrie's pioneering account. Baumgartel compounded the problem, however, in that she not only ignored the Palaeolithic but focused on developments in Upper Egypt at the expense of important discoveries in the Delta and the Fayum. Émile Massoulard's *Préhistoire et protohistoire de l'Égypte* (1949) is perhaps the most complete review under one cover of all prehistoric research conducted in Egypt and was partially duplicated by a several-volume work, *Les Peuples de l'Orient méditerranéen*, by E. Drioton and J. Vandier, which appeared in 1953. In 1970 Baumgartel published an updated account of "Predynastic Egypt" and Kurt Butzer discussed Egyptian paleo-environment in the third edition of the *Cambridge Ancient History*. Unfortunately, these accounts are not integrated and were often somewhat outdated by the time they were published. Published posthumously, in 1965, W. C. Hayes's incomplete synthesis *Most Ancient Egypt*, even in its unfinished form, is one of the most useful works of its kind and a monument to the versatility, thoroughness, and intellectual breadth of its author. Its principal limitation is that it appeared just before the impact of the Aswan Dam studies could be incorporated into the syntheses of Pleistocene archaeology. Three important summaries have appeared since 1968 as the result of work done under the auspices of Fred Wendorf in the Sudan and southern Egypt: a two-volume work entitled *The Prehistory of Nubia* (1968), a single volume edited by Wendorf and Marks, *Problems in Prehistory: North Africa and the Levant* (1975), and a recent tome edited by Wendorf and Schild, *Prehistory of the Nile Valley* (1976). While much of the material contained in these works is revolutionary, it tends to focus on the earlier, Palaeolithic phases of Egyptian prehistory and is aimed at the specialist. Thanks to such valuable and timely technical analyses by archaeologists working in Egypt and the Sudan, Egyptian prehistorians finally find themselves today in a position similar to that occupied by Breasted seventy years ago—confronted by a huge amount of undigested information that needs desperately to be culled and summarized and related to older work before we can go on to investigate new horizons of the past.

If there is now a clear and recognized mandate for a general prehistory of Egypt, the problem of how to organize such an account is not so easily solved. To those familiar with the literate prose of Breasted, or the epic accounts of Thucydides, Gibbons, or Toynbee, prehistorians often appear overly dry and pedantic—even to each other! All too often we either bore our audiences with laundry lists of countless archaeological sites or preach to them like modern Savonarolas, denouncing or ignoring all that has gone before in the name of a narrowly based conception of scientific rigor. Perhaps this is why it is painful to read, let alone understand many contemporary prehistorians. As one historian colleague of mine once quipped, "Because you prehistorians deal with preliterate cultures is no excuse to write *illiterate* books!" Although, as this remark implies, some of the differences between history and prehistory may stem from the traditional educational contrasts between literary humanism and materialistic science, the real culprit operates at a much deeper and more intellectually subtle level. The reason that prehistorians do not write good history in the manner of Breasted is not only because they do not have the same educational background as historians but because they often deal with different types of information. Also, the basic tools of our trades usually differ—epigraphy and historiography in the case of history, archaeology and ecology in the case of prehistory.

Finally, prehistorians routinely consider larger blocks of time than historians, and because their dating techniques do not allow them to stipulate the year or even the decade or century of a particular find, they must perforce be more "impersonal" about the past and a good bit more vague and general about the causes and effects of particular events than the oft-envied historian. These underlying differences then will have important consequences for the way that we approach the prehistory of Egypt.

Following the contrasts I have drawn between history and prehistory, the fact that prehistory was still in its infancy in Egypt when Egyptology attained maturity has had an important impact on the progress of research and, ultimately, upon our knowledge of the past. Modern archaeology in Egypt is an outgrowth of Western science. In Europe the first stirrings of what can be called scientific antiquarianism or scientific prehistory can be detected in the late seventeenth and early eighteenth centuries. As long as prehistorians investigated peoples and traditions at least mentioned in the ancient literature of the West (the Greek and Roman classics or the Bible) there was little opposition to the study of "Barbarians." But when some pioneers began to argue that man had existed for countless hundreds of thousands of years, the orthodox ecclesiastical view that human history began in 4004 B.C. was threatened. As we shall see in Chapter 3, it was only after the Biblical "time barrier" had been shattered by prehistoric archaeologists like Boucher de Perthes in the mid-nineteenth century, that there could be prehistoric archaeology in Egypt. Long before this time, the presence of numerous Biblical references to ancient Egyptians and nasty pharaohs had sanctioned the science of Egyptology. The strikingly different experience of prehistory and prehistorians, beginning as an "antiestablishment" discipline, has left a peculiar impact on our history. Unlike Egyptologists, prehistorians of Egypt do not now and never have possessed a conscious unity of purpose. Egyptologists may study different periods, but they all deal critically with the texts and with the fabric of a defined society. Prehistorians, on the other hand, have tended to be identified, grouped, and isolated according to the particular period which they study. As we have seen, what Petrie meant by prehistory was far different from what Wendorf means by the term. Contemporary prehistorians, investigating different periods, such as the Predynastic and Palaeolithic, seldom if ever attend the same conventions as their third cousins in Egyptology, nor do they usually publish in the same journals. For this reason, the history of the discipline, and of research, assumes great significance for understanding Egyptian prehistory. For Egyptian prehistory is a collection of individual researchers, not, like Egyptology, a discipline whose members talk and dispute regularly with one another. Thus, in our account of the prehistory of Egypt, individual excavators, their foibles, finds, and interpretations will be as important as the material which they have unearthed.

As a sign or perhaps a reflection of the newness of the field, it is still not possible to talk about consensus of opinion or even of a single shared sentiment about how prehistory should be done in Egypt. In tracing the story of Egyptian prehistory, therefore, we will also be tracing the story of many of the archaeologists who made the discoveries, the mistakes, and breakthroughs which have placed us today on the threshold of a unified approach to Egypt's prehistoric past.

In addition to its comparative youth and lack of unity, Egyptian pre-history suffers from the more fragmented and incomplete nature of its basic information—the archaeological remains. Although Breasted could lament the "sad state of the historical records of ancient Egypt," he readily conceded that "papyri when mounted between hermetically sealed glass plates survive indefinitely" (Breasted 1906, I: 16-17)—an accomplishment never quite attainable with archaeological evidence. In marked contrast to the task of the copyist or translator of ancient papyri who ultimately preserves the record of the past in a reasonably exact facsimile of its original form, the work of the archaeologist is, by its very nature, destructive, requiring us to literally pick apart the remains of the past in order to understand them. Unlike Breasted, who could usually return to the documents and monuments and recopy and retrans-late their inscriptions, old archaeological sites are often lost forever. A site or a portion of a site once excavated can survive only through the records kept by its excavators. If, as has occurred all too frequently in the past, an archaeologist neglected to record thoroughly and publish everything he removed, then it is irretrievably lost. It has taken archae-ology a long time to learn this lesson, often after bitter experience. In a sense, archaeology has grown up in Egypt, beginning with the depre-dations of adventurers and exploiters like Belzoni and Vyse in the early nineteenth century and coming of age with the triumphs of Petrie, Reisner, and Carter. But progress has not been continuous nor com-petence spread equally throughout the profession. Ironically, some of the best archaeological sites are now lost not because of the wanton looters, greedy peddlers of antiquities, and swarms of promoters who plagued Egypt throughout much of the nineteenth century, but rather because of self-proclaimed archaeologists, incompetent in the field and dedicated more to the spectacular museum find or academic pedantry than to science, who excavated sites badly or published finds incom-pletely. If prehistory often strikes the critical reader as a thing of bits and pieces or as being overly attendant on the importance of individual artifacts, it is, as we shall see in examining many problems and contro-versies in Egyptian prehistory, because an excavator has taken his task too lightly and failed to record and publish the total context of his material. Ultimately, it is our concern with the context of material ob-jects that sets the tone of archaeology.

Although we share with historians a fundamental interest in reconstructing man's past, prehistorians have to depend much more on the often unimpressive scraps of material evidence discarded by our ancestors in their camps, towns, cemeteries, and garbage heaps. To us, the key to the study of humanity's past revolves around the investigation of material remains, while to the historian a critical analysis of written documents ideally constitutes the proper study of mankind. It is only logical, therefore, that the principal tool of prehistory is archaeology—a science that employs special techniques and methods to recover and interpret the *material* remains of the human past. Because of our concern with the commonplace, the ordinary, often we have been dubbed "ditch diggers with degrees" or "yesterday's garbage men." Strictly speaking, archaeologists do not always confine their activities to prehistoric periods, but deal with any job that involves recovering and using the material remains of culture to reconstruct the past, regardless of whether that past existed 50 years ago or 500,000 years ago. In point of fact, however, most are trained in prehistory or at least utilize techniques developed by prehistoric archaeologists. The reason for the precociousness of prehistoric archaeology is the relative poverty of the sites we study. Because archaeology is absolutely vital to prehistory (although merely an adjunct to history), prehistoric archaeologists characteristically try to push their scanty evidence as far as possible, and often a good deal farther.

In extracting from archaeological discoveries the maximum amount of information, we often turn to the natural and social sciences for additional clues to human behavior and in so doing have discovered that we are able to explore problems and seek solutions once thought comprehensible only through the use of written documents. For instance, prehistoric archaeologists now discuss freely ancient social organization, economy, and polity without so much as a scrap of contemporary documentary evidence. They dare to approach such formerly esoteric or speculative arguments thanks to a whole new battery of recording and dating techniques aimed at recreating more faithfully the original and total context of archaeological sites. Such reconstructions are still most successful, however, when documentary evidence can be projected backward into a late prehistoric or protohistoric era immediately prior to the introduction of literacy.

The protohistoric approach is aided and abetted by ethnohistory—the method of employing oral accounts and recorded behavior of contemporary peoples to reconstruct the life-style of their immediate ancestors. Ethnohistory combines the anthropological science of ethnography—the study and description of relatively contemporary, nonindustrial cultures —with traditional history. The ethnohistoric method is especially useful and relevant in a land like Egypt, where valuable details of everyday life are depicted in tomb paintings and house models which show activities like the harvesting and threshing of grain, the preparation of foodstuffs, crafts, games and social events like weddings, funerals, coronations, and festivals as well as by actual hieroglyphic documents that shed revealing if all too occasional light on aspects of ancient Egyptian social and economic organization. The fact that some physical aspects of Egyptian village life have changed but little over the millennia permits us to use controlled analogy and comparison employing ancient paintings and models, modern ethnographic parallels and archaeological remains to study the prehistory of Egyptian settlements. When we add to this wealth of potential information the uniquely arid climate of Egypt that has preserved a greater amount and variety of cultural and organic remains than the other great civilizations of antiquity, the possibility of extending by analogy ethnographic and ethnohistoric facts back into prehistoric times grows stronger all the time. The promise of such a multidisciplinary approach to the past is one of the great contributions of contemporary prehistoric archaeology to the study of man—a promise that offers a tangible link between the disciplines of history and prehistory and that ultimately constitutes one of the major themes of this book.

If, as Egyptologists tell us, the Third Dynasty (ca. 2700–2620 B.C.) shaped the canons of classical Egyptian art, architecture, politics, and religion for the succeeding 2,500 years, then the Predynastic era (ca. 5500–3100 B.C.) laid the foundations upon which the unique culture of pharaonic Egypt was built. Considering the close connection in time between Predynastic and Dynastic periods and the greater amount of archaeological research done in the later as opposed to earlier (Palaeolithic) phases of Egyptian prehistory, it is only natural that a large portion of this book is devoted to the Predynastic era. This does not mean, however, that the vast periods of time represented by the Palaeolithic will be ignored. As I have stated before, the aim of a general prehistory of Egypt is to overcome the barriers that have stood for so long between Palaeolithic and Predynastic specialists and thereby make available to students of ancient Egypt the rich heritage of all of Egyptian prehistory—a period that comprises 98 percent of mankind's experience in the Nile Valley. To even ponder such vast increments of time will transport us philosophically and intellectually from the bounds of hundreds or even thousands of years into a realm where magnitudes of tens and hundreds of thousands of years of human experience bend the familiar patterns by which we judge our short historical past and open to us horizons in time as vast as those revealed by Einstein's theory of relativity.

The first remains of man are crude stone artifacts, greatly disturbed by eons of climatic and geological change. For this reason, Palaeolithic archaeologists are more dependent on the natural sciences of geology, ecology, and climatology than their colleagues who work with later periods, like the Predynastic, from which a wealth of remains has been preserved. Without settlements, dwellings, tombs, large cemeteries, and art, Palaeolithic archaeologists have been limited until quite recently to the imperishable stone tools and what these artifacts, in combination with associated geological strata, tell us about technological responses to eons of climatic change. Thanks to the work of paleoanthropologists like the Leakeys in Kenya and to modern archaeologists in Egypt and the Sudan—Wendorf, Hassan, Phillips, and Marks—we have been given renewed hope of recovering additional traces of Palaeolithic culture so that the people of this long-forgotten era will no longer appear as fleeting shadows dimly mirrored on the Sahara's timeless sands, but as flesh-and-blood predecessors of later Egyptians, whose achievements were as respectable in their own way as the pyramids were in theirs. Our increasing ability to relate Palaeolithic cultures to the main threads of Egyptian culture-history and to treat Stone Age developments as necessary precursors of Egyptian civilization is an outgrowth of modern multi-disciplinary research that is bringing together for the first time scholars and scientists who study the diversity of the past in its myriad forms— from climate to architecture, from potsherd to pyramid. Far from studying the campsites, villages, towns, cemeteries, and tools of Palaeolithic and Predynastic Egyptians as things in themselves, quite apart from the spectacular developments and failures of pharaonic civilization, we are now beginning to realize the essential continuity that bridges the different epochs of prehistory and history, so that we now seek the over-arching cultural processes that led ultimately to the emergence of Egyptian civilization. Unlike traditional "historical" accounts, this book sees Egyptian civilization as an end rather than a beginning—a result of pre-historic development during which the first Egyptians adapted their societies to the evolving river Nile and to the radically changing climatic regimes that together forged a distinctively Egyptian cultural template.

An undertaking as extensive as this owes its appearance to a number of individuals. First and foremost, I would like to thank those relatives and friends who were encouraging at times when support was hard to come by. Many friends and colleagues have read and commented on parts of this manuscript, including Professor Klaus Baer, Professor Walter A. Fairservis, Professor William McHugh, Professor Fekri Hassan, and Stefan Bonfiglio. I owe an especial debt to Professor Baer for reading and commenting critically on the entire book while we were in Egypt in 1978. Professor Fairservis, who first made my career in Egyptian archaeology possible, has encouraged my efforts constantly and supported my research. Out of our long association in the field, in Egypt and Pakistan, have emerged several of the intellectual themes that appear throughout this book. I wish also to thank my editor, Angus Cameron, for his support and encouragement in organizing *Egypt Before the Pharaohs*. Throughout three years of preparation he and his wife Sheila have become valued friends.

Many of the illustrations have been made available by colleagues. I would like to thank Professors Fred Wendorf and Anthony Marks especially for their prompt and unstinting assistance in obtaining most of the photographs and line drawings used in Chapters 4, 5, and 6. Much of the original manuscript was typed by Ms. Lani Higgins of the University of Virginia, who offered useful comments on style and patiently dealt with the often odd array of names and spellings in the book. Generally speaking, in spelling the names of archaeological sites, I have followed historical rather than linguistic precedent, using the forms preferred by the original excavator or the writer most prominent in the original archaeological literature.

MICHAEL A. HOFFMAN

PART I

INTRODUCTION

1
DINNER ON THE NILE: EGYPTOLOGISTS, ARCHAEOLOGISTS, AND PREHISTORIANS

WHEN George Edward Stanhope Molyneux Herbert, fifth Earl of Carnarvon, gave a dinner party he did it in style. Although within months he would die of an infected mosquito bite while the international press wrote banner headlines about "Tut's curse," Lord Carnarvon was not to be denied his moment of glory. The recent discovery of the nearly intact tomb of Tutankhamon on November 4, 1922, had electrified the world and justified years of expensive and seemingly fruitless excavation. But Carnarvon's faith in archaeologist Howard Carter had finally been spectacularly justified and the wealthy peer was in an expansive mood as he entertained Carter's field crew and two visiting Egyptological firemen—James Henry Breasted of the University of Chicago and Sir Alan Gardiner of Oxford. The diners seemed little concerned by the prospect of the dead pharaoh's wrath as they sipped wine and posed for photographs around a small table set up in an adjacent tomb in the Valley of the Kings. Dressed in jackets and ties and waited on by two servants, the guests would have seemed more appropriate at an English hunt party than on an archaeological excavation. But the manners and customs of the day prescribed formality, and the strict rules of etiquette that separated European administrators, aristocrats, and professional men from native Egyptians were conscientiously observed—even in the field. Especially when dealing with a royal burial, archaeologists and their staffs affected the guise if not the manners of gentlemen. It was as if only an aristocrat could unearth the remains of another. Egypt in the early 1920's was still the undisputed domain of archaeologists and Egyptologists who established themselves by studying massive tombs and temples and who supervised large work crews on behalf of noble patrons like Lord Carnarvon, much in the way pharaoh's officials must have done thousands of years before.

Sitting at Lord Carnarvon's table, in the literal lap of luxury, Howard Carter cannot have avoided contrasting his present surroundings to the conditions that prevailed thirty years before when he first came to Egypt as a young man to work under Sir Flinders Petrie. If Lord Carnarvon's luncheon was a model of good form and upper-class English gentility, then Petrie's dining habits were, to put it kindly, notorious. The story is told that Sir Flinders would set out a number of cans of food at a convenient spot, open them, and then he and his wife would eat their fill. Each member of the crew was then expected to do the same. Petrie's frugal habits began in Egypt in 1880, when he lived in poverty in a small tomb near the Great Pyramid, but by the 1920's it was felt that the old master clung with unjustified tenacity to his Spartan ways. Still, the cranky Petrie remained convinced that the younger generation had grown soft and effete. Whether Petrie's longevity (he lived to be eighty-nine) had anything to do with these habits cannot be determined, but his rough life-style differed radically in table manners and methodology from those of the archaeologists and Egyptologists who attended Lord Carnarvon's party. Unlike most of his contemporaries, Petrie believed that worth was to be found in all manner of archaeological remains, from potsherd to pyramid, and was not averse to dirtying his hands in the refuse heaps and graveyards of the common man and his prehistoric antecedents. When he left Egypt in a huff in 1926 and moved his operations to Palestine, he left an archaeological community divided into prehistoric and historic (Egyptological) camps. For years afterward, few men, with the partial exception of Breasted, dared bridge the widening gulfs among Egyptologists, archaeologists, and prehistorians. Despite the fact that the disciplines made tremendous advances between the two world wars, there was no attempt to integrate findings or cooperate in solving common problems and, indeed, until recent times, the study of Egyptian culture-history remained the realm of specialists.

Almost half a century after Carnarvon dined with his guests in a tomb in the Valley of the Kings and after the redoubtable Flinders Petrie left Egypt, Professor Walter Fairservis, Jr., Director of the American Museum of Natural History Expedition to Hierakonpolis, gave a party in honor of Professor John Wilson of the University of Chicago. The staff gathered in the dining room of the remodeled Cook's steamer, *Fustat*, a ship that had carried her first passengers up the Nile when Carter and Carnarvon were celebrating the discovery of Tutankhamon's tomb. The *Fustat*'s boilers were gone, and the paddle wheel as well. She had long since been refitted as a floating houseboat to accommodate archaeologists working on the Aswan Dam project in the mid-1960's. In 1969, the ship played host to a totally new kind of expedition—one composed of Egyptologists, archaeologists, and prehistorians, working toward a common goal. Gone were the jackets and ties of the old days, along with the stingy meals and severe discipline of Petrie's camp. The staff was healthy and worked hard. John Wilson, who began his career in Egyptology under Breasted a year after the discovery of Tutankhamon's tomb and who would later succeed his mentor as Director of the Oriental

Institute, provided intellectual perspective and acted as a personal link
between the present and the past. Having just retired from the university,
Wilson was serving as consultant on the project and in his autobiography, *Thousands of Years*, reminisced fondly:

> The group was young and blessed with a combination of enthusiasm
> and businesslike methodology. They were much better trained than
> we had been at their age. Five nationalities were represented, but there
> was little of that polite wariness common on mixed digs of the past.
> The running series of little personal jokes was most intense at the
> expense of the youngest American man, but democratically included
> everybody and was enjoyed by everybody. *(Wilson 1972: 189)*

In addition to Wilson and Fairservis, the group included Egyptologist
Klaus Baer of the University of Chicago and a graduate student, Jan
Johnson, who has since become a full-fledged Egyptologist at Chicago.
Cultural anthropology was represented by Winifred Lambrecht—Belgian
by birth, trained at Berkeley, who had already worked in Peru and
Africa. Kent Weeks worked as field archaeologist, architect, and part-
time physical anthropologist. His wife, Susan, along with Englishwoman
Claire Sampson, served as expedition artist and assisted Klaus Baer in
drawing tomb inscriptions. The Egyptian Antiquity Service's representative, Abdul Fattah, served cheerfully in the capacity of field archaeologist
and part-time translator, while S. P. Jain of the Archaeological Survey
of India worked on mapping. Finally, the writer, an eager graduate
student in anthropology from the University of Wisconsin—"the youngest American man"—bore up tolerably well under the joking and, in
addition to excavation responsibilities on the Dynastic town site, assisted
Fairservis on the prehistoric survey.

Walter Fairservis's style in running his expedition was noticeably
different from that of Carter or Petrie. As Wilson recalled:

> The field director used to be the absolute authority. Often he was
> the only experienced person on the expedition. His assistants were
> students or volunteers. In any case, they became his disciples. The
> pattern was set by Flinders Petrie. . . . In these days of professional
> specialization it is no longer possible to treat the field director as
> omniscient and infallible . . . since he has become the leader of inde-
> pendent-minded craftsmen, he can succeed only if he respects the
> opinions of his staff members. *(Wilson 1972: 190)*

As a field archaeologist, I am not sure that I agree with Wilson that
changing patterns of authority on archaeological projects are, necessarily,
a sign of the times. There is always a good deal of the personality of the
director injected into the style of any expedition, regardless of the era.
In this sense, much of the conviviality and banter that accompanied
dinners on the *Fustat* was a direct reflection of Fairservis's attitudes—

1   The staff of the Hierakonpolis Expedition on board the *Fustat*. Front row, left to right: Claire Sampson, servant, Professor John Wilson, Mrs. Mary Wilson, Mrs. Susan Weeks, Ms. Jan Johnson, Dr. Winifred Lambrecht, servant, Mr. S. P. Jain, cook, captain. Back row: Professor Walter A. Fairservis, Professor Klaus Baer, Professor Kent Weeks

2   The Nile at Hierakonpolis, showing the *Fustat* and the local ferry

both social and personal. On the other hand, what motivated Walter Fairservis—what motivated most of us—was something rather new in Egyptian archaeology: an interdisciplinary spirit that has spread throughout archaeology since the Second World War. In his formative years, Fairservis had seen the birth of that spirit. He had always felt an attraction for Egypt. As a young boy he corresponded with the great American archaeologist, George Andrew Reisner, and at the age of sixteen he ran away from home and reached Egypt before being apprehended. During the war he served in the armed forces in Mongolia and Japan. Later, when he returned to graduate school at Harvard, the lure of unknown civilizations took him first to Afghanistan with Louis Dupree and then to Pakistan and India. Over the years Fairservis became an acknowledged expert on the transition from village life to urban civilization in South Asia, but he always dreamed of returning to Egypt—his first love. After a preliminary effort in 1967, he assembled a staff trained to cope with a wide range of periods and problems and returned to Hierakonpolis in southern Upper Egypt. As we shall see later on, the focal points of this expedition were the archaeological remains of the Predynastic and Archaic periods (ca. 5500–2700 B.C.), while secondary stress was placed on Egyptological, Palaeolithic, and ethnographic evidence. In all our minds was an awareness of what similar research projects had already accomplished in other areas of the Middle East.

Thanks to pioneering work in the Tigris-Euphrates river valleys by Robert Adams of the University of Chicago in the 1950's and early 1960's, and later by Frank Hole, Kent Flannery, and James Neely of the University of Michigan in the mid-1960's, the interrelated processes by which civilization or "complex urban society" arose in Mesopotamia had been outlined successfully. The roles of plant and animal domestication, economic organization, settlement geography, ecology, and demography were pieced together into a general picture or model, which explained the rise of cities and states. This was fine for Mesopotamia, but it left us in the dark about other areas of the world where civilization seems to have developed on its own—Egypt, the Indus Valley, China, and highland Peru. Only in Mesoamerica—an area stretching from the Valley of Mexico in the north to Guatemala in the south—have archaeologists amassed information comparable in quantity and quality to that recovered from Mesopotamia. Based on the Mesopotamian and Mesoamerican precedents, Fairservis realized that the development of a program of interdisciplinary, problem-oriented archaeology in Egypt had to be his first objective. Along with many of us, he was bothered by what seemed to be an overemphasis on Mesopotamian developments at the expense of other areas of the Middle East.

At the heart of the problem, of course, was the spectacular success of Mesopotamian research which, often unwittingly, biased our evaluations of other, neighboring areas. We tended, for example, to equate the rise of civilization everywhere with the rise of cities, even though Egyptian scholars like John Wilson had long argued that Egypt possessed no precise equivalents to the great urban centers of Mesopotamia during her formative years. There was also a personal factor. During his lifetime, James Henry Breasted had dominated the Oriental Institute, and the institute had dominated American research in the ancient Middle East. Breasted was an Egyptologist and many scholars reacted (sometimes unconsciously or unfairly) to what they perceived as an Egyptian dominance of Middle Eastern research between the world wars by pushing Egyptology aside or ignoring it. Between 1939 and the beginning of the Aswan Dam rescue project in 1961 Egyptian research also lagged behind research in neighboring areas because of the international political situation. And to make matters worse, fifty years ago a number of amateurish English anthropologists known as heliocentrists maintained that all "high culture" diffused from Egypt to the rest of the world. The scholars' reaction to this, quite expectedly, was to cast suspicion on all things Egyptian and they devoted a good deal of time and energy to refuting the extreme claims of the heliocentrists.

From his earlier experiences in Pakistan and India, where he believed he had traced an essentially independent development of civilization, Fairservis felt that the reaction to the Egyptian evidence on the part of many Middle Eastern archaeologists and prehistorians had been too strong. As we shall see later, he was not alone in his beliefs, and scientists like Karl Butzer of the University of Chicago and Fred Wendorf of Southern Methodist University, to name but two, have played major roles in the recent revolution in Egyptian prehistoric archaeology.

To unravel the processes of culture change from the time humanity itself was evolving in the Lower Palaeolithic period (ca. 2 million–100,000 B.P.) through the rise of the state under the first two dynasties (ca. 3100–2700 B.C.) is an immense task beyond the mere abilities of one person; specialists are essential. As Wilson realized, this is the real reason that the organizational flavor of most modern archaeological digs has changed radically from the days of Petrie and Carter. The modern expedition leader, stripped of his jacket and tie and exposed to constant intellectual banter, to on-the-spot creation, testing, and rejection of working hypotheses, has become as much arbiter as lofty leader—even though in Egypt he may be called by the old Ottoman Turkish term *Bash Mudir* (head leader). Although Middle Eastern archaeology still has its share of narrow minds, stuffed shirts, and white-haired eminences who pontificate from giddy intellectual heights, the successful leader's image is gradually changing to one of first among equals. The American image has replaced the British. The new ways, to be sure, are fraught with problems; sometimes changing goals and new scientific methods threaten to overwhelm us with their variety and complexity. But what has been called the new archaeology, when purged of its hot air, grounded solidly

3   The Grid System at the early Dynastic town of Hierakonpolis in 1969

MODERN EXCAVATION TECHNIQUES IN EGYPT

4   Screening backdirt at the Predynastic town site at Hierakonpolis in 1978

in the scientific technique, and tempered by imagination, is helping spawn a new intellectual synthesis that might be called "scientific humanism." The new methods demand rigor in description and quantification and a readiness to test hypotheses statistically and reject them. Periodically, in scientific endeavor, it is necessary to pause and take stock of our progress and errors so that new hypotheses may be generated and tested and new conclusions drawn.

Attempts to synthesize Egyptian prehistory date back only to 1920, when Petrie published *Prehistoric Egypt*. That work, like many of its successors, totally ignored the Palaeolithic period and concentrated on the latest Predynastic phases of Egypt's rich prehistoric past. More recent and more complete summaries than Petrie's have usually lacked theoretical orientation and are now outdated by a rash of recent discoveries. This is as it should be.

This book is offered with the conviction that the time has come to step back and examine the ground we have traversed and to offer fresh conclusions and insights into a wide variety of problems. To this end, I have organized my presentation around two principles: first, the importance of the interpersonal, historical, and sociological circumstances surrounding particular key archaeological discoveries, and second, the period-by-period presentation of Egyptian prehistory in terms of a series of ongoing cultural processes stretching from the first entry of our human ancestors into the Valley of the Nile perhaps a million years ago, to the spectacular emergence of Egyptian civilization under the pharaohs of the first two dynasties, between about 3100 and 2700 B.C.

For scientists and humanists it is satisfying to realize that the speculations and findings of prehistorians, historians, and archaeologists over the last century or so have given us a tremendous appreciation for the total sweep of the ancient Egyptian past—one that far surpasses the much-touted wisdom of the priests of old. Those priests, as far back as the time of Herodotus in the fifth century B.C., were notorious for the ways in which they callously manipulated tradition to hoodwink naïve Greeks, Romans, and even native pilgrims—notorious for the uses they made of their own past. This book is submitted in the spirit of scientific humanism with the hope that our own knowledge of Egypt's past (prehistoric as well as historic) will enable us to render it the true servant of the present and future, rather than its master.

2

TIME BEYOND RECKONING:
FROM MANETHO
TO DE PERTHES

The two men had almost nothing in common, except a passion for time. They were separated by over 2,000 years and almost as many miles. One was a devout priest, the other a religious skeptic. While Manetho was a native of Egypt and almost certainly never left his country, Boucher de Perthes never once set foot on Egyptian soil. Despite this, both men made major contributions to chronology, providing a framework for almost all modern approaches to the study of Egypt's past. About Manetho, we know very little. He was probably born in the late fourth century B.C. during the lifetime of Alexander the Great (356–323 B.C.). As a boy he undoubtedly heard eyewitness accounts of the Macedonian king's entry into Egypt. If Egyptian and Greek shared anything in common at that time it was a healthy dislike for the Persian barbarians who had effectively dominated the Middle Eastern and eastern Mediterranean worlds for almost two centuries. Even when Egypt had been an independent nation, as far back as 600 B.C., Egyptian kings employed Greek mercenaries and settled them in colonies in their land, and later, on more than one occasion, Greek money had financed native Egyptian uprisings against Persian rule. When Alexander the Great reached Egypt, therefore, he was greeted as a liberator and almost immediately visited the oracle of Amon at the oasis of Siwa where he was, with true political foresight, proclaimed divine.

If the Egyptian priests thought they knew a good thing when they saw it, Alexander's opportunistic Macedonians—especially General Ptolemy—never forgot the immense agricultural wealth of Egypt. Ptolemy returned there after his commander's death and in 305 B.C. proclaimed himself king in the fashion of the ancient pharaohs. His son, Ptolemy II Philadelphus, became a great patron of the arts, and under his rule Alexandria flourished as a center of Hellenistic learning and science.

At the same time (around 280 B.C.) Manetho wrote a condensed history of his native land for its new rulers. Manetho was a native of Sebennytos in the Delta and a priest or "prophet" who had been educated in the old scribal traditions. The temple had been famed for over 2,000 years as a center of learning and doubtless contained records passed down from earliest historical times. Although Egypt's priests had occasionally passed out tidbits of garbled information to curious visitors like Herodotus, no one had ever compiled a complete history, especially one for foreigners. In addition to writing in Greek—a foreign tongue—Manetho's task must have been compounded by the fundamental differences between ancient Egyptian and Greek concepts of history. Since the time of Thucydides in the late fifth century B.C., Greek authors had striven to write history in terms of cause and effect relationships—a scientific method that foreshadowed modern historiography and contrasted radically with the Egyptian approach that stressed the central and mystical role of the divine pharaoh as a preserver of traditional values. Manetho was, first and foremost, an Egyptian, and so when he wrote his history it was little more than a chronicle in which events were arranged from oldest to youngest, according to the reign of a particular king. The kings were grouped into thirty dynasties—a technique that has remained characteristic of Egyptian histories ever since Manetho's time.

Unfortunately, no complete copies of Manetho's work have ever been found. The earliest reference is contained in the writings of Josephus and dates to the mid-first century A.D.; and our principal sources are even later than that, ranging from the third through ninth centuries A.D. These authors—Africanus, Eusebius, and Syncellus—do not even agree with one another on the periods of time that Manetho assigned to each dynasty. Although, roughly speaking, each of Manetho's dynasties represents a separate ruling family, it is unclear whether Manetho himself realized that, during periods of civil war, several dynasties ruled at the same time. This makes it impossible to reconstruct an accurate chronology for Egyptian history by simply stringing together all the reigns of all the kings of the thirty dynasties and then counting back from a known date, such as Alexander's conquest in 332 B.C. Several earlier historians who tried this approach overestimated the beginning of the First Dynasty by as much as 2,500 years! Despite these pitfalls, modern Egyptologists have converted Manetho's system into a viable chronology whose accuracy is the envy of archaeologists all over the Mediterranean and Middle East and is an invaluable tool to prehistorians seeking historical "controls" on their own, less accurate dating techniques.

One reason that Manetho's system has proved so durable is that it was based on much older documents, or king lists, to which, as a learned priest, he had access. Archaeologists and Egyptologists have discovered five such lists which, despite some discrepancies, support Manetho in general. The oldest document dates to the Fifth Dynasty (ca. 2400 B.C.) and includes fragments in Palermo, Cairo, and elsewhere. Although badly damaged, they preserve the names and principal events of kings from the Fifth Dynasty back *before* the unification of Egypt by the legendary Menes, founder of the First Dynasty (ca. 3100 B.C.). Other lists include the Karnak Tablet, compiled under Thutmose III, about 1450 B.C., which lists a selection of kings back to Menes; the Abydos Tablet compiled under Seti I, about 1300 B.C., which also lists all the kings back to Menes; the Saqqara Tablet compiled under Rameses II, about 1250 B.C., listing most of the kings back to the late First Dynasty, and the Turin Papyrus written sometime during the Nineteenth Dynasty (ca. 1300–1220 B.C.). The Turin Papyrus, which has suffered severely, resulting in the needless destruction of over half the document, goes back well before the First Dynasty, giving the names of mythical divine rulers of prehistoric Egypt. It also lists the exact length of each king's reign and divides rulers into different groups, foreshadowing the dynastic approach used by Manetho.

By far the most useful record for the earliest dynasties is the Palermo Stone and the fragments in Cairo, parts of which are now distributed among various museums. This record was engraved in the Fifth Dynasty (ca. 2400 B.C.) at a time when memories of the earliest dynasties were relatively fresh and still older lists probably available. As we have said, the Palermo Stone and its counterparts in Cairo record the names of late Predynastic rulers of the separate kingdoms of Upper and Lower Egypt and so provide a slim but tantalizing protohistoric link between the historic and prehistoric periods. Both documents also purport to list the exact number of years that each pharaoh occupied the throne. Since Egyptian kings from at least Middle Kingdom times (ca. 2130–1785 B.C.) dated events from their own year of succession to the throne, the Palermo Stone and Turin Papyrus are invaluable clues to the absolute chronology of Dynastic Egypt and potentially could provide a relatively exact starting point for prehistorians and historians alike. Unhappily, there are serious problems involved in using these documents. First, both are badly fragmented with large gaps and substantial inaccuracies. Second, the Palermo Stone ends its account with the reign of Neferirkare, third king of the Fifth Dynasty, although originally it may have included the names of three of his successors. Even supposing that the last missing name was that of Niuserre, sixth king of the fifth Dynasty, we still must determine when Niuserre and Neferirkare reigned in relation to our own era. To do this we have to assign an absolute date to some point in the Dynastic period so that we can begin to count backward to prehistoric times. Fortunately, we are able to locate some such points which enable us to navigate up the river of time thanks to the peculiar nature of the Egyptian calendar and the so-called Sothic cycle.

Today, the world officially reckons time according to a complex calendrical system based both on natural divisions, like the solar year and the lunar month, and on civil or artificial divisions, like the hour, day, and civil month. We reckon a year by the length of time it takes the earth to make a full circuit of the sun. By our most precise scientific estimates, one year consists of 365 days, 5 hours, 48 minutes, and 46 seconds of mean solar time. Our own calendar goes back to a prototype introduced under Julius Caesar in 45 B.C. and reformed by the scientists of Pope Gregory XIII in A.D. 1582. Even today, because of minor inaccuracies in the Gregorian computations, it is necessary to make periodic adjustments in our calendar. Throughout the millennia, mankind has devised a number of ad hoc calendars based on the cycles of the sun, moon, and stars, the harvest and the hunt. In a sense, all these are arbitrary and have enjoyed varying degrees of success and failure. The earliest example of a solar calendar comes from Egypt, where the first day of the new year was reckoned from the annual heliacal rising of the star Sothis, known to us as Sirius. A heliacal rising occurs on the day on which a star appears in the sky just before dawn, after having been invisible for some time. The fact that the heliacal rising of Sothis corresponded roughly with the beginning of the annual, life-giving Nile inundation probably suggested its utility and potency to the ancient Egyptians.

Unfortunately, they reckoned a year at 365 days, neglecting to account for the extra quarter-day on each year. Thus, every four years the so-called Sothic calendar slipped behind the actual solar year by one full day. The error multiplied over the years, throwing certain seasonal feasts hopelessly out of kilter. Every 1,460 years, however, the error corrected itself so that New Year's Day found itself once more coinciding with the heliacal rising of Sothis. Since the Roman author Censorinus recorded such a "coincidence" in A.D. 139, it is possible to derive a number of similar coincidences by simply subtracting 1,460 years from A.D. 139. This produces dates of 1321 B.C., 2781 B.C., and 4241 B.C. (or 1313, 2773, and 4238 B.C. according to another reckoning). Since we know from documentary sources that the Sothic calendar existed before 1321 B.C., we are left with two possibilities for the starting point of the Egyptian solar calendar. If we accept the date 4241 B.C., then we are faced with the likelihood that the Sothic calendar can be extended far back into the Predynastic era. One school of Egyptologists argued that this date must be accepted, since one could not have a civilization without a calendar. Since the Egyptian state was already many centuries old in 2781 B.C., they thought that the Sothic calendar must date back into prehistoric times. Although such an invention seemed to them an astounding proof of the intellectual leadership of ancient Egyptian culture, this tentative link with the prehistoric past proved to be as illusory as the logic of its proponents. Ignoring the obvious fallacy of their basic assumption that the Egyptian state required a solar calendar from its inception, other authorities pointed out that it would have been possible for the Egyptians to pick an arbitrary starting point, like the heliacal rising of Sothis at virtually any point in their early history and then subject it to minor shifts.

It is therefore entirely possible that we cannot even extend the calendar back to the mystical date of 2781 B.C. What direct evidence we have on the matter, however, suggests that the solar calendar came into use in the Third Dynasty (Wilson 1951: 60-61) and a date of 2781 would fall comfortably within this period. This is not to say that the prehistoric Egyptians and their immediate descendants of the first two dynasties completely lacked calendars. There is strong evidence that the Egyptians once employed a lunar calendar since they continued to use a lunar calendar for liturgical purposes through Ptolemaic times, and such a system almost certainly dates to prehistoric times. Alexander Marshack has recently demonstrated that the Upper Palaeolithic hunters of France, people who lived between 12,000 and 30,000 years ago, probably counted time by marking the phases of the moon on pieces of bone. But for now the significance of ancient Egypt's solar calendar is not in its prehistoric antecedents but rather in the possibility that it can be correlated with our own calendar and the Dynastic chronology of Manetho unraveled.

Egyptologists have been surprisingly successful in this enterprise and in their painstaking researches have laid the foundations for a reliable prehistoric chronology. Since we know some dates for Sothic risings from the New and Middle Kingdoms (see Table I) in the form of regnal dates (e.g., the seventh year of the reign of Senwosre), we can determine the absolute value of that date in years before Christ. The earliest fixed

TABLE I DYNASTIC CHRONOLOGY OF ANCIENT EGYPT

Period Name	Absolute Date (B.C.)	Dynasty
Archaic*	3100–2700	I *and* II
Old Kingdom*	2700–2180	III–VI
First Intermediate Period	2180–2130	VII–X
Middle Kingdom	2130–1785	XI–XII
Second Intermediate Period	1785–1550	XIII–XVII
New Kingdom	1550–1080	XVIII–XX
Third Intermediate Period	1080–664	XXI–XXV
Saite Period	664–525	XXVI
Late Period	525–332	XXVII–XXXI
Ptolemaic	332(323)–31	XXXII

* Some authors refer to the Archaic as the Early Dynastic Period (Frankfort 1948b) while many authorities remain uncertain about the status of the Third Dynasty. Most often the term "Early Dynastic" is now used for Dynasties I-III.

date in the Dynastic Egyptian chronology at present is the seventh year of the king Senwosre III, now calculated to have fallen between 1877 and 1872 B.C. Egyptologists, by counting back from Senwosre's reign and allowing for the overlapping reigns of different dynasties, have arrived at a date of approximately 3100 B.C. for the beginning of Manetho's First Dynasty, setting the stage for the prehistorians with their more imprecise archaeological and radiochronometric techniques to fill in the previous gap of 750,000 years.

Returning to Manetho himself for a moment, it is amazing to consider the impact on our view of history of a man about whom we know so little. Regrettably, categories like dynasties often divide or group events in ways that obscure trends or events that did not interest the ancient scribes or square with the official concept of what history should be. The Dynastic approach to the past overemphasizes political history, for example, at the expense of social, cultural, economic, and technological developments. That, in fact, is probably why it survived, since Manetho confused historical breaks with changes in family. For this reason, modern Egyptologists and archaeologists usually assemble Manetho's dynasties into broader categories, like the Archaic Period, Old Kingdom, Middle Kingdom, New Kingdom, and Late Period (see Table I). Unfortunately, like the dynasties themselves, these divisions are not mutually exclusive. They often tend to obscure real cultural relationships and not all Egyptologists agree on their definition. Generally speaking, however, Table I presents the system widely used by Egyptologists and Egyptian archaeologists when dealing with the historic period.

In addition to his role as historian, Manetho exerts a surprising influence on our view of later Egyptian prehistory. For instance, in the 1890's, when Sir Flinders Petrie and his associates discovered a rich prehistoric culture immediately preceding the First Dynasty, they immediately

TABLE II   PREDYNASTIC CHRONOLOGY OF ANCIENT EGYPT*

Date (B.C.)	Upper Egypt	Lower Egypt
3100	Protodynastic	Protodynastic
3300	Late Gerzean (Naqada II)	Late Gerzean/Maadian
3500	Early Gerzean (Naqada II)	Omari B?
4000	Amratian (Naqada I)	Omari A?
5000	Badarian	Merimden/Fayum A
(5500 ?)		

* Traditionally, prehistoric chronological charts list the earliest periods at the bottom in imitation of their archaeological-stratigraphic position, in contrast to historical chronologies such as Table I, which place the earliest phase first.

labeled it Predynastic and thus cast it irrevocably in the shadow of its successor. As we shall see in later chapters, the Predynastic period began about 5500 B.C. and lasted until the beginning of the First Dynasty around 3100 B.C. (see Table II). After more than eighty years of archaeological discoveries and research, it is now clear that the Predynastic era was a critical time for the formation of later ancient Egyptian culture—a time during which the economic, political, and social underpinnings of pharaonic culture took on a distinctively Egyptian form. It is a period that witnessed the introduction and formative development of the mainstays of later historic ancient Egyptian society: effective farming and herding, metallurgy, pottery making, the shaping of hard stone by grinding, ceremonial architecture, elaborate burials, effective river-going sailing craft, long-distance trade, and stratified political and social systems.

Instead of dividing the Predynastic (ca. 5500–3100 B.C.) according to historical events or dynasties, prehistorians use the chronology originally devised by Sir Flinders Petrie and revised on a number of occasions. Each of the Predynastic periods is named after an archaeological site where an important discovery was made. Later, in relating the stories of how these sites were discovered and excavated by archaeologists, I will review what they were like and the important issues they raise. For now, the different periods are listed separately for Upper and Lower Egypt in Table II. In Upper, or southern Egypt, the sequence begins with the Badarian, continues through Amratian (or Naqada I) and terminates in the Gerzean (or Naqada II). In the Delta, or Lower Egypt, the earliest Predynastic period is known as Merimden. This is followed by Omari A, then Omari B. The latest prehistoric phase is sometimes called Maadian or Late Gerzean because of the similarities it had come to share with the cultures of the south. Even though these terms bear no relation to Manetho's system, they do preserve the spirit of his chronology in the term Predynastic. Although Manetho and his fellow priests would never have dreamed of such a scheme, they probably would not have had any problem accepting the Predynastic peoples as their ancestors; there is, after all, a strong continuity between the village farmers of the Predynastic and their Dynastic counterparts since the change from Predynastic to Dynastic society was largely organizational and political, not technological and cultural, and the Egypt of the pharaohs remained down through Manetho's time an essentially village farming society.

Such continuity is much harder to demonstrate between the Predynastic peoples and their Palaeolithic hunting, gathering, and fishing predecessors. We will probably never know if they were from the same ethnic and linguistic stock. Palaeolithic cultures were fundamentally different from those of the Predynastic and Dynastic villagers; their settlements were smaller, relatively impermanent, and there were few inherited social differences among men. Wealth was neither conspicuous nor consumed. Then there is the matter of time. While traditional priests like Manetho, or anyone trained in the Middle Eastern ecclesiastical learning, had little trouble conceiving of some type of prehistorical ancestors, these were usually mythical and there was no way available to determine just how long ago such quasi-historical peoples lived. Our own Bible reflects such a tradition. Basing his estimates on the genealogies listed in Genesis, an early seventeenth-century Irish archbishop, Ussher, decided that the earth was created in 4004 B.C. Such a conclusion was perfectly logical in light of the information available to him. Even the interests of the eighteenth-century antiquaries in Western Europe seldom strayed beyond the monuments of early farming peoples (like Stonehenge) and even the great antiquarian of the Age of Reason, William Stuckeley (1687–1765), incorrectly attributed these to the Celts or their Druid priests—an estimate that missed the mark by over a thousand years. When early archaeologists like Father McEnery in England found stone tools associated with bones of extinct prehistoric animals as he did in 1825 at Kent's Cavern, the extreme antiquity that the association implied aroused a storm of controversy. His opponents argued that human tools could not possibly be contemporary with extinct animals and that the association must have occurred by accident when ancient Britons of Caesar's day dug their ovens into the lower layers of the cave. Even the idea of extinct animals caused trouble. Some eighteenth-century scientists thought that they represented earlier stages of development of modern animals. But the ecclesiastical apologists and their allies maintained that all species were created independently and could not change—hence the strong opposition to Darwin. Those traditionalists who admitted that fossils of extinct animals were genuine, explained the problem in terms of series of catastrophes, *pace* Sodom and Gomorrah, which periodically wiped out some original creations. Evolution was still held to be as impossible as "pre-flood," or "ante-Diluvian," artifacts.

Such opinions did not bother the early Palaeolithic archaeologist Boucher de Perthes, who, although he never saw Egypt, brought about changes in our conception of time that would liberate prehistoric archaeologists and give them guidance in the same way that Manetho's fragmented history acted as a springboard to the most recent, Predynastic epoch of the prehistoric period.

Jacques Crèvecoeur Boucher de Perthes was born in 1788, one year before the storming of the Bastille unleashed the French Revolution, toppling Europe's old regimes and ripping apart a social, economic, and spiritual order that had prevailed since the fall of the Roman Empire. Boucher de Perthes was a child of that revolution; but it is not for his mildly liberal social philosophy that he is known to modern science as a revolutionary, but for the role he played in smashing the Biblical "time barrier" that denied the existence of Stone Age man. Europe in the early nineteenth century seethed not only with political dissent but with a conflict that had been building for a century and a half, ever since the Copernican and Newtonian revolution had set rationalistic observation and experimentation above older beliefs and conventions. The new natural science that arose during the so-called Age of Reason began to seek new explanations for the bewildering varieties of "new" plants and animals that were being reported by explorers like Captain James Cook and Carsten Niebuhr. One of the greatest problems encountered in explaining the variety of life on our planet was the traditional Biblical view that things were created separately and were immutable. Even so distinguished a scientist as Linnaeus, who devised the modern taxonomic system used in biology, refused to believe that living forms could have evolved. Rather, people of his day referred to "the great chain of Being" or the *Scala naturae* in which God created an evenly graded progression of living things, from algae to angels. For many years before the eighteenth century, however, scholars, including Leonardo da Vinci, had reported extinct fossils in ancient geological strata. Da Vinci even observed that in order to explain the presence of certain geological beds containing sea mollusks on top of modern mountains, we would have to accept the notion of vast changes on the face of the earth. This observation posed no difficulty for those ecclesiastical and secular authorities who interpreted the Bible literally. After all, the Bible mentions numerous cataclysms. The existence of extinct animals could be explained by the operation of floods, earthquakes, and fire from heaven. But certainly, no new forms of life ever appeared after the initial creation.

The cataclysmic view of the earth's history was bolstered by authorities like Archbishop Ussher who, as we have seen, proclaimed that the world was created in 4004 B.C. If the world were only 6,000 years old, then surely not enough time existed for major evolution to have taken place and any changes in the earth's crust must have been cataclysmic, not gradual.

But of course Ussher was wrong. Beginning in the late eighteenth century, scientists like James Hutton (the father of modern geology) began to study the records of the rocks and to publish treatises that proclaimed the great age of the earth. The capstone of their arguments was provided by Charles Lyell, who published his three-volume classic, *Principles of Geology*, between 1830 and 1833, and buried the old-time catastrophists beneath a mountain of incontrovertible facts. Lyell's work opened the intellectual floodgates. Armed with his book, young Charles Darwin set out on a course of research that would eventually disprove the old idea that species (and ultimately man) did not change or "evolve." And another group of scientists, the founders of modern Palaeolithic archaeology, took heart at Lyell's findings. For hundreds of years there had been reports of tools associated with extinct animals or apparently old geological strata. This implication that man himself preceded all known accounts given in the Bible was strongly rejected by the establishment (deans of universities were particularly notable in the opposition). In 1859 Sir Joseph Prestwich, one of the most prestigious natural scientists of his day, and a young archaeologist, John Evans, traveled to France at the request of Dr. Hugh Falconer to investigate the persistent claims of Boucher de Perthes that he had found "ante-Diluvian" tools in direct association with extinct animals in the gravel terraces of the Somme River. De Perthes had been working and publishing for twenty years but was consistently ignored by the French scientific community. Now in the same year that Darwin's *Origin of Species* shook the foundations of Western science, the French prehistorian was exonerated before the Royal Society by Prestwich in a meeting attended by the greatest scientists of the day—Lyell, Thomas Huxley, Michael Faraday, and Roderick Murchison.

Although de Perthes's claims were still disputed for another decade in France, Lyell enthusiastically welcomed the discoveries and stated that the material found in the river terraces exceeded 100,000 years in age. Subsequent work by archaeologists like Édouard Lartet confirmed de Perthes's findings and established sequences relating tool development to animal evolution and climatic change and wrote the preamble to the first and longest chapter in man's prehistory—the Old Stone Age or Palaeolithic era.

More than a hundred years ago, the Palaeolithic was divided by de Perthes's successors like Lartet and Louis de Mortillet into a number of stages and substages. The principal stages—the Lower, Middle, and Upper Palaeolithic—which are used all over the Old World, were introduced to Egyptian archaeology as early as 1869 (Table III). Unlike Manetho's dynasties, the divisions have no historical basis and the assignment of a given site to a particular period is dependent on establishing approximate correlations among types of artifacts and geological strata or, more recently, by employing radioactive dating methods like carbon-14 analysis, thermoluminescence (TL), fission track dating and, with the most ancient Palaeolithic materials, potassium-argon dating. Although archaeologists often like to call such radioactive methods *absolute* dating techniques because they give us readings in years relative to our own time, we will see that they are hardly absolute by contrast to Dynastic estimates and characteristically, even at their best, vary from fifty to several hundred years with carbon-14 to several thousands or tens of thousands of years in the case of potassium-argon estimates. Because of the pitfalls in dating prehistoric societies, there are problems to be faced and special techniques that prehistorians use that seem strange to historians. Because of our inability to speak in terms of specific years or even decades, the individual and his role in changing

TABLE III GEOLOGICAL AND CULTURAL STRATIGRAPHY IN EGYPT AND NUBIA THROUGH THE LATE PLEISTOCENE

Geologic Time	Cultural Time	Nile Phases	Major Nilotic Stratigraphic Units	Environmental Conditions	Date (B.C.)
Upper Pleistocene	Late Palaeolithic	Neonile	Sahaba-Darau Formation	semiarid, high flood	10,000
			Ballana-Masmas Formation	semiarid, high flood	14,500
			Debeira-Jer Formation	arid, high flood	17,500
			Korosko Formation	arid, high floods	24,000 / 30,000
				Mousterian Subpluvial	
	Middle Palaeolithic	Prenile/Neonile Interval	Makhadma Formation	arid	50,000 / 90,000
			Abbassia Formation	Abbassia Pluvial	120,000
		Prenile	Dandara Formation	semiarid	150,000
Middle Pleistocene / Lower Pleistocene	Lower Palaeolithic	Protonile	Qena Formation	semiarid / pluvial	500,000 / 700,000
	"Villa-Franch-ian"*	Paleonile/Protonile Interval	Issawia Formation	arid	2,000,000
late Lower Pliocene		Paleonile	Armant Formation	semiarid, Armant Pluvial	10,000,000
Lower Pliocene		Neonile/Paleonile Interval		arid	15,000,000
Upper Miocene		Neonile		arid?	20,000,000

* *Sensu strictu*, a faunal assemblage.

the world around him fades into the background. Even if we are limited in this way, we most certainly are able to take a grander view of the processes of the past, both human and ecological—a view that complements the findings of the historian.

3

THE TWO LANDS:
AN ECOLOGICAL PERSPECTIVE

To an ancient Egyptian, reverence for his native land was more than an obligation, it was a religion.

> Whichever god decreed this flight, have mercy, bring me home! Surely you will let me see the place in which my heart dwells! What is more important than that my corpse be buried in the land in which I was born! (Trans. Lichtheim 1973: 228)

Sinuhe, who wrote these words almost 2,000 years before the birth of Christ, had fled Egypt as a young man, on learning of the assassination of King Amenemhat I in 1962 B.C. To what extent he had been involved in or party to the plot is unclear, but eventually he managed to make his way to Syria or Palestine, where he married the daughter of a chief and became a successful leader and wealthy man. As old age approached, however, he felt more keenly than ever the pangs of loneliness for his own people and their comforting death rituals. He wrote to the reigning pharaoh, Sesostris I, son of the slain Amenemhat I, and begged to be readmitted to his homeland. The king replied graciously and Sinuhe's story ends with his honored return to Egypt. The strong affection shown by Sinuhe for his land underscores the unique importance of the environment to the ancient Egyptians and has led the noted environmental archaeologist, Karl Butzer, to remark: ". . . major segments of ancient Egyptian history may be unintelligible without recourse to an ecological perspective" (Butzer 1976: 15). The ecological perspective—a view that attempts to understand the complex interrelationships between cultural and physical and biological systems—is a modern, scientific way of expressing the old reverence for what we once called the "balance of nature" or "man's place in nature." In the last fifteen to twenty years our consciousness of the need for such an approach to the world around us has grown steadily as we have begun to realize that man and his technology are not independent but subject to the limitations of a fragile and imperiled ecosystem. The new reverence for the physical and biological world and our curiosity to understand the limits and potentials of human growth have given rise to a number of new disciplines, including what Butzer has called "environmental archaeology."

> The relations of man to the land in prehistory are, as yet, poorly understood. But with the growth of interdisciplinary interest for the many kinds of problems involved, a fuller understanding is bound to emerge. *(Butzer 1966: 471)*

The same author, in a recent study of the "cultural ecology" of ancient Egypt, has reached a conclusion that emphasizes the links between the world of Sinuhe and his prehistoric ancestors of Predynastic and Palaeolithic times. According to Butzer (1976: 111), Egypt

> showed an unexpected continuity in environmental exploitation strategies between prehistoric communities of the Pleistocene and the much more complex and sophisticated cultures of historical times.

Such a continuity really should not come as a surprise. Ancient Egyptian literature is replete with praises of the geography of the homeland and suspicion of the outside world. Of all the peoples of recorded history, the Egyptians were among the most insular and self-satisfied. While Phoenicians, Mycenaeans, and later Greeks explored the far reaches of the Mediterranean from Sidon to the Pillars of Hercules, planting countless colonies in their wake, Egyptians stayed at home, contemplating the glories of Tawy—the Two Lands. Even in the imperial days of the New Kingdom (ca. 1550–1080 B.C.) when Egyptian ships plied the Mediterranean and sailed down the Red Sea to trade with the peoples of Somalia for precious spices, we hear of no intrepid adventurer who sailed off to found a colony or forge his own life freely in a new land. So strongly were the geography and environment of Egypt imprinted in the ancient Egyptian mind that we read of people who literally feared the dark forests of Syria, where a man could not see from horizon to horizon and where rivers ran backward. In Egypt there was only one river, the Nile, and it flowed from south to north. Hence, we speak of southern Egypt as Upper Egypt because it is upriver, while Lower Egypt refers to the north (or the Delta). This division was as important to the Egyptian self-image as the dichotomy (real or imagined) between northerner and southerner still employed by citizens of the United States. Even the ancient Egyptian's word for the nation, "Tawy," suggests a parallel to the "United States" in that it admits geographical and cultural plurality while affirming political unity. In Egypt, that unity arose from the Nile, while the geographical and cultural divisions implicit in terms like Upper and Lower Egypt were likewise products of cultural-ecological differences created by the river and climate. On the one hand there was the fertile alluvium, the black land, which contrasted strikingly to the barren desert frontiers, the red land. The tension created between these

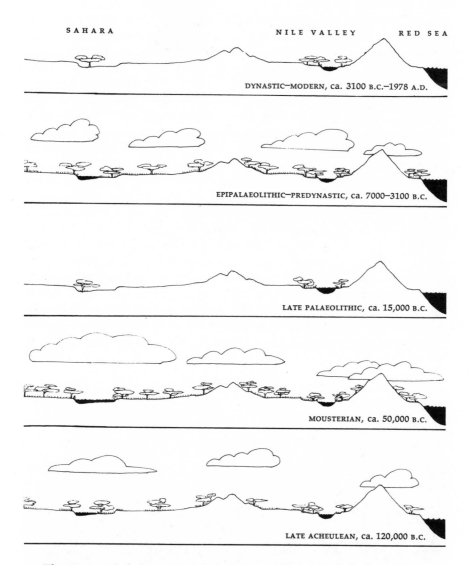

SAHARA   NILE VALLEY   RED SEA

DYNASTIC–MODERN, ca. 3100 B.C.–1978 A.D.

EPIPALAEOLITHIC–PREDYNASTIC, ca. 7000–3100 B.C.

LATE PALAEOLITHIC, ca. 15,000 B.C.

MOUSTERIAN, ca. 50,000 B.C.

LATE ACHEULEAN, ca. 120,000 B.C.

5   The impact of changing climate. Schematic diagram showing the effect of
alternating rainy and arid periods on the plant communities and water
resources of southern Upper Egypt since late Acheulean times

two environments and the cultures that grew up in them dominated
Egyptian prehistory for tens if not hundreds of thousands of years and
is one of the strongest links between ancient Egyptian history and
prehistory.

The geographical divisions of Egypt—both ancient and modern—provide spatial starting points in much the same way that Manetho's chronology and its modern permutations give us a framework for studying

change through time. Until recently, however, geography was often viewed as a one-dimensional factor. Some extreme interpretations made all cultural factors subservient to the physical and biological environment while others chose to regard geography merely as a convenient back-drop against which was played out the drama of history and prehistory. The truth is that neither extreme comes close to the mark. That is why prehistorians prefer to use the term "cultural ecology." This concept does not imply one-way relationships or posit simple answers. Rather it emphasizes the complex interrelationships between human behavior and the particular physical and biological environment in which it develops. As exemplified by the work of Butzer, the approach is so broad that it attempts to draw together an unusual range of specialists. It focuses on materialistic and measurable types of evidence such as that traditionally available to the prehistoric archaeologist. Cultural ecology helps compensate for the time-consciousness of archaeologists by forcefully interjecting the idea of space into our musings over the development of human society; it forces us to see ancient historic and prehistoric societies in something approaching their total context and avoid overly simplified explanations that invoke "sweeping invasions and hungry hordes." The cultural-ecological continuity that Butzer has proposed between history and prehistory in Egypt is still bold speculation pinned

6   An eastern view toward the Nile Valley of the desert in southern Upper Egypt, showing looted Predynastic graves on the banks of the once verdant Great Wadi

to new and often controversial discoveries and interpretations, but it has given renewed impetus to the search for the underlying processes of cultural and social change and has sharpened our awareness of the long-term environmental possibilities and limitations of human life in northern Africa while helping to correct a number of inaccurate stereotypes about Egypt's ancient environment.

Had you purchased a general history of Egypt more than ten years ago, chances are it would have begun with an introduction to the prehistoric environment and its effect on the development of Egyptian civilization. The chances are also good that this introduction would be totally inaccurate. As we shall see in our review of the prehistoric foundations of Egyptian civilization, many of these misconceptions have been cleared up by the work of scientists like Karl Butzer. For example, one of the most persistent errors made in the past was to view the prehistoric environment of the Nile Valley as thoroughly inhospitable to man. Historians, beginning with Herodotus, usually portrayed the prehistoric Delta as a virtually uninhabitable swamp whose early sites (in the unlikely possibility that they ever existed at all) would invariably be buried beneath countless meters of alluvium. South of Cairo, the Upper Egyptian Nile Valley was supposedly a steaming jungle analogous to the pestilential, vegetation-choked *sudd* of the southern Sudan. It is little wonder that our older assessments of Egypt's role in world *pre*history have been so disparaging. Fortunately, modern geological research has disproved both of these environmental stereotypes and given us a reliable baseline for evaluating the cultural-ecological differences between the Two Lands. For example, the Delta, although marshy, boasted a number of elevated hillocks and a fair amount of dry land in its central and southern parts which supported habitation from early times. Moreover, the deposit of alluvium in the Delta was not uniform, so that at least some prehistoric sites there must still survive near the modern surface. To the south, Upper Egypt, far from being an inhospitable, swampy jungle, was a well-drained floodplain that supported with ease Palaeolithic hunters and fishers as well as Predynastic and Dynastic farmers.

Another major misconception about the ancient environment of Egypt concerns the nature of the River Nile, most especially its source and causes of its annual inundations. Herodotus tells us:

With regard to the sources of the Nile, I have found no one among all those with whom I have conversed, whether Egyptians, Libyans or Greeks, who professed to have any knowledge, except a single person. He was the scribe who kept the register of the sacred treasures of Minerva in the city of Sais, and he did not seem to me to be in earnest when he said that he knew them perfectly well. His story was as follows:—"Between Syene, a city in the Thebais, and Elephantine, there are," he said, "two hills with sharp conical tops; the name of the one is Crophi, of the other Mophi. Midway between them are the fountains of the Nile, fountains which it is impossible to fathom. Half of the water runs northward into Egypt, half to the south towards Ethiopia." *(Trans. Rawlinson 1932: 89-90)*

Herodotus proved his suspicions when he visited Elephantine (Aswan) and learned from the natives there that the river extended at least forty days' journey to the south. The great historian was forced to conclude ". . . but of the sources of the Nile no one can give any account. . . ." (Trans. Rawlinson 1932: 92). It was only in the nineteenth century, as Britain pushed her colonial frontiers to the limit, that explorers learned that the Nile flowed from two distinct sources. Eighty percent of its volume is accounted for by the waters of Lake Tana, high in the Ethiopian highlands. Once a year, during summer, the monsoon rakes the peaks of Ethiopia, filling Lake Tana and sending down the Blue Nile the rich silt that made the annual inundation in Egypt the cause of unexampled agricultural prosperity. The source of the White Nile, Lake Victoria in Uganda, was only discovered in 1862–63 by the explorers John Speke and James Grant after a controversial and much-publicized journey. It contributes a far smaller volume to the Nile than its Ethiopian twin, which it joins at the modern city of Khartoum in the Sudan, where General Charles Gordon met his death at the hands of the Mahdi's followers in 1885.

In Herodotus's day no one understood the cause of the annual floods and this gave rise to some truly wild speculations. Herodotus himself sought to explain the annual flooding of the Nile between July and November as the result of decreased evaporation of river water by the sun during wintertime. As if never to be satisfied, now that we know the true source of the inundations, we have turned our inquiries to the very age of the Nile itself. Herodotus estimated 20,000 years for the river to have formed the Delta. He was, of course, wrong. Nevertheless, the answer to this question, of such concern to prehistorians, is still far from settled. At the turn of the century, a German scientist, M. L. P. Blanckenhorn, speculated that a huge ancestral Nile of tremendous volume—an Ur Nil he called it—once flowed to the west of the present river. He based his conclusions in part on the occurrence of ancient gravels in the Western Desert. For years he was disbelieved. Now, scholarly opinion, like a great, slow-moving pendulum, is swinging back toward a kind of Ur Nil interpretation, although no one employs the term itself.

The reason for all our uncertainty about the age of the Nile and its early course lies in the difficulty of tracing a river's history. To learn the age of a water course we must read the message of the deposits of alluvial soils deposited by running water over hundreds of thousands of years. But in many cases such a task of dating is made difficult by subsequent erosion of the oldest features. As we shall see in Chapter 4, there has been a river corresponding roughly to the Egyptian Nile for many millions of years. The link with Lake Tana, however, is much more recent, dating perhaps to between 50,000 and 25,000 years ago. It is the phenomenon of the annual flood and its life-sustaining silt that fascinated the curious from Herodotus's day on and this question, like so many in Egyptian prehistory, has yet to be resolved. Yet the fact that we are now at least able to offer intelligent guesses about the river's age and course of development is forcing us to reconsider one of the greatest environmental misconceptions in Egyptian prehistory—the myth of the benign Nile.

Since the times of Herodotus 2,500 years ago, historians have characterized the Nile as a regular and predictable element in the Egyptian cosmos and attributed to its influence much of the balanced, pragmatic, and ultimately confident outlook of Egyptian philosophy. Although it is true that the Nile is a relatively tame stream compared with the Tigris and Euphrates rivers of Mesopotamia, we now realize that its influence on Egyptian history and prehistory has been neither passive nor wholly benign. For instance, the annual inundations that are the backbone of Egypt's phenomenal fertility are, or rather were, until the construction of the first Aswan Dam in the late nineteenth century, the cause of much public anxiety. If the floods were unusually low, there was drought and famine; if the inundations were too high, whole towns could be wiped out and thousands would perish in sudden deluges or later of starvation.

The fears confessed by pharaoh to Joseph in Genesis were not merely idle dreams: they constituted one of the principal threats to the security of Egypt and, ultimately, of any dynasty that wished to rule the country. So it was in historical times; so it had been throughout prehistory since the upper reaches of the Nile had established that fateful link with the waters of Lake Tana. Throughout this book, we will encounter a number of instances in which the size and timing of Nile inundations have played crucial roles in some of the most important dramas of Egyptian prehistory and early history: The research of astronomer Barbara Bell with the Palermo Stone (ca. 2400 B.C) has enabled her to reconstruct the relative heights and fluctuations in the annual inundation all the way back to the reign of Djer, second or third king of the First Dynasty (ca. 3050 B.C.), and suggests some rather startling explanations for the rise and tribulations of the early Egyptian state. And recent speculation by archaeologist and prehistorian Fekri Hassan suggests that a precocious development of agriculture in late Palaeolithic times (ca. 16,000–10,500 B.C.)—one of the earliest such attempts in the world—was cut short by a series of disastrous floods.

As a final example of how our changing ideas about Egypt's environmental history are today forcing us to reevaluate many of our most cherished notions about the basic patterns that underlie early Egyptian history and prehistory, we need only consider the problem of the "nome." Nome was a word that the Greeks used for the ancient Egyptian provinces. In New Kingdom times (ca. 1550–1080 B.C.) there were roughly eighteen nomes in Lower Egypt and twenty-two in southern or Upper Egypt. It is clear that although these administrative units underwent alteration throughout Dynastic times, several date back to at least the Fourth Dynasty (ca. 2650–2500 B.C.). There has been a long-standing argument among Egyptologists as to which, if any, might have been actual survivors of earlier, prehistoric political divisions and what role, if any, they might have played in the unification of the Egyptian state under Menes. To date, most of these disputes have centered on two types of evidence: the hieroglyphic texts and the archaeological material. It is one thing to argue that nomelike divisions probably existed in Predynastic times but quite another to prove which of the pharaonic provinces were products of later artificial political redistricting and which reflected older units. Gerrymandering—the process of manipulating boundaries for political advantage—is not a new practice and, the historians might well argue, must have occurred in the long history of Dynastic Egypt. On the other hand, the Egyptologist and social philosopher Henri Frankfort has presented a good case for the prehistoric origins of at least some nomes by pointing out

> the ease with which these provinces became independent under their own local chiefs whenever the central power weakened; their representation by standards or emblems connected with a local cult; and the varying groups of these same standards—indicating an unstable and changing political conformation—which appear on predynastic monuments restraining enemies or demolishing cities.
>
> *(Frankfort 1948b: 17)*

Although the presence of apparent nome standards on Predynastic pottery and ceremonial maceheads and slate palettes reinforces the argument for the prehistoric origin of nomes, it still leaves open the question as to whether or not such standards really symbolized something different in prehistoric and protohistoric times than they did from the Fourth Dynasty on. Although some careful studies of Predynastic pottery styles suggest distinct but minor regionalism in prehistoric Upper Egypt, until recently these arguments have lacked a persuasive economic explanation and were not grounded in ecological considerations.

By restudying the historical evidence and comparing it to new paleoenvironmental information, Karl Butzer has provided Egyptian prehistorians with just such an explanation by demonstrating a link between traditional nomes and localized systems of irrigation and by suggesting a tantalizing if still highly tentative reconstruction of relative population densities in early historic Egypt. His conclusions that "these nomes, as basic territorial entities, originally had socioeconomic as well as ecological

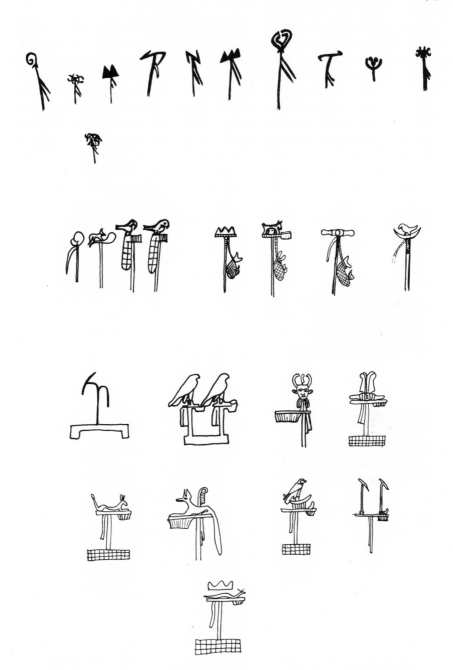

7   Selected nome standards of historic Egypt and possible proto- and prehistoric
antecedents. Top row: Late Gerzean "ship standards." Middle row:
Protodynastic signs from the Narmer Palette. Bottom row: Early Fourth
Dynasty nome standards from the reign of Snefru

overtones, but then became increasingly administrative in nature" (Butzer 1976: 105) is far from proved, but it is significant because it marks the application of the new cultural-ecological approach to a classic Egyptological problem. The extension backward in time of traditional cultural-ecological categories raises hopes that very soon our understanding of Egyptian prehistory will be transformed from an exercise in chronology and site excavation to a full-scale analysis of the cultural processes which helped to weld the different environmental spaces of Delta, valley, and desert into the land Sinuhe knew as Tawy—a land where age-old cultural dichotomies persisted alongside the new pharaonic order—a land where, as he put it, the epitome of cultural shock still remained one rooted in environmental contrasts: "As if a Delta-man saw himself in Yehu (Assuan), a marsh-man in Nubia" (Trans. Lichtheim 1973: 225).

PART II

THE PALAEOLITHIC AGE
IN EGYPT,
ca. 700,000–5500 B.C.

4
PALAEOLITHIC ORIGINS: POMP, CIRCUMSTANCE, AND PREHISTORY

KHEDIVE ISMAIL had outdone himself. On that sunny afternoon of November 17, 1869, the French imperial yacht *Aigle*, carrying the beautiful Empress Eugénie, led a magnificent regatta formally dedicating the Suez Canal. In an era addicted to pomp and pageantry, Egypt declared her entry into the modern world with an unabashedly enthusiastic celebration of the technological wonder of the age. Even England, which had long sought to block the Franco-Egyptian venture, saw fit to send as envoy the royal heir, the affable and diplomatic Prince Edward, to grace the pageant, and later that year in London Queen Victoria herself wined, dined, and knighted the canal's brilliant builder, Ferdinand de Lesseps. A new opera house, the first ever built in the Middle East, had been rushed to completion for the gala opening, and if Giuseppe Verdi's specially commissioned work *Aïda* was not ready for the occasion, the opera did at least manage to open in time for the festivities with *Rigoletto*.

In that year French influence in Egypt was considerable and it seemed for a brief moment that old dreams of imperial expansion in the East, thwarted by Britain for a hundred years, were about to be realized. No one, except possibly the Prussian Chancellor Otto von Bismarck, could have foreseen that within a year France's vaunted Second Empire would lie in shambles, with Napoleon III and Eugénie in exile and Paris itself besieged by German guns.

France's long and checkered career on the Nile began spectacularly in 1798 with Napoleon's attempt to conquer Egypt and isolate the English mercantile colonies to the East. Although a political failure, Bonaparte's expedition was a scientific triumph. Fired by the idealism of the French Revolution and a belief in a science that would serve all mankind, hundreds of scientists, scholars, and engineers flocked to Egypt to study, measure, and observe the land, its people, and its ancient monuments. Beginning in 1809 they produced the first book of the twenty-four-volume *Description de l'Égypte*, giving the outside world its first reliable account of the ancient monuments and undecipherable hieroglyphs of the Nile Valley. With the defeat of the French Mediterranean Navy in 1799 by Lord Nelson, the British presence temporarily replaced the French in Egypt. The Rosetta Stone, a black basalt stele inscribed in 196 B.C., in Greek and Egyptian demotic and hieroglyphic script, passed into the hands of the victors. Eventually it found its way to the British Museum, where a number of scholars immediately recognized the potential of the bilingual tablet and set about trying to translate from the known Greek into the unknown ancient Egyptian. When the French linguist Jean-François Champollion deciphered the mysterious hieroglyphic text in 1822 and published a preliminary account of Egyptian grammar two years later, the science of Egyptology was officially born. Thus had a Frenchman bested Britain in the opening round of a scholarly rivalry that was to persist for over a century—a rivalry that was but a pale reflection of a deeper colonial contest between Britain and France for the domina-tion of the minds and markets of the nonindustrial world. Ultimately, this contest would divide Africa in the nineteenth century between a "British vertical" and a "French horizontal" and bring both nations to the brink of war in 1898 at the obscure Sudanese outpost of Fashoda.

In the scholarly and scientific arenas, the rivalry played itself out against the backdrop of Egypt's archaeological treasures. At the begin-ning, the French could reflect with satisfaction that although they had lost the Rosetta Stone to the British Museum, it took a French scholar to decipher its riddle. In 1858 the French achieved another signal victory with the appointment of Auguste Mariette as Conservator of Egyptian Monuments. Mariette was able to obtain his position through the good offices of the ubiquitous de Lesseps, who was a close personal friend of the monarch at that time, Said Pasha. In 1854 Said Pasha had become ruler of Egypt unexpectedly after the assassination of his unpopular uncle, Abbas. As a young man he had been overweight and overshadowed by his elder brothers, who were in line for the throne. Then he was befriended by de Lesseps, who was special French emissary to Said's famous father, Mohammed Ali. In their different ways, both men were dreamers. De Lesseps dreamed of building a canal to link the Red Sea and the Mediterranean; and Said, like another Egyptian younger son 3,300 years before (Pharaoh Thutmose IV), dreamed of the throne. Once Said became Pasha he was easily persuaded by his old friend of the wisdom of building the Suez Canal. Despite the opposition of England and Turkey and despite staggering financial problems, the canal was begun by de Lesseps and completed during the reign of Said's successor, the Khedive Ismail. Throughout Egypt, the presence of French scientists, scholars, engineers, diplomats, and military advisers foreshadowed in a strange way the later Soviet presence of the late 1960's and early 1970's and proved to be as long-lasting.

Although Mariette owed his position to de Lesseps's and France's growing influence, once established he ruled over the archaeological scene in Egypt independently—even autocratically—for the next generation, and he managed at least to curb the wholesale looting of Egypt's antiquities which had been perpetrated before his arrival by men like Howard Vyse and Giovanni Belzoni. Mariette's impact on the growing science of archaeology was reflected in pioneering laws he had passed limiting the destruction and appropriation of Egypt's antiquities, often to the detriment of his own nation. So strong a precedent did Mariette set that when the British established a protectorate over Egypt in 1882, they were formally forced to recognize the right of a Frenchman to occupy the dominant administrative position in archaeology—a practice that remained in effect until 1956.

Although overshadowed by other events—the opening of the Suez Canal and Mariette's spectacular discoveries—the year 1869 is notable in another regard. In that year, three Frenchmen—Adrian Arcelin, Ernest Hamy, and François Lenormant—published the first account of Palaeolithic chipped stone implements found in Egypt and launched the science of prehistoric archaeology in that country.

According to the noted European prehistorian, Geoffrey Bibby, prehistoric archaeology itself had just come of age two years before in 1867 (Bibby 1956: 45), when the Exposition Universelle was celebrated in Paris with a sense of public showmanship and a consciousness of progress appropriate to Napoleon III's Second Empire and with a flair that must have impressed Khedive Ismail. The khedive, in office but four years, attended the exposition and must have been pleased by the presence of an Egyptian temple and statue of the pyramid-builder Khafre located in the oval garden in the center of the exhibition palace. More important to our story is the fact that at this same exhibition, for the very first time, were displays of prehistoric artifacts, including early tools of chipped stone classified by archaeologist Louis de Mortillet as Old Stone Age or Palaeolithic.

Unlike pyramids, tombs, and inscribed monuments, the earliest human tools are not enormously impressive nor are they always recognizable as the handiwork of man. In fact, it was only a decade before the discovery of Palaeolithic tools in Egypt in 1869 that the world's scientific establishment had accepted officially the existence of such implements and the extreme antiquity of human culture which they implied. Several finds of stone tools with extinct animal remains had helped prepare for the recognition of our Palaeolithic past: the discovery of hand axes at Hoxne, England, by John Frere in 1797; the excavations of ancient artifacts and bones from sealed cave deposits at Windmill Hill, England, by William Pengelly in 1858 and 1859; and the discovery in France of Palaeolithic art at Massat and Aurignac by Édouard Lartet in 1861. Important as these finds were, however, as we have seen, it was the persistent work of one man, Jacques Boucher de Perthes, which epitomized the struggle and triumph of prehistory in the nineteenth century and which paved the way for serious Palaeolithic archaeology in Egypt.

Sandford and Arkell and the First Prehistoric Survey: The Wheels of Progress

Even though archaeologists since de Perthes had recognized the potential of the Nile's terraces for dating the remains of Palaeolithic man and appreciated the general value of geology, it took the organizational genius and promotional ability of James Henry Breasted to initiate the first exhaustive archaeological-geological survey of the Nile Valley. Breasted, it will be recalled, had dined with Lord Carnarvon in the tomb in the Valley of the Kings in 1922 as an honored guest. As Director of the Oriental Institute of the University of Chicago aided by Rockefeller funds, he had built a research empire that was unsurpassed between the First and Second World Wars. Not only were the epigraphic methods used by the Chicago school of Egyptologists considered the most scientifically advanced and refined of their day, but the establishment of a center at Luxor (called, appropriately enough, Chicago House) has provided a meeting place for scholars and scientists interested in Egypt's past for over fifty years. Countless visitors have appreciated the cool, shaded verandas and peerless library of this great institution, the brainchild of the versatile Breasted. The prehistoric survey was another of Breasted's innovations—one for which he has received too little credit. In 1926 he commissioned geologist-archaeologists K. S. Sandford and W. J. Arkell to undertake an extensive prehistoric survey of the Nile Valley and its river terraces under the sponsorship of the Oriental Institute.

8 Acheulean hand ax from Upper Egypt

9 Acheulean hand ax on surface near Dungul Oasis

One has to admire the foresight of Breasted (long known as a master epigrapher and historian) in encouraging Palaeolithic research. As early as 1919, in a speech before the National Academy in Washington, D.C., he had suggested

> the possibility of a rough parallelism between the then-known Nile terraces and the succession of glaciations in Europe; but the knowledge of Nile geography then available was far too incomplete and imperfect to give such a reconstruction a stable basis.
>
> *(Breasted 1928: vii–viii)*

The use of river terraces to date Palaeolithic tools was a technique that originated in de Perthes's work in the Somme River Valley. Lacking any written records, coins, or calendars and the modern techniques of radioactive carbon-14 and potassium-argon dating, de Perthes and his successors worked out a sequence of relative dates for the material from the Somme Valley by the ingenious use of river terraces—a method that would later be used by Sandford and Arkell. Through careful field studies, geologists learned that river terraces like those of the Somme

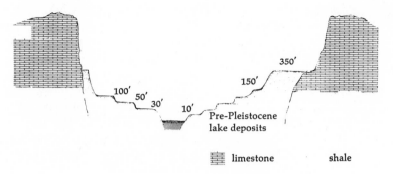

10   Idealized geologic cross-section of the Nile terrace system

represent earlier stages in a river's history. A simplified view of river terrace evolution envisions a river in its first phase as occupying a narrow V-shaped valley which it gradually reduces to a "mature" U-shape through erosion. In the base of this mature valley, the river occupies a wide, shallow bed that it has built up through aggradation, or deposition of water-borne materials. If and when the volume of the river decreases or the base level of the sea to which it ultimately flows drops, it will attempt to maintain its velocity and, in so doing, cut through its old bed, leaving it high and dry as a terrace above its new course. Variations in the volume and the load of materials transported by a river, especially when associated with fluctuations in sea level (relatively common occurrences during the Pleistocene) can bring about several cycles of aggradation and down-cutting and produce a whole series of terraces along a river's course. Thus, over hundreds of thousands of years, as the world's seas rose and fell, as snow in the north and rainfall in the south increased and decreased and as glaciers advanced and retreated across the landmasses of the Northern Hemisphere, terraces developed along many of the great river valleys of the earth. In general, the highest terraces are the oldest, and the lowest are the most recent.

Behind Breasted's enthusiasm for the Nile terraces was a desire to explore the earlier phases of Egyptian culture which he felt had been so "seriously neglected" and link these to the known Dynastic and Predynastic periods.

In terms of culture the present state of our knowledge carries us back only to an already existent Egyptian civilization based on cattle-breeding, agriculture, metal, and writing. We have never been able to push behind these possessions of the earlier Nile dwellers, to investigate the origins of cattle-breeding and agriculture, and to link up this stage of settled agricultural civilization with the hunting stage which preceded. (Breasted 1928: vii)

Over the next decade, Sandford and Arkell produced a landmark, four-volume study of the geology and archaeology of the Nile Valley, and although many of their conclusions have been substantially revised by paleoclimatologists like Karl Butzer and Carl Hansen and geologists like Rushdi Said, their contributions cannot be underestimated and many of their ideas continue to dominate the discussion of Nilotic origins and the Palaeolithic period in Egypt.

Looking at the four nicely bound and profusely illustrated scientific reports written by Sandford and Arkell and published by the Oriental Institute between 1929 and 1939, it is easy to ignore the difficulties that confronted them. The first step in undertaking any major archaeological and geological field survey, after defining one's problem, is to organize an expedition as efficiently as possible within the constraints of a budget. As we have seen, the history of Egyptian archaeology has seen a variety of field camps and living conditions, from the luxurious sailing *dahabiyehs* of the middle nineteenth century to the unbelievably Spartan and penurious conditions favored by Sir Flinders Petrie. In beginning their fieldwork in the 1926–27 season, the biggest problem facing Sandford and Arkell, was mobility:

> The plan of work necessitated covering as much ground as possible. . . . In the previous year one of us (K. S.) had used camel transport exclusively for the same type of work; this, though sure, is slow, wasteful of time, and involves much unnecessary exertion. This year it was determined to sacrifice the high reliability of camel transport for the rapid, though much more hazardous, progress of motor transport. In view of the nature of the work and the type of country to be covered, it was, however, essential to keep the outfit to the smallest proportions in both personnel and equipment.
>
> (Sandford and Arkell 1928: 28)

TABLE IV OLD METHOD OF RELATIVE DATING BASED ON THE ELEVATIONS OF NILE TERRACES

Terrace	Period	Date*
320 foot (northern Egypt)		660,000 B.C.?
200 foot (northern Egypt)		500,000 B.C.?
100 foot (southern Egypt)	Lower Palaeolithic	476,000 B.C.
100 foot (northern Egypt)	Lower Palaeolithic	270,000 B.C.
50 foot (southern Egypt)	Lower Palaeolithic	230,000 B.C.
30 foot (southern Egypt)	Middle Palaeolithic	187,000 B.C.
50 foot (middle Egypt)	Middle Palaeolithic	150,000 B.C.
10 foot (southern Egypt)	Middle Palaeolithic	70,000 B.C.

* All dates highly speculative—those marked with "?" probably much too young.

Unfortunately, the best-laid plans often go awry:

> It had been intended originally to take two Ford ton-trucks adapted
> for desert work; but a storm in the Mediterranean prevented an im-
> portant letter from reaching its destination, and on our arrival in Cairo
> we found neither cars nor servants at our disposal.
> *(Sandford and Arkell 1928: 28)*

After searching around Cairo for a few days, they were able to obtain
the services of an old Ford touring car that had been used by the prehistorian Gertrude Caton-Thompson in her survey in the Fayum and to
purchase a small, seven-horsepower Jowett. The next step was to obtain
a crew. Unlike the great traditional excavations of Carter and Carnarvon
in the Valley of the Kings which often employed hundreds of workmen
and scores of foremen, the requirements of the prehistoric survey were
minimal:

> A driver-mechanic was found, thanks to the good offices of our friends,
> who also produced a cook. The latter was a portly Nubian of enormous
> bulk and stature; he deserted as soon as he saw the cars, which was
> fortunate, as he probably weighed little less than a couple of hun-
> dredweight. The driver came to the rescue and introduced a friend and
> colleague, who filled the onerous post of cook-mechanic to perfection.
> *(Sandford and Arkell 1928: 28-29)*

Instead of sending the cars south by rail as was customary in their day,
the two men resolved on driving to Chicago House in Luxor. All archaeologists who have conducted prehistoric surveys are aware that, at
any moment, they must be prepared to travel without benefit of roads.
Unfortunately, given the nature and state of roads in rural Egypt in
1926, Sandford and Arkell were to encounter as much difficulty in their
drive south as in their later desert exploration.

> Roads in Egypt are the banks of irrigation ditches, and they follow
> therefore the needs of irrigation and not of getting from north to
> south in a straight line. Of recent years these canal banks have been
> made into excellent mud tracks in northern and middle, and much of
> southern Egypt; and, so far as we knew, the route to Luxor held no
> terrors for the motorist. We were to be disillusioned.
> *(Sandford and Arkell 1928: 30)*

After numerous breakdowns, the tiny expedition finally arrived at Luxor
and began the survey. They surveyed the desert on both banks of the
Nile, setting up their highly mobile camp in a likely locality and using
this as a base of operations for exploring the surrounding region. Their
actual work involved studying and mapping the remnant terraces near

11 A tree blocks the road in Upper Egypt, 1978

the Nile and exposed geologic beds in the desert hinterlands in order to reconstruct accurately the stratigraphy of the Nile Valley and its complete geologic history. At one point, the surveyors reached the site of Hierakonpolis, where a number of important Predynastic and early Dynastic remains had been unearthed thirty years before by the British excavators J. E. Quibell and F. W. Green.

> As the evening shadows were lengthening we drew up under the ruins of the protodynastic fortress and pitched our tents in the shelter of its massive mud-brick walls. Tea had been brought, and we were resting from our day's exertions at the door of the tent, when a figure was seen making toward us from the cultivation. When he approached we saw that he wore the badge of the Department of Antiquities, and he demanded solemnly if we had our antiquities tickets for visiting ancient monuments. We had camped in his ruins!
>
> *(Sandford and Arkell 1928: 36)*

After traversing the Nile several times in the course of their survey, Sandford and Arkell finally wound up on the Red Sea coast where they discovered the first *in situ* (undisturbed) flint implements in that area (p. 50): ". . . even had we found nothing else of importance they alone would have justified our journey."

There is a prevalent feeling—or superstition—among field archaeologists that the last days of an expedition are the most critical. Often, just as you are closing down your season's operation, an important find is made that requires spending added hours, days, or weeks just to ensure that this last bit of evidence is saved. In other situations, after a hard field season, when tempers and constitutions have been strained to the breaking point, everything seems to fall apart at once. Having had a number of these experiences myself, I find the final comments of Sandford and Arkell on the 1926–27 season (p. 52) especially poignant:

> . . . it was the very last day, only twenty-five miles from Luxor, when both rear springs on our small car snapped simultaneously, twisting the rear axle out of alignment and obliging us to crawl, crabwise, into town. We had actually ferried across the Nile and were within a few miles of Chicago House when the differential of the Ford also gave out, such a noise issuing from it that our approach could be heard from afar.

Behind the Aswan Dam: Tactics, Strategy, and Salvage Archaeology

Despite the valuable contributions of Sandford and Arkell's survey, in the long run, Breasted's fond hope of reading the chronology of Palaeolithic man from the river terraces (Table IV) has proved unfeasible. Rushdi Said, the contemporary Egyptian geologist who, perhaps more than any other person, has provided a fresh and revolutionary revision of the geological history of the Nile has noted:

> The futility of using elevations in correlations is obvious in a valley with as complex a history as that of the Nile Valley which was formed by several streams following one another and separated by long periods of intense tectonics and erosion. (Said 1975: 28)

Although many prehistorians are disappointed at being unable to use traditional geological techniques based on terrace positioning to date their artifacts, the last fifteen years have witnessed a quantum jump in our knowledge and understanding of Egypt's Palaeolithic prehistory. Crucial to recent progress has been a uniquely productive personal friendship between an American archaeologist and an Egyptian geologist and an international archaeological crisis brought about by the construction of the Aswan High Dam. Dr. Fred Wendorf of Southern Methodist University and Dr. Rushdi Said of the Geological Survey of Egypt met and became friends as students while attending Harvard University.

Some years later, in the late 1950's, Egypt realized that a new high dam at Aswan was needed to furnish the food and energy needs of the rapidly growing population. The proposed dam would flood an immense expanse of the Egyptian and Sudanese Nile Valley and destroy or permanently cover great numbers of valuable antiquities. In order to meet the crisis, a call went out for an internationally funded scientific expedition to save the monuments of Nubia. Under the auspices of UNESCO, a multinational commission of archaeologists and Egyptologists was formed. For their part in this massive rescue operation, Egypt and the Sudan relaxed their antiquity laws and agreed to permit large numbers of foreign archaeologists to work in the threatened area (Wilson 1972: 145-165). Before it was through, at least $50 million had been spent on the operation, and scientific teams from the United States, the Soviet Union, Great Britain, France, Germany, Italy, Poland, Japan, Australia, and India had participated. Active fieldwork began around 1961 and lasted for roughly ten years. Many of the discoveries still await publication. The most important point about this effort is that it marks the beginning of a new phase of prehistoric work in Egypt. The massive amounts of money and resources pumped into the threatened area resulted in the discovery of hundreds of sites spanning several hundred thousand years. The fact that so much new and diverse material has been uncovered is due in part to a new attitude toward archaeological exploration and excavation that has grown up since the Second World War—

12   Salvaging a Palaeolithic campsite in the Batn el Hajar, Nubia

an attitude epitomized in the work of Dr. Wendorf and his American, Egyptian, British, French, Belgian, and Polish colleagues in the Combined Prehistoric Expedition.

Instead of restricting their work to impressive monuments and graves, the Nubian campaigns of the sixties learned much from a special sub-discipline known as *salvage archaeology*. This approach was first developed in the industrialized nations where the "march of progress" in the form of large-scale construction projects destroyed ancient sites and monuments at an alarming rate. The building of new dams, roads, housing subdivisions, and factories has long been recognized as a hazard to archaeological data, and the salvage archaeologist tries to recover and record a maximum amount of information before the bulldozer does its work. Since extensive regions are often threatened and a variety of archaeological sites are usually present, the old approach of finding and digging only the biggest and richest site (often in helter-skelter fashion) has been scrapped. Instead of ignoring many sites because they are too early, too late, or too small, the good salvage archaeologist approaches his task much as a good general might approach a battle—with a complete arsenal of tactics organized around an overall strategy based on a commitment to recover and reconstruct as much as possible of the culture-history of a given region over the entire span of human occupation. Scholarly problems are seen in terms of the overall pattern of human adaptation to a particular environment, and individual historic or prehistoric periods are not viewed in isolation.

Where appropriate, specialists are called in to deal with particular periods or types of sites (e.g., architectural ruins versus small campsites) but, at some level, the archaeologist adopts a general approach to his area. Since he faces such a vast task, he must constantly strive to recover a representative sample of every settlement type from every time period as well as representative artifacts. This requires estimating the comparative frequency of sites in any given period and this, in turn, presumes that the archaeologist has conducted an accurate site survey and made a good map. In a place like the Nile Valley, where sites vary from a few centuries to hundreds of thousands of years in age and from small hunting stations to large towns, cemeteries, and temples, special skills were required to rescue the archaeological treasures of Nubia. Architects and artists were needed to map and draw buildings, epigraphers copied and translated inscriptions, engineers moved whole temples, physical anthropologists analyzed human skeletal material, paleobiologists studied ancient plant and animal remains, geologists recorded the stratification and comparative age and geoclimatic history of localities and Palaeolithic archaeologists (often known as "lithic" specialists from their main pastime of analyzing stone tools) explored the small hunting and gathering campsites of the earliest inhabitants of the Nile Valley.

It is in this latter category that Dr. Wendorf and his colleagues have made their great contributions. Even after the Nubian rescue operation ended, the approach to archaeology pioneered by Wendorf and Said and their associates has continued in Upper Egypt, the Fayum, and several oases of the Western Desert under the auspices of the Combined Prehistoric Project. Their cooperative efforts have enabled Said to rewrite the story of the evolution of the Nile. This information, when related to Palaeolithic sites, even sites found on the surface, has permitted more reliable dating and a new appreciation of the environmental context of ancient cultural development.

In a sense, the new sequence of geological stages that Said and his colleagues have proposed to explain the evolution of the River Nile and Wendorf's geoarchaeological periodization of the Palaeolithic function are much like the dynasties devised by the Egyptian priest Manetho. As we have seen, Manetho's division of ancient Egyptian history into thirty dynasties was based on the records available to him 2,300 years ago, and, although known to be imperfect, his arrangement of the Egyptian kings in a relative chronological order has been accepted historically. Modern science is more demanding than Manetho was, however, and the geological record of the Palaeolithic is much less well documented than the succession of Egyptian pharaohs. Although we now believe that we are closer to an appreciation of the rhythm and tempo of the Palaeolithic past, we still tolerate a great deal of uncertainty with the understanding that, as the result of the contributions of a number of scholars and scientists, we are closer to the past today than the ancient Egyptians, with their love of old things, origin myths, and primeval waters, could ever have dreamed.

Interlude: The Leakeys at Olduvai Gorge—Early Man in Africa and the Nilotic Corridor

Though Sandford and Arkell's sequence of river terrace dating is not generally applicable to the entire Egyptian Nile Valley, it has retained some value when used to arrange tools from one vicinity in an approximate chronological order (see Table IV), and in its day it effectively quashed rash speculation about "eoliths." Eoliths, or "dawn tools," were reported in the nineteenth century from extremely old pre-Pleistocene gravels all over the world and, for a time at least, held to be the earliest tools of man. Unfortunately, careful examination of these tools showed them to be as genuine as their namesake, Dawn Man (*Eoanthropus dawsoni*), the famous Piltdown fraud. Most eoliths were, in fact, nothing more than products of natural flaking in running water, where stone abrades against stone. Although eoliths often are a source of amusement, embarrassment, or derision to modern archaeologists, it must be said in all fairness that the earliest stone tools are not always easy to distinguish from the products of natural weathering and that often their status as tools rests on the examination of the total context of an undisturbed site and analysis of thousands of pieces of stone for the signs of regular or patterned alteration that will differentiate them from the works of nature. Beginning in the 1880's, Dr. Georg Schweinfurth, a German geologist and archaeologist, reported such eoliths from different vicinities in Egypt, including the 200- and 150-foot terraces which Sandford and Arkell later found to be sterile. Although Schweinfurth's pioneering studies place him among the founders of Egyptian Palaeolithic archaeology, after Arcelin, Hamy, and Lenormant, he had, according to another prominent archaeologist and anthropologist, Charles G. Seligman, a tendency to "see eoliths everywhere" and to classify much later implements as eolithic (Seligman 1921: 116). Today, although the "eolith" has been assigned to the scientific graveyard, the search for the earliest men and their tools goes on. To date, the earliest tools yet known from the lower Nile Valley come from the cliffs of Abu Simbel, across the river from the spectacular temple of Rameses II. Based on geological evidence, they date to the Lower Pleistocene, about 700,000 years ago, and were deposited during a rainy period or pluvial when the gigantic Protonile flowed 10 to 15 kilometers west of its present course and stood as much as 100 meters above the modern Nile bed (see Table III). Slightly later in time, perhaps dating to 500,000 years ago, are stray finds of stone tools, including Lower Palaeolithic "hand axes," found by Sandford and Arkell in the so-called 50-foot and 100-foot Nile river terraces.

The first scientific description of the Chellean and Acheulean hand axes reported by Sandford and Arkell was offered by Boucher de Perthes in the second quarter of the nineteenth century after material he discovered in his Somme River gravels. De Perthes called them *coup-de-poing*, which is rendered hand ax in English, though some later nineteenth-century archaeologists used the word *boucher* in honor of the French archaeologist.

As I mentioned before, there were earlier reports of such hand axes, but they were largely ignored because of the predominant belief in a short, Biblical chronology. One of the most famous and precise of these early accounts was penned by the Englishman John Frere and appeared in volume 13 of the journal *Archaeologia* in 1800 under the title, "Account of Flint Weapons Discovered at Hoxne in Suffolk." The account was in the form of a letter dated June 22, 1797, and is notable for its advanced use of geological stratigraphy and associated extinct animal remains in attempting to date the implements in question. Frere describes the flints as evidently weapons of war, fabricated and used by a people who had not the use of metals. They lay in great numbers at the depth of about twelve feet, in a stratified soil, which was dug into for the purpose of raising clay for bricks.

The strata are as follows:
1. Vegetable earth 1½ feet.
2. Argill 7½ feet.
3. Sand mixed with shells and other marine substances 1 foot.
4. A gravelly soil, in which the flints are found, generally at the rate of five or six in a square yard, 2 feet.

In the same stratum . . . and in the stratum of sand (No. 3), were found some extraordinary bones, particularly a jaw-bone of enormous size, of some unknown animal, with the teeth remaining in it.

The situation in which these weapons were found may tempt us to refer them to a very remote period indeed; even beyond that of the present world. . . .

Although Frere's discovery was greeted with polite silence, he was to be vindicated 150 years later in a personal way when his direct descendant, Dr. Mary D. Leakey, and her husband, Louis Leakey, discovered the oldest archaeological site in the world at Olduvai Gorge in Tanzania and, in so doing, revolutionized the study of the past. So important are the finds at Olduvai for world prehistory in general and African prehistory in particular, that any attempt to understand the earliest age of man in Egypt must begin there.

In 1959, after they had operated for years on a minuscule budget, Louis and Mary Leakey's persistence was richly rewarded. Working in the lowest geological stratum (Bed I) almost 100 meters below the canyon rim, they discovered the remains of a large hominid or manlike fossil almost two million years old, which they called *Zinjanthropus boisei*. Even more important for archaeology was what the Leakeys found along with their ancient hominid. Thousands of animal bones and crude stone tools remained in place, preserved by solidified volcanic ash in much the same way that Pompeii was sealed eons later. By employing potassium-argon dating, scientists determined that the DK site—the oldest living floor in the world—was about 1.75 million years old. Taken together, the stone artifacts comprise what archaeologists call the Olduwan Industry and include a variety of piercing, cutting, and scraping implements made either on crudely flaked, fist-sized cobbles or by simply utilizing the sharp flakes that were detached from their "cores" by percussion. Louis Leakey believed that some chipped stone balls in the site were used in crude bollas and Mary Leakey has argued that many of the splintered bones at the DK site show signs of use—a view not readily accepted by most archaeologists. On the same occupation level, the Leakeys uncovered what many then believed to be the oldest building ever found:

> The circle of lava blocks was discovered on the occupation floor during 1962. . . . The circle measured approximately 14 ft. in diameter from east to west and 12 ft. from north to south. It was formed by blocks of vesicular basalt, loosely piled round the circumference to a maximum height of just under 1 ft. . . . On the north side . . . there were groups of stones piled up into small heaps. It is possible to identify six of these piles which rise to a height of 6-9 in. and are spaced at intervals of 2-2½ ft., suggesting that they may have been placed as supports for branches or poles stuck into the ground to form a windbreak or rough shelter.
>
> In general appearance the circle resembles temporary structures often made by present-day nomadic peoples who build a low stone wall round their dwellings to serve either as a windbreak or as a base to support upright branches which are bent over and covered with either skins or grass. (Leakey 1971: 24)

Who built this structure, if that indeed is what it was, and who manufactured the stone tools—whether Zinjanthropus or a meat-eating cousin —is still a matter of debate. But one thing is certain: the Leakeys revealed at Olduvai one of the oldest and perhaps the most continuous stratigraphic records of human cultural evolution ever found. Beginning at the base of Bed I about two million years ago, man's tools and fossilized remains are associated with four thick layers and numerous climatic episodes, culminating in the microlithic stone blades of Capsian peoples dating to about 10,000 years ago. The layers of Olduvai are like a book on whose pages is printed in boldface the outline of Palaeolithic evolution, chapter by chapter.

The Olduwan Industry underwent gradual change over a million years, slowly acquiring sophistication and, presumably, increased efficiency, so that we speak of its later stages (between about one million and 750,000 years ago) as Advanced Olduwan. The creatures who used these tools and built their crude shelters on the shores of the ancient lake at Olduvai stood only four or five feet tall but already possessed the hallmarks of humanity—large brains and two-footed locomotion. Their fossilized remains are now well known from several sites in South Africa, from Olduvai Gorge and Lake Rudolph in East Africa, and from the Omo and Afar river valleys in Ethiopia. At present, two or perhaps three types are thought to have existed simultaneously in the late Pliocene and early Pleistocene geologic periods (ca. 5–1 million years ago)—a large, presumably vegetarian form (like Zinjanthropus) generally called *Australopithecus robustus* that seems to have died out; and a smaller form, *Australopithecus africanus*, that hunted as well as browsed, and which many believe was our ancestor. A third form, *Homo habilis*, has also been proposed as our ancestor on the theory that its brain was significantly larger than that of *africanus*.

To date, neither australopithecines nor Olduwan tools have been found in the lower Nile Valley (Egypt and the Sudan), but despite this disappointing lack of evidence, there is now reason to suspect the presence of man's earliest ancestors in Egypt.

Over a hundred years ago Charles Darwin speculated, without fossil evidence, that the cradle of humanity might lie in the African continent. In the last fifty years many anthropologists have come to believe that man indeed did originate in Africa in the late Pliocene or early Pleistocene and slowly spread out from there, so that by 750,000 years ago he had settled northwest Africa, southern Europe, and much of tropical and subtropical Asia. Other experts believe that we will eventually find the early hominid remains in any tropical or subtropical area of the Old World during the late Pliocene–early Pleistocene period, providing conditions permitted their preservation. Regardless of which view we accept, we can build a strong circumstantial case for the presence of early australopithecine ancestors along the Nile. If our ancestors really did originate in southern and eastern Africa and spread over much of the habitable world by 750,000 years ago, then the Valley of the Nile would have been an ideal route of migration. Although that river was still not connected to its Ethiopian sources, it did drain all of Egypt and reached well into the Sudan. Beyond this, to the south, other streams would have flowed into closed drainage basins, forming a chain of rich lakes and river systems that led into eastern Africa. This period was characterized by abundant and prolonged rainfall in Egypt and Nubia, so that we can easily envision northeast Africa as rich in tropical and subtropical plants and animals. The shores of the Protonile, and the bordering grasslands, must have acted like a giant corridor providing entry to the north for tropical African plants and animals. In a way roughly analogous to the Bering land bridge that permitted man and other animals to populate the New World, the valley and hinterlands of the huge Protonile, watered by abundant rains throughout the year, must surely have felt the footsteps of man well over a million years ago.

To imagine what it must have been like in those times, we must picture some of the rolling semiarid savannas of eastern and southern Africa today, such as the Serengeti Plain. Giraffes, gazelles, and even hippopotami abounded on the now arid margins of the Nile Valley during the periodic rainy or pluvial periods that prevailed in the Southern Hemisphere as glacial advances and retreats in the north altered worldwide patterns of rainfall during the Pleistocene. Our ancestors followed the game and plant life and congregated around good fishing holes, expanding and contracting their wanderings in response to the pressures exerted by local climatic conditions.

Although still speculation, the idea of a Nilotic corridor is also supported by the continuous distribution of fossil hominids from South Africa to Ethiopia, suggesting that if paleoanthropologists were able to locate and explore appropriate geological beds in the Sudan and Egypt, they would find australopithecines there. Those of us who are optimists like to think that the absence of such geological beds rather than the real absence of fossil hominids accounts for our failure to date to uncover Olduwan industries in Egypt. With the major revisions being made today in our understanding of the Nile's history, perhaps such tools even now await a young John Frere or Mary Leakey, hidden in remnant shore deposits of the ancient Protonile somewhere in the Western Desert.

5

WHEN THE DESERT BLOOMED

**Hand Axes, Inselbergs, and Fossil Springs:
In Search of Acheuleans**

AT ROUGHLY the same time Sandford and Arkell were conducting their epic-making prehistoric survey on behalf of the Oriental
Institute of the University of Chicago, Gertrude Caton-Thompson and
Elinor Gardner were exploring Kharga Oasis in the Western Desert for
the Royal Anthropological Institute. Caton-Thompson, whose pioneering
researches in the Fayum and at Hemamieh in Upper Egypt I will
discuss later, was probably the first modern archaeologist in Egypt to
report late Lower Palaeolithic (Acheulean) (ca. 250,000–90,000 B.P.) and
Middle Palaeolithic (Mousterian) (ca. 90,000–30,000 B.P.) industries far
out in the desert and to carefully record the relationship between prehistoric implements and the geological-ecological context in which they
were found. It was Caton-Thompson and her geologist colleague, Gardner, who first discovered the peculiar way in which stone tools were often
cemented inside calcareous deposits from fossil springs that had been
active during late Lower and Middle Palaeolithic times.

This information provided the key to locating some of the earliest
known sites in the Western Desert after the Second World War when
systematic exploration of that inhospitable region resumed on a large
scale. Sponsored by Fred Wendorf and Rushdi Said, between 1963 and
1965, James Hester, Philip Hoebler, and Frank Eddy set out to explore the
prehistoric settlement patterns of a huge area around Dungul Oasis about
75 miles from the Nile, deep in the wastes of the Western Desert.

> The area of study being isolated, it was necessary that all food, water,
> gasoline, spare parts, etc., be brought in to the base camp. . . .
> *(Hester and Hoebler 1970: 18)*

Like the nomads who live in the desert and like Sandford and Arkell
forty years before, mobility was one of the principal concerns to the
members of the Dungul project:

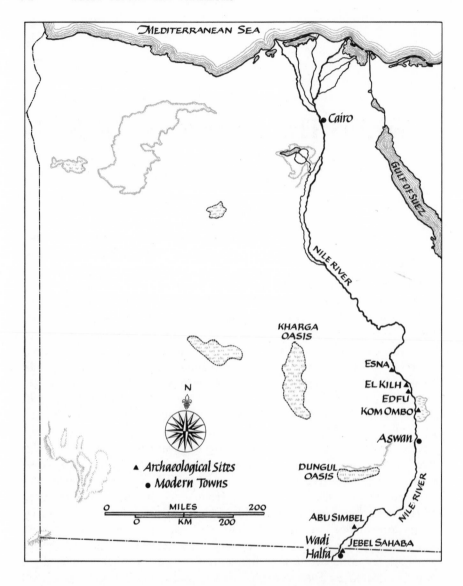

13   Distribution map showing the location of important Palaeolithic sites in
     Egypt and Nubia

A total of six trucks (two 5-ton lorries and four pick-ups) and two
trail cycles were used. Three of the pick-up trucks were generally available for field work with one normally being down for repairs. The
cycles were used for emergency transportation and occasional field
work. *(Hester and Hoebler 1970: 18)*

Six trucks and two motorcycles—how things had changed since Sandford and Arkell first struggled back to Chicago House with two battered and ruined cars!

Palaeolithic sites in the desert are generally found in one of two situations: around dried-up springs, ponds, and lakes or where raw materials for making stone tools abound. More often than not, manufacturing sites in the Western Desert (also known as the Libyan or Nubian Desert; the part of the Egyptian Sahara west of the Nile) generally occur on eroded hilltops or *inselbergs*, while habitation sites are found in lower-lying areas near former sources of water. Although modern archaeologists make much of the need to reconstruct ancient patterns of settlement and characteristically try to relate these to the biological and geographical characteristics of an era, this is often quite difficult in dealing with extremely old sites, like those of Acheulean times, which have been subjected to

14   View of Dungul Oasis in the Western Desert, one of the last remnants of the vegetation which covered the Sahara during the Pluvial periods

massive, long-term geological and climatic change. Such massive erosion has also prevented the development of deeply stratified sites, like Olduvai, in Egypt and in Nubia. For example, at Dungul

> most sites consisted of surface concentrations of artifacts lying upon bedrock, because extreme deflation had removed the soil. There were few sites with cultural fill which could be excavated. A second limitation, interfering with typological analysis, was presented by artifacts with eroded chipping scars due to sand-blasting. Along with erosion, deposition had also affected the possibility of locating sites; undoubtedly many are buried beneath the alluvial fans and pediments resulting from mass wasting of the adjacent buttes.
>
> *(Hester and Hoebler 1970: 18)*

Umm Shagir (also known as Site 8715) provides an example of the practical problems created by the sparse and eroded nature of even the best Acheulean locality in Dungul. The site was discovered on top of a 150-meter hill and consisted of a scatter of 159 artifacts spread out over a 400 by 700 meter area—hardly a rich site. Unfortunately, none of the stone tools recovered by Hester and Hoebler consisted of the "classic" Acheulean hand axes—a fairly common disappointment in Egypt that makes even approximate dating of sites difficult. At Umm Shagir the presence of shallow pits containing fresh artifacts led Hester and Hoebler to observe that people originally visited this hill in order to mine the native quartzite for tools.

Fortunately, not all late Acheulean sites are so poorly preserved and heavily weathered, as demonstrated by the work of the Polish archaeologist Waldemar Chmielewski in the middle 1960's. His site, called Arkin 8, lies near the town of Wadi Halfa close to the Nile Valley. Chmielewski dug and reported Arkin 8 with a degree of care and thoroughness seldom seen in earlier Palaeolithic work in Egypt and Nubia. He was also fortunate in that, unlike the sites in Dungul Oasis and the stray finds of hand axes made earlier by Sandford and Arkell in the 100- and 50-foot gravel terraces of the Nile, Arkin 8 was astoundingly rich; for example, 2,754 artifacts were recovered from an area 64 meters square and only 20 to 25 centimeters deep (Chmielewski in Wendorf 1968: 110-117), and this area represents only one-eighth of the entire site! In addition to its size and richness, Arkin 8 boasts the earliest known shelters or houselike structures in Egypt and the Sudan, which, next to the Leakeys' stone ring at Olduvai, are among the earliest dwellings in the world. One structure was an oval pit 30 centimeters deep and 1.8 by 1.2 meters across. The depression appeared to be partly lined and floored with flat sandstone slabs. Another structure was more difficult to define, comprising a scatter of several large sandstone blocks which appeared to the excavator to form an irregular circle. From such finds, it seems possible that at Arkin 8 we are dealing with the remains of one or more "tent rings," in which heavy rocks were used to tack down skins or brush that formerly were stretched over a makeshift frame. Although it is true that such stone circles could also be the product of mining operations or even of chance erosion, the existence of a tent ring at Arkin 8 is logical given the prevalence of similar buildings among modern hunting and gathering and nomadic peoples and the presence of a similar feature at Dungul Oasis (Site 8817) tentatively dated to the Khargan period (perhaps 40,000 to 50,000 years ago). Unlike the earlier Arkin 8 structures, the Dungul ring is indeed impressive, consisting of vertically laid tufa slabs carefully placed in the earth to form a circular enclosure 11 meters in diameter—an area big enough to enclose an extended family. In addition to tent circles, the presence of distinct artifact clusters at Arkin 8 also gives us an unusual insight into the daily life of Acheulean times, hinting at the very places where ancient craftsmen squatted and chipped their stone artifacts, and suggesting in a general way early divisions of labor in evolving human society.

"Surely one of the most isolated and desolate places on Earth" is how excavator Fred Wendorf describes another Acheulean locality, Site BS-14, located in the Libyan Desert in the now parched Bir Sahara depression (Wendorf *et al.*, 1976: 103). The depression is a flat-bottomed, shallow basin which supported artesian-fed lakes during late Acheulean and Mousterian times (ca. 120,000–40,000 years ago). Site BS-14 lies around and in an ancient spring vent similar to those found by Caton-Thompson at Kharga Oasis and Hester, Hoebler, and Eddy at Dungul Oasis. Its early date (final Acheulean—ca. 100,000+ years ago) as well as the association of early faunal remains including ostrich eggshell and the bones of a horselike creature (possibly *Equus asinus*—the wild ass) make it, along with Arkin 8, one of the few and most important Lower Palaeolithic sites in Egypt. The presence of ostrich eggshell recalls a custom employed by the contemporary bushmen of the Kalahari Desert, who use these objects as water canteens on hunting trips into the desert, while the equid bones may suggest that the late Acheuleans had migrated out onto the grassy plains of the Sahara during the Abbassia Pluvial, or rainy period. This pluvial, which prevailed for nearly 30,000 years between about 120,000 and 90,000 years ago, succeeded a 400,000-year drought and in its wake sent late Acheulean peoples out onto the former wastes in search of large grazing animals. The manner of hunting must have been based on driving and trapping game—a technique attested from earlier Acheulean sites like Torralba-Ambrona in Spain (ca. 275,000 years ago) and by much later historic "game trap walls" discovered in Dungul Oasis. In any event, the limited pasturage, few reliable water holes, and seasonal rainfall available during the Abbassia Pluvial would have created conditions whereby the men of that era (who were just making the transition between what anthropologists call *Homo erectus* and *Homo sapiens neandertalensis*) would have traveled seasonally onto the open grasslands, retreating to permanent watering holes during the dry season. Around such springs the presence of fossil pollen and plant remains indicates that plant food was abundant at oases like Bir Sahara, Dungul, and Kharga during the Palaeolithic pluvials. We might conjecture that, during the dry season when groups concentrated around permanent water holes like Bir Sahara, women, children, and older males would have browsed for the bulk of a group's food in the immediate vicinity of the oasis while the adult males hunted the farther peripheries.

While sites like Bir Sahara-14 and Arkin 8 reveal something of the rhythm and organization of late Acheulean life, they are surface sites without significant stratification and cannot be dated with any precision. The need to devise a chronology for the Acheulean has led the French archaeologists Guichard and Guichard to propose early and late variants of the Acheulean based on stylistic and technological differences between assemblages of stone tools (e.g., Guichard and Guichard 1968: 148-163). Unfortunately, the artifacts found on most Egyptian and Nubian late Acheulean sites are not stylistically sophisticated and, especially in the absence of local, stratified sites (like Olduvai in eastern Africa), most archaeologists feel that it is nearly impossible to date Lower Palaeolithic sites in relation to one another. From the viewpoint of establishing an effective relative chronology for the Acheulean the most important breakthroughs have come from recent investigations in the Western Desert that link geological-climatic epochs like the Abbassia Pluvial with certain well-defined later Acheulean tool assemblages and provide a rough estimate for the end of the Lower Palaeolithic. Sadly, it is virtually impossible to relate any Lower Palaeolithic dates to our own calendar because the radioactive-dating techniques most frequently employed with prehistoric material, carbon-14 and potassium-argon, are not useful in dating the period of time between about 250,000 and 70,000 years ago—i.e., the late Lower Palaeolithic and early Middle Palaeolithic eras. The dates presented in this book therefore (e.g., Table III), are highly tentative and before 45,000 B.C. based on liberal assumptions and cross-dating with better-known sequences in other parts of the world. As new techniques are discovered and old ones refined, it is hoped this chronological gap will be filled so that archaeologists will have a reliable guideline as they plumb the depths of the earlier Palaeolithic prehistory of Egypt.

Enter the Spear: The Middle Palaeolithic

One of the most striking scenes awaiting the unwarned traveler coming to the depressions of the Bir Sahara–Bir Terfawi area are large dark portions of deflated floor literally covered by carpets of Mousterian artifacts.

(Schild and Wendorf in Wendorf and Marks 1975: 98)

Such were conditions at the height of the Mousterian Pluvial, between about 50,000 and 30,000 years ago, when springs, lakes, and lush grasslands covered much of the Sahara, even surpassing the conditions that had prevailed in the heyday of the earlier Abbassia Pluvial. But the Middle Palaeolithic or the Mousterian, as it is sometimes called after the type-site in Le Moustier, France, did not begin on such an optimistic note. About 90,000 years ago the Abbassia Pluvial drew to a close and the Sahara returned to desert conditions. Initially, the Neanderthaloid peoples who had evolved out of *Homo erectus* during the late Acheulean took refuge in the Nile Valley and the great oases like Kharga.

At about the same time a change in technology occurred involving the development of a more efficient stone-tool industry generally known as Levalloisian after the site in France where it was first officially described. Simply put, the levallois technique involves the production of a special tortoise-shaped core from which relatively symmetrical, relatively thin flakes are removed. The flakes, in turn, are used to make the majority of tools. The advantage of the levallois technique was that it represented an advance over older methods which either demanded that a large hunk of raw material be flaked down to form a single core tool, or that the

15   A typical levallois core from Thebes

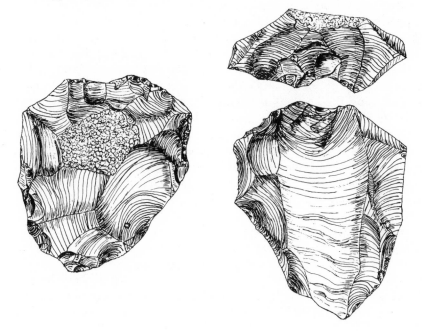

16 Levallois points from Egypt

highly varied flakes produced in this fashion be retouched or used as is. With the levallois technique, however, thin, sharp flakes of predictable and standardized shape could be made and later retouched from one (unifacial) or both (bifacial) directions, creating a more diversified tool kit in which individual tool types were more effectively standardized.

Among the new tools manufactured by the levallois process, one especially heralded a new efficiency in hunting that must have been of revolutionary importance—the stone projectile point. Levallois points were not only preshaped but often retouched to facilitate hafting them to wooden shafts. It is difficult today to appreciate the impact of such a discovery, but the superiority of stone projectile points over the old fire-hardened wooden spear must have permitted a great increase in hunting efficiency as well as a change in hunting tactics and strategies. It was perhaps this invention that was responsible for Middle Palaeolithic hunters in some areas of the world focusing their attention increasingly on one type of game (for instance, sheep and goats in the highland Middle East)—an early step on the long road to domestication. In addition to stone points, better and more specialized scrapers and borers were possible using the levallois technique. Bifacially worked tools were no longer as common as in the Lower Palaeolithic and when they were made, they were generally smaller and more carefully worked than in earlier times. Although some tools made on blades (long, narrow, parallel-sided flakes at least twice as long as they are wide) foreshadowed later technological developments of the late Upper Palaeolithic in the same way that forerunners of the levallois technique can occasionally be found in late Lower Palaeolithic industries, they are not statistically important until much later times.

Perhaps it was the fortunate coincidence of this series of technological inventions linked with the major climatic change brought on by the Mousterian Subpluvial that permitted a real flowering of later Middle Palaeolithic cultures. Egypt is covered with Middle Palaeolithic sites, some in the most unlikely places. It was not really until the 1920's and

1930's that we began to appreciate the true distribution of Middle Palaeolithic cultures through the surveys of Sandford and Arkell, who reported finds from various Nile terraces below the 30-foot level, from the Eastern Desert all the way to the Red Sea coast and, most surprisingly, in the barren Liqiya depression in the southern Libyan Desert. At the same time, Caton-Thompson's prehistoric survey produced a number of Middle Palaeolithic (Mousterian) sites at Kharga Oasis and in the Fayum, including the first apparently undisturbed (*in situ*) Middle Palaeolithic sites at Kharga. From the first, it was apparent that these localities were associated with a moist climatic episode, being located around fossil springs and along the scarp of the depression. Caton-Thompson's biggest problem—similar to that encountered by other Palaeolithic archaeologists like the Guichards—was that, lacking carbon-14 dating and superimposed sites, there was no way of determining which of her sites were early and which were late. She did not know then as we do today that the Mousterian Subpluvial came in the latter half of the Middle Palaeolithic (ca. 50,000–30,000 B.C.). All she had to work with were her separate surface sites. By arranging her collections according to stylistic characteristics, she proposed that the earliest variant, which she called "lower Levalloisian," was characterized by fairly crude tortoise-shaped cores which became more refined by "upper Levalloisian" times. Unfortunately, her collections were so small that the scheme was not statistically valid. Since that time, especially in the last decade, the specter of small collections that do not comprise valid statistical samples has come to haunt all archaeology, and especially Palaeolithic archaeology, where generalizations of sweeping changes were made often on the basis of a few, fancy artifacts. Obviously, the solution is to collect larger samples and to count everything. This is precisely what Dr. Chmielewski did in 1965 at Arkin 5, a generation after Caton-Thompson's pioneering study at Kharga.

Chmielewski's approach to Arkin 5 was similar to that used on the earlier Arkin 8 site. An area of 100 square meters between 5 and 40 centimeters deep was excavated and yielded a very large sample: 9,769 artifacts of ferrocrete sandstone. In fact, this material clustered in three distinct concentrations. According to his report (Chmielewski in Wendorf 1968 I: 134–147), only 165 of these, or 1.58 percent, were deliberately worked "tools." On the basis of such a low percentage of finished artifacts, it was believed that Arkin 5 had been a manufacturing locality. Although such may well be the case, the fact that the so-called waste flakes were not checked for signs of use suggests that perhaps the sharp edges of flakes that are commonly used as tools might have been put to some use directly connected with nonmanufacturing activities like hunting, food processing, shaping of wood or skins or the like. Recently archaeologists have begun to realize that the study of waste is as necessary as the study of well-made artifacts and have even taken to chipping and using their own stone tools in order to determine experimentally the relationship between tool manufacture and tool use. The worked tools at Arkin 5 included levallois cores; small, "foliated" hand axes and points; knives; picks; bifacial and transverse scrapers; denticulates and truncations. Some of the knives and points had crude stems for hafting, perhaps foreshadowing the tanged points of the somewhat later Aterian Industry. One of the exciting features of Arkin 5 was the existence of distinct artifact clusters located in shallow depressions dug into the underlying red sand and Nubian sandstone. These depressions were about 2.5 meters in diameter and occasionally their sides were lined with slabs of ferrocrete sandstone. The function of the depressions is unclear; they may have been shelters of the type seen in the Acheulean site at Arkin 8 or mining pits like those found by Hester and Hoebler at Dungul Oasis.

Whatever the reason for the clusters of Mousterian artifacts at Arkin 5, such features are common occurrences on shallow sites where hunting and gathering peoples returned periodically, pitching their tents, building their hearths, making and sharpening their tools, and scattering their debris in roughly circular or oval concentrations. We have almost come to anticipate the presence of horizontal clusters, so it was quite surprising to the Polish scientist Romuald Schild and his American colleague Fred Wendorf when recently excavated Mousterian sites in the Bir Sahara depression of the Libyan Desert failed to yield such concentrations:

> Most important of all is the positive lack of any traces of clustering which could have suggested smaller homogeneous occupation units within areally extensive settlement mantles, a situation highly divergent from those found at several Upper and Late Paleolithic sites in Europe and North Africa, where scatter-patterning of artifacts was put into operation. This observation might suggest, in spite of the very limited experience with Mousterian spatial distribution of artifacts, a radically different social and/or functional patterning of the settlements from Bir Sahara from all other Middle Paleolithic settlements. Small, internally contained, homogeneous occupation units, which often make up the larger settlements of Upper or Late Paleolithic, are frequently interpreted as representing closely tied small social units partially isolated within larger structures and identified with families.
>
> *(Schild and Wendorf in Wendorf and Marks 1975: 105)*

Whether we accept the reality of the lack of internal patterning at Bir Sahara or ascribe it to natural (i.e., geological) agencies, the type of speculation represented by Schild and Wendorf's hypothesis is at least based on the careful mapping of practically every flake and promises to stimulate an active if not heated debate about aspects of human prehistory seldom thought liable to the deductive approach of archaeology.

In addition to intrasite differences at sites like Arkin 5 and the Bir Sahara, archaeologists have detected a number of regional variants or "facies" during the Middle Palaeolithic, including a distinctive denticulate Mousterian in the Western Desert. Perhaps these facies represent different traditions of different peoples or different environmental adaptations of the same people. Perhaps the puzzling number of Mousterian variants now being reported is more an artifact of our meticulous taxonomic "splitting" of stone-tool assemblages and perhaps it reflects the multiethnic and multicultural roots of the Middle Palaeolithic. Whatever the case, we cannot but appreciate the far-flung radiation of human populations that was accomplished by the Neanderthaloid peoples of the Middle Palaeolithic as they colonized almost every available niche of North Africa in the wake of the great Mousterian Subpluvial.

Aterian Archers and the Impact of Radiocarbon Dating

The Assyrian came down like the wolf on the fold,
And his cohorts were gleaming in purple and gold;
And the sheen on their spears was like the stars on the sea,
When the blue wave rolls nightly on deep Galilee.
                    —Byron, "Destruction of Sennacherib"

In the prestigious Huxley Memorial Lecture for 1946, Gertrude Caton-Thompson addressed herself to "The Aterian Industry: Its Place and Significance in the Palaeolithic World." In some ways, her interpretation of the processes of cultural change set into motion by the Aterians recalls Byron's famous poem.

And when, as in the Aterian, the tanged point is accompanied by unmistakable arrowheads of more than one sort, and spear blades up to 22 cm.—nearly 9 ins.—long, it needs no imagination to visualize not only a new and formidable mechanical force let loose in the African world, able, if its possessors so desired, to impose their territorial or other wishes upon neighbors, as well as to outdo them in hunting prowess; but, for good or evil, a palaeolithic group collectively or individually endowed intellectually beyond its contemporaries, being capable of extending the age-old simple contrivance of the sling-stone or bolas into the complex and far more accurate and deadly propulsive force of the bow and arrow. (Caton-Thompson 1946b: 88)

Caton-Thompson's insight seems less significant when we recall that the invention of stone and bone-tipped lances had already occurred in Mousterian times. However, her characterization of the far-reaching technological impact of the Aterian technology on northern Africa treats a central theme about which questions of chronology, technology, climatology, cultural change, and the very notion of human progress have been united.

Earlier I touched on the importance of time to prehistorians and historians alike, and the critical role dating plays in our interpretation of ancient events and processes. Only a year after Caton-Thompson's lecture on the Aterian, Willard F. Libby of the University of Chicago announced a major breakthrough of truly revolutionary import for archaeology in general and the dating and evaluation of the Aterian in particular—the discovery of carbon-14 dating.

Carbon-14, or radiocarbon dating, originated as a byproduct of Libby's nuclear research in the Second World War and is based on the fact that all living things maintain a relatively constant amount of the unstable isotope carbon-14 within their systems. At death, the intake of carbon-14 ceases and the remaining amounts within the plant or animal tissue begin to decay at a constant rate. Within a period of 5,730 years, half the specific carbon-14 radioactivity will have changed into nitrogen-14 and carbon-12, a more stable isotope of carbon. This period is known as a half-life. Obviously, if we can determine the relative proportion of radioactivity present in any ancient organic matter, we will be able to calculate the number of years that have elapsed since death. There are several important limitations to this process, however: first, after a certain amount of time so much carbon-14 will have decayed that it becomes impossible to measure the infinitesimal residual radioactivity and therefore impossible to estimate the age of the sample. The carbon-14 technique, therefore, is seldom accurate beyond about 50,000 years ago. In some special cases, by using what is called an enrichment technique, certain laboratories are able to push carbon-14 dates back as far as 70,000 years.

Second, all radiocarbon dates are really averages, and they are accompanied by a plus or minus factor of from 50 to several thousand years (e.g., 5645 ± 150 years B.P.). Generally speaking, the farther back in time we go, the greater the statistical margin of error. Thus, a date 2,000 years ago may be within 75 years of the "true" date, whereas a date 50,000 years ago might vary 1,000 years or more from the "true" date.

Third, one out of three carbon-14 dates is inaccurate due to contamination of the sample and similar problems. A fourth and rather recently discovered factor affecting the accuracy of radiocarbon dates is a flaw in the basic assumption that makes the method possible. Heretofore we believed that the production of carbon-14 in the atmosphere was constant through time. We now realize, however, that variations in the magnetic fields of the earth in the past have altered this rate slightly and introduced certain errors into our dating formula. These errors have recently been revealed by comparing carbon-14 dates with known

Egyptian Dynastic dates and tree-ring dates from the long-lived bristle-cone pine of the American Southwest. By means of these checks, it has been possible to construct a correction factor for radiocarbon dates back to 5145 B.C.

In dating Predynastic and early Dynastic sites, therefore, we should remember that many of Libby's carbon-14 estimates for Egypt are from several hundred to a thousand years too late—a factor appreciated by many Egyptologists who were subjected to often severe and unwarranted criticism for their "unscientific" and "outmoded" dates in the early days of carbon-14 estimation. A final factor affecting the accuracy of carbon-14 dates should be considered. When we date a large wooden beam from an ancient tomb, for example, we are dating the time at which the tree was cut down but *not necessarily* the time at which the beam was carved or installed in the tomb. Many years may have passed before the wood was used, and it might have been reutilized many times before arriving at its final resting place. We know that the reuse of a predecessor's monuments and possessions was a common habit of pharaohs, who seemed to have worried little about prior ownership. Given such problems, archaeologists often favor the use of short-lived plants like reeds or twigs and artifacts manufactured from them, like baskets or cloth. Any organic material, though, is potential fodder for the carbon-14 technique, including bone, shell, hair, skin, and related materials as well as soil carbonates.

Despite the difficulties involved with carbon-14 dating, it has given us a control over time unimagined 30 years ago. One of the unexpected byproducts of this control has been a wholly new status for the Aterian. In Caton-Thompson's time—indeed, until ten years ago—we believed that the Aterian was contemporary with the Upper Palaeolithic cultures of Western Europe, that is, it flourished from about 30,000 to 15,000 or 20,000 years ago. Since Aterian technology was strongly rooted in earlier Mousterian or levallois practices, its late date seemed to be yet one more example of the essentially backward nature of the non-European world during the Upper Palaeolithic. When *our* ancestors were painting those pretty pictures at Lascaux and Altamira and fashioning beautifully made flint spearheads and bone harpoons and needles, other peoples' ancestors were still living in the long night of a moldering Mousterian tradition.

This metaphor of European progress contrasted to Third World cultural lag found perhaps its most ludicrous expression in attempts to derive *Homo sapiens sapiens* (modern man) from non-Neanderthaloid precursors, which evolved first in Western Europe. Such was the prejudice that dominated Middle Palaeolithic research until a generation ago, that Neanderthal finds were even misreconstructed and badly described to emphasize the differences from, rather than the similarities to, modern man. Modern research by physical anthropologists like C. Loring Brace and M. Wolpoff and archaeologists like David Brose has shown that in Europe the supposed break in tool traditions and bodily appearance that heralded the arrival of Upper Palaeolithic "modern man" and separated him from his "brutish" Middle Palaeolithic Neanderthal cousins was an artifact of poor archaeology and paleontology coupled with inadequate dating of the finds. Thanks in part to the radiocarbon revolution and in part to more careful archaeology and physical anthropology, the slow and fairly continuous evolution of Middle Palaeolithic culture and physique to Upper Palaeolithic culture and physique has been demonstrated. The modern cultural and biological catastrophists have been defeated. But for long years our conviction of the cultural superiority of Upper Palaeolithic Western European culture remained. Ignoring the fact that most of the research has been done in Europe and most of the scientists studying other areas understandably compared their discoveries to better-known European sites, we have often fallen into the trap of relegating the Palaeolithic cultures of other lands to second-place positions while viewing all progress as the product of a semimystical "diffusion" of "higher culture" from mother Europe. Just as recent radiocarbon dates have toppled the Middle East from its position of cultural preeminence, new estimates for non-European assemblages have shown surprisingly early dates for certain technological innovations. For instance, blade technology, a hallmark of the Eurasian Upper Palaeolithic, seems considerably older in the Levant than in Western Europe. And now, since 1968, a series of radiocarbon dates have forced us to push the Aterian back at least 10,000 years, to over 40,000 years ago and to place its demise at just under 30,000 years B.P. In Western European terms, then, the Aterian is late Middle Palaeolithic and not, as once believed, Upper Palaeolithic.

The new dates for the Aterian Industry have raised new problems. In Caton-Thompson's day, when all we had to work with were the tools themselves, our explanations were, perforce, oriented toward artifact typology and cultural diffusion. Today, with a better idea of the true age of Aterian assemblages and more refined techniques of excavation, recording, and analysis, we are turning away from diffusion and invasion-oriented explanations to consider in more detail the technological and environmental significance of the Aterian Industry.

The first problem raised by the newfound antiquity of the Aterian concerns the "unmistakable arrowheads" which Caton-Thompson characterizes as ". . . a new formidable mechanical force let loose in the African world, able, if its possessors so desired to impose their territorial or other wishes upon neighbors as well as outdo them in hunting prowess . . ." (Caton-Thompson 1946b: 88). From a purely technological viewpoint, if one reexamines the original drawings of Aterian tanged points at a one-to-one scale these artifacts seem at once too big and too bulky to have been used as projectile points on primitive arrows. Moreover, 45,000 years ago seems considerably too early for the bow and

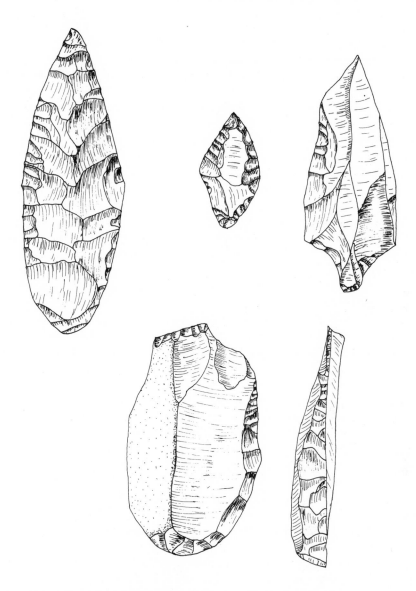

17   Assorted Aterian artifacts. From left to right and top to bottom: large
     foliate biface, small tanged point, large tanged point, end scraper

arrow—an invention first attested in Egypt from the end of the Late
Palaeolithic (ca. 10,000–12,000 B.C.) at Jebel Sahaba (see Chapter 6) and
dating several thousand years later in Europe (ca. 7000 B.C.). If Aterian
tanged points do represent a real technological advancement, they were
probably employed as dart points in spear throwers, certainly not as
arrowheads. Like the Mousterian tradition from which the Aterian In-

dustry apparently derived, it may be that the invention of the spear thrower, like the development of the stone-tipped thrusting spear at the beginning of the Middle Palaeolithic, made possible new hunting strategies, thereby affecting deeply the life-styles and social organizations of its possessors.

A second factor that must be considered when trying to understand the Aterian is that its spread occurred in conjunction with the climatic improvement brought about by the Mousterian Subpluvial, and followed hard on the heels of a slightly earlier expansion of Mousterian peoples out on to the newly greened savannas of the Sahara. The relationship between the Mousterian and Aterian industries and the people who used them around 45,000 years ago foreshadows a much later Saharan development that occurred at the beginning of the Neolithic Subpluvial (ca. 7000–6000 B.C.) when farming and herding replaced hunting and gathering and ultimately laid the foundations for the agricultural civilization of the Nile Valley itself (see Chapter 16). The repetition of such relationships at times of periodic environmental change gives Egyptian culture-history much of its feeling of continuity and constitutes what archaeologists and anthropologists refer to as cultural process. Although one can certainly not predict *when* events like rainy periods will occur so that they are not really cyclical in the true sense, the ecological and cultural tensions and relationships that occur on newly opened frontiers have provided ideal and recurring stages for the drama of human inventiveness and adaptation throughout the millennia. For the present, we assume that the new Aterian technology permitted a more efficient way of hunting the large grazing animals that roamed the Saharan grasslands in the closing years of the Mousterian Subpluvial. This interpretation is lent credence by the site of BT-14, a recently discovered and excavated archaeological locality at Bir Terfawi, 350 kilometers west of the Nile. The place has been described as a "huge Aterian kill site with numerous bones scattered over an area measuring a few thousand square meters" (Schild and Wendorf 1975: 93). So far one radiocarbon date of 44,190 ±1,380 years ago has been obtained from shell associated with the site, but it may have been somewhat contaminated by later materials. Therefore, a date of at least 45,000 years ago is probable.

BT-14, which lies on the beach of an ancient, dried-up lake, is the earliest site discovered so far in Egypt to yield extensive faunal remains and this factor, plus its great size and the presence of internal artifact clusters within the site distinguish it as one of the most important Palaeolithic finds in Egypt. The bones from BT-14 indicate that the Aterian settlers exploited both large game of the savanna and smaller oasis species. The faunal remains so far reported include white rhinoceros, extinct Pleistocene camel, a large bovid (possibly *Homoiocerus antiquus*), wild ass, two species of gazelle (*Gazella rufifrons* and *Gazella dama*), fox (*Vulpes ruppeli?*), jackal (*Canis aurenus lupaster?*), warthog, antelopes of different sizes, ostrich, turtle, and bird (Wendorf *et al.*, 1976: 106).

Although BT-14 has greatly enlarged our knowledge of the Aterians and given us new respect for their efficiency as hunters, its surprisingly early date, when compared to the estimates on Mousterian sites at nearby Bir Sahara, only 14 kilometers to the west, suggests that a more typical Mousterian tradition managed to persist in spite of the presence of the Aterians, creating a kind of cultural mosaic across the inhabited face of the Sahara during the Mousterian Subpluvial (ca. 50,000–30,000 B.C.). The side-by-side persistence of strikingly different technological (and possibly cultural?) traditions is not unique to this period in Egypt but, as we shall see, characterizes the late Palaeolithic sequence in the Kom Ombo Plain in southern Upper Egypt and probably continued through Predynastic times to be echoed in Dynastic traditions of the cultural duality of Upper and Lower Egypt. Recently, additional fuel for the fires of Middle Palaeolithic cultural diversity has been provided by the work of Anne Attebury of Southern Methodist University, who, following Caton-Thompson at Kharga, has excavated an Aterian workshop site (E-76-4) the environmental and stratigraphic context of which suggests a good deal of regional, cultural, and environmental diversity among the sites in the Bir Terfawi depression.

All of this is as it should be. Such revisionism is an integral part of modern archaeology. The Aterian, which was first officially defined by the archaeologist M. Reygasse in 1919 on the basis of his finds at the type site of Bir-el-Ater in Tunisia, has grown unwittingly beyond the strict technological-typological criteria envisioned by Caton-Thompson in 1946. Its regional distribution—rather, that of its distinctive tanged points—has grown by accretion until it reaches across thousands of square miles. It is grossly illogical to believe that the people who shared this technological characteristic necessarily shared a common language and material culture. After all, because twentieth-century people use cars, are they part of the same culture? And yet, the sharing of an important technological system and all the attendant adjustments it requires does impose certain similarities on vastly different peoples.

Thanks to increasingly refined dating techniques and important new finds that allow us to reconstruct the ecology of Aterian sites like BT-14 and E-76-4, we are moving toward an appreciation of the depth of cultural diversity that developed on the savannas and around the oases of Middle Palaeolithic northeastern Africa. As we learn to appreciate this diversity and its contributions to cultural change, we will move away from the unimodal, unidirectional concepts of cultural evolution so popular with Palaeolithic archaeologists and prehistorians toward a more balanced interpretation. As with evolutionary genetics, which emphasizes the value of diversity in the survival and adaptation of a species, prehistorians are finally realizing that labels like Aterian or Mousterian cover a multitude of differences and that sites and regions must be studied under the archaeologist's and paleoecologist's microscope before we can observe the full panorama of cultural diversity and change.

The Khormusan: The Art of Definition

Most laymen and a good number of professionals, when confronted with the bewildering variety of technical terms used by archaeologists to describe what they dig out of the earth, throw up their hands in dismay, convinced more than ever that ours is truly a nonliterate tradition. Although terms and terminology do often create confusion, when properly defined they establish standards that, as in the case of the Aterian, for example, can be revised as more information is discovered. This is the essence of the scientific method.

An excellent illustration of the utility of the method whereby archaeologists create technical terms and then drastically revise them is provided by the Khormusan Industry. Until the last few years, it was widely believed that the Khormusan exemplified the earliest Upper or late Palaeolithic phase in Lower Nubia and southern Upper Egypt. Most carbon-14 dates indicated a range from 25,000 to 14,000 B.C., and the stratigraphic evidence was accordingly interpreted to indicate a period of extreme aridity. Thanks to drastically revised radiocarbon estimates, however, it is now known that the Khormusan dates back to at least 45,000 B.C., making it largely contemporary with the Aterian.

The Khormusan Industry was officially born in 1968 when Dr. Anthony E. Marks of Southern Methodist University published a monograph-length article entitled "The Khormusan: An Upper Pleistocene Industry in Sudanese Nubia." In the same way that Caton-Thompson's landmark work on the Aterian summarized and critically evaluated the past work done on that industry and produced a set of criteria and hypotheses that defined an archaeological industry (a collection of similar assemblages of tools from different sites), Marks presented a definition of the Khormusan Industry. Rightly pointing out that "the designation of a new late Upper Pleistocene industry along the Nile . . . is not done lightly," Marks proceeded to define the Khormusan according to the two primary dimensions dealt with by archaeologists: time and space. In space

the Khormusan industry, named after the type site 1017 in a bank of the Khor Musa, is represented in the archaeological record by five sites, all *in situ*, which are rich in chipped stone tools and faunal remains and contain rare examples of worked bone and ground hematite.

Technologically and typologically, the Khormusan industry exhibits at each site unifying characteristics which set it apart from other industries and which demonstrate that these sites represent a single lithic tradition. *(Marks in Wendorf 1968b: 315)*

Unlike many archaeologists who are maddeningly vague with technical terms, Marks was quite explicit about the criteria that distinguish a site as Khormusan, listing nine technological, five typological, and three residential characteristics.

The technological criteria included: (1) a strong levallois flake tradition, (2) few true blades but a number of laminary flakes, (3) a high percentage of all flakes with faceted butts, (4) very carefully prepared levallois cores, (5) a predominance of oval to pointed oval-shaped cores, (6) use of a wide range of raw materials, (7) use of different raw materials for different tool types, (8) a wide range in tool size, and (9) the predominance of a unifacial flaking tradition, with bifacial retouch being rare (Marks in Wendorf 1968b: 329).

Marks's typological criteria specified that (1) the Khormusan Industry is dominated by three tool types: levallois flakes, burins, and denticulates; (2) end and side scrapers, although never common, are always present during the main stages of the Khormusan; (3) between half and three-fifths of all tools are unretouched levallois flakes; (4) notched flakes or simple truncated (snapped) flakes are rare; (5) a number of tools are not found in Khormusan sites, including backed blades or microblades, borers, backed knives, backed points, geometrics and large bifacial core tools (Marks in Wendorf 1968b: 329).

Khormusan settlements are (1) very large, covering thousands of square meters; (2) all close to the Nile and oriented parallel to it on sand formations; and (3) comprised of a number of artifact clusters about individual hearths, rather than continuous scatters of debris.

Today, a number of new sites have been added to Marks's original five, but still the basic criteria which he originally defined for the Khormusan ten years ago stand. That is the good news. The bad news, as I noted before, is that the original chronology for the Khormusan (ca. 25,000–15,000 B.C.) has undergone severe revision. Now that the Khormusan has been catapulted backward in time by as much as 25,000 years, prehistorians have been permitted a rare glance into early Egyptian cultural diversity undreamed-of even a decade ago. The possibility that in Middle Palaeolithic times a major cultural division existed between a basically Nilotic Khormusan tradition and a basically desert-savanna Aterian tradition suggests that there might be an enormously long background to some of the historical-geographical distinctions so basic to Dynastic civilization. The problem of the Khormusan also illustrates nicely the arguments that can be caused by vague dating and the alternative interpretations to which even the most carefully described and well-excavated archaeological material can be subjected.

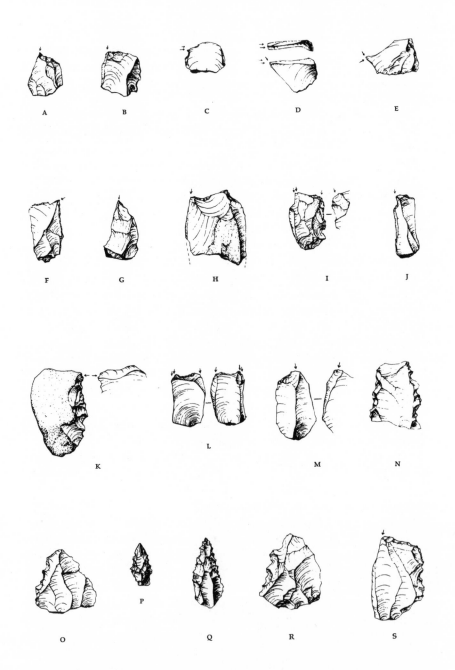

SELECTED KHORMUSAN ARTIFACTS

18   Site 34D: a–j, l, m, burins; k, s, burin-denticulates; p, q, denticulate points; n, o, r, denticulates

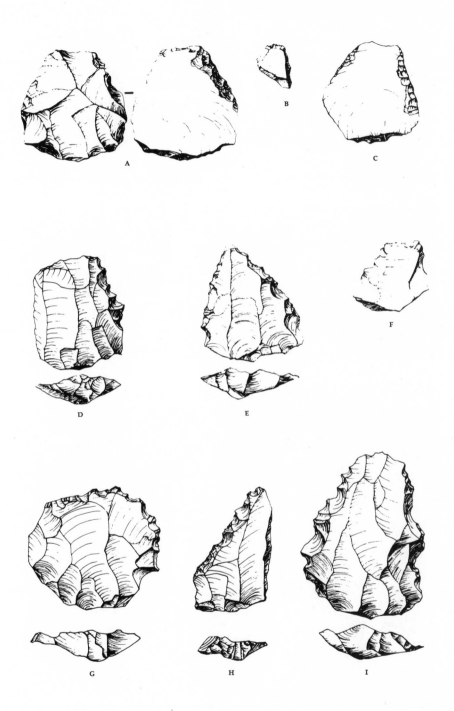

19   Site 1017: a, c, side scrapers; b, end scraper; d–i, denticulates

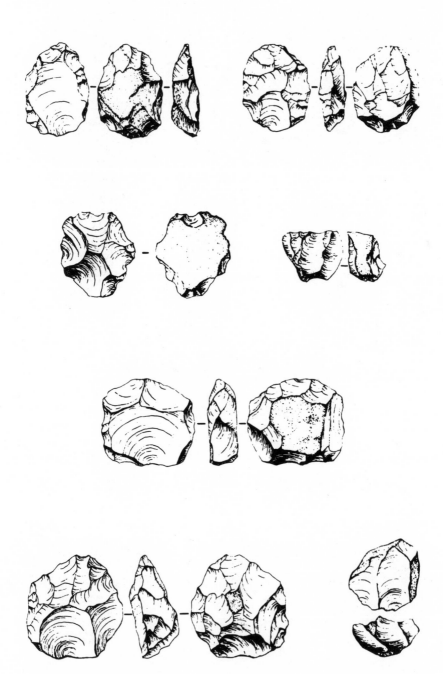

20 Cores from Site 34D

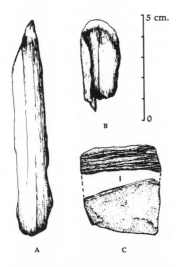

21   Site ANW-3: a–b, bone tools;
c, ground hematite

For instance, Fred Wendorf and Romuald Schild in a recent interpretation of the evidence prefer to arrange the three major Middle Palaeolithic
industries in sequential order, beginning with Mousterian, continuing,
after a brief arid spell, through the Aterian, and culminating, finally, in
the Khormusan. Since the radiocarbon dates and the geostratigraphic
correlations are neither clear nor consistent, I believe that it is safest and
most logical to interpret these industries as overlapping somewhat in
time and space. Although we may never know what relationship tool
industries bore to real human groups, if we can assume that they did
represent different cultural traditions, it is likely that an area as vast as
Egypt saw the coming, going, and overlapping of different traditions
over the vast stretches of time represented by the Middle Palaeolithic.
    Despite the present vagueness of carbon-14 dating and the flexibility
of human groups, I do believe that a useful contrast can be drawn
between the two most distinctive Middle Palaeolithic traditions currently
known—the Aterian and the Khormusan. Assuming that both overlapped in time for about 10,000 years, the early contrast between two
different technological traditions sets the stage for one of the more important tasks of this book: tracing the known distinctions in Dynastic
civilization to their earliest prehistoric counterparts and explaining the
reasons why such distinctions arose and persisted. An archaeologist
viewing both the Aterian and Khormusan industries from a purely
technological perspective might easily be tempted to regard the Khormusans as peaceful, unarmed Nile-dwellers, fishing and gathering along
the river while the bow-and-arrow-wielding Aterians carried out a
Middle Palaeolithic blitzkrieg on the grassy savannas of the Sahara.
Obviously, such an extreme explanation of cultural diversity seems exag-
gerated in light of modern explanations of the reasons why cultures

change. Not only is it highly unlikely that the Aterians "came down like wolves on the [Khormusan] fold" to paraphrase Lord Byron, but there is now little reason to believe that the Aterians were the sole possessors of the bow-and-arrow technology as implied by Caton-Thompson in 1946. In the Khormusan stone-tool assemblage we are struck by the popularity of the small, sharp, stubby burin. This tool is known to have actually tipped arrows or darts in the Egyptian late Palaeolithic (see page 97) and probably performed the same function in the Khormusan Industry.

Fortunately, the revised view of Khormusan technological competence does not, for once in the Palaeolithic record, rest merely on some archaeologist's notion of the possible function of a stone tool like the enigmatic burin, but on a much more solid ground—the food remains of Khormusan camps. Faunal remains are one of the most important sources of information available to an archaeologist.

> Any routine competent identification of faunal remains—both hard and soft parts—from an archaeological site can reveal which species of animals are represented in the excavated materials. But a proper faunal analysis merely begins at this point, and goes on with appropriate analytical techniques, to make a truly significant contribution to the overall understanding of the site's prehistory.
>
> For instance, a thorough faunal analysis could help tell how the remains of such species present in the deposit were introduced there; the dietary and culinary preferences of the aboriginal inhabitants; customary hunting areas and seasons for different types of game; the approximate population of the site and how long the inhabitants had been there; which parts of the site were in use at which times; ritual or totemic uses of animals; climatic or other ecological changes in the site region; the existence and extent of prehistoric trade routes; and even aboriginal domestication practices and animal diseases.
>
> *(Ziegler 1975: 183)*

Obviously, any knowledge of ancient diet allows us a deeper and more sophisticated insight into economy than mere stone tools, but such remains are seldom preserved in Palaeolithic sites in Egypt. Even when bones can be recovered, we generally lack plant or pollen remains, so our opinion of ancient Palaeolithic man as a hunter par excellence is certainly overrated. Nevertheless, the faunal remains discovered at many Khormusan localities plus the newly reported Aterian finds from the Libyan Desert make possible a gross evaluation of each industry's hunting competence. We have already seen that the Aterians did well by themselves. The Khormusans, however, were also redoubtable hunters as well as fishers and gatherers whose menu included wild cattle (*Bos primagenius*—animals about twice as big as our modern, docile domesticates), large catfish (*Clarus sp.*) over two feet long, large *Synodontis* and *Barbus* fish from the Nile, and supplementary amounts of wild ass, gazelle, large antelope, and even hippos. Judging from the different habitats favored by these animals, the Khormusans must have ranged from the savanna grasslands on the border of the Nile Valley to the river itself and possessed a variety of strategies for obtaining their varied sources of food. Their campsites, although large, indicate recurrent occupancy by small groups over many hundreds if not thousands of years.

Although the Khormusan economy was closely tied to the Nile Valley, we should not overlook its hunting proficiency, judging from the types and numbers of animals consumed. If we now return to the Aterian, we will recall that it too was an efficient hunting tradition, but that it lacked the riverine focus of the Khormusan. It is true that Aterian sites have been reported along the Nile, but the fact that there might have been some Nilotic peoples using this technology does not obviate the fact that many peoples on the desert plains were relatively more dependent on hunted animals than the peoples who dwelt near the Nile Valley, which abounded in edible plants, fish, and fowl. It cannot be doubted that Aterian peoples were efficient hunters and successful as long as the tenuous environmental conditions that supported their way of life survived. But sometime between 30,000 and 40,000 years ago the Sahara dried up and these peoples lost their livelihood. Even the great oases like Kharga were apparently abandoned for the next 25,000 years or so. Where did the Aterians go? To be sure, many of the savanna hunters must have perished of starvation, as in the recent great African drought, but surely many more managed to gravitate slowly to the great oasis of the Nile. There they encountered peoples using both a Khormusan technology and riverine Aterians as well (and probably a host of other areal traditions). At that time there must have been sufficient plants, game, and room in the valley to support small groups of immigrants. Without efficient river transport, however, these local groups were unable to establish and maintain regular contact. Their differences persisted and grew, giving rise to the numerous areal traditions of the later Palaeolithic, when the peoples of the Nile Valley adapted to the increasing aridity of the Sahara that sent sand dunes into the valley and to occasionally drastic changes in the annual inundation which extended or reduced the biosphere—the environmental container within which Egyptian civilization would germinate.

6

THE LATE PALAEOLITHIC: OF FLOODS, DROUGHTS, AND A PROMISE UNFULFILLED

Vignard in the Kom Ombo Plain: Were the Late Palaeolithic Egyptians Laggards or Innovators?

U NTIL 1920, when a young Frenchman, Edmund Vignard, reported finding stone implements in the bleak plain of Kom Ombo in Upper Egypt, there was, for all practical purposes, no Egyptian late Palaeolithic. In marked contrast to better-known areas like Western and Central Europe, where spectacular cave paintings, sculpture, and beautifully made stone and bone tools characterized what de Mortillet called the Upper Palaeolithic, the latest phase of the Egyptian Palaeolithic was a blank. Most experts expected to find the same types of tools in Egypt that typified the European Upper Palaeolithic: long, symmetrical, parallel-sided blades; large, beautifully flaked stone points and large numbers of burins; bone needles, barbed harpoon heads and the like; and, of course, the striking animal art and "Venus" figurines. Such was not the case. The lack of similarity between European and Egyptian Upper Palaeolithic industries, combined with the absence in Egypt of sites with long, deeply stratified sequences like the famous French caves, delayed the application of the usual methods of stratigraphic cross-dating, until Vignard's discoveries at Kom Ombo.

Kom Ombo is a great embayment of the Nile Valley, located on the east bank of the river in southern Upper Egypt. Over the years it has filled with alluvial silts and developed into a small, well-defined topographic and environmental zone. During the 1920's, Vignard located and excavated a number of prehistoric sites there and became convinced that they dated to the Upper Palaeolithic period, first, because of their geological context and, second, because of the presence of burins at many sites. Burins are small, stubby, pointed tools made of flakes or blades and characterized by one or more distinctive burin spalls—long, narrow flakes forming a point. He christened his new industry Sebilian and divided it into three distinct phases. The Lower Sebilian (or Sebilian I) began with an essentially levallois industry, using Mousterian-like retouched points and a few microburins. Tools were manufactured from a locally obtained diorite—a hard, black igneous rock. As time went on, the Sebilian tradition gradually developed through Stages II (Middle Sebilian) and III (Upper Sebilian) into a true microblade industry, employing flint instead of diorite and displaying a high percentage of microburins and true microblades. Vignard felt that when compared to other Upper Palaeolithic industries in Europe, like the Aurignacian or Solutrean, the Sebilian retained many Mousterian characteristics and was, therefore, technologically conservative. This fact, he believed, showed that Africa in general and the Nile Valley in particular constituted cultural backwashes at the time. Unfortunately, despite Vignard's excellent descriptions and pioneering methods, he did not find stratigraphic evidence to support his conclusions, so that more recent work, most notably by P. E. L. Smith of the Royal Ontario Museum in Canada, has turned the tables on Vignard's reconstruction in a wholly unexpected way and forced us to view the late Palaeolithic Egyptians *not* as cultural laggards but precocious innovators.

Both Vignard's description of the Sebilian Industry and his evolutionary scheme have been revised by Smith and Fekri Hassan. The situation turns out to be much more complex than Vignard ever imagined and suggests a good deal of technological if not ethnic variation in the Kom Ombo Plain during late Palaeolithic times. It seems that around 13,000 B.C., coexisting with the earliest phase of Vignard's Sebilian, was a sophisticated blade and microblade industry which Smith calls Silsillian. Whoever made the Silsillian tools clearly understood blade technology and exploited the fine-grained flints and chalcedonies found in local gravels. The Silsillian tool kit was varied and included truncated blades (blades that have been snapped intentionally to produce a desired size or shape), backed bladelets, notches and denticulates, altered base blades and bladelets modified for mounting onto spears, darts and arrow shafts, and an occasional well-made burin. There is virtually no trace of levallois technology and indeed the Silsillian Industry can hold its own with any Upper Palaeolithic industry from Europe or western Asia, while it actually leads those areas by several thousand years in pioneering the use of microlithic tools. Microliths—literally miniature tools made from small blades—are yet another one of those vital inventions that gave early man the ability to exploit his total environment more efficiently. Microliths, with their regular shapes and sharp edges, are ideal for use in compound tools like arrows, darts, harpoons, and sickles and have the added attraction of requiring relatively small amounts of raw material. This latter advantage must have been quite important in the Kom Ombo area, where some of the finest (glassiest) stone was available only in small, stream-worn nodules. The adaptation of microliths to compound tools involved a far-reaching technological reorganization requiring the fastening of preshaped stone blades into wooden or bone handles or shafts by means of a natural adhesive like tar or prepared animal glue (fish glue was especially popular). As fishing weapons or as arrow points such small, sharp and lightweight tips were considerably more efficient than the larger, bifacially-worked points like those used by the Aterians and they were considerably cheaper to produce. When dipped in poison (a practice frequently employed by recent hunting peoples), they certainly improved the efficiency of the hunt. Perhaps more important than the use of microliths in projectile weapons was their use as sickle blades, set into straight or slightly curved wooden or bone handles and used to harvest wild plants, especially grains. This source of food provided a boost to the gathering component of late Palaeolithic economy in Egypt and, as we shall see shortly, accompanied one of the earliest experiments in "protoagriculture" known anywhere in the world.

As if the picture of cultural diversity in the plain of Kom Ombo is not sufficiently complicated by overlapping Sebilian and Silsillian technologies, Smith has proposed yet a third industry for the area which he calls Sebekian. Although it produced nice blades, the Sebekian lacked geometric forms, microburins, and the pointed, backed blades found in Silsillian sites. Unfortunately, the distinction between the two industries is clouded by the lack of precise dating and well-defined stratigraphic relationships. Although at one site the Sebekian overlies the Silsillian, other localities nearby suggest that the two coexisted, probably together with the oft-studied Sebilian, which has now been located in many regions of southern Upper Egypt. Just how such industries managed to remain distinct for as much as several thousand years is illustrated in the preferences they showed for different types of raw material for their stone tools. The fact that all three industries drew on distinctly different deposits of stone suggests a relationship known to biologists as "sympatric" in which members of the same or closely related species live in the same large territory but manage to exploit different ecological niches. It is certainly too early to claim with certainty that such was the case in the marshes and salt pans of the late Pleistocene Kom Ombo Plain some 15,000 years ago. However, it is not too far-fetched to imagine many separate groups, perhaps no larger than bands of 30 to 50 individuals, occupying the area at roughly the same time, each practicing a kind of transhumance—a seasonal round of hunting, fishing, and gathering—which, for a time at least, allowed each group to keep pretty much to itself. If their territories overlapped, it was probably only on the peripheries, and as long as the region was large enough and population growth, climate, and river relatively stable, several cultural traditions persisted side by side. As we shall see throughout this book, the picture of cultural diversity and varying rates of technological change seen in Kom Ombo 15,000 years ago has broad implications for all of the late Palaeolithic prehistory of Egypt as well as later Predynastic times.

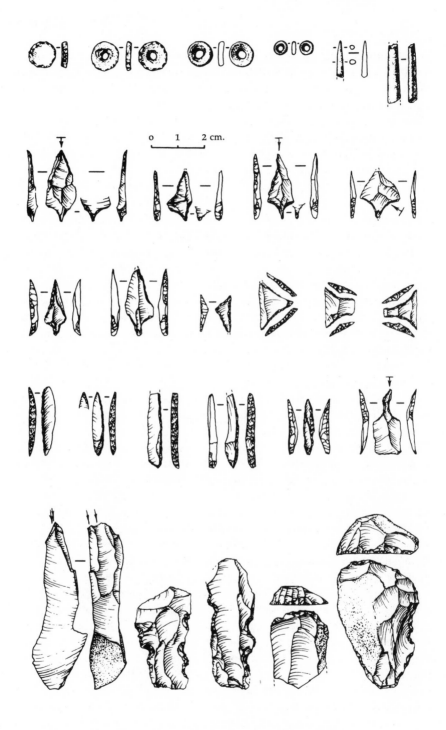

22   Tools from terminal Palaeolithic level at Site E-75-6, Nabta

A World of Diversity

The multiplication of stone tool traditions and the creation of diverse, localized cultures that it reflects was not restricted to the Kom Ombo Plain, but characterized Egypt as a whole during the late Palaeolithic; but just how useful was such diversity? We might compare the cultural diversity of late Palaeolithic Egypt and Lower Nubia to what biologists call a "gene pool." Generally speaking, the more diverse or varied the sum total of genetic traits possessed by a given species, the better that species' chances of survival, since adaptation is ultimately based on variation. Variability, either genetic or cultural, is healthy in that in times of environmental change it provides alternative pathways by which a species or a culture can adapt and avoid the trap of extinction. The cultures of the late Palaeolithic, spawned in the adversity of a rigorous climate and schooled in a tradition of making the best of locally available resources, constituted such a varied and ultimately healthy pool. Some groups clung to old ways, while others moved headlong into a new microlithic technology—the earliest of its kind in the world—while others charted a middle course between conservatism and innovation. Broadly speaking, the period after about 30,000 B.C. witnessed marked environmental deterioration, pronounced technological innovation, and the regionalization of social groups. All these factors were related to one another and combined to produce a cultural mosaic in the Nile Valley that gave rise to two precocious developments: the invention of the world's first microlithic technology and one of the world's earliest attempts to domesticate plants.

As we have seen already, thanks to the vagaries of carbon-14 dating it is difficult to know when the desiccation of the Sahara actually took place. Some experts would place this event as early as 40,000 B.C., but for the time being at least a lower estimate of about 30,000 B.C. will be adopted. Throughout the better part of the period between 40,000 and 17,000 B.C. our information is poor and our dates unreliable. The safest bet is that Nilotic industries like the Khormusan survived and gradually changed. As one would expect, a number of localized tool industries, still vaguely in the Levalloisian technological tradition, appeared, some contemporaneous with later "conservative" Khormusan industries. The earliest of these industries known is called Halfan because its sites were first found around the town of Wadi Halfa in the Sudan. Halfan sites stretched from the Second Cataract in the south to north of the Kom Ombo Plain in Egypt, a distance of 362 kilometers, and appear to have flourished between about 18,000 and 15,000 B.C., although one date as early as about 24,000 B.C. has been reported. The Halfan is known from over seven sites and is especially important because it exhibits a pioneering trend toward miniaturization of its tool kit. In its earliest forms, the

Halfan Industry begins with a specialized levallois technology which produced small, nicely worked artifacts and finishes with a blade technology that produced even smaller, highly specialized flakes for use in compound tools, like the bow and arrow, the harpoon, etc. These tools represent a refinement over the Khormusan and as we have seen already in Kom Ombo are generally made of finer materials like flint or even agate. The later appearance of microlithic tools in Europe and the Near East (ca. 12,000–6000 B.C.) is usually interpreted as a response to a changing climate that saw the disappearance of the Pleistocene herds and an increased reliance on the stalking of solitary forest game and/or the development of new and better fishing and fowling techniques. Such does not seem to have been the case in Egypt. Hunting of big herding animals and fishing remained important, with savanna types like wild cattle and ass common on Halfan sites, as well as catfish, the old Khormusan favorite. Halfan campsites cover relatively small areas compared with Khormusan settlements, but are densely cluttered with material, perhaps suggesting greater permanence and a more limited range of seasonal wandering.

In Upper Egypt at least three local archaeological groups flourished between about 17,000 and 15,000 B.C.—the Fakhurian and two variants of the Idfuan. While all made at least some use of blades and blade cores, the Fakhurian (ca. 16,070–15,640 B.C.) was the only industry that was out-and-out microlithic. Working with tiny blades often under 3 centimeters in length, Fakhurian craftsmen displayed a skill that belies their extreme antiquity and bleak environment. Restricted to a small region around the modern town of Isna, Fakhurians divided their time between two distinct but overlapping habitats. In the winter and the spring, between November and June or July, they camped on the borderlands between the dune fields and the floodplain of the Nile—a position that enabled them to exploit both the fish and game of the river and any grazing animals that might range into the hinterlands after a rare winter shower. As the annual inundation began in late June, the Fakhurians retreated farther back into the dune fields. Because the Nile floods of the time were higher than those of the recent past, the hyperarid conditions that had dominated northeastern Africa since the end of the Mousterian Subpluvial were somewhat moderated. Prehistorians call this phase of the Nile's history the Ballana or Ballana-Masmas Aggradation and believe it prevailed between about 18,000 and 15,000 B.C. One of the interesting side effects of higher floodwaters was a higher groundwater table. This in turn created small ponds in low spots among the dunes—seasonal mini-oases that attracted plant and animal life and acted as welcome havens for humans fleeing the damp air and swampy ground created by the annual floods in the bottomlands.

Distinct from the Fakhurians technologically, the Idfuan industries existed contemporaneously in southern Upper Egypt (ca. 15,850–15,000 B.C.), preserving more of the flavor of an older, essentially Middle Palaeolithic way of life. The absence of microlithic tools suggests a less efficient adaptation to fishing and fowling than the Fakhurian technology and, perhaps, a desire to continue to rely on hunting, trapping, and snaring, in the old way. The Halfa variant of the Idfuan retained an advanced levallois technology using the Halfa core and flake technique and employing long, pointed blades whose bases were blunted, apparently to facilitate hafting or use in the hand. A second variant, which Fekri Hassan has called the "non-Levallois, non-Halfa variant," used opposed platform blade cores, showed a strong preference for burins and employed retouched blades and flakes as tools as well as the familiar basally blunted blades, notches, and denticulates. The two variants reflect the now familiar pattern of regionalization so characteristic of the late Palaeolithic and so suggestive of later territorial, subcultural divisions like the Dynastic nomes.

We do not know if the trend toward local diversification seen in Upper Egypt was also taking place in the north; however, to the south, in Nubia, the process was repeated in industries like the Dabarosa Complex, dated as early as 16,000 B.C. Located across the river from Wadi Halfa, this archaeological grouping is restricted to three sites, all concentrated in a small area—a good indication that we are dealing with one group of people. The Dabarosa Complex is one of the earliest Nubian microlithic assemblages. A number of specialized points manufactured by a prepared core technique reminiscent of a refined levallois method are typical of Dabarosa sites and show the persistence of older hunting traditions. The rest of the stone industry includes a few burins, denticulates, and notches with, once again, older Middle Palaeolithic forms like sidescrapers and, more rarely, levallois and Halfa flakes. Another, somewhat later, local Nubian variant known as the Gemaian (ca. 15,500–13,000 B.C.) is represented by eight sites strung out along an old channel of the Nile. Although the levallois technique was still occasionally employed, new microlithic and geometric forms were coming onto the scene, differentiating innovative from conservative neighbors just as in Upper Egypt to the north. Like the earlier Halfans, the Gemaians hunted the large grazing animals of the savanna and fished for catfish; but unlike the Halfans, their camps were both small in area and relatively light in the amount of debris within them.

A third highly localized microlithic industry (the Ballanan) has been identified by prehistorians near Ballana in Egyptian Nubia, on the west bank of the river and dated slightly later than the Gemaian, between 14,000 and 12,000 B.C. Ballanans lived in small, compact camps and hunted both large, wild cattle and ass and fished for Nile catfish. Their tools are noteworthy for a number of forms made on truncations (deliberately snapped blades), for the popularity of burins (perhaps used as punches and arrow points), and for the technique of "backing." Backing a blade is a fairly simple process by which one edge is dulled by deliberate, controlled flaking (sometimes the flake scars are quite tiny as in the so-called Ouchtatta retouch) so that the implement can be used in the hand much in the manner of a pocketknife or more easily hafted into a compound tool like an arrow or sickle shaft. The fact that many late Palaeolithic industries in both southern Upper Egypt and northern Nubia, although adjacent and sharing the same environment, differed in seemingly little ways, like the frequency of microliths or backing on blades, illustrates the difficulty and challenge that face the archaeologist in trying to reconstruct the past from the scantiest of clues. Yet it is only by paying attention to the differences between assemblages of stone tools that we are able to glimpse dimly the outlines of emerging societies that would soon contribute their collective diversity to the culture of ancient Egypt.

The Early Farmers of Tushka and Idfu: An Experiment That Failed

After a short "recessional" period during which the high Nile floods of the Ballana-Masmas Aggradation declined, a new phase of high seasonal floods, named the Sahaba-Darau Aggradation by geologists and archaeologists, commenced. Although the exact dating of all these geologic events is tenuous, the Sahaba-Darau was in full swing by about 13,000 B.C. and lasted to around 10,000 B.C. The climate was essentially arid as in preceding periods, although there may have been intermittent and brief periods of rainfall, varying from region to region as in the modern Arabian Desert. Several major industries, some of which are fairly widespread, are well known from this period: (1) the Qadan in Lower Nubia is represented by over 20 sites stretching from the Second Cataract north to the town of Tushka, about 250 kilometers upriver from Aswan; (2) the Sebilian, which we have encountered before in Kom Ombo, has been found in three concentrations in Upper Egypt; (3) the Afian, found around a pond at Thomas Afia village near Isna in southern Upper Egypt; and (4) the Isnan, reported so far from three areas in southern Upper Egypt: Isna, the famous Predynastic locality of Naqada and Dishna. There are other, mercifully unnamed industries that have been reported, but it is clear that, at this highly descriptive stage of our work, many of these industries are merely seasonal or functional variants of larger complexes, while others, like the Qadan, Sebilian, and Isnan probably represent major chronological or territorial groupings.

With the Qadan, we are fortunate in possessing a number of unusual bits of evidence, such as cemeteries, that allow us, for the first time, to look at nontechnical aspects of Palaeolithic man and his societies and appreciate the broader ramifications of his culture and its links to its

Predynastic-Neolithic descendants. Most Qadan sites that have been radiocarbon-dated lie between 13,000 and 9,000 B.C., but some later dates are known, including a reading of 4500 B.C. Although most experts are now inclined to reject the later dates, the question is still not fully answered and could have important consequences for the interpretation of much of our evidence.

Although Qadan stone technology is basically microlithic throughout, there is an increasing preference for blades over flakes and, at the latest sites, a definite decline in the quality of stone tool manufacture. The levallois technique characteristic of Middle Palaeolithic times finally disappeared from the industrial repertoire and characteristic tools include scrapers, semicircular lunates, a variety of burins, backed and truncated microflakes, and partially backed points.

A rare insight into many features of Qadan life in particular and late Palaeolithic life in general is provided by a site uncovered a decade ago by Dr. Fred Wendorf near Tushka. Here, in an ancient embayment intersected by an abandoned river channel, stand a number of low mounds—the remains of fossil ponds whose floors were cemented by minerals and left high and dry as the surrounding sand dunes were blown away. Some of the material that washed into one of these interdune ponds has been radiocarbon-dated about 12,500 B.C. and on the basis of other geological evidence prehistorians believe the sites could not have been later than about 10,500 B.C. Near Tushka, farther down toward the river, archaeologists have located more than 100 distinct hearths surrounded by rich assemblages of microlithic tools. Although the area is barren and stark today, an abundance of animal remains attests a wide range of human activity there about 12,000 to 14,000 years ago. Near the old river shoreline sites have yielded the head and foreparts of catfish skeletons, indicating that the hapless fish, after being speared or netted, were quickly decapitated and cleaned and possibly smoked over the fires and consumed elsewhere (very few remains of the main body of the fish have been found at shoreline sites). The fish were probably caught in the late summer and early fall when they were trapped in pools by the retreating floodwaters of the Nile. Farther back from the water's edge, around ponds collected in the hollows on rolling, grass-covered sand dunes, Qadan sites are littered with bones of large grazing animals of the savanna. Giant wild cattle appear to have been the favorite item on the Tushka meat menu, followed by wild ass, gazelle, and occasional hippo.

The high numbers of animals whose favorite habitat would have been the grassy savanna reflect either the effects of a raised water table or a cooler, cloudier, and somewhat wetter climatic interlude. Such a pattern of seasonally available foodstuffs located in different areas hints that the Qadans practiced limited movement between the areas from the banks of the river out onto the low desert. As we have seen earlier in discussing

Kharga, such a transhumant pattern of settlement need not involve moving the entire population between river and desert throughout the course of the seasons, but it does require a social group flexible enough to break apart and join together at particular times during the year and a sophisticated knowledge of habitats and animals. Today, now that they are nearly extinct, we are beginning to realize just how subtle and complex a knowledge of their environment and food resources nonfarming peoples had. In the past, there was a kind of agricultural-industrial snobbery at work when speaking of hunters and gatherers that portrayed these peoples as trapped in a hopelessly traditional way of life in which the options for change and adaptation were extremely limited. This stereotype is probably as invalid as the old attitude that depicted Egypt as a bastion of Middle Palaeolithic conservatism—an attitude shaken by the discovery of a sophisticated and remarkably early microblade technology and, at Tushka, an even more innovative and daring development whose full course and meaning we do not yet understand.

According to most modern authorities, agriculture and animal domestication originated outside the Nile Valley. It is argued that these crucial economic inventions originally took place in areas native to the wild ancestors of later domesticates. This view is based on several assumptions that might be inaccurate, however. Admittedly, if domestication did start at the very end of the Pleistocene, about 10,000 years ago, then the climate and presumably the wild ancestors of domesticated animals and plants were roughly what they are today, in the Middle East at least. But if the roots of domestication reach back into earlier epochs—into the late Palaeolithic—then the climate and the distribution of plants and animals would have been far different from what they were around 8000 B.C. In Egypt in Isnan sites at Isna, Naqada, and Dishna and in Nubia at sites like Tushka, Professor Wendorf and many of his associates now believe that late Pleistocene peoples were experimenting with potential plant domesticates by 12,000 B.C. and that these precocious experiments eventually faltered. This in itself is a radical idea that shakes the very basis of much modern social, economic, and historical thought with its implicit belief in continuous technological progress. But, when we think about it, it is really more logical than the older view that domestication was something completely new—a view that greatly underestimated the technological sophistication of late Palaeolithic peoples not only in Egypt but over much of the inhabited world. Physically, these were fully modern men and women who had long studied the plants and animals around them, accumulating a rich knowledge of different techniques useful in extracting the maximum amount of food (excluding tabooed materials) with the minimum amount of effort. Second, they possessed an incredibly efficient hunting (and gathering) technology. However, tools associated with hunting, like stone points and scrapers, preserve better than woven nets and baskets; so we shall never know the full extent of gathering technology. But to appreciate the hunting skills of Palaeolithic peoples all around the world, we have only to recall the magnificent cave paintings of Europe or the great elephant kills of Siberia and North America or the Aterian kill sites in the Bir Terfawi. As the prehistorian Chester Chard has pointed out, since the Middle Palaeolithic, many groups were already concentrating on certain types of animals (and probably plants), so all that was needed to develop effective domestication was lots of time for trial and error experimentation and a little luck. Apparently, the late Palaeolithic Egyptians possessed neither, although our evidence shows that they made an extraordinarily early attempt at domestication and that its failure was accompanied by some rather traumatic side effects.

Shortly after 13,000 B.C. grinding stones and sickle blades with glossy sheen on their bits (the result of silica from cut grass stems adhering to a sickle's cutting edge) appear in late Palaeolithic tool kits. At Tushka both grinding stones and sickle blades were numerous and it is clear that the grinding stones were used in preparing plant food and not, as some have suggested, pigment: they are very common, their grinding surfaces ample and heavily worn and lacking in the telltale stains found on pigment palettes.

But do grinding stones necessarily indicate domestication? The answer is, like most answers in archaeology, equivocal. In the Appalachian Mountains of the United States, the first grinding stones were used by prehistoric peoples to process plant food like nuts and sunflower seeds long before the arrival of full-fledged agriculture, reflecting a tendency to use local foodstuffs before the introduction of the more productive maize. The evidence at Tushka and many Isnan sites probably reflects such an experimental stage in the domestication of local plants. The line between intensive "caring for" and out-and-out "domestication" of both plants and animals is thin and blurred by the degree to which a given species responds genetically to tending and to the selective pressures created by human interference. If a plant yields too little or is prone to die out easily, then it is unlikely that people will continue to invest time and energy in tending it. In both Old and New Worlds, successfully domesticated plants like wheat, barley, millet, and rice underwent important genetic changes before they achieved dominant positions in local social, economic, political, and religious life. These changes in the case of wheat and maize took thousands of years. In Egypt, as in many other areas of the world like the Appalachians, where experiments in the tending of local plants never produced effective domesticates, the grinding of grass or grain lasted for thousands of years without ever causing an economic revolution. Similarly, in prehistoric California, where Indians depended on acorns for their staple food, the acorns themselves were never manipulated genetically to yield surpluses comparable to and as flexible as those produced by wheat, barley, maize, rice, and millet.

In addition to the grinding stones and sickle blades found at Tushka, there is actual firsthand evidence of the plants involved in the Qadan experiment. Pollen from pond sediments shows the presence of an unidentifiable large *Graminae* (a wheatlike grass) and a type of fungus that grows on wheat and other related grasses; and Isnan sites contain the pollen of possible wild barley. Although far from imposing, such rare archaeological information suggests a reason for the apparent expansion of population in the Nile Valley between about 13,000 and 10,500 B.C. when large and intensively occupied sites flourished in present-day northern Sudan and southern Egypt.

Our view of early agricultural experimentation on the late Palaeolithic peoples of the Nile first sketched at Tushka has been sharpened by Fekri Hassan's recent discoveries in the Isna area.

> ... the sites are surprisingly large, without any indication of internal clustering, as might be expected if they represented numerous repeated occupations. They seemingly represent a constant and long-lasting settlement of a large population. The fact that sites are both numerous and large suggests a demographic explosion that may find its explanation in a new economic base. *(Wendorf and Schild 1976b: 289)*

This description reminds us more of a Neolithic farming village than a Palaeolithic campsite. In terms of the faunal remains found at Isnan sites, there is also a strange break with tradition.

> One of the surprising features of the Isnan sites is the absence of fish remains. Unlike the previous occupants of this area, these hunted only large mammals. The decline in fishing as a source of food may be related to the appearance of the new food resource represented by ground grain. The associated pollen strongly suggests that this grain was possibly barley, and significantly, this large-grass pollen, which is tentatively identified as barley, makes a sudden appearance in the pollen profile just before the time when the first settlements were established in the area. This may indicate a change in local conditions favorable for this particular grain that permitted it suddenly to colonize the area, and this, in turn, attracted the new settlers.
> *(Wendorf and Schild 1976b: 291)*

Although there may be too many "ifs" in the current status of early agriculture and the Isnan Industry in the Nile Valley, the circumstantial evidence is building up to support Wendorf's early claim that the primacy of the hilly flanks from the Balkans to Baluchistan in agricultural origins will have to allow at least temporary rivalry from the southern horn of the old Fertile Crescent.

As apparently spectacular as the rise of protoagriculture in the late Palaeolithic Nile Valley was its precipitous decline. No one knows exactly why, but after about 10,500 B.C. the early sickle blades and grinding stones disappear, to be replaced throughout Egypt and Nubia by Epipalaeolithic hunting, fishing, and gathering peoples who used tiny, geometrically shaped stone tools reminiscent of those in vogue elsewhere in Africa, Europe, and the Middle East. Based on evidence of truly massive Nile floods in the late Sahaba-Darau period, Fekri Hassan has speculated that a prolonged series of such natural disasters would have discouraged the Nilotic peoples from continued reliance on grain foods that had to be cultivated in the dangerous and periodically scoured or buried bottomlands. Whether his explanation is sufficient or whether it places too much emphasis on catastrophic events cannot be told at present. For now, however, it is one of the few explanations based upon both geological and archaeological evidence. Unexpectedly, a small cemetery at Jebel Sahaba in Nubia has contributed a new dimension to our understanding of the demise of late Palaeolithic societies.

Cemetery 117: An Epitaph to Violence at Jebel Sahaba

The discovery of an important archaeological site often begins in a most routine way:

This site was initially noted in January, 1962, during the preliminary survey of the reservoir area. At that time R. Paepe and Jean Guichard discovered a fossilized human femur in the bottom of a small tributary wadi on the east bank of the Nile, north of Wadi Halfa. Paepe and Guichard also found a group of thin sandstone slabs which seemed to have been purposefully arranged on the surface. . . . The slabs were removed and a small pit was excavated, 0.1 m. wide, 1.5 m. long, and 0.3 m. deep. Fragments of three human skeletons were recovered from this pit. (*Wendorf 1968 I: 954*)

What would later be called Site 117 belonged to the late Palaeolithic Qadan culture.

A total of 58 [sic] skeletons were recovered from all three projects at the site. Most of these were in excellent condition, and included both males and females, infants and adults . . . the skeletons are believed to date somewhere between 12,000 and 10,000 B.C. They are particularly significant in that they provide an unusual opportunity to examine a sizable population of late Pleistocene age.

(Wendorf 1968 I: 954)

Site 117 is so vital to prehistorians not because, as some outsiders are wont to believe, we prefer our informants dead to alive, but for the diverse types of information that ancient graveyards and skeletal remains provide. From cemetery sites, when properly preserved and excavated, it is possible to relate both biological data like population demography and pathology and cultural information like wealth differentials, status and occupation, and religious beliefs. In the past, much information was thoughtlessly wasted when archaeologists, especially those trained in disciplines like art history, did not record information on skeletal remains, ignoring them in favor of pretty pots and ornaments to be displayed like trophies in the museums of the world. Unfortunately, in divorcing the artifacts from their former owners, archaeologists lost a rare opportunity to relate human biology to social and cultural organization. Thanks to the modern, interdisciplinary approach taken by Wendorf and his colleagues, following in the long and honorable tradition begun by Petrie and Reisner, these earliest Egyptian and Nubian cemeteries have been rescued for science.

The burials at Site 117 were loosely flexed and frequently multiple. In general, Qadan graves were simply shallow, oval pits covered by flat slabs of rock. It is possible that small mounds of dirt were once piled over the slabs, but these have long since eroded away. In a few instances the large horns of giant wild cattle were found just above a grave, suggesting that at least some burials were marked with these horns in a manner reminiscent of the early Dynastic use of such ornamentation for royal graves and the long-standing Egyptian religious concern with cows cited by Herodotus:

> ... the Egyptians, one and all, venerate cows much more highly than any other animal. . . . When kine die, the following is the manner of their sepulture: The females are thrown into the river; the males are buried in the suburbs of the towns, with one or both of their horns appearing above the surface of the ground to mark the place. When the bodies are decayed, a boat comes, at an appointed time, from the island called Prosopitis—which is a portion of the Delta, nine schoenes in circumference—and calls at the several cities in turn to collect the bones of the oxen. (*Trans. Rawlinson 1932: 95*)

Three Qadan cemeteries are known to date: Site 8905 at Tushka, which had 21 burials; Site 117 near Jebel Sahaba in Lower Nubia with as many as 59 interments, and one across the river from Site 117, with 39 graves. The physical anthropologists who examined Wendorf's sites were able to reconstruct what the paleodemographer Dr. Lawrence Angel has called "death curves"—a cemetery population's demographic, age-sex profile.

The age and sex ratios of individuals buried at Sites 8905 and 117 are given in Tables V through IX and illustrate an end product of modern physical anthropological analysis which gives archaeologists and evolutionary human biologists an invaluable baseline from which to begin the in-depth analysis of ancient demography and social organization. The close bond between archaeologists and physical anthropologists, as exemplified in the work of Wendorf's expedition, is not new in Egyptian archaeology but can be traced back to the turn of the century when the

TABLE V AGE AND SEX COMPOSITION
OF BURIALS AT SITE 117

Age	Male	Female	?	Total
Infant*			1	1
3–5			1	1
6			2	2
7			2	2
10			1	1
11			1	1
12?			1	1
Young Adult	2	3	0	5
Middle Adult	8	9	1	18
Old Adult	5	2	0	7
? Adult	5	3	6	13
TOTAL	20	17	16	52(1)

* Less than six months.
(1) The total of 52 individuals given by Anderson is at variance with the total of 59 given by Wendorf and cited in Table VII.

TABLE VI FREQUENCY OF PATHOLOGY
OF BURIALS AT SITE 117

A Cutting—8
B Degenerative Joint Changes
    1 Osteophytosis—on vertebrae, 7/29 or 24.1 percent, but only 3/29 or 10.3 percent severe
    2 Arthritis—12/34 individuals or 35.3 percent, but only 3/34 or 8.8 percent severe
    3 Sacroiliac problems—5/18 individuals, 4/18 severe
    4 Early Spinal Tuberculosis?—2 individuals
    5 Osteitis—1 individual
C Dental Pathologies
    1 Lost teeth—7/34 individuals
    2 Caries—4.3 percent of all teeth
    3 Alveolar abscesses—10 individuals

TABLE VII FREQUENCY OF ARTIFACTS AT SITE 117

Age Group	Total	No. with Artifacts	Percent of Age/Sex Group	Embedded Points
Children	11	4	36.4	
Adult Male	20	9	45.0	2
Adult Female	21	10	47.7	2
Adult ? Sex	7	1	14.3	
TOTAL	59	24	40.7	

TABLE VIII AGE AND SEX COMPOSITION OF BURIALS
AT SITE 8905 BASED ON TRADITIONAL CRITERIA

Age	Male	Female	?	Total
Children			1	1
Adult	2	3	15	20
TOTAL				21

TABLE IX AGE AND SEX COMPOSITION OF BURIALS
AT SITE 8905 BASED ON NEUROCRANIAL DIMENSIONS

Sex	Number	Neurocranial Range	Mean	S.D.
Adult Male	12	1320–1587	1452	73
Adult Female	8	1273–1371	1311	35
? Infant	1	—	—	—
TOTAL	21			

great British anatomist Grafton Elliot Smith was first retained by Reisner to work on the skeletal material from the First Archaeological Survey of Nubia (1907–12). Unfortunately, like many scientists of his day, Elliot Smith was more interested in problems of cultural and racial origins than in modern human biological concerns like demography and statistical frequencies and so too often emphasized rare and bizarre pathologies, idealized racial types and rather abstruse metrical indices, like the cephalic index which describes head shape, rather than the total make-up of an ancient population. Despite the excesses of Elliot Smith, it is much to his credit that he recognized the great potential of ancient Egyptian skeletal material in revealing the interrelationship between culture and biology.

Although the poor state of preservation and small number of individuals buried at Site 8905 made it difficult to draw broader, demographic inferences, Site 117 allowed a number of quite unexpected insights. The people buried there doubtless represented an active, breeding population, rather than a special group of retainers, such as found in some Dynastic graveyards, since roughly equal numbers of adult men and women were interred and since a wide and varied range of subadult age categories are represented. The one exception to this, and one that demands explanation, is the puzzling rarity of children under age three in the cemetery. Only a single infant burial was found at 117, a situation paralleled at 8905. Since infant mortality is usually quite high in both ancient and modern nonindustrial societies, we suspect that the very young individuals must have been excluded systematically from the cemeteries, perhaps because they were not regarded as fullblown members of the social group or perhaps because they were buried somewhere else, possibly underneath the floors of dwellings—a common practice in Predynastic times. At any rate, the burial of a single infant in each cemetery is the type of anomaly that attracts our attention and may be explained by some sort of ritual, dedicatory behavior. The absence of children under age three from Qadan cemeteries also prevents us from properly estimating the mean life expectancy of the ancient populations or of gauging the approximate birthrate. This latter fact is of more importance than one might readily suspect, because of the known tendency of hunting and gathering groups, as opposed to farming groups, to limit population size. In this regard, hunters and gatherers are closer to industrial peoples than to farmers—a fact that might well be recalled by those who try to portray high birthrates and large populations as the natural state of man.

In terms of the pathologies that plagued the Qadans (see Table VI), familiar diseases like arthritis, sacroiliac problems, osteitis and, possibly, spinal tuberculosis as well as a variety of dental disorders, including missing teeth, cavities, and abscesses were noted by Dr. J. E. Anderson of McMaster University in Canada, who analyzed the material.

23, 24   The late Palaeolithic cemetery at Tushka, Site 8905

25   A late Palaeolithic double burial of adult and child at Jebel Sahaba

The presence of incisions or cuts on human bones in eight burials is somewhat surprising, and might reflect attempted cures or, more probably, the pervasive violence that is attested to at Site 117.

One of the unusual features of the burials was the direct association of 110 artifacts, almost all in positions which indicate they had penetrated the body either as points or barbs on projectiles or spears. They were not grave offerings. Many of the artifacts were found along the vertebral column, but other favored target areas were the chest cavity, lower abdomen, arms, and the skull. Several pieces were found inside the skull, and two of these were still imbedded in the sphenoid bones in positions which indicate that the pieces entered from under the lower jaw. *(Wendorf in Wendorf 1968 II: 959)*

Slightly over 40 percent of the burials were accompanied by small flake points, some of which were nothing more than stubby burins that had once been inserted in arrow shafts as points. In the case of four persons (some of whom suffered multiple wounds) points were actually embedded in the bones. In other cases, simple association of such points with skeletal remains has been interpreted as the result of violence (Table VII). This assertion is hard to deal with archaeologically; if soft tissue is lacking it is normally difficult to prove that such injuries actually caused death, but the location of stone points near vital organs or the simple fact that they seemed to have remained in the body's tissue suggests that most wounds were ultimately fatal. In the case of the points embedded in bone, the absence of extensive bony calluses around the intrusive objects clearly supports the conclusion that death followed rapidly upon injury, since bone starts to heal itself rather quickly by redepositing bony tissue around the injured area. The magnitude of violence in an essentially hunting and gathering society is difficult to explain in terms of the classic anthropological ideas about the low incidence of large-scale warfare and raiding among such peoples. Initially, one could reject the evidence from Site 117 on the grounds that those stone points not actually embedded in bone (the vast majority) were either grave offerings or accidental inclusions from underlying or overlying strata. This argument can be rejected because of the careful recording of the graves—an example that I wish more archaeologists would follow. Wendorf's observations revealed that there were no overlying or underlying occupation strata, so that contamination is unlikely. That leaves the possibility that the points were deliberately included as grave offerings as the one remaining stumbling block to the violence interpretation. This explanation is also highly unlikely, however, because the points were not carefully arranged inside the grave in the manner of offerings and they were generally located near or in vital parts of the body. Finally, there is the example of the four individuals who still retained points embedded in their bones.

Assuming then that about 40 percent of the people buried at Site 117 actually did perish from arrow or dart wounds from spear throwers (the points are clearly too small for thrusting spears), we must return to the problem of why such a hunting and gathering people were so prone to violence. Wendorf once proposed that the fighting might reflect strain brought about when increasing aridity after about 10,500 B.C. began to take its toll on the overextended, protoagricultural Qadan population.

According to this view, the large size and wide extent of Qadan (and Isnan) sites are due, in part at least, to experiments in primitive agriculture. When the moisture (be it rainfall or high floodwaters) that nourished this precocious revolution disappeared and plant and animal communities shrank, the Qadans were forced back on remaining, limited resources. The fight for limited resources and living room would then be viewed as the culprit. However, if Hassan is right and giant floods and not aridity eliminated protoagricultural experimentation around 10,500 B.C., then we must reject the first explanation in favor of floods. As a third alternative—one that avoids totally environmental determinism— we might imagine that even experimenting with agriculture generates the kind of internal social and economic stress that leads to increased violence, but before we can accept or reject such a sweeping generalization there are other possibilities that have to be considered.

The first goes back to a classic difficulty encountered by prehistorians: dating. If Site 117 was used by only one social group (and that seems logical based on the fairly even ratio of males to females and the normal distribution of age categories above three years), then we must be dealing with a graveyard used for only a handful of generations—perhaps no more than a century, even assuming the group was small. Spread over the course of several generations, it is easier to attribute 40 percent violent deaths to a slow accumulation, rather than a high endemic rate of violence or to sudden slaughter. Second, recent ethnographic studies have shown that, in point of fact, violent deaths—usually by ambush— are more common than once believed among known hunters and gatherers (obviously, it is hard to get statistics). Viewed in this light, the varied ages and sexes of the victims at Site 117 are better explained by conditions of endemic raiding and ambush than regular, organized warfare, which usually takes its highest toll in young to middle-aged adult males.

Finally, there is a third and highly unlikely archaeological explanation for the violence at Site 117 that deserves mention. Since the site is only dated on the basis of stone tool typology, it could conceivably fall anywhere between about 12,000 and 4500 B.C. If it were abandoned very late in that era (and that is highly unlikely based on most accepted dates for the Qadans), there is an outside chance that the people fell victim to changes accompanying the arrival of intensive farming and herding in the Nile Valley. We should not be too quick to adopt the view that radical change is necessarily caused by an outside factor or people. Migration has long been the Holy Grail of prehistorians unwilling to tackle the deeper complexities of how and why cultures change. However, we do know that massive social and economic change and one-sided exploitation do often promote conflict. For instance, in the Dynastic period, whenever Egypt was politically powerful, she preyed off Nubia for desired raw materials and luxury goods like gold, conducting regular military campaigns and even establishing a virtual no-man's-land to secure her own southern frontier, recalling Tacitus's characterization of Roman military imperialism: "They make a wasteland, and they call it peace." In Egypt this exploitative policy dates back to earliest historic times. If Site 117 was abandoned at late as 4500 B.C., it is possible that its inhabitants might have suffered from similar competition with larger, more politically centralized societies like the Badarians of Upper Egypt. The dominant agricultural-pastoral groups need not have been outside immigrants in the sense of many of the barbarian tribes which invaded the Roman Empire, but merely other indigenous Nilotes or desert peoples who adopted farming and animal domestication first, as it spread into Egypt after 5500 B.C. The possibility that some people accepted innovations sooner than others is not only logical but in a land characterized by the extreme cultural variability of late Palaeolithic Egypt, it is a virtual certainty, as demonstrated by the conservative peoples of El Kab who retained an essentially Palaeolithic way of life at the same time that the peoples of Nabta Playa in the Libyan Desert were adopting agriculture and animal husbandry (see Chapter 16).

The Epipalaeolithic Peoples of El Kab: The End of the Beginning

Until Dr. Paul Vermeersch's discovery of 1968, few Egyptian prehistorians would have believed El Kab a likely place for a Palaeolithic site, especially a well-stratified one. Hugging a narrow strip of land on the eastern bank of the Nile and hemmed in by the towering Red Sea Hills less than a kilometer to the east, El Kab is surrounded by a massive mud-brick wall 450 meters by 550 meters on its sides, built probably in the tenth century B.C. At the center of the ancient town stands an older circular wall (thought by the controversial and eccentric architect Sommers Clark to be of protohistoric date but probably of early New Kingdom vintage) and the stone walls and toppled columns of once imposing temples devoted to Nekhbet, the vulture-headed patron goddess of Upper Egypt—a deity so important that pharaoh himself wore her image on his crown beside Wadjet, the cobra goddess of Lower Egypt. Together they were the Two Ladies. El Kab rose to prominence at the end of the Old Kingdom, with the decline of neighboring Hierakonpolis, across the river, and is best known to historians through the writings of two of its sons who served in the successful war of liberation against the Hyksos in the early sixteenth century B.C. Like other provincial centers, the town's notables were buried in tombs carved out of nearby cliffs and recorded the honors, real or symbolic, which they obtained from the king.

Beginning in 1967 the site was visited by a Belgian team of epigraphers, architects, and archaeologists bent on reopening major excavations in the area. Fortunately for Egyptian prehistory, the group included a man well versed in the careful techniques of European Palaeolithic archaeology. While mapping the region around El Kab, Dr. Paul Vermeersch discovered some geometric microlithic tools in the lower levels of an exposed ditch just inside the circuit walls. He immediately recognized their importance. Thanks to the finds made by the Nubian campaigns and earlier French work all over North Africa, Vermeersch knew that these tools must date from the latest epoch of the Palaeolithic—a period often called the Epipalaeolithic. With Wendorf and his colleagues pushing back and extending forward the record of Palaeolithic development, El Kab offered an exciting opportunity to fill in a major gap in Egyptian prehistory: the period between the end of classic late Palaeolithic culture and the appearance of village farming Predynastic cultures after 5500 B.C. The finds at El Kab also refuted the claims of many older archaeologists and geologists that Palaeolithic material would not be found on the floodplain of the Nile. They had argued that these deposits were either fairly recent or that older material would be deeply buried or washed away in the course of millennia. Like so many ad hoc conclusions based on blanket statements and assumptions, this view was misleading and ignored the subtleties and nuances of geologic processes.

Armed with information gleaned from actual field investigation, Vermeersch returned to El Kab in December 1968, and initiated large-scale test excavations in the floodplain in search of his Epipalaeolithic site. An area 20 meters square was explored and yielded an unexpectedly clear sequence of cultural development. Near the top, just below the Dynastic debris, were found three Predynastic burials. Below these were three sealed occupation levels dating from Epipalaeolithic times. The soil profile showed that the tools came from campsites located on the old channel of the Nile. As the river shifted to the west in succeeding years and continued to deposit soil by its annual floods, the campsites were buried. The lowest occupation (radiocarbon-dated to about 6400 B.C.) was somewhat disturbed and lay at the bottom of the old channel. The artifacts had not been moved far, however, and the accuracy of their date was confirmed by two higher Epipalaeolithic campsites still *in situ* on the old riverbank. The middle camp dated to 6040 B.C. and the upper occupation to 5980 B.C. Although the stone waste was not analyzed nor checked for utilization, Vermeersch carefully classified over 4,000 artifacts, most of which were carefully made and minutely retouched blades and microblades. Flake points of many varieties were common, as were burins and scrapers. Ostrich shell beads indicate ornamentation and badly decayed fish bones suggest the ultimate reason for the Epipalaeolithic stations along the Nile. Since we know that occupation of such riverside camps would have been impossible during the annual inundation, it is almost certain that the El Kabian campsites were seasonal affairs lived in during spring or summer.

The pattern of Epipalaeolithic life suggested by Vermeersch's finds is

TABLE X ARCHAEOLOGICAL INDUSTRIES FROM LATE MIDDLE PALAEOLITHIC THROUGH EPIPALAEOLITHIC TIMES IN EGYPT AND NUBIA

Date (B.C.) & Period	Lower Nubia	Kom Ombo	Upper Egypt
5,700	Sharmarkian ?		El Kabian
6,700 Epipalaeolithic	Arkinian		Fayum B (Qarunian)
9,500	?	Isnan	
12,000	Ballanan ? — Qadan / Gemaian	Sebilian / Silsillian / Sebekian ?	Affian ?
Late (Upper) Palaeolithic	Dabarosa Complex ?		
15,000	Halfan ?		Fakhurian / Idfuan (Halfan Variant) ? / Idfuan (non-levallois, non-Halfan Variant)
24,000	Khormusan ?		
34,000	?		
40,000 Late (Middle) Palaeolithic	Aterian ?		

(*N.B. All correlations are very tentative.*)

echoed by two roughly contemporaneous industries in the northern Sudan near Wadi Halfa—the Arkinian and the Sharmarkian.

The Arkinian, which is known from only one site and dated at 7440 ± 180 B.C., was microlithic but had a fairly large number of blades and two-ended or double-platform cores. A great variety of fish were caught in the Nile and wild savanna grazing animals such as wild cattle, ass, gazelle, and riverine hippo hunted. The existing settlement consists of a cluster of thirteen oval concentrations of debris, probably a seasonal camp by a small group of people. The Sharmarkian spans a longer time, from 5750 ± 120 B.C. to at least 3270 ± 50 B.C. and may in fact be a later variant of the Arkinian. The principal tools were microlithic flakes and blades at first, but in the latest sites there was a decline in the quality of stone working. Settlements were located on the high water or recessional beaches left by the flooding Nile and were probably occupied seasonally during inundation. As time went on, sites developed from small, compact camps to large concentrations. Considering the time these late sites were occupied, it is almost certain that there had been a population increase brought about by the introduction of agriculture and animal domestication after 5500 B.C. The well-made microlithic tools of the El Kabian, Arkinian, and early Sharmarkian in Upper Egypt and Lower Nubia and of Fayum B (Qarunian) in Lower Egypt underscore the efficiency of the Epipalaeolithic adaptation to the riverine environment. This way of life was so well suited to the Nile and the climatic barriers so forbidding in the deserts of this time, that any experiments that earlier Egyptians might have made with plant domestication were never revived. The hunting-fishing way of life of Nilotic Egyptians continued until the rapid introduction of Near Eastern village farming culture into the Nile Valley on the heels of the Neolithic rainy period around 5500 B.C.

We still know little about exactly when or how effective agriculture and animal domestication spread to Egypt. There is still a mysterious gap of approximately 1,000 to 1,500 years between Epipalaeolithic industries like the El Kabian and full-fledged early Predynastic cultures like the Badarian in Upper Egypt and the Merimden in Lower Egypt. There are tantalizing clues at sites like Catfish Cave in Nubia, carbon-14 dated to 5110 ± 120 B.C., of domesticated animals that might have been brought into the Nile Valley from the Sahara during the Neolithic Subpluvial and there has been speculation for years that cattle might have been domesticated independently in Africa. For the time being, the Epipalaeolithic-Predynastic gap remains one of the least known and most important research problems facing prehistorians and archaeologists working in northeastern Africa. Despite this gap, one thing is certain: thanks to the wealth of new archaeological information and dates that have accumulated over the last 15 years, the Palaeolithic era is more understandable and in many ways foreshadows the spectacular Predynastic cultures that flourished in Egypt between about 5500 and 3100 B.C.

PART **III**

THE PREDYNASTIC PEOPLES OF UPPER EGYPT: THE EMERGENCE OF THE VALLEY TRADITION, ca. 5500–3100 B.C.

7

THE IRASCIBLE
PROFESSOR PETRIE AND
HIS CEMETERY AT NAQADA

T HE DISCOVERY of the Predynastic cultures of Upper Egypt
began on a far from auspicious note:

> Whatever we left was sure to be lost for ever, as any cemetery known
> to the natives is completely grubbed out very soon. The hundreds—
> thousands—of open tomb-pits all along the desert, rifled and refilled
> in recent years, show this only too plainly. . . . Whatever we left un-
> worked was therefore irrevocably to be destroyed, after we had once
> shown the way. *(Petrie and Quibell 1896: x)*

In 1894 William Matthews Flinders Petrie was forty-two years old and
at the midpoint of a long and eventful career. In fourteen years of digging he had already painstakingly mapped and described the great pyramids of Giza, discovered the lost ancient Greek colony of Naucratis, and
founded the Egypt Research Account—one of the most important spon-
sors of archaeological work in Egypt for the next two generations. The
thousands of graves he excavated at Naqada, therefore, were neither the
most startling nor the best known of his finds. In fact, he was so puzzled
by the strange pottery and ornaments that he initially believed the cemeteries were built by a "new race" that had invaded Egypt in the troubled
times following the collapse of the Old Kingdom around 2180 B.C.

In addition to being an acute observer, an incredibly energetic worker,
and a methodical genius, Flinders Petrie was an outspoken critic of incompetence and had a way of getting involved in feuds that followed
him throughout his long life. In the mid-1890's, one of the incidental
targets of his professional wrath was the brilliant and flamboyant French
archaeologist, Jacques de Morgan. If Petrie is remembered as the father
of modern, scientific archaeology in the Near East, de Morgan must be
reckoned a pillar of the old school—a master of the well-turned phrase,
an aficionado of the spectacular site. To appreciate the differences between the two men one must understand in a real way the intellectual
and scientific foundations of Predynastic research in Upper Egypt as well

26 In the wake of grave robbers. A looted Predynastic grave at Hierakonpolis in 1978

as the future directions that archaeological fieldwork and interpretations would take. The methods employed by Petrie and de Morgan contrast sharply in the following excerpts from their reports. First, Petrie is talking in 1896 about the mysterious and unimpressive cemeteries he had just found at Naqada:

> In the first place, strict discipline was maintained among the men, and new comers were carefully allotted with old hands, so as to be educated. Carelessness in breaking up skeletons was punished, sometimes severely. . . . The constant rule enforced on the diggers was that any bones once disturbed must never be put back in place unless the cast of them remained in the earth. . . . In the best part of the cemetery, which I had most continuously in my own hands, and where the work was most completely organised, the system of a compound gang was as follows: The whole party consisted of two pairs of boys, two inferior pairs of man and boy, two pairs of superior men, Ali [Petrie's foreman] and myself. First a pair of boys were set to try for a grave, and if the ground was soft they were to clear around up to the edges of the filling, but not to go more than a couple feet down. At that point they were turned out to try for another, and an inferior

man and boy came in to clear the earth until they touched pottery or bones in more than one place. They then turned out to follow where the boys were working, and the pair of superior men came in to dig or scrape out with potsherds, the earth between the jars. While they were at work Ali was in the hole with them, finishing the scraping out with a potsherd, or with his hands, his orders being to remove every scrap of loose earth that he could without shifting or disturbing any objects. When he had a favourable place his clearing was a triumph. . . . Lastly, when I came up to the party I found several graves thus prepared. *(Petrie and Quibell 1896: viii-ix)*

Now de Morgan in 1906 discusses his work at the ancient Persian metropolis of Susa:

I thought that I was going to find some large building that would at least be in good enough condition for the plan to be studied, which would have involved a special method of working. . . . But I soon realized that everything was in the greatest disorder and that significant objects, however large, were sparsely distributed among a great deal of rubble. This realization led me to adopt a working method that might be termed "industrial."
(De Morgan 1906: 1-37 in Huot 1965: 54)

De Morgan decided to reduce the 35-meter-high ancient acropolis of Susa in seven 5-meter levels in order to implement his industrial methods:

A general excavation (in five meter levels) was therefore called for without taking into account the natural levels, which are imperceptible and which it would be childish to try to distinguish . . . experience (showed) that if the workmen threw the dirt into the wagons from a height of five meters, the materials would not suffer. *(De Morgan 1906: 1-37 in Huot 1965: 54)*

And finally, in contrast to Petrie's small crews and highly structured organization, de Morgan believed "A thousand men are no more difficult to organize than 200. You simply arrange them in squads and group these squads according to major excavation points."

Given such startling differences in competence, one may imagine Petrie's consternation when de Morgan, excavating at Abydos in 1896, found graves similar to those at Naqada and *immediately* recognized them as prehistoric, "though," as Petrie wryly adds, "by happy guess without any evidence" (Petrie 1932: 167). And what did Petrie think of de Morgan? Elsewhere he castigated de Morgan's appointment as Director of the Cairo Museum in 1891 (a post traditionally held by a Frenchman) in belittling tones (p. 147). "Really he was the son of Jack Morgan, a Welsh mining engineer and a brother of a Parisian dealer in antiquities. He knew nothing whatever about Egypt but, as a capable business man, made the most reputable head that the French could find."

27 Distribution map
showing location
of important
Predynastic sites

So it was that a mere businessman, an untrained and sloppy excavator and, worst of all in Petrie's estimate, a Frenchman, must get the credit for discovering the Predynastic cultures of Upper Egypt. Despite his precocious guess at Abydos, de Morgan did not follow up on his prehistoric finds, and quickly relinquished the scientific arena to his irascible and more thorough English critic. Even if de Morgan had correctly guessed the prehistoric date of the Naqada material, he had not, as Sir Flinders observed with obvious relish, really "proved" anything. The final proof came after almost six years of hard work, analyzing and reanalyzing Naqada and an additional 1,200 graves dug up by Petrie and his associates at Abadiyeh and Hu in 1898 and 1899.

The greatest problem facing Petrie as a prehistorian was one thrust on him by the peculiar nature and immense size of the Predynastic cemeteries at Naqada, Ballas, Abadiyeh, and Hu. At Naqada, for example, a staggering total of 2,149 graves was packed into approximately 17 acres on the low desert spurs overlooking the cultivated land of the Nile Valley. In taking advantage of the soft subsoil on these spurs, the prehistoric Naqadans had placed their graves side by side until the area was literally saturated with tombs—like a Land of the Dead on the western bank of the river foreshadowing the Western Land of later Egyptian mythology.

Most Naqadans were buried in simple rectangular pits, three to four feet deep, which were roofed with crude ceilings of interwoven branches and brush and capped by low mounds of dirt. As time passed, the ceiling collapsed and the dirt fell into the grave. When Petrie's workmen were

28   An intact Late Gerzean grave at Hierakonpolis

cleaning out the pits, they used potsherds for scraping through the sand and gravel and cleaning around the skeletons and grave offerings. Sometimes they found and reused prehistoric sherds, rounded from previous use in the same task—suggesting that little changed in the art of grave-digging over 6,000 years.

The dead were placed in a contracted position, reclining on their left side with legs flexed at a 45-degree angle to the chest and arms bent so that the hands lay in front of the face or neck, the overall impression recalling a fetal crouch. With very few exceptions, the head lay at the southern end of the tomb while the face looked west—once again, an anticipation of later Egyptian beliefs concerning the location of the Land of the Dead. In the rare instances where people did not look west, it is possible that they were regarded as outsiders or outcasts in the community and denied some of the comforting last rites of Naqadan society. Although the Predynastic Egyptians did not practice mummification, the hot, dry sands of the desert often preserved their flesh and other organic parts better than the fanciful chemical concoctions of later times. From these natural mummies we get a vivid portrait of the ancient Naqadan peoples. Both men and women wore their hair long, often braiding or plaiting it in some fashion. Men were beardless and both men and women short by modern Western standards. When we compare their faces to portraits and sculptures of Dynastic Egyptians, the resemblance is strong; indeed, we would probably lose a Predynastic Naqadan among a group of modern rural southern Egyptians.

Before 4000 B.C. the Predynastic peoples of Upper Egypt had already developed a strong belief in burying their surplus wealth with them, in strong contrast to their neighbors in the Delta, whose graves contain scarcely any material. Tombs were kinds of minihomes, with great attention given to the needs of the dead—another custom that became a hallmark of Dynastic Egyptian society. The deceased were laid on reed mats and invariably accompanied by grave offerings that reflected their relative wealth and aspects of their daily life: tools such as flint knives, scrapers, and arrowheads; green slate grinding palettes with accompanying malachite or hematite pigment stones; copper punches, awls, and adzes; ornaments (many of which were imported) like shell and stone beads; containers fashioned from hard and attractive stones like diorite, porphyry, and syenite; and a bewildering variety of fine, handmade polished red ware and black-topped red ware jars as well as more enigmatic artifacts that throw light on individual differences and personal preferences, like baked clay figurines, amulets, and carved ivory plaques—objects often relegated by the archaeologist to the mystical category of "ceremonial objects."

It is the arrangement of all these types of artifacts in relation to the body that ultimately enables archaeologists to evoke some of the long-dead customs of prehistoric Naqadans and, at the same time, causes a

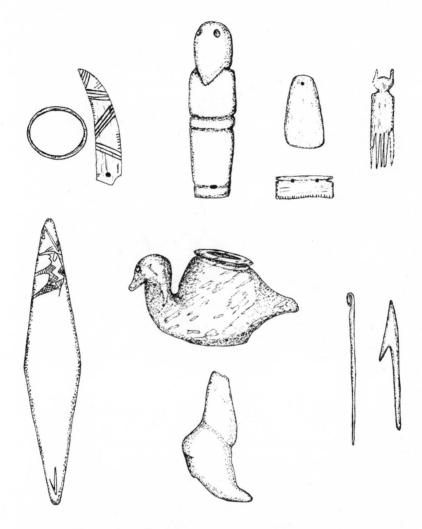

29 Predynastic artifacts from the cemeteries of Abadiyeh and Hu in Naqada.
From left to right and top to bottom: ivory bracelet, ivory pendants or
amulets (3), ivory combs (2), incised slate palette, stone effigy duck vase,
clay figurine, copper pin, barbed point

good deal of controversy. For one thing, many of the graves Petrie and
his co-workers uncovered had already been looted long before the first
pharaoh ascended his throne. Petrie observed that several graves were
robbed only in the spots where valuable objects like personal ornaments
would have been placed. The conclusion was obvious: these robbers
knew what they were doing because they were familiar with Naqadan
burial rites; they were, in fact, Naqadans. Thus, tomb robbery was
already a well-established national pastime a thousand years before

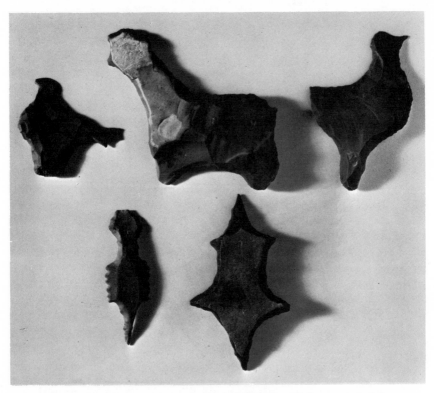

30 Predynastic animal figurines of chipped flint. Top (left to right): falcon, unidentifiable animal, unidentifiable bird. Bottom: lizards (?)

31 Predynastic slate pigment palette ground in the shape of a fish

Khufu (Cheops) strove vainly to preserve for eternity his body and treasures within an impregnable mountain of stone at Giza.

The widespread looting of Predynastic tombs resulted in the frequent contamination of graves by later objects that happened to fall in either during or after robbery. For an archaeologist like Petrie, this must have been a discouraging problem, especially in light of the time required to carefully clean a grave before being able to determine whether it had been despoiled. Unlike de Morgan, who used the apparent disturbance

32 Selected examples of Petrie's Predynastic pottery types. Top row: Class B, black-topped pottery. Middle row: Class C, white cross-lined pottery. Middle row (last form): Class B. Bottom row: Class N, incised black pottery; Class W, wavy-handled pottery; Class P, polished red pottery (after Petrie 1901)

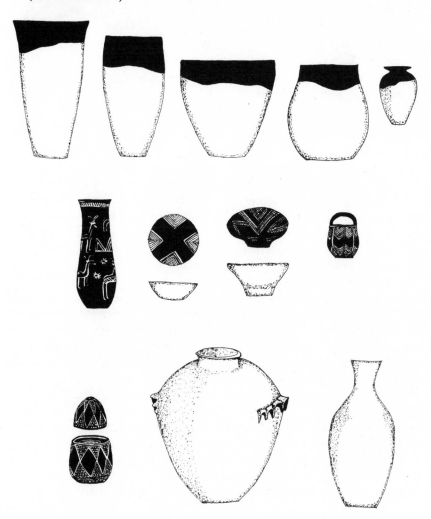

33 Flint "fishtail lanceheads" of Predynastic date. It is possible that these artifacts were not primarily utilitarian but intended instead for a ritual connected with the afterlife

of Susa as an excuse to initiate reckless industrial archaeology, Petrie insisted that even a looted tomb, if properly recorded, would often yield enough information to justify its careful excavation. As a result of his thirst to learn all the facts, he discovered that not all the disturbances had been perpetrated by looters. In a small number of unrobbed tombs (perhaps 10 percent), Petrie thought that the ways the bones were distributed in the grave indicated that they had been deliberately placed there after the flesh had rotted away. Anthropologists call this practice secondary burial and it is a fairly common practice in many societies. The reason for the custom varies: it may be that the bones of either relatives or enemies are kept around the house for a while for good luck, to honor or placate the spirit of the dead, to acquire some of the power once possessed by an unusually successful person or simply because one does not wish to part quickly with an old friend. The particular reasons are legion, but the fact is that at some point the remains of the dead are disposed of—often through formal burial.

Obviously among the Predynastic Upper Egyptians this custom was not common but did occasionally occur. The problem is to determine the peculiar social conditions that could have accounted for occasional resort to secondary burial. Sadly, the information available on Petrie's Naqada finds is not complete enough to begin to propose an explanation that would be scientifically grounded, except in one case where Sir Flinders's description of a large tomb (T. 5) is detailed enough to pose some tantalizing possibilities. Petrie believed that tomb T. 5 reflected not only secondary burial of several individuals but cannibalism as well! Inside this unusually large grave he found the scattered and rearranged remains of at least six individuals. Since the grave was still sealed and the rich grave offerings intact, he ruled out the possibility that tomb robbers could have disturbed the original position of the bones. Detailed exam-

34 Two large Late Gerzean tombs. Top: Tomb T.5 at Naqada, scale 1:40. Bottom: The Painted Tomb from Hierakonpolis, scale 1 : 50

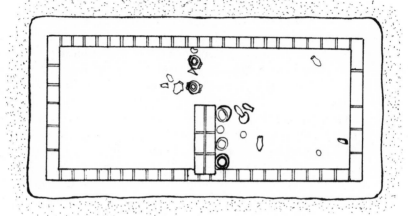

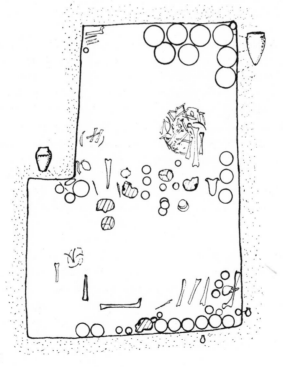

ination of the human long bones showed teeth marks (whether from human or nonhuman agency is unknown) and clear signs that the marrow inside the shafts had been carefully scooped out with tools—clearly a human practice. Unfortunately, none of the human bones showed signs of burning and this fact, overlooked by Petrie, argues against cannibalism, although it does leave two other possibilities open: multiple reburial or human sacrifice. In many societies it is common to reuse the same burial vault for several generations. In such cases, the bones of dead ancestors are swept aside to make room for the most recently deceased member of the family. Although this custom may explain tomb T. 5, the fact that none of the burials were left in a normal position when we should expect the most recent interment to be undisturbed, argues against it. If we consider the possibility of deliberate human sacrifice, however, the puzzle begins to make more sense. Tomb T. 5 was located in a decidedly wealthy cemetery at Naqada and, judging by the types of pottery and other grave goods found inside, was built in Late Gerzean times (ca. 3300–3100 B.C.) when differences in wealth and social position in Egyptian society had already become marked. It is therefore quite possible that the inhabitants of the tomb were victims of human sacrifice— a practice that reached its peak early in Dynastic times and then quickly disappeared. Sacrificing one's slaves or servants to demonstrate wealth and power is common in societies undergoing the transition from chieftainship to state, but in the long run is wasteful and dangerous since it ultimately does away with the ruler's most loyal followers and craftsmen who are capable of producing an excess of wealth for their patron and his successors.

Despite occasionally spectacular customs like mass reburial or human sacrifice, it is the more normal everyday behavior of the Naqadans that ultimately attracts our attention. Their values and customs and the cultural differences that animated their society can still be traced thanks to Sir Flinders's careful mapping of their tombs, and we only regret that such a small portion of his carefully collected information (a mere 6.2 percent of all the graves) was ever published. Tombs varied a good deal in size, from humble pits just big enough to accommodate a single body and a few pots to large, brick-lined sepulchers 13 feet long by 9 feet wide. Although many of the biggest tombs were looted, some idea of their comparative wealth may be gained by noting that one grave of medium size contained upward of 80 separate pottery storage jars. Such containers were not simply laid haphazardly in the grave, but were placed according to a deliberate formula—a formula discovered by Petrie in carefully excavating thousands of tombs—and one that sheds light on the nature and meaning of ritual and belief in Predynastic times. The northern end of the grave was reserved for long, conical, or cylindrical jars of polished red or black-topped polished red ware:

These were filled with grey ashes of wood and vegetable matter. Such ash-jars were typical of the New Race graves, and occur in all tombs except the very poorest. The ashes were very carefully winnowed by us at first, but nothing distinctive was ever found in them, except a few bits of broken bones of animals; no trace of human bones occurred, nor were any of the human bones in the burials ever calcined or discoloured. In every case we emptied out these ash-jars and looked over the contents, often dozens in a single grave; but amid the tons upon tons of ashes searched not a single object of human work was found. *(Petrie and Quibell 1896: 19)*

What did this mean?

We learn, however, that a great burning took place at a funeral, and the ashes of the vegetable matter and even the burnt sand beneath it, were gathered up and buried in the grave. In some cases a layer of some vegetable paste had been poured on top of the ashes; perhaps a libation of thick beer, of which the solid part lay on top, while the liquid filtered down. *(Petrie and Quibell 1896: 19)*

The opposite or southern end of the tomb around the head of the deceased was reserved for the now-famous wavy-handled jars. In the earliest burials at Naqada these jars were filled with a scented vegetable fat. As time went on, first the amount of scented fat was reduced and the remainder of the jar sealed with mud until finally, at the very end of Predynastic times, only mud filled the jars. Although we might most easily explain this in terms of the gradual debasement of real goods for cheaper, symbolic equivalents, it is also possible to read in this trend evidence for increasing poverty in the graves of the general populace at a time when "the rich were getting richer and the poor, poorer." Body ornaments such as necklaces or bracelets were placed around the necks and arms of the deceased while slate pigment palettes, baked clay figurines, stone vases, chipped stone knives and other ornamental and occupational materials do not show careful or deliberate placement. Either the location of these goods was not as essential to the Predynastic Naqadans as the placement of the storage jars containing food and ointment for the afterlife, or the later disturbance of such small, valuable objects was so general that it is difficult now to detect any special location in the tomb.

Despite the vast number of graves at Naqada and Ballas and the vast period of time spanned by the cemeteries, we are struck by the overall similarity in artifact types and their slow stylistic evolution over time. This fact also impressed Petrie. The evidence of the tombs points not to a catastrophic change, but to the slow development of one tradition in the Egyptian Nile Valley—a tradition that began with the appearance of farming villages around 5500 B.C. and which ultimately produced one of the most distinctive civilizations the world has ever seen.

The picture of basic cultural harmony and continuous development that came from Petrie's work at Naqada must be qualified to a degree by taking into account the differences Petrie found in the four cemeteries he dug at Naqada. The largest contained 1,953 recorded burials, while cemetery B had 133 graves and cemetery T 57 burials. Besides these, Petrie's assistant, Grenfell, dug six graves in cemetery G. By far the richest group of tombs, and one of the latest, came from cemetery T. For some archaeologists this suggests a separate caste of rulers, although most people now follow Sir Flinders's original conclusion that cemetery T was the area reserved for the more wealthy and powerful residents of Naqada—people who were the real forerunners of later Dynastic pharaohs.

In 1901 Petrie once more made archaeological history by announcing to the world that he had finally cracked a problem that had puzzled and fascinated him ever since de Morgan pointed out that the Naqada graves dated to the prehistoric period. After six years of hard work, he felt confident that he could finally assign relative dates to the thousands of graves he and his assistants had unearthed. Without written records and without benefit of such modern devices as radiocarbon dating, he had reconstructed the complex sequences of stylistic change through which the grave goods of the Naqada people had developed. The ingenious technique of sequence dating involved using his detailed notes, so arduously and rapidly taken in 1894–95 at Naqada, and devising a crude kind of statistical analysis that was based on two operations. First, he split broad categories of artifacts such as pottery into several types. In the case of ceramics, nine types were devised. He then repeated the method for other classes, like slate palettes, flints, figurines, and ivories. Next he recorded the contents of each tomb on a card and noted the way in which certain types of artifacts clustered together. By assigning sequential numbers from 31 to 80 to each object, based upon its relative position on a stylistic scale running from simple to complex, he worked out his system of sequence dating. By employing this, an excavator could now take a given object, compare it to Petrie's "corpus" or list of types, and immediately assign it a number that indicated its age relative to the First Dynasty. Objects with designations in the 70's were latest and those in the 30's earliest.

Ironically, the success of Petrie's system hinged on how well he could guess the correct direction in which a given artistic or technological characteristic evolved. For instance, he made much out of the fact that wavy ledge handles (his class W) declined through a series of stages until they became useless decorative motifs painted or molded in low relief on the sides of jars. But how did he know the functional handles were earliest and the decorative ones latest? We can, of course, explain

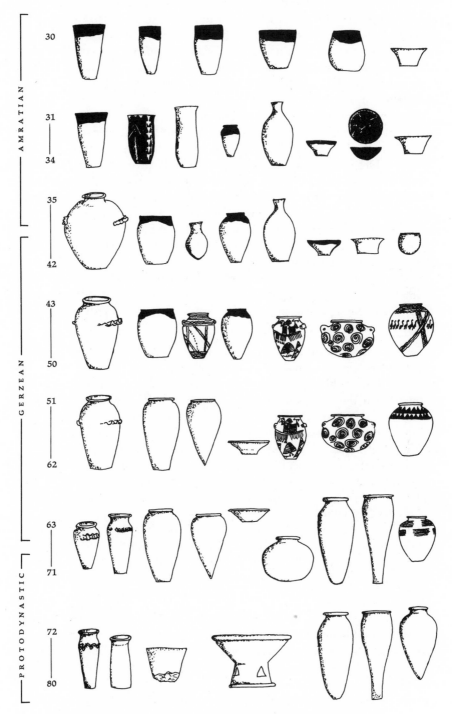

35   Petrie's original sequence dating chart for Predynastic pottery

his insight as an outcome of the careful analysis of his hundreds of carefully prepared index cards and his huge corpus of illustrated pottery types. Petrie himself implies this. However, lurking in back of many of his "hard" scientific statements and pronouncements on statistics and art history we get the suspicion that Petrie knew all along that the wavy handles were earliest and the molded and painted wavy lines latest. And he did!

Two years after Sir Flinders abandoned Naqada, the irrepressible de Morgan visited the site, and with his instinct for the theatrical, unearthed the rich tomb of Queen Neith-hotep, dating to the beginning of the First Dynasty. Despite de Morgan's sloppy methods of excavation, the fact remains that he found the jars with Petrie's "degenerate" wavy lines in direct association with datable early Dynastic artifacts—proof positive, so it seemed, that wavy lines were indeed the endpoint of a stylistic trend. Twice in the course of a few years Petrie owed the success of his carefully worked-out analysis of Naqada to the lucky insights of the son of a Welsh mining engineer.

In the years since Petrie proposed his original scheme, fate has taken another ironic turn, casting doubt on some of his most brilliant deductions. Elise Baumgartel, a long-time student of the Predynastic, has recently pointed out that

> Petrie's division of the material into two main sections still holds good, but the system of sequence dates is in need of complete revision and can be used only after checking each individual case. The reason for this is that the two main classes of pottery which were used as foundations for the system are now known to have ranges different from those originally assigned to them. The white cross-lined pottery, to which Petrie gave a very short life from S.D. 31-34, in fact continued into the later stages, as Brunton maintained. In consequence, some of the tombs which Petrie dated to S.D. 31-34 on the strength of the discovery in them of white cross-lined pottery may have to be dated considerably later.
>
> For the later period Petrie took the wavy-handled pottery as his characteristic type, and assumed for it a development, or rather deterioration, in form on which he based his dating. This assumption also proved to be mistaken and the sequence dates assigned to the graves on the strength of this argument have to be altered.
>
> (Baumgartel 1970: 464)

Despite problems as the result of sequence dating, prehistorians who followed Petrie were able to date their finds to one of two major periods, called either Naqada I and II after the original find spot, or Amratian and Gerzean, after other sites where Predynastic cemeteries were unearthed. The earlier Amratian period (ca. 4000–3500 B.C.) is characterized by a fancy white cross-lined on polished red ware, black-topped red burnished pottery, stone vases and small, rhomboidal slate palettes. Today we believe the Amratian period began around the turn of the fifth millennium B.C. and lasted approximately 500 years. It was followed by the Gerzean epoch, lasting from about 3500 to 3100 B.C.—a time that witnessed increasing foreign influence, the introduction of a new red-on-buff painted pottery featuring realistic representations of processions of boats carrying shrines as well as geometric motifs, the use of fine ripple-flaked flint knives, animal and fish effigy slate palettes, more widespread use of copper and precious metals like gold and silver, improved fancy stone vases and changes in shape and the reduction of the extent of blackening around the tops of the standard burnished red ware vessels. These periods finally were defined by Petrie himself during the First World War when events forced him to remain in England, where in 1920 he published his *Prehistoric Egypt*, the first attempted synthesis of the Predynastic information. Unfortunately, this work, the culmination of Petrie's long and personal involvement in Predynastic archaeology, reads more like a catalogue of important and impressive finds from Naqada than a balanced appraisal of all the major sites dug up to that time. As we noted earlier, the title is also somewhat misleading. Petrie had ignored the entire Palaeolithic era, or 98 percent of human history.

When we stop to realize that for a generation Sir Flinders Petrie's view of Egyptian prehistory was the only one available to most interested English-speaking peoples and that his own work as represented in *Prehistoric Egypt* drew so heavily on the original site of Naqada, that place takes on an added significance and raises a number of still unanswered questions. The fact that the standard 1896 report on the work of Naqada discussed only a minute fraction of what was found should have called for a later, more complete "final" publication which presented all the information. Such at least was the practice of George Andrew Reisner, an American, who became Director of the Nubian Archaeological Survey in 1909 and two years later chief of the Harvard Naga-ed-Der expedition. Reisner brought archaeology one step closer to true science by insisting on complete recording and publication of all information that was excavated. But the impatient Sir Flinders (once he fancied the historical problem solved by the invention of sequence dating) saw no reason to reproduce pedantically all the evidence from those thousands of tombs so carefully cleaned in 1894 and 1895. He remained a busy man almost until the day of his death in 1942; but a man overlooked not by one but two generations of successors. Through the years colleagues and friends (the two were not often synonymous) urged the aging master to return to the Naqada material, but as long as Petrie remained entrenched in London he showed no interest in the project and forbade anyone else even to touch the artifacts from the site. When at last he was succeeded in his post by a former student, Margaret Murray, in 1932, hard times had come on the university and space was needed. The extra room was to be had at the expense of Petrie's donated collection of papers, and accordingly a decision was made to throw away all notes from published excavations, only a small fraction of which, as I noted, had ever really appeared in print. This was a disastrous decision even by the great Murray, who outdid her master by living to the ripe old age of one hundred and one.

What might be called the second discovery of Naqada occurred in 1969 totally by accident, 5,000 miles from the site of the original excavations. Almost miraculously, one box of Petrie's notes and papers (the "London box") and those of several of his early collaborators escaped destruction in 1932 and lay all those years forgotten "under a telephone in University College, London." Elise Baumgartel relates her joy and amazement at such serendipity—having at the time of the find already spent the better part of her life locating and recording the scattered collections from the Naqada cemeteries. Baumgartel was an interesting successor to Petrie and a study in contrasts. Unlike the master, she had little field experience and even less desire to play the role of universal genius. Her scholarly life was spent trying to recover, reanalyze, and explain much of the unpublished Predynastic information from Petrie's and Quibell's excavations. Between 1947 and 1960 she published her own summaries of Egyptian prehistory—*The Cultures of Prehistoric Egypt*—which included much of the work done since Petrie's volume appeared in 1920.

Unfortunately, Baumgartel was guilty of the same shortsightedness as Petrie in that she not only ignored the Palaeolithic cultures of Egypt but also made short shrift of the exciting finds in the Delta and the Fayum. These areas, which were occupied by a strikingly different cultural tradition in Predynastic times, were believed by Baumgartel to be unimportant backwaters, but as we shall see later, they were to play an important role in the emergence of pharaonic culture at the end of the prehistoric period. The basic problem with Baumgartel's study was that it was blinded to the overall cultural and environmental setting of the Predynastic societies of Upper Egypt by the brilliance of Naqada funeral practices. Like many prehistorians before and since, Elise Baumgartel saw the uniqueness of the culture that arose in the Nile Valley after the coming of the Neolithic Subpluvial, but she did not appreciate how such an artistically precocious people could be tied to their neighbors in the Delta and the peoples of the desert frontiers.

What she has shown by her careful research is that Sir Flinders's work at Naqada deserves all the acclaim it has received over the years, and that the 1896 report did not do proper justice to Petrie's labors. In rereading the actual texts of Petrie's notebooks and examining his ground plans for each tomb, the Naqada culture assumes a vividness and complexity not hinted at in *Naqada and Ballas*. A case in point is cemetery T —the group of 57 wealthy graves whose clearance was so meticulously

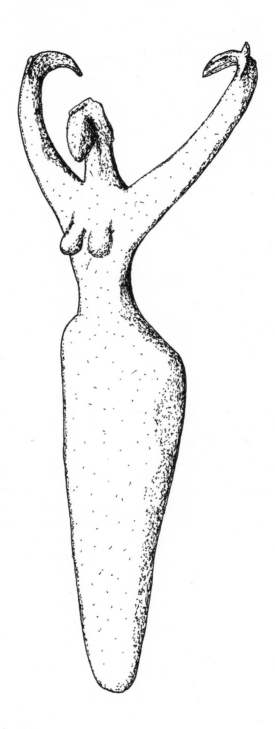

36 An Amratian figurine

supervised by Petrie himself. Nowhere in the published reports is there a hint that this cemetery contained tombs as large and impressive as some that are drawn in Petrie's notebooks, tombs whose size and sophistication foreshadow the magnificent graves of the earliest pharaohs. Perhaps Sir Flinders can be excused for failing to grasp the connection between the emerging Naqadan ruling class that segregated itself in death from its poorer neighbors in tombs of unusual size and wealth, and the earliest pharaohs who carried social distance and "conspicuous consumption" of wealth to monumental extremes. Beginning in 1900, even before he had published his final report on sequence dating, Petrie managed to obtain permission to redig the recently looted royal tombs of the first dynasties at Abydos.

In mapping and redigging Abydos, it is somewhat puzzling that Petrie never saw the relationship between the wealthy tombs at Naqada and the tombs of the first pharaohs (see also Chapter 18). Both were unusually large and built for elite personages. Both contained relatively massive quantities of grave offerings. Both were physically separated from graves of commoners, and contained evidence of human sacrifice. Perhaps, in the end, it was the very massiveness, the scale, of the buildings at Abydos with their thousands of finely wrought stone vases and hundreds of sacrificed retainers that dissuaded Petrie from making the comparison to Naqada. At the turn of the century, the idea that the social and economic function of a class of remains was as important as the date and size of those remains had not yet made an impact on archaeology. There was still a world of difference rather than an underlying similarity to be seen in a comparison of cemetery T at Naqada and the royal tombs at Abydos.

There may be a final reason why Petrie never returned to his Naqada notebooks and attempted to rework the evidence contained in their pages. He always claimed he was too busy for such work; but in the back of his mind must have been the knowledge that time was passing him by and an ultimate fear that his genuinely masterful work might be subjected to undue criticism if he dared to republish a more complete report a generation after the site had been dug.

8

QUIBELL AND GREEN AT HIERAKONPOLIS: THE PATH OF EMPIRE

IN ADDITION to Petrie's excavation notebooks, the "London box" has yielded a wealth of original field notes taken by many of his early associates. It is an unwritten rule among experienced archaeologists that a researcher's competence (or lack thereof) may be measured by his excavation notes and records. On this score, Petrie deserves every bit of credit traditionally accorded him for his work at Naqada. Puzzlingly, this praise cannot be extended to many of his students and co-workers. When we recall his temperamental and critical nature, it is especially hard to understand how Petrie could have overlooked the mistakes and carelessness of his young associate Quibell, who was working but two miles away at Ballas and who shared authorship of the Naqada report in 1896. James Edward Quibell, who had just taken his university degree in chemistry and classics, excavated over 900 graves at Ballas and part of a prehistoric settlement (the so-called north town), but he reported even fewer graves than Petrie and these were poorly illustrated. He apparently did not even bother to make a plan of the town. The recent discovery of his field journal from Ballas has confirmed a long-held suspicion that his recording left much to be desired. Whereas Sir Flinders drew scaled-down plans of each grave he excavated and carefully rendered on paper the location of even the most inconsequential object, Quibell was often satisfied with the mere outline of the tomb pit and seldom bothered to draw accurately the skeletal remains or grave offerings within. In fact, even his published plans in *Naqada and Ballas* are far inferior to Petrie's "little masterpieces of archaeological illustration."

Despite his failure to measure up to the master, Quibell must still be reckoned one of the better excavators of his day, especially when compared with E. Amélineau or de Morgan. Along with another of Petrie's students, F. W. Green, he also occupies an important place among the discoverers of Egypt's prehistoric past for his pioneering work at the site of Hierakonpolis. To the ancient Greeks Hierakonpolis meant city of the hawk and to the ancient Egyptians it was Nekhen, city of falcon-headed Horus. Hierakonpolis held an especial attraction for the educated Englishmen of Quibell's day. In the last decade of the nineteenth century Britain basked in the full light of a far-flung empire on which the sun never set. The elegant Prime Minister of Cape Colony, Sir Cecil Rhodes, embodied the popular essence of civilized man and epitomized the Victorian notion of social progress. The fledgling empires of England, France, and Germany, ensconced in what historian Barbara Tuchman has called their Proud Tower, looked upon their own cultures as culminations of long sequences of progressive social evolution that stretched back to the Stone Age. Society, according to the popular social Darwinian doctrines of the day, did not become civilized until the evolution of the earliest literate states and empires. With Egypt's hoary antiquity, splendid temples, imposing pyramids, mysterious hieroglyphic writing, and precocious and efficient government, it seemed to many historians to stand at the very wellspring of Western civilization. We all tend to see the past as a reflection of our own incident glory, and late Victorian England was no exception. In a way, therefore, for an Englishman to find the birthplace of what many believed to be the world's oldest civilization, might justify an unpopular British colonial rule in Egypt before the eyes of a scientific world, whose coffers were kept filled by rewards from grateful governments and well-to-do private citizens who liked to cast themselves as the new guardians of man's civilized heritage.

In the broader sense, therefore, Hierakonpolis offered much more than tangible archaeological and historical rewards. It promised its excavator the chance to link the known to the unknown and thereby make the world of the ancients intelligible to the citizens of an industrialized, imperialized world. But if Quibell was drawn to Hierakonpolis by the lure of finding the birthplace of Egyptian civilization, he was impelled by a more immediate concern as well—the bazaars and antiquity markets of Egypt were beginning to overflow with illicit loot from Predynastic tombs, justifying Petrie's worst fears. Thus, motivated by a combination of scientific curiosity, nationalistic pride, and legal concerns over looting and smuggling, Quibell sailed upriver to Hierakonpolis one cool, clear December day in 1897. What greeted his eyes as he disembarked must have been a quite different sight from what our own expedition beheld 72 years later. In Quibell's day, the first Aswan Dam was just being built and the tremendous population explosion that would ultimately frustrate dreams of agricultural and economic prosperity was unsuspected. A thin strip of cultivation barely a kilometer wide fringed the western bank of the river, much as it does today. But in 1897 there were no deep canals that ran with water year-round and the water table was somewhat lower and the land not yet plagued with major problems of salinization. The mud-brick walls of the early Dynastic town, known by its Arab name as the Kom el Ahmar, or red mound, stood largely intact on the edge of the Western Desert—as yet untouched by the moisture that has reduced it to shapeless heaps in a mere three-quarters of a century. Beyond the Kom el Ahmar, in the low desert, the land was littered for a million square yards with the debris of the largest Predynastic settlement ever discovered in Upper Egypt. Within this so-called Gerzean town lay several contemporary cemeteries and a mysterious stone mound that still defies explanation. A great wadi cut the northwestern end of the settlement and along its western bank, on top of an earlier Predynastic cemetery, towered the massive 30-foot-high mud-brick walls of the so-called fort of Khasekhemui, last ruler of the Second Dynasty—a monument still reckoned one of the oldest standing ruins in Egypt. Beyond the fort, the wadi led into eroded red sandstone hills that border the Western Desert. These jagged *inselbergs*, it will be recalled, were often covered by Palaeolithic tools. Their upper slopes were pocked with tombs dating to the New Kingdom (ca. 1550–1080 B.C.) when Egypt ruled an empire that stretched from the Fourth Cataract in Nubia to the Euphrates River in northern Syria. Ironically, although Quibell and Green, following a good nineteenth-century archaeological custom, actually lived in one of these tombs (in 1978 Professor Klaus Baer and Mrs. Jan Fairservis found nails driven into a wall and a powder box left by the pair) they either failed to notice or neglected to record the Predynastic and Palaeolithic sites that dot the area: sites that remained undetected by scientists for the next sixty years.

Despite the fact that much was overlooked, the finds made by Quibell and his colleague F. W. Green have shaped our ideas about the origins of Egyptian civilization ever since. Like many nineteenth- and early twentieth-century excavators, Quibell believed that the most profitable digging would be within the walls of the ancient temple where rich offerings were most likely to have been buried. Often when the Egyptians chose to build or restore a temple, they dug a pit near the foundations and placed inside offerings to commemorate the occasion. Since finding such objects would please the many financial backers of the Egypt Research Account—private individuals and institutions which believed that history and prehistory were best exemplified by impressive objets d'art— Quibell's choice can be understood. After all, what museum director wants to settle for hundreds of thousands of prosaic potsherds when he can have a golden statue instead? The temple at Hierakonpolis was not difficult to find. Despite the fact that the town had lain almost completely deserted for over 4,000 years, pharaohs down through the ages had continued to heap gifts and honors upon the home of the legendary founder of their line and his patron god, Horus of Nekhen.

It is hard for us today to appreciate the concern felt by ancient Egyptian rulers for Hierakonpolis. But the pharaoh himself bore an official name—one of five—derived from the Horus of Nekhen and was careful to bestow on selected officials the honored title of Protector of the Precinct of Horus of Nekhen. In lavishing presents on the shrine, pharaoh was really lavishing public praise on himself as a proper and just king who duly honored the institution of the monarchy. For a pharaoh not to pay homage to Horus of Nekhen would have been like a president or prime minister refusing to take his nation's oath of allegiance. In addition to being intimately bound up in the symbolism of the Egyptian kingship, the sacred sanctuary of Upper Egypt itself, the *Perwer*, was linked to the site of Nekhen via its neighbor El Kab, so that the place represented to ancient Egyptians all of Upper Egypt and the unique cultural traditions that had been developing there since the coming of the village farming way of life around 5000 B.C. Because of the symbolic importance of Hierakonpolis, some scholars believe that it was not important in any actual historical sense—that Menes, or whoever his real historical equivalent was, did not actually issue forth from its gates to subdue and unify the Two Lands. They feel that Hierakonpolis was somewhat arbitrarily selected by the Egyptians to symbolize the narrow, desert-bound valley of Upper Egypt in the same way that the town of Buto in the Delta officially represented the open marshlands and special cultural identity of Lower Egypt.

We will return to these arguments later in trying to understand just how the various traditions of Predynastic Egypt fused at the beginning of the Dynastic era. Many of the problems we have in trying to relate the half-legendary accounts of the ancient Egyptians to the archaeological material from Hierakonpolis stem directly from Quibell's excavation procedures. In the 1897–98 season, as soon as he had settled in at the site, Quibell directed his workmen to start digging within the massive enclosure walls of the temple precinct. These walls, which are still visible, albeit in a highly eroded state, were perhaps raised by the great warrior pharaoh Thutmose III in the middle of the fifteenth century B.C. during a major renovation of the entire temple. As the adzelike *fuss* of Quibell's workmen bit deeper and deeper into the earth, they revealed a whole succession of building levels from earlier Middle and Old Kingdom shrines. With the kind of blind luck that causes modern archaeologists to go green with envy, Quibell stumbled on two extremely rich finds. First, in what we now believe were the storerooms of an Old Kingdom temple, he found a golden hawk—a representation of Horus of Nekhen—and a near life-size copper statue group depicting King Pepi I and his young son Merenre, rulers of the Sixth Dynasty. This piece is the earliest known example of large-scale metal sculpture in the world. In adjoining storerooms were found a number of fancy stone vases of alabaster and limestone which had probably once been used in rituals performed in honor of Horus of Nekhen on behalf of his loyal servants, the god kings Pepi and Merenre.

The second astounding discovery was made under highly confusing circumstances between two walls of an Old or Middle Kingdom temple and has been labeled the Main Deposit. It is fairly clearly a collection of "antiques"—artifacts either broken, out of style, or of no immediate use but of sufficient value to the ancient Egyptians that they were deemed worthy of burial in sacred ground. Fortunately for us, the relics so thoughtfully preserved have turned out to be of unique importance to the early history of Egypt: commemorative palettes and maceheads of the Protodynastic kings of Nehken, Narmer and Scorpion, documenting their attempts to subdue the Delta and their concern for promoting agricultural production through irrigation; some of the earliest examples of hieroglyphic writing in its crudest stage; and carved scenes in stone and ivory of fantastic animals, recalling the art styles of contemporary Sumeria and Elam—countries that lay far to the east. Such objects raise a number of critical questions. Was this spot actually the first capital of Menes and did his historical counterparts, Narmer and Scorpion and Aha, use Hierakonpolis as a base of operations in their conquest of the Delta? And finally, what does the presence of Middle Eastern artistic motifs indicate about the origins of Egyptian civilization? Did Easterners really invade the Nile Valley as some Egyptologists have contended? Were the early urban societies of the Iranian Plateau and Mesopotamia, which flourished in the fourth millennium B.C. at sites like Susa and Uruk, linked to the Late Gerzean kingdoms of the Nile between about 3300 and 3100 B.C., and if so, how?

Sadly, we do not even know for sure where the most graphic piece of evidence, the Narmer Palette, actually came from. It was evidently found near the Main Deposit but not actually with the other material. From Green's field notes (Quibell kept none!) it seems to have been found a meter or two away, and Green noted in the 1902 publication that it was found in a place directly associated with an apparently Protodynastic level, which would date it a generation or two before the unification of the Two Lands in 3100 B.C. But two years earlier in the first report published on Hierakonpolis by Quibell, it was labeled as coming from the Main Deposit proper, a feature that may be as late as the Middle Kingdom (ca. 2130–1785 B.C.). One can clearly appreciate the frustration of modern archaeologists over such sloppiness! For if we knew for certain that the magnificent palette came from a securely dated stratum clearly associated with the Protodynastic temple (ca. 3100 B.C.) then it would be fairly certain that Narmer himself had deposited this monument in the temple of his capital to commemorate his conquests in the north. If, on the other hand, the palette came from the Main Deposit, we may never know what journeys it experienced on its way to its last resting place. We do know that the Main Deposit itself was buried in Old or possibly even Middle Kingdom times, between 500 and 1,000 years after the death of Narmer.

And what does it show that makes knowledge of its origin so vital? The Narmer Palette is a carefully carved, roughly triangular shaped slab

37 The Narmer Palette

of dark green slate, on one side of which the king, wearing the high-peaked crown of Upper Egypt, ritually bashes in the head of a northern enemy beneath the protective gaze of the hawk Horus, while on the reverse face the king, now bedecked in the red crown of Lower Egypt, impassively reviews his beheaded opponents on the battlefield, accompanied by his allies and members of the court while a rampant bull (another traditional symbol of the pharaoh) smashes in the walls of an enemy town. Although the most important document linking the silent prehistoric past to the historic world of pharaonic Egypt, the Narmer Palette is only one of many such commemorative objects found by Quibell and Green at Hierakonpolis—objects that we shall see again when we try to piece together the events that led to the unification of Egypt.

Quibell did not return to Hierakonpolis for the second and final season's work but accepted a post as inspector of monuments and took over the compilation of a catalogue for the Giza Museum. The remainder of the work was supervised by Green. Happily, F. W. Green believed in taking copious notes and now that these have been published, we are able to compare them to recent work carried out by the American Museum of Natural History Expedition in 1969 and vindicate many of

Green's original observations. Beneath the level of the Old Kingdom temple, Green discovered a sloping, semicircular stone wall or revetment constructed of small sandstone blocks. The revetment encased a mound of clean white sand and stood about two and one-half meters high. He believed this structure had served as a base for a Protodynastic reed temple similar to the types represented on the walls of later Egyptian temples. Beneath the revetment Green found New Race pottery (remember, Petrie was still analyzing his Naqada material) showing that the town had been occupied since Predynastic times and that this one spot had remained sacred for thousands of unbroken years. Around the revetment, badly disturbed and cut into by later building operations, Green found a paved area and bricked approaches which he thought led to the original temple. Despite the fact that he was a vastly superior field archaeologist to Quibell, Green's observations have been largely ignored and mercilessly picked apart in the years following the publication of his findings. Many people simply refused to accept a Protodynastic date for something as complex as the mound and revetment structure. As for the presence of Predynastic settlement on the floodplain, that idea was rejected on the false theoretical assumption that annual flooding and the wild, junglelike nature of alluvium would have rendered it practically uninhabitable and because of the nearness of the huge Gerzean town.

However, Green was right. Between March 2 and 12, 1969, I had an opportunity to observe on my own the complex stratigraphy of the town not 50 meters from the spot where Green discovered the revetment. Working within a 10-meter square, we encountered a large area of eroded mud-brick paving (possibly an ancient platform) just underneath a later Old Kingdom level. The paving was joined at one point by a narrow but carefully laid walkway, and sitting near the juncture of paving and walkway was a line of sandstone boulders of the type used in the revetment. One of these bore a shallow depression—the remnants of a door socket—suggesting that access to the platform had been controlled by a gate or door. Not only did this architectural complex relate clearly to what Green had found in 1898–99, but by digging in controlled units and collecting all the sherds this time we could be sure that the remains dated to the Protodynastic era.

As the workmen scraped away the soil in arbitrary 10-centimeter levels just to the west of the paving, my crew chief, Abdul Kader, and our stately *Reis* or foreman, Sheik Hussein, excitedly called my attention to a "wall" emerging from a light yellow layer of earth. Both Abdul Kader and Sheik Hussein were professional archaeological foremen, or Guftis—so called because most come from the central Egyptian town of Guft. They are a tight-knit and proud group of craftsmen who trace their origin back to fathers, grandfathers, and even great-grandfathers trained by Sir Flinders Petrie. One of our Guftis claimed, probably incorrectly, to have worked for Petrie as a basket boy. In Egypt one learns quickly to value a Gufti's judgment and to pay attention to his observations. The only danger in this is when an archaeologist, untrained himself in the manual skills of excavation, is unable properly to evaluate the strengths and weaknesses of his workmen. I had seen enough demonstrations of Gufti skill that I responded immediately to Hussein and Abdul Kader's summons. When I jumped into the square and quickly cleaned the surface with my trowel, I noted with surprise that the dark line both men identified as a wall was not a wall at all, but a wall trench. Having worked several seasons in the southeastern United States as a laborer and foreman myself, I realized the unique importance of what we had found. Two parallel trenches, about 2 meters long and 40 centimeters across, enclosing an area about 1½ meters wide by 2 meters long, were intersected at their ends by large, circular holes that had once accommodated posts. Another such posthole was placed in the center of the structure. We carefully collected all pottery and stone objects from the immediate area and mapped two or three hearths that had lain just outside the post building. The evidence was conclusive. The structure dated to the Protodynastic period and was either contemporary with or slightly earlier than the mud-brick pavement. Could this be the decayed remnants of the post and reed shrine—similar to the *Perwer* of neighboring El Kab—so often depicted by later Egyptian artists? Had we found archaeological proof linking the holy shrine of Upper Egypt to the specific site of Nekhen? When we recall Green's discoveries, the closeness of the stone revetment and the ancient Egyptian legends, it is tempting to see our humble building as a real example of a traditional shrine of Upper Egypt.

But 72 years earlier, Green could not be sure about the dating of his revetment and could place even less confidence in the amazing discoveries made by Quibell the year before. Once he had satisfied himself of the importance of the early Dynastic town and the apparent antiquity of the temple area, he moved his workmen about a thousand feet to the west, out on to the desert where the pottery and stone debris of the prehistoric town are still so thick that one cannot take a step without crushing a piece of Egypt's past underfoot. Here, following Petrie's example at Naqada, Green searched for the telltale depressions that would reveal the location of an ancient cemetery. Amid the ruins of the Predynastic town, he found over 200 burials, mostly from the Gerzean period, with their typical painted pottery, beautifully wrought flint knives, animal-shaped pigment palettes, and crouched skeletons. And once more, Hierakonpolis yielded the totally unexpected. In one corner of the cemetery a group of five large tombs was found. Today most people remember only the most spectacular—the Painted Tomb—but the cluster of rich graves recalls Naqada and several other Predynastic sites where wealthy and powerful citizens held themselves apart from their neighbors and tried to take a portion of their wealth with them into the afterworld. All to no avail. When Green gazed into the rectangular Painted Tomb, he discovered that tomb robbers had preceded him by several thousand years. Fortunately, enough remained to date the structure to the close of the Predynastic epoch—to the Late Gerzean.

Even more exciting than the unusual size and solid mud-brick construction of tomb 100 were the lively scenes painted on its walls. It is clear that the prehistoric artist who decorated the tomb of some well-to-do patron derived his inspiration from the painted pottery of the day. First, the walls of the grave were coated with white or light buff plaster, recalling the buff exterior of Gerzean pottery. Over this base the artist applied a wide variety of designs ranging from simple lines in red and blue-black pigment to complex scenes of men wearing strange costumes —some fighting and one holding back two animals in a motif typical of Iranian and Mesopotamian art at this time. Also portrayed are high-prowed ships with cabins and ensigns. Here is the earliest known attempt at mural painting in Egypt and an immediate forerunner of one of the most important and long-lived traditions in classical ancient Egyptian art. From this point on, pottery decoration declined rapidly as the professional craftsmen of the day turned their attention to decorating the palaces and tombs of an emerging aristocracy. Artistic energies that had once been devoted to producing fancy containers that would capture local trade markets in the Early Gerzean period, now came to be dominated by the interests of the same local magnates who would soon unite Egypt by force of arms.

But for all their pretensions of wealth and power, the occupants of tomb 100 had been relieved of their worldly riches by humble grave robbers, so that all that remained in the end was a scatter of pulverized bone and bone dust. Since most of the 200 graves that Green dug were not published, we will never know the vital biological and demographical information so necessary in reconstructing the daily lives of the Predynastic citizens of Nekhen. We do not know their life expectancy, their actual diet, the diseases that plagued their lives, or the effect of their occupations on their health and physical appearance. The lack of appreciation of the overall biological and cultural value of the graves in Green's time is understandable. Even sadder, however, is the record of two later expeditions to Hierakonpolis, one directed by John Garstang in 1905 and the other under the supervision of Ambrose Lansing of the Metropolitan Museum of Art in 1934. Despite the fact that these ventures recovered an additional 400 Predynastic skeletons, many of which were in fine shape, not one scrap of useful biological and demographic information was published from their work. In fact, it is suspected that many of the skeletons were so poorly regarded by their excavators that they were simply ditched at the site, while the pretty pots were taken and distributed as booty to the museums of the world.

Locating the several cemeteries unearthed at Hierakonpolis over the years itself poses a problem. According to most experts, one of the hallmarks of Upper Egyptian Predynastic culture is the interment of most members of the community in formal cemeteries located away from the actual settlement, in contrast to the Lower Egyptian custom of intra-settlement burial. But at Hierakonpolis three different cemeteries with a total of over 600 dead were scattered within the vast area traditionally known as the Gerzean town. Does this mean that the Predynastic inhabitants of Hierakonpolis buried their dead within the precincts of the town? Probably not. The very size of the Predynastic town as well as the uneven distribution of household debris hints that we are dealing with the remnants of scattered hamlets or outliers clustered about the Great Wadi and Dune Wadi on the elevated ground of the low desert. Green believed this and says in his notes that grinding stones, darkened earth, and general household midden, or garbage, were not uniform over the entire area but concentrated at several points. Succeeding prehistorians who have explored the area, including Karl Butzer in 1958 and Walter Fairservis and myself in 1969, have located patches where, almost certainly, old mud-brick walls have been worn down by wind and sand, leaving dense concentrations of debris. In one case, I recall seeing square or rectangular concentrations of such debris interrupted by clean lines of eroded mud or mud-brick, clearly indicating Predynastic house sites. The clustering of houses within the town area promises to tell us something useful about the types and arrangements of social groups in Predynastic times. Perhaps these hamlets were concentrations of quasi-independent kin-based groups or factions of kinsmen and nonrelated hangers-on who gathered about the dwelling of a rich and powerful man —a pattern known from contemporary Upper Egyptian villages. Questions like these, questions that go to the very heart of ancient society, can only be answered by carefully planned and organized archaeological excavations.

Even with the most sophisticated techniques in the world, however, we must bear in mind that towns, villages, and hamlets are extremely complex groupings of human activities. Such activities might be rather simple and straightforward on one level—let us say the preparation of food in an oven—but on another level they might involve sets of highly formalized symbolic social relationships that are difficult if not impossible to reconstruct from the archaeological remains. An example of such a relationship, to stick with our example of food preparation, would be the redistribution of food prepared in an oven to the members of a social group in accordance with their age, sex, and rank or, an even more abstract level, the preparation of "food for the dead"—offerings to be placed at the grave of the deceased. In several cases, archaeologists have actually found fires and food remains on the edges of Predynastic graves so that interpretation of social custom is something we must always be ready for. To infer social relationships—the very glue that held ancient societies together—requires not only careful excavation and recording but the deliberate testing of ideas or hypotheses about social life. In Egypt we are fortunate in being able to use written texts and scenes and models of daily life from Dynastic times to lend direction to our inquiries into Predynastic social, economic, and religious structure. Other hunches come from observation of contemporary or historical village life and its relation to the environmental setting. An example of the usefulness of this approach that illustrates what almost certainly happened at Hierakonpolis is a phenomenon known as "settlement drift." Today, in towns along the Nile you can often see how, over the years, the better and newer quarters have moved upwind while the downwind extremities of the settlement have gradually fallen into disuse and abandonment. Besides being a testimony to the role of garbage in human housing choices, the drifting pattern of residence can create the impression that a given settlement sheltered more inhabitants than it actually did. How much of the settlement (or settlements) was occupied at any one time is a question complicated further by the length of time Predynastic peoples have been at Hierakonpolis and by discoveries made since Green's day. Beginning in the late 1920's, archaeological explorations of the area have added a whole new dimension to the picture by showing that Predynastic settlement in the region was much older than was formerly believed and dates from the inception of agriculture in Upper Egypt. We now know that the earliest agricultural peoples at Hierakonpolis belonged to a culture totally unknown until thirty years after the discovery of Naqada.

9

BRUNTON AT BADARI
AND CATON-THOMPSON
AT HEMAMIEH:
VINDICATING PETRIE

G UY BRUNTON had first come to Egypt in 1914, when Europe
was on the brink of the Great War. He began his long apprenticeship
under Petrie in a most spectacular way. While digging a plundered
Middle Kingdom royal tomb, a glint of gold came to light. Petrie
immediately cleared the area of workmen, setting a trustworthy Gufti
and Brunton to work in utmost secrecy. Brunton spent an entire week
in the tomb, even sleeping there at night for fear the treasure might be
plundered. His pains were rewarded by an extraordinary cache of personal jewelry belonging to the Eleventh Dynasty Princess Sit Hathor
Yunet.

After the war, Brunton continued working under Sir Flinders until
1922, when he and his wife were sent off to dig their own concession
on the eastern bank of the central Nile Valley. There, between 1922
and 1925, the Bruntons and the indefatigable prehistorian Gertrude
Caton-Thompson recorded almost 650 prehistoric graves and a staggering number of settlements perched above the modern floodplain on desert
spurs. Although 308 of the graves could be assigned to known Predynastic periods, more than half contained artifacts never before recorded
in Egypt. Brunton tells us that his suspicions were originally aroused
even before he understood the unique quality of the "new" graves when
he noticed pottery of a wholly unfamiliar type weathering out of a
ditch in a modern village. Although handmade, like other Predynastic
wares, the pottery was very hard and thin walled, indicating that it had
been well fired. Three main types of fancy wares were found: polished
red, polished black, and black-topped polished red or brown pottery.
The outer surface of many pots bore a type of finish which Brunton
called "rippled" or "combed." These ripples were usually quite prominent, although in some instances they had been partly erased by burnishing of the pot's surface. Brunton examined his new finds carefully and
decided that the rippling effect was caused by trailing a serrated length

of bone or a wooden comb over the surface of the pot before firing. So different and so striking was this new pottery that he suspected almost at once that it must predate anything then known from the Predynastic era. His hunch proved correct when he and his wife located and carefully cleaned over 300 burials, each of which contained sherds or unbroken bowls and plates of rippled ware. In some instances, finer vessels were decorated with incised designs of crossed palm fronds or six-rayed stars. That the combed ware was somehow tied to the Predynastic tradition of pottery making was immediately obvious because of its frequent association with characteristic polished red and black-topped red ware jars of Amratian vintage. Once more, Petrie's insight in leaving 30 open slots in his system of sequence dates for undiscovered, earlier cultures paid off. Brunton immediately assigned his Badarian pottery sequence dates ranging in the 20's, and although several prehistorians doubted the extreme age of his material, he was completely vindicated by the unprecedented excavations conducted by his colleague and houseguest, Gertrude Caton-Thompson.

In 1922 women were still a novelty in archaeology. True, many archaeologists took their wives into the field, and in the case of Lady Petrie and Mrs. Brunton, women even attained a certain amount of fame and professional recognition. For those women who chose to operate on their own, however, the more gracious pursuits of art historian or museum conservator were the rule. But Gertrude Caton-Thompson was not to be confined to the dusty recesses of a museum laboratory nor would she be bound by the restrictions of a polite society that demanded lady-like inactivity. Her interests lay in the active field disciplines of excavation, geology, and ecology, and between the two world wars she demonstrated her versatility and energy not only in the excavation of Hemamieh but, as we said earlier, in extensive archaeological surveys at Kharga Oasis and the Fayum where she became perhaps the first Egyptian archaeologist to deal with the entire spectrum of the prehistoric past from Palaeolithic through Predynastic. In combining careful excavation techniques with extensive regional surveys and a concern for the natural setting of ancient societies she was a generation ahead of her time and paved the way for later environmental archaeologists.

Caton-Thompson dug Hemamieh with a care accorded no site in Egypt before, and few since. She marked off the low debris mound in strips 35 feet long and 10 feet wide and subdivided these units into 5-foot intervals marked along the length. Thus, each strip was divided into seven 5 by 10 foot squares. These, in turn, were slowly and carefully excavated in arbitrary 6-inch levels and any variations in soil cross-sections recorded after each level was completed in each square. With the exception of the "rough ware" sherds, the exact position of each artifact was recorded to at least the nearest foot and its exact depth

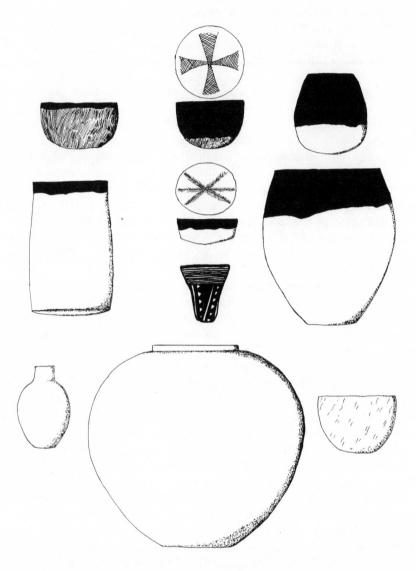

38   Assorted Badarian pottery, ca. 5500–4000 B.C.

registered. Today, modern archaeologists lament the lack of attention paid to the rough ware sherds (they comprised 99 percent of the pottery), but in Caton-Thompson's time, digging the site unassisted by other professional help and excavating Hemamieh were triumphs of scientific archaeology. Caton-Thompson was so far ahead of her time that she sieved or screened the soil from hearths and rooms, searching for minute seeds and small artifacts otherwise missed in the normal excavation procedure. Although time and lack of skilled help did not permit her to screen the whole site, the very fact that she even conceived of this method, still considered daring in most of the Middle East, sets her apart from her contemporaries and the majority of her successors.

39   Assorted Badarian artifacts, ca. 5500–4000 B.C. From left to right and top to bottom: ivory spoon, wooden throwing stick, ceramic figurine, slate palette, ivory comb, bone needle, seashell hook, ivory wand (?), bone animal effigy pendants (2), banded alabaster pendant

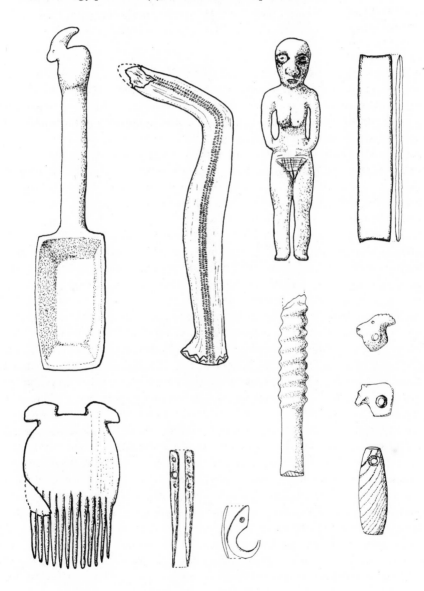

40   Badarian stone projectile points. From left to right: hollow base point from
El Badari, hollow base point from Hemamieh, triangular point from
Hemamieh, willow-leaf-shaped flake point from Hemamieh

At Hemamieh, between 5½ and 6 feet of debris had accumulated between about 5000 and 3500 B.C. As Caton-Thompson analyzed her
material so carefully collected level by level, she slowly unraveled the
story of those undocumented years. The first occupants had camped for
only a short time on the edge of the desert, leaving no architectural
remains but merely a scatter of broken pottery and flint tools. These
clearly belonged to what Brunton called the Badarian culture: rippled
pottery was common and there was a large number of rather crudely
made flint tools, the most common of which was a steep-ended scraper
made from a heavy nodule or core of flint. The crudeness of the stone
tools contrasted strongly with the finely made flint sickle blades and
bifaces that Brunton found buried in the tombs of adult Badarian men.
However, the beautiful hollow-based arrowheads found all over Egypt
at this time were present in both settlements and tombs. Curiously
enough, the Badarian residents of Hemamieh preferred to use nodules
of weathered chert and flint for their stone tools, despite the fact that a
much better grade of raw material was available in nearby Eocene cliffs.
Since later Predynastic peoples knew about and used this better grade
of stone, Caton-Thompson believed that the Badarian farmers must
have been comparative newcomers to the Nile Valley, since they seemed
unfamiliar with the area's resources. Although her Sherlock Holmes-like
reasoning is rather hard to evaluate in purely archaeological terms, the
environmental evidence does support the idea that the Badarians, or at
least many aspects of their way of life, appeared rather suddenly in the
Nile Valley. The fact that Neolithic cultures were established in the
Western Desert at places like Nabta by 6000 B.C. (see Chapter 16) and
that there were several fluctuations in the rains of the Neolithic Subpluvial between about 7000 and 2500 B.C. might explain both the origins
and the sudden arrival of the Badarians. The discovery by the Bruntons
of large numbers of fossil tree roots near Hemamieh, one of which had
been cut by a Badarian grave while the tree was still alive, and the
finds of extensive Predynastic sites along the Great Wadi at Hierakon-

polis leave us with the impression that climatic change was a major factor in the genesis and initial expansion of Predynastic culture in Upper Egypt.

Above and beyond its environmental significance, the most important facet of Hemamieh is that it was the first and, to date, only well-stratified Predynastic site excavated in Egypt, boasting a sequence running from Badarian on the bottom, through Amratian, to Gerzean at the top (ca. 5000–3500 B.C.). The lowest stratum of Badarian materials, 6½ feet beneath the surface, was sealed by a foot of sterile breccia. Above the breccia was more Badarian material, then a mixed stratum overlaid by Amratian and Gerzean pottery. Half a century after Caton-Thompson's excavations, Hemamieh remains the only site in Egypt to produce clear stratigraphic proof for Petrie's system of sequence dating. It is perhaps appropriate that, while these words are being written, Dr. Fekri Hassan of Washington State University is planning to return to the site and thoroughly reexamine the chronological and cultural problems it raises.

Recent radiocarbon estimates performed by Dr. Hassan on a number of Upper Egyptian Predynastic sites have raised the possibility that Badarian and Amratian might overlap, at least partially, in time—a suggestion originally offered by Egyptologist Werner Kaiser, based on his stylistic analysis of the Predynastic pottery from Armant. The situation has been further complicated by the recent use of a new dating technique that suggests that Hemamieh might have been settled originally around 5600 B.C., only a few centuries after the El Kabians were hunting, fishing, and gathering along the Nile.

Almost twenty years ago, scientists at the University of Wisconsin began experimenting with a technique known as thermoluminescence dating. The scientists noted that all clay contains radioactive energy in minerals that is driven off when the clay is fired. As time goes by, the minerals (like quartz) continue to accumulate radioactivity which is, once again, trapped in the crystalline lattice of the mineral. If we reheat this baked clay to about 500°C. and measure the radioactivity released as light, we can theoretically calibrate the number of years elapsed since original firing. Ideally, any ceramic should yield a TL date, but in reality there are many technical problems that limit the use of this method. We have now reached a point where the technique is applicable under special circumstances in which contaminating factors can be controlled or excluded. Fortunately, some of the sherds from Hemamieh, long in storage at Oxford, meet these criteria and have recently provided some excellent and rather startling TL dates that push back the Badarian in one instance to the middle sixth millennium B.C.—substantially earlier than most Predynastic archaeologists believed. The dates in question range from 5580 ± 420 B.C. on a rough ware sherd from Caton-Thompson's 6 foot 6 inch level below the breccia, to 4450 ± 365 B.C. on a rippled ware sherd in the 5 foot to 5 foot 6 inch level to 4360 ± 355

B.C. on another rippled ware sherd from the 3 foot 6 inch to 4 foot level. Undoubtedly these estimates will be subjected to the usual scientific criticism and it may be that some or all of them will be rejected. It is also true that we do not really know the exact relationship between carbon-14 and thermoluminescent years. In their support, however, the dates are internally consistent, ranging from oldest at the bottom to youngest higher up. They suggest that the Badarian epoch was long-lived, and that it may indeed have overlapped late Epipalaeolithic cultures, making the sixth millennium before Christ possibly one of the most interesting and certainly one of the least understood periods in the last 10,000 years of Egyptian prehistory, and the one most crucial to the formative phase of Predynastic development.

Taking at their face value the new TL dates from Hemamieh and comparing them to two known carbon-14 dates on Badarian material (one of 3160 ± 160 B.C. corrected to 3920 ± 190 B.C. from El Badari and one of 4875 ± 108 B.P. corrected to 3892 ± 108 B.C. from Locality 11 at Hierakonpolis), the Badarian epoch can be dated between about 5500 and 3800 B.C.—a much longer and older span than traditionally believed. Before the advent of carbon-14 and TL dating, Guy Brunton attempted to make a similar point by proposing the existence of an early predecessor to Badarian culture, called Tasian:

> He based his identification of this culture very largely on a particular type of pottery consisting of deep bowls with a small flattish base and angular sides narrowing towards the mouth. These vessels, divided by Brunton into two classes according to their colour—brown, or grey-black—seem to be cooking pots. All the other objects tentatively assigned to the Tasian culture (limestone axes, palettes of hard stones, and black-incised beakers) could not be proved to be specifically Tasian by the original excavations at El-Mustagidda or the subsequent work at El-Matmar. (Baumgartel 1970: 468)

Considering the lack of stratigraphic evidence, the clear "mixing" of Badarian and Tasian graves in the same cemeteries and the reliance on only one main indicator—pottery—to define the new period, Elise Baumgartel concluded some years ago, "It is too early to speak of a 'Tasian civilization' as distinct from the Badarian." Based on the rather extensive, if shallow, remains of Badarian villages Brunton found on the spurs around El Badari and the new TL and corrected carbon-14 dates, the time has come to reevaluate the Badarian and to search for important chronological divisions within the epoch that will reflect the long time depth that Brunton thought exemplified by his Tasian culture. Such differences can only be documented satisfactorily at stratified sites like Hemamieh and by employing careful and up-to-date methods comparable to those employed by Caton-Thompson fifty years ago.

A final contribution of Hemamieh, a number of small, circular dwellings of Amratian date uncovered in the middle levels of the site, will be discussed in the next chapter in considering the patterns of settlement and architecture characteristic of Predynastic Upper Egypt.

Our overall impression of the Badarian culture from both Hemamieh and a number of Brunton's cemeteries in middle Upper Egypt is of a developed farming and herding society—the earliest yet known in the Upper Egyptian Nile Valley—which foreshadows in technology, economy, and custom later Predynastic cultures and early pharaonic civilization. The Badarian contrasts strongly with the terminal Palaeolithic or Epipalaeolithic cultures of Upper Egypt that flourished between about 10,000 and 5500 B.C., but at this time we are unable to determine whether or not it was completely foreign to the valley or whether it represents an adaptation of new ideas and technologies by an indigenous folk.

From the beginning, the Badarian, like other Predynastic cultures, exhibited a tendency toward ornamentation and display that distinguished it from contemporaneous groups in the Western Desert and the Delta to the north. The pottery was well made and frequently decorated. Oval slate palettes often still bear traces of red ocher or malachite green on their surfaces, while pots have been found filled with prepared pigment. The beautifully made, hollow-based arrowheads are also found in Lower Egypt and perhaps indicate contact between these two cultural areas in the late sixth and fifth millennia before Christ. Countless shell and stone bead necklaces were buried with the dead, as were well-made ivory spoons, strange humanoid figurines of baked clay, animal amulets and carved throwing sticks used in the hunt. A few graves contained small copper tools or ornaments like pins which were hammered or annealed rather than being cast as in other areas of the Middle East, where copper metallurgy was already 1,000 years old.

Another hallmark of later, ancient Egyptian civilization that first appears during Badarian times is tomb robbery. This practice is linked intimately to mortuary practices that required substantial offerings be interred with the dead. It is ironic to think that Brunton found fairly clear indications that many Badarian graves had been despoiled soon after their completion. The fact that both practices persisted—rich grave offerings and tomb robbery—side by side down to the triumph of Christianity in the fourth century A.D. reminds us of the flexibility of human belief. For nearly 5,000 years, piety and pragmatism survived side by side within the context of Egyptian Predynastic and pharaonic culture, much like two heads of the same coin: the one ideological and the other economic. Another familiar theme of later, historical times that first appears during the Badarian period is the beginning of marked differences in wealth as evidenced by the quality and number of exotic prestige goods found in Badarian graves. Throughout the following chapters, and especially in Chapters 18 and 20, I will return to the role played by the developing cult of the dead in the shaping of the political, social, economic, and ideological order that emerged around 3100 B.C. under the first kings of the First Dynasty and which became typical of Egyptian civilization over the succeeding three millennia.

10
HOUSES, HAMLETS, VILLAGES, AND TOWNS: THE TEXTURE OF PREDYNASTIC EGYPTIAN SETTLEMENT

IN 1928 Guy Brunton published the final report on his finds near El Badari in a book entitled *The Badarian Civilisation*. In the same volume Gertrude Caton-Thompson wrote an extremely lucid account of her excavations at Hemamieh. Not only did their work set a new standard of excellence for Egyptian Predynastic archaeology, but it revealed for the first time glimpses of an early Predynastic settlement. Although, as we shall see shortly, larger, more impressive settlements had been tested earlier by Petrie and Quibell, these were poorly reported and still remain little understood because of the vagueness of published accounts. Such criticism cannot be leveled against Caton-Thompson, and although her settlement is obviously a relatively unimportant one in terms of what must have been the general trend in Amratian times, its careful documentation renders it invaluable to an understanding of the settlement archaeology of that era.

Scattered in apparently random fashion on the low desert spur at Hemamieh and associated with artifacts of late Amratian date, Caton-Thompson unearthed several "hut circles," varying from about 1 to 2.3 meters in diameter. Some were clearly dwellings, as indicated by the presence of a hearth, while others were extremely small and contained in one instance desiccated sheep or goat dung. While many believe that this material was being stored for fuel, its presence and the location of the settlement on the desert borderlands may also indicate a seasonal herding encampment to which a portion of the community repaired after the seasonal (summer or winter?) rains to pasture their sheep, goats, and cattle on the desert grasses. The walls of the hut circles were about 35 centimeters thick and built of a mixture of mud and local limestone chips and blocks. We believe the huts were covered by conical roofs of straw and reeds, since impressions of these materials were preserved on the dried mud exteriors of the buildings' walls. There were no doorways in any of the structures, prompting Elise Baumgartel to draw a comparison with earlier Neolithic houses found by Professor Hermann Junker

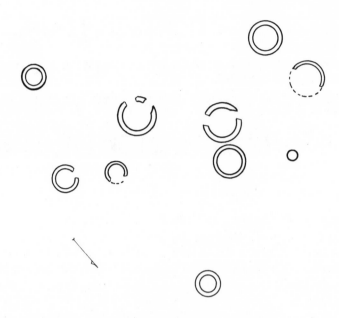

41 Schematic plan of the dwellings at the Predynastic hamlet at Hemamieh

at Merimde beni-Salame in the western Delta (see Chapter 12) where
". . . the tibia of a hippopotamus was used as a step" (Baumgartel 1970:
475). When we consider that at the time the hut circles in the tiny
hamlet of Hemamieh were occupied during the Amratian period (ca.
4000–3500 B.C.), developed farming and herding culture was only about
a thousand years old in the Nile Valley, the contrast to earlier late
Palaeolithic or Epipalaeolithic peoples (ca. 10,000–5500 B.C.), such as the
fishermen of El Kab, is all the more striking. The contrast is particularly
tangible when comparing the relatively abundant garbage of village
farming sites with the usually meager remains of hunting and gathering
localities!

The overall impression given by the Amratian settlement at Hemamieh
is of a small community, living in circular, probably dome-roofed huts
with a number of small outbuildings of similar plan but smaller dimension surrounding the dwelling proper. This barnyard type of settlement
plan, with free-standing houses separated from neighboring dwellings
is, as we shall see in Chapters 12 to 15, paralleled in Lower Egypt at
sites like Merimde and El Omari, but there is reason to suspect that it
is not truly representative of all types of Upper Egyptian Predynastic
settlements for reasons that I will review below. At present, even though

the evidence is only indirect, I suspect that the architectural or human-spatial dynamics of southern or Upper Egypt tended toward a more compacted or "agglutinated" settlement and that this pattern was an important element in the development of a distinctive social, political, and economic ethic for the region.

The open or barnyard settlement plan of Hemamieh contrasts strongly with that of modern Egyptian villages as well as their Dynastic antecedents, in which rectangular mud-brick houses with walled courtyards are arranged one against the other along winding lanes or in deliberately (i.e., government) planned communities, along regular, gridlike streets. Many Egyptian prehistorians and architectural historians have concluded from Hemamieh and from Lower Egyptian Predynastic sites like Merimde and El Omari (see Chapters 12 and 14) that Predynastic peoples did not use mud-brick and that their settlements consisted mainly of post, wattle, and daub houses of round or semicircular plan. Although this type of construction is admittedly typical of Hemamieh and sites in Lower Egypt, the question is, how characteristic was it of all Upper Egypt during the Predynastic period? Until more settlements are carefully dug, recorded, and published we will not be able to answer this question definitively.

However, we do have good reason to suspect that mud-brick construc-

42   Clay model of Gerzean house at El Amrah

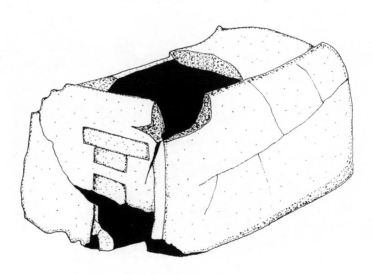

tion and substantial buildings existed in Predynastic times. At El Amrah, the site that gave its name to the Amratian epoch, Petrie found a miniature clay model of a house in a grave of Gerzean date that looks like a typical Dynastic mud-brick dwelling, while at the Predynastic town of Nubt (the south town) near Naqada he located part of a civic wall and rectangular mud-brick houses of possible Amratian date. Baumgartel (1970: 484) mentions a Gerzean rectangular house with typical Dynastic room and forecourt plan under the temple at Badari, while Petrie's dig at Abadiyeh produced a broken model of a late Amratian walled town with two men (presumably lookouts) peeping over the crenelated wall. In Protodynastic times, depictions of walled towns are found on the Narmer Palette and, finally, the hieroglyph for town in ancient Egyptian ⊕ almost certainly derives from late prehistoric times.

In Predynastic Upper Egypt, villages grew up either parallel to the river on elevated hillocks in the alluvial bottomlands or on raised portions of the low desert, or they followed the channels of the larger wadis a few miles out into the desert until the limits of cultivation had been reached. The wadi settlements provided access to the seasonal pasturage of the newly greened borders of the Sahara and the highland valleys of the Red Sea Hills and allowed easy cultivation of the soft wadi silts during the rainy season of the Neolithic Subpluvial. On the other hand, the larger valley sites afforded easy access to the rich bottomlands and

43   Model of a Predynastic town wall with sentries found in a grave at
     Abadiyeh

placed the river's food and transportational resources within reach of the townsmen. While in Lower Egypt the late prehistoric population was concentrated in large, fairly deep sites which were occupied for long stretches of time (e.g., Merimde and Maadi), in Upper Egypt sites tended to be spread out and shallow, like Hierakonpolis and El Badari, with the result that structural remains were often not preserved. The fact that most Predynastic archaeologists focused their efforts on grave-yards and that, with the notable exception of Hemamieh, settlement sites have been either badly excavated or poorly preserved, makes it extremely difficult to reconstruct the relative population density of different regions in Upper Egypt to determine their impact on the development of Egyptian civilization. Recently Dr. Karl Butzer of the University of Chicago attempted to solve this problem by using both Dynastic records and prehistoric archaeological information (including more than 15,000 recorded graves and 50 settlements) and reached the rather surprising conclusion that some of the regions of southern Upper Egypt previously thought by Egyptologists like Professor John Wilson to be among the poorest in agricultural potential were, in reality, the richest and supported the largest populations. Later on we will learn the implication of Dr. Butzer's findings in discussing the rise of Menes and the political unification of Egypt at the end of the Predynastic era. For the time being, we will return to some of the pioneering work done at two very different types of Predynastic settlements—Hierakonpolis and Abydos.

Given the high standards of his work at El Badari and his close personal association with Caton-Thompson, it is a shame that Guy Brunton was unable to undertake a large-scale investigation of the Predynastic town site at Hierakonpolis. Instead, he conducted only a casual reconnaissance in 1928, after finishing his work at Badari. Certainly, much existed there in his day that has since disappeared or decayed. From his observations it seems clear that the town was really a hodgepodge of smaller settlements and special features, and not at all like Hemamieh. He noted that the ground was "seamed with little trenches," some of which were 100 feet long, and thought that they might have been dug to accommodate fences or boundary walls. In 1969, inexplicably, no trace of them remained, but

perpahs the most striking feature of the place was a mound about half-way across from north-east to south-west, but nearer the north-west than the south-east end (of the site). The mound is covered with a great accumulation of stones, partly natural pebbles, but chiefly broken pieces of sandstone, quartzite, and granite, about fist-size. Mixed with these are a few small sherds, charcoal, and a fair number of animal bones in small pieces, apparently of oxen or some other large ruminant. An excavation has been made in the mound, and we picked out the sherds and bones from the scarp of the undisturbed portion. . . . This extraordinary pile lies on the highest part of the site: the ground is covered with broken bones to a depth of two or three feet over an oval area about 170 by 120 feet, sloping up from the edges to the centre, where the layer of stones rises suddenly to over 5 feet. Possibly this was originally much higher and the stones all around have gradually rolled down and spread out from it. . . .

Another, much smaller, area covered in a similar way with stones, lay to the west of this. (Brunton 1932: 273)

Although this enigmatic mound still stood in 1969, erosion and the earlier "excavations" reduced its dimensions rather substantially since Brunton's visit. Brunton also saw "at least six pottery kilns," but not all of these can be located today, and in many cases it is difficult to prove their date, let alone their identity as kilns. However, if some of these structures are indeed Predynastic kilns, they would be yet another evidence of the internal complexity and industrial-architectural sophistication of large Predynastic centers like Hierakonpolis. For the time being, we are limited in our understanding of the Predynastic town at Hierakonpolis by the same difficulties that hampered Brunton—a lack of reliably excavated architectural remains and, most important, the lack of a detailed map of the site.

To get a clearer idea of spatial arrangements within Predynastic Upper Egyptian settlements we are forced to abandon the large centers and focus on the very small and very late prehistoric site of Abydos. Referring to the artifacts found at the Predynastic-Protodynastic hamlet of Abydos in 1913, T. Eric Peet, one of Petrie's brightest young associates, wrote:

The interest of these is that they represent the objects used by predynastic man in his everyday life, whereas his products are generally known to us only from his tombs. The great lesson that they teach is that the objects deposited by the dead are not necessarily a fair sample of those used in ordinary life. (Peet 1914: 2)

Despite the fact that Peet's site was only about 30 meters in diameter and excavated by relatively primitive techniques (two trenches), his interest in reconstructing the total context of the settlement has made it possible to suggest the types of social-economic, spatial arrangements of the tiny community. A grain-parching kiln stood on the northeast perimeter of the village and when the settlement is viewed as a whole it seems as if human activities were arranged like a series of concentric circles, one nested inside the other. The heaviest midden was found just around the outside of the circle, suggesting a trash dumping zone. Inside was another circle, this time of hearths, indicating the area where food was prepared. And finally, at the center of the settlement, Peet found

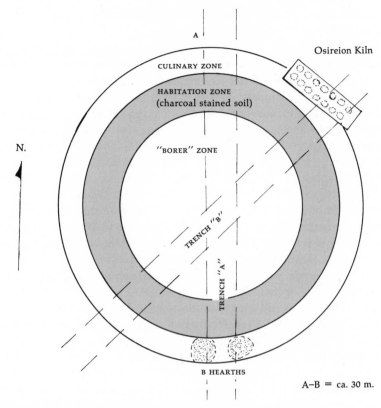

44   Schematic plan of the Late Gerzean hamlet at Abydos

the habitation zone—a gray stratum of powdered mud—". . . probably
the remains of huts built of wattle and covered with mud" (Peet 1914:
2), and over 300 tiny stone microblade points which were identified as
borers or punches but which, judging from a similar concentration reported by Butzer from the Predynastic town of Hierakonpolis, may have
been drill bits for making stone beads.

We can imagine this hamlet at Abydos as reflecting the life-style of a
rather specialized component of rural Upper Egyptian culture at the
close of the Predynastic era, it being likely that we are dealing with
either a specialized service community analogous to those maintained in
later times to build and service pharaonic tombs and temples, or with a
lower economic class. In societies as internally complex and stratified as
Egypt must have been in the late prehistoric period, one of our greatest
archaeological problems is knowing what segment of the greater culture
we are dealing with. Although we may assign approximate dates on the
basis of sequence dating or more modern but less accurate chronometric
means, it is sometimes difficult to determine whether sites owe their
differences to chronological, regional, or social-economic factors. Until

many more settlement sites of Predynastic vintage are excavated in Egypt, we will continue to be plagued by such problems.

As part of his desire to reconstruct the total context of Predynastic village life, Peet took care to have the animal bones identified by a specialist, Miss K. Haddon of the Zoological Laboratories, Cambridge, in one of the earliest examples of the application of faunal analysis to Egyptian prehistoric archaeology. At Abydos, the community maintained a mixed herd of sheep, goats, oxen, and asses for food and other by-products and transportation. This pattern dates to the inception of Predynastic culture around 5500 B.C. and must have diffused from already established Neolithic communities in the Middle East or in the Sahara (see Chapter 16). Since herds were an important investment or insurance against crop failure and hard times, we may imagine that animals were slaughtered infrequently and were most valued for their dairy products. We do not know how far increasing centralization of wealth and power by late Predynastic times (ca. 3300–3100 B.C.) had restricted the protein intake of the average farmer, but this factor had probably become a serious problem by Archaic times (ca. 3100–2700 B.C.), with the solidification of formal social and economic classes.

The same aristocrats who were to be buried in bigger and better tombs, with richer and more ostentatious grave offerings, were also doubtless helping themselves to more and more of the herds and other valuable possessions of their subjects (see Chapter 20). Judging from the fish bones at Abydos, at least, the ordinary people continued to catch or trade for Nile fish like their Palaeolithic ancestors and their later Dynastic descendants. They produced an abundance of emmer wheat and barley in their fields and, at certain times of the year, brought the sifted and winnowed grain to the community parching kiln on the edge of the settlement and emptied it into one of twenty-three vases, arranged in two rows. Each vase was set on the hard, virgin sand and supported all around by fire bricks placed on end and propped inward. In the habitation debris of the hamlet, a number of tools were found that round out the story of the daily life of the average Egyptian of about 3200 B.C. Milling stones were used to transform parched wheat and barley into flour, which could then be used in unleavened loaves of bread baked over the hearths that burned outside each dwelling. Flour already had become the mainstay of the common man's diet, the heart of his existence. Spindle whorls of groundstone and bone as well as bone tatting needles and loom weights made from pierced, rounded sherds show that a little weaving was still done at home, although the number and quality of textiles from other sites indicate that weaving of flax had already become a sophisticated industry during Predynastic times (ca. 5500–3100 B.C.) and may well date back into the Palaeolithic.

Most of the debris at Abydos, like other farming villages, consisted of broken pottery sherds and flints. Ninety-nine percent of the pottery in such sites was coarse utilitarian ware, the fancier red polished and black-topped red wares and painted potteries accounting for the remaining one percent.

This is in striking contrast to a small Amratian settlement that I tested at Hierakonpolis, where over 50 percent of the pottery recovered from a test square consisted of finer quality ceramics. Does this suggest that the people of Hierakonpolis were richer, or that they indulged in an inordinate fondness for fancy pottery, or that this pottery was more common in earlier times when wealth was more widespread? Since the excavators of the other village sites in Upper Egypt worked in an era when counting and tabulating all finds was considered unimportant, we cannot yet determine to what extent differences in artifact percentages reflect genuine regional subcultures or to what extent they are due to the error of the excavator. This is one reason why modern archaeologists insist that things be counted. Despite problems that beset comparison, most Egyptologists and archaeologists suspect that along the 400-mile stretch from Cairo to Aswan some important differences in life-style should have occurred even among the seemingly similar peoples of Predynastic Upper Egypt.

The chipped stone tools from Abydos are quite undistinguished when compared with those from earlier Predynastic periods and may reflect the increasing importance of copper cutting and piercing implements just before the beginning of the pharaonic epoch. The origin and rise of metallurgy in Predynastic Egypt, as we shall see in discussing the Lower Egyptian site of Maadi in Chapter 15, is a complex topic. Although copper tools are known throughout the Predynastic, very few examples of metal artifacts survive from before the First Dynasty (ca. 3100 B.C.). There is some reason to believe that in Upper Egypt at least copper tools were extremely scarce and imported from manufacturing centers like Maadi in the north. Nevertheless, we should not be too hasty in under-estimating the role of copper tools in Predynastic times, since by the First Dynasty (ca. 3100–2900 B.C.) the working of this metal, as demonstrated by Walter Emery's excavations at Saqqara (see Chapter 18), was surprisingly advanced.

Returning to the stone assemblage of the late Predynastic hamlet at Abydos, sickle blades, often equipped with saw edges and characteristic use sheen are common, as are scrapers and borers used in the production of hides and textiles (and possibly stone vases). The decline of hunting is suggested by the fact that only two broken arrowheads (one stone and one ivory) were found in the two long trenches that Peet dug through the settlement. Compared to finds from earlier Predynastic sites in both Upper and Lower Egypt, the rarity of hunting implements is unusual but does make sense when related to the low frequency of game animals in the site's kitchen middens. Because Abydos is so small, because it was excavated so many years ago with comparatively primitive techniques and because it was so late in the Predynastic sequence (ca. 3200–3100 B.C.) there are many explanations that might be posed for the apparent decline in the consumption of hunted game. Perhaps it reflects a general decline in rainfall on the borders of the Sahara, perhaps it is the result of the monopolization of this prestigious food source by the new ruling class, or perhaps it is related to the geographical situation of the site. It may even be that our impression of conditions at Abydos is wholly inaccurate due to the limited area dug or simply to statistically invalid sampling procedures or mistaken or incomplete faunal analysis.

Flint knives were made on the spot, but the radical differences in craftsmanship suggest that the large, well-made specimens that were still used for butchering animals in Dynastic times were produced by full-time stone-knappers whose shops turned out hundreds if not thousands of these artifacts in a year. As mentioned before, the only surprising aspect of the stone industry of Abydos is the occurrence of over 300 small flint borers in the center of the settlement circle. These implements are generally believed to have been used as drill points for piercing stone beads, although Peet preferred to interpret them as leather punches. Unfortunately, no microscopic analysis of possible wear patterns was ever performed so their true function remains a mystery. Their clustering at the center of the hamlet suggests that the task in which they were employed was a matter of public concern and if they were used in the manufacture of stone beads, then this would help to explain the great number of unworked, exotic stones like agate, carnelian, quartz crystal, and diorite located at the site and perhaps indicates that the small settlement served a highly specialized function. The distinctive Upper Egyptian interest in ornamentation and decoration is evident at Abydos despite its small size and apparent poverty: red ocher and malachite provided pigment when ground on the familiar slate palettes of the day, bone and ivory were fashioned into pins and even used in inlay work, clay was molded into animal figurines and little erratically shaped flints were kept, possibly as amulets. Metal was rare but included a ring, two small copper chisels, possibly for fine woodworking, and fish hooks. The rise of the state and the imposition of taxes and record keeping on even the humblest citizens is dimly echoed in a clay label and slab that bear the indistinct impressions of a cylinder seal.

It is a sad but painfully true principle in archaeology that even the most promising and well-dug sites often produce completely different types of information, making their comparison extremely difficult. Thus, Hierakonpolis, one of the best known and most studied Predynastic sites in Upper Egypt, has not yet produced evidence of the internal arrangement and planning of the settlement, while the Abydos area, famous for its impressive Dynastic temples, has given us a glance into the daily life of a prehistoric community and tiny Hemamieh has provided our only good example of Predynastic domestic architecture and stratigraphy.

11
BACK TO HIERAKONPOLIS:
THE METHODS
OF ENVIRONMENTAL
ARCHAEOLOGY

HAD IT NOT been for a walk in the desert taken by two young German archaeologists in 1958, the full archaeological potential of Hierakonpolis would not have been realized. When the Egyptologist Werner Kaiser and his geologist-archaeologist colleague, Karl Butzer, arrived at Hierakonpolis, they had come not to dig but simply to look in a systematic way. Their interest in the distribution and accurate dating of settlement sites in the entire region around the ancient town reflected two new trends in archaeology: the analysis of prehistoric settlement patterns and paleoenvironmental studies.

By the mid-1950's, archaeology was becoming both a natural and a social science. It was no longer enough to dig the biggest and best sites but necessary to study culture in all its many forms, from city to campsite, from columned temple to mud sanctuary, from pharaoh to commoner. In order for the new approach to work, however, archaeologists needed to know the entire range of ancient social and cultural development—not just the rich and impressive. Kaiser and Butzer were pioneers in this new style of studying the past. During their few hours at Hierakonpolis, they became the first archaeologists to record the presence of Predynastic sites out in the desert—sites that stretched far beyond the town on the edge of the desert for perhaps a few kilometers up the Great Wadi into the borderlands of the Sahara. Butzer, whose training in the natural sciences predisposed him to environmental interpretations, saw in this surprising find further proof for an old and cherished notion. Ever since the explorations of Brunton and Caton-Thompson, Egyptian prehistorians had debated the pros and cons of climatic change and tried to reconstruct what role it could have played in Predynastic society and economy. Butzer saw the pattern of Predynastic settlement in the Hierakonpolis region as a testimony to the impact of increased rainfall on the human ecology and cultural development of village farming life in the Nile Valley.

Having visited Hierakonpolis in the fall of 1959—over two years after

Butzer and Kaiser walked the site—Walter Fairservis was taken with
the idea of studying Egypt's early civilization with the same techniques
he was then developing in Pakistan to analyze the Indus Valley culture.
Almost a decade later he realized his dream, returning to Hierakonpolis
with a large, modern expedition. The aim would be no less than a
massive study of the cultural history and paleoecology of the entire
region drained by the Great Wadi—from Palaeolithic beginnings through
the Predynastic and Dynastic periods. To aid in this multidisciplinary
approach, a team of specialists was assembled, ranging from Egyptologists and artists to read, decipher, and record Dynastic tomb inscriptions,
to ethnographers to describe the contemporary life and technology of the
Saidis of Upper Egypt. After a preliminary effort in 1967, a full crew
(including the author) set to work in the early months of 1969 in an
attempt to solve simultaneously several major problems that had long
vexed both historians and prehistorians. A most important adjunct to
our work was the extension of the preliminary reconnaissance of Butzer
and Kaiser into a full-scale archaeological survey. This aim was nearly
accomplished in the brief field season by Fairservis and myself, devoting
every minute of our spare time to the survey. On Fridays, our day off,
and on holidays, we plodded out into the desert every morning, starting
at the base of the Great Wadi where it debouched onto the cultivated
soil of the floodplain, following it past the Gerzean town, past early
New Kingdom tombs ensconced high above in the sandstone hills, out
toward the Sahara proper. Occasionally, our pace was hurried by the
telltale patter of little feet running behind us, as children sought to tag
along.

In surveying large sites like the Gerzean town, we arbitrarily divided
up the area, noting unusual structural features and collecting separately
flints, sherds, and groundstone in an attempt to locate settlement clusters.
As we ventured farther and farther up the Great Wadi, the Predynastic
debris stretched almost unbroken before us, along the flat terraces that
bordered the wadi. Geologists believe such terraces to be composed of
silts deposited far up into the larger wadis of Egypt by the extremely
high floods of 13,000 years ago. Six thousand years later Predynastic
farmers were attracted to these banks and built their villages there, growing their crops of wheat and barley in the loose soils of the wadi bottom.
They worked the land, now a stark desert wilderness, and then moved
away, as suddenly as they had come. Since their departure, no farming
people has ever been able to support itself this far from the Nile. For
nearly two miles, their sites stretch out into the wastelands, defying
explanation and contradicting some of our most cherished ideas about
Predynastic patterns of settlement. Based on the work of an earlier
generation of archaeologists, we have long seen Predynastic peoples as
essentially river-bound—with their settlements perched on the low desert
escarpments paralleling the rich alluvial soils of the Nile Valley proper.

At Hierakonpolis, however, settlements extended *both* parallel and per-pendicular to the river's banks. Why?

Compared with Caton-Thompson's efforts at Hemamieh, my own test square along the banks of the Great Wadi was a meager effort. Never-theless, it was a beginning of a deliberately environmental approach to the excavation of Predynastic sites. It also proved to be an unexpected exercise in personal ingenuity. Since Egyptian workmen commonly dig with adzes, I had to scour the hold of our boat to find a digging tool that was more familiar—a shovel. The next step, selecting an appro-priate place to dig, was actually less of a problem. Our previous week's explorations along the terrace had located a number of promising Pre-dynastic sites. At a spot we had designated Locality 14, recent, illicit digging by *sebakh* or fertilizer hunters had tapped a buried layer of charcoal-stained midden, thick with broken pottery, charred seeds, bones, and flint chips. In inspecting the face of the pit dug by the *sebakhin*, Fairservis and I even discovered a small flint sickle blade with a piece of vegetable material still adhering to its edge: an ancient moment in time, frozen for nearly 6,000 years. Here, then, seemed an excellent spot to recover a controlled sample of the living debris of a Predynastic living site.

After laying out a test square 2 meters on each side, I began to dig alone with my familiar shovel and trowel in a manner that aroused no little professional curiosity among our Gufti foremen, who paid me the courtesy of an afternoon visit one Friday. Since I had already seen the stratigraphy or layering of the soil in the scarp of the *sebakh* pit, I deter-mined beforehand the thickness of my excavation levels so they would best exploit the natural strata of the soil. Because the dark-stained occu-pation zone was quite deep (about 50 centimeters), I suspected that it might actually represent several years' deposit. Since there were no obvious soil differences that would indicate natural subdivisions within the occupation stratum, I imposed my own divisions, separating the midden layer into three arbitrary zones. The general succession of soil layers did reveal some interesting facets to the history of Locality 14. The modern surface was littered with between 5 and 15 centimeters of Predynastic debris thrown up from the adjacent *sebakh* pit. Beneath this was the old natural surface consisting of about 10 centimeters of clean, yellow sand. Sealed underneath the sand was the occupation layer itself —50 centimeters of light to dark gray ash, carbonized plant remains, bones, and a wide variety of artifacts mixed with sandy soil. Reflecting perhaps the arid conditions that prevailed in Upper Egypt before the coming of agriculture was a thin layer of clean, yellow sand and sand-polished rocks immediately below the occupation midden. This, in turn, sat perched atop the late Pleistocene silts of the wadi terrace. In a geo-logic sense, Locality 14 can be seen as a kind of miniature summary of the recent climatic history of Upper Egypt. Unfortunately, it is still a

45   A western view toward the Sahara of the Great Wadi, showing Palaeolithic
inselbergs

46   Locality 14: An Amratian midden excavated by the author in 1969, shown
in relation to the Great Wadi at Hierakonpolis

history with many pages missing; but enough remains to help piece together a fascinating outline of the rise and fall of a way of life that prevailed in Egypt for 2,000 years before the advent of the pharaohs and helped pave the way for classical, Dynastic Egyptian civilization.

As I carefully shoveled out the loose, sandy soil from the 2 meter square, I sorted all cultural material, including artifacts, bones, and vegetable remains, into separate bags and labeled them according to the level from which they were taken. The white cross-lined pottery and rhomboidal slate palette immediately dated the site to Amratian times. The arbitrary levels that I dug within the apparently homogeneous mass of occupation midden proved my initial suspicions were correct. There was *not* a single occupation, but two light Amratian periods of settlement separated by a very brief interval during which the site lay abandoned—a possible indication of a seasonal pattern of life. In a larger sense, the cultural material showed that the Amratians at Locality 14 possessed an amazingly varied and complex subsistence economy—one that we cannot dismiss with our usual generalizations about village farming societies. Within the two occupation horizons were found abundant amounts of emmer wheat (*Triticum dicoccum*) with many of the seeds still encased in their original glumes or seed pods, traces of barley (*Hordeum sp.*), a piece of unidentified animal hide, bones of a large fish, a few mussel shells, and a number of animal bones. Preliminary identification of the bones indicated that the people of Locality 14 possessed dog, pig, cattle, and possibly sheep or goat and they may have hunted gazelle.

Five human coprolites (dried feces) showed that the diet consisted primarily of starchy and vegetable foodstuffs—another sign that the herds were already being treated as "capital" wealth and that meat was not commonly consumed (at least during the time that people were occupying Locality 14). A trace of sphagnum moss in one of the human coprolites was somewhat of a surprise and may reflect the proximity of swamps, probably on the nearby floodplain, and a somewhat cooler climate.

Large numbers of burned and unburned twigs have been identified as coming from the tamarisk tree (*Tamarix sp.*). Today, tamarisk and acacia forests represent what botanists call the natural or climax vegetation in the more well-watered wadis of northern Egypt where the rainfall averages about 2.5 centimeters a year, and the presence of tamarisk at Hierakonpolis in Predynastic times is another good indicator of the effect of climatic change on the dry borderlands of Upper Egypt. Preservation conditions at Locality 14 were so good that we were even able to recover and identify insect remains, including the ubiquitous scarab (*Heliocopris gigas*), a favorite artistic and mythological theme in later Egyptian culture, and a specimen of *Pimelia* as well as some still unidentified larvae.

Most of the organic material was recovered because I took soil samples from each level. Ideally, after returning to the laboratory, these samples would be carefully sorted by hand for recognizable seeds, small mammal bones, insect parts, coprolites, and the like. Once this tedious process of dry sorting was completed, a flotation process would be used on the remaining soil to separate out leftover plant parts and extremely small seeds. Unfortunately, we did not have either the time or the equipment to do this important job on the spot, so it was necessary to take the soil samples back to the United States for analysis. Ordinarily, one would imagine, this should not have been much of a problem. However, archaeologists do not live in the best of all possible worlds and United States Customs officials are prone to frown on funny-looking plastic bags containing dark, powdery substances, even when the bearer is carrying official letters of explanation. The year 1969 had seen an increasing row over the international drug traffic, and so I was understandably nervous that Customs might look with disfavor on a student returning from the East bearing small bags of dirt! Luckily, my letters convinced the officials of my legitimacy, but there remained another barrier.

The U.S. Department of Agriculture regulations expressly forbid the import of soils from areas of the world inhabited by crop pests that might infect this country. This is a sensible regulation, but requires either shipment of exotic soil samples to a specially designated, bonded laboratory or heat treatment of the specimens on the spot. After much checking and rechecking in the circus that is Kennedy International Airport, I was told that I must leave my precious cargo in the hands of U.S.D.A. officials. My uneasiness was somewhat relieved by the politeness and efficiency of the agents and by the official receipt which they provided for my material. Despite these assurances, however, I spent several uneasy months awaiting my specimens. My feelings of ill ease were made more acute by constant lighthearted chiding by my colleagues about my "dissertation in a box" being misshipped by the postal service to a little old lady in Peoria who would use my precious dirt to fertilize her begonias.

Fortunately, the much-dreaded disaster never happened and the box arrived intact. By combining all the organic analyses with our site distribution maps for the Hierakonpolis area, we are now fairly confident that our evidence proves the old contention of climatologists and prehistorians that a rainy period that began about 7000 B.C. and ended between 3000 and 2500 B.C. had substantial effects on ancient Egyptian cultural development. To try to picture the effects of such rainfall, Karl Butzer has made an educated guess that the Hierakonpolis region would have received about 5 centimeters of rain per annum—a mere two inches. This amount only slightly exceeds the modern annual precipitation in Cairo.

To those of us used to 30 or 40 inches of rain a year, such amounts seem trifling. But all things are relative, and what would be one week's average precipitation in the southeastern United States or northern Europe, can nourish enough vegetation in normally arid or semiarid zones like the Sahara to turn apparent wasteland into verdant pasturage almost overnight. To appreciate just how much vegetation can grow under such a regime, we have only to look at the situation that prevails today in the wadis around Cairo—wadis that, if anything, are much poorer than their prehistoric counterparts because of overexploitation by grazing and charcoal gathering. At the Wadi Gebel Ahmar (or Red Mountain Gulch, to use the more prosaic English translation), the Egyptian ecologist M. Kassas recorded 22 separate plant species in 1952 under conditions where the annual rainfall was probably well below the 5 centimeter figure reconstructed by Butzer for southern Egypt during Predynastic times. Today, the absence of tamarisk groves from Wadi Gebel Ahmar has been explained by the wadi's proximity to a large urban center whose citizens and dependents have destroyed the natural forest cover in their insatiable search for pasturage and cheap fuel. William McHugh, who has spent years studying the prehistory of the peoples of the Western Desert frontiers, believes that Butzer's reconstruction is much too stingy and, on the basis of ancient rock drawings of animals that can still be seen in the desert, he would provide a generous 25 centimeters of rain per year for the Hierakonpolis region at the beginning of the Neolithic rainy period. The implications of his climatic arguments for the tempo of prehistoric human ecology in northern Africa are rather novel and revolutionary and will be considered at some length when we turn our attention to the role of the frontier peoples in the rise of Egyptian civilization. For the time being, we can rest assured that even allowing for the minimum increase in rainfall proposed by Butzer, the Great Wadi at Hierakonpolis during much of the Predynastic period received a regular seasonal runoff from the surrounding highlands. It is also clear that this rainfall enriched the surrounding environment to the point where plant and animal life flourished in unprecedented abundance.

We know now that timing was an especially crucial factor in the birth and growth of Predynastic Upper Egyptian culture, balanced as it was on a precarious peak of a climatic optimum. For a time between 7000 and 2500 B.C. the deserts bloomed and human societies colonized areas that have been unable to support such dense populations since. Yet, within that gross 4,500-year period, there are important distinctions that we must draw with respect to the yearly timing and effect of rainfall if we are to understand the processes of social and economic change that worked upon the people of Predynastic Egypt. An initial distinction has to do with the question of the relative permanence of the residential sites along the Great Wadi. Were they occupied throughout the year by a representative cross-section of the area's population, or were they seasonally transhumant camps, which harbored only a small number of hunters, herders, or harvesters? Although we cannot yet answer all these questions for all the localities along the wadi, we can make an educated guess that many of the sites were occupied for periods of at least several months (during the rainy season) and possibly for several years at a time by men, women, and children. Because several Predynastic burials were found in these wadi sites, we are able to infer that adults of both sexes and their offspring lived and died in the small hamlets that dotted the banks of the stream course. We can also be fairly sure that mothers bore their infants here and considered the area home, because infant burials, characteristically placed within the precincts of the dwelling in other Predynastic and Dynastic sites, were located in the course of our survey. A final argument for relative permanence of at least some sites along the wadi is the very nature of the foodstuffs found in the living sites—grains and herding animals being present in abundance and large storage pots being a common type of vessel encountered in the occupation debris.

The next question of timing involves the larger question of the particular time of year during which the rains fell. Egypt is not today and never has been like the temperate areas of the world in which most of us were reared. Rainfall, when it does occur in arid and semiarid regions with any regularity, is restricted to a particular season of the year. The livelihood of peoples in such areas, therefore, depends on a rather precise knowledge of just when such rains will come—this kind of timing is absolutely critical to survival. If we look at the distribution of rainfall today in the central and eastern Sahara, there is a definite division between winter and summer regimes. North of the Sudanese Egyptian city of Wadi Halfa (about 22° latitude) rainfall comes during the winter months, from January through March. Most rain actually falls nearer the beginning than the end of this period and none falls south of Cairo on a regular, yearly basis. South of Wadi Halfa, the rains come in summer.

Although most prehistorians who have studied the Predynastic agree that a startling increase in rainfall took place in Upper Egypt between about 7000 and 2500 B.C., they are not unanimous about where it came from, how consistent it was, or at what time of the year it would have fallen. Karl Butzer sees the northerly rain belts that today water the Mediterranean coast of Africa shifting south, providing Hierakonpolis with about 5 centimeters of winter rain, probably in January and February. McHugh disagrees, preferring to believe that the southerly rains shifted north, dumping as much as 25 centimeters of rain on Hierakonpolis during the summer months (June through September). The disagreement here is important because the seasonal timing, as well as the magnitude of rainfall, certainly affected the life-style and social and economic organization of ancient Hierakonpolitans on a year-round basis.

At present the question cannot be resolved, partly because different types of evidence have been marshaled by the disputants—Butzer relying strongly on formal geological stratigraphy and soil analysis and McHugh reconstructing rainfall at different latitudes on the basis of water requirements of animals depicted in prehistoric rock drawings in the deserts of Egypt, Nubia, and Libya. A third alternative of both summer and winter rainfall is possible but extremely unlikely. This problem will have to be set aside for future researchers to resolve.

In the meantime, however, there was another natural cycle that remained critical to Egyptians from prehistoric times right down to the present: the timing of the annual Nile floods. Since this timing was established by the Upper Pleistocene, well before the coming of agriculture to Egypt, we know that the floods of Predynastic times occurred, as now, from late June through late September. Traditionally they provided the new soil upon which the phenomenal agricultural wealth of Egypt was based. Before the first Aswan Dam in the late 1890's altered the traditional floods, visitors to Egypt reported that wheat was sown in either late October or November and barley shortly thereafter, usually at the end of November. Harvest time came in late March or early April, just as the hot wind of fifty days (the *khamsin*) swept down upon the land. If Butzer is correct and the Neolithic rains fell during January and February, the people of the Hierakonpolis district planted and tended their crops according to two basically different agricultural regimes: dry farming in the wadi and basin irrigation cultivation on the bottomlands of the Nile. Under such circumstances, it is unlikely that the same people could have tended both areas, separated as they were by a substantial distance and each area requiring its own special method of cultivation at the same time of the year.

The bones found at desert sites suggest that residents, in addition to their farming responsibilities, herded their flocks of sheep and goats (and probably their cattle and donkeys) on the seasonal pastures that fringed the Sahara, and hunted and fished around the small catchment basins and water holes that dotted the sandstone hills of the Hierakonpolis region. Regardless of how we reconstruct the subsistence economy and divisions of labor that were used by Predynastic peoples to take advantage of their complex environment, it seems apparent that they were scattered widely from the banks of the Nile out into the hills of the Western Desert, exploiting a variety of ecological niches with a variety of different subsistence techniques and modes of social organization.

As summer approached and the Nile overflowed its banks, the low-lying sections of the floodplain had to be abandoned in favor of sites sitting on elevated hillocks or desert escarpments. At the same time, along the Great Wadi, if we follow Butzer's interpretation of winter rainfall, then after March the plant life would have dried up and the animals retreated toward the river or more permanent water holes in the desert hills. Nevertheless, the wadi could have remained an attractive alternative for settlement when compared to the increasingly humid and insect-ridden floodplain. People in the desert could have continued to support themselves on the gazelle that they trapped around the permanent water holes and found diversion in the change of seasons and still supported themselves on the stored surpluses of grain that they so prodigally tossed out in their trash at sites like Locality 14.

If the rains visited Hierakonpolis in the summer rather than the winter, the tempo of life would have been different. The same people could have harvested their winter crops in the bottomlands and been able to move a part of their numbers or even their whole population out into the Great Wadi to cultivate the dry crop there. A more practical arrangement would have seen the division of the local Predynastic society into two units—one that subsisted in the desert borderlands by farming, hunting, and herding, and another that lived on or very near the floodplain in areas like the Gerzean town and practiced more intensive basin irrigation agriculture and fished and traded along the Nile River.

It was doubtless the diversity of such Predynastic peoples that ultimately enabled them to develop a prosperous society and outward-looking economy that exploited connections with both the Sahara to the west and the Red Sea to the east and plied the Nile with high-prowed sailing vessels from Aswan to the Delta, and perhaps beyond. It was this prosaic pattern of broadly based economic and social networks linked with more inexplicable cultural factors like the preference for elaborate ornamentation and public display and an unusual fascination with accumulating goods for the afterlife that ultimately laid the foundations for classical Dynastic civilization. It was this fact that Petrie first glimpsed at Naqada 80 years ago. If, over the years, we have expanded our vistas to include other peoples and traditions that coexisted with the Naqada culture in the Delta and on the frontiers and if we have been able to see more clearly the role of climatic change in the beginnings of Egyptian civilization, then we still return, time after time, to Petrie's classic descriptions, painstakingly penned in that hectic season at Naqada as he raced the tomb robbers and antiquities dealers, to salvage for future generations a critical chapter in Egyptian prehistory.

PART IV

THE PREDYNASTIC PEOPLES OF LOWER EGYPT: THE DELTA TRADITION, ca. 5500–3100 B.C.

12

FATHER JUNKER
AT MERIMDE BENI-SALAME:
FARMING COMES TO THE DELTA

HERMANN JUNKER was the model of a successful German university professor. His career in Egyptology and archaeology was as stable and stolid as Petrie's was erratic and colorful. Like Petrie, he was long-lived and a good organizer, but unlike the self-taught Englishman, his scholarly and scientific skills were products of a long, carefully pursued and highly disciplined academic career. While Petrie, then at the peak of his powers, was unraveling the secrets of Naqada, Junker, a young student at the Catholic seminary at Trier, was mastering a host of modern and ancient Oriental languages, including Hebrew, Aramaic, Arabic, Ethiopian, and Sanskrit. He was ordained in 1900, but soon tired of parish life and the following year enrolled as a graduate student in Berlin to study under Adolf Erman, the greatest Egyptologist of the day. In an era when German scholarship and universities led the world and American colleges imported German scholars en masse, Junker enjoyed a degree of steady success that would do credit to any man of letters. In 1907 he matriculated to the University of Vienna, became an assistant two years later, a full professor in 1912, and dean of the faculty in 1921–22. To anyone familiar with the ins and outs of academic promotions, this pace indicates that Hermann Junker was not only a successful scholar but a competent politician as well. Father Junker's track record as an active philologist and field archaeologist is similarly impressive. Between 1908 and 1911 he undertook a mission to Nubia for the Prussian Academy of Science as part of an effort to rescue monuments threatened by an expansion of the ten-year-old Aswan Dam. In Nubia he was exposed to many of the same problems and demands that forged the American George Andrew Reisner into a premier field technician. Although Junker never attained the heights of technical expertise reached by Reisner, his experience in Nubia seems to have instilled in him a respect for systematic excavation and kindled an interest in settlement sites, anticipating his pioneer work at Merimde a generation later.

Hermann Junker had a good year in 1912. Secure in his new professional status, he was appointed Director of the Vienna Academy of Natural Sciences' expedition to Egypt—a position he filled with distinction for the next twenty-seven years. Between 1912 and 1929, with an interruption for the First World War, he dug at Giza, uncovering and scientifically measuring, recording, and copying temples, texts, and burial chambers and adding immensely to our knowledge of the culture of the Old Kingdom and its most magnificent architectural and artistic achievements.

In 1929, amid a storm of protest, Junker succeeded Ludwig Borchardt as Director of the German Archaeological Institute in Cairo. Borchardt had created a cause célèbre some years earlier by discovering the famous bust of Nefertiti in a sculptor's studio at Tell el Amarna. The fact that Germany had been awarded the head infuriated many Egyptians and in the increasingly nationalistic atmosphere of the 1920's, possession of Nefertiti's head became an international issue and a source of constant professional embarrassment to Borchardt. Junker's diplomatic disposition made him a natural candidate for the older scholar's position. While this trait is apparent in almost everything he did, its more negative aspects are apparent in the ease with which he accommodated himself to the Nazi government, in contrast to Borchardt's stubborn opposition to the new order—a capitulation that was not to endear Junker to his Western European colleagues.

As the 1920's drew to a close, Junker began to search for new areas in which to dig. One might have expected him to choose an Old Kingdom site related to his past triumphs at Giza, or at least to dig at a Dynastic site where his brilliance and versatility as a linguist and translator would find fulfillment, especially since he was one of the very few Egyptologists of modern times to aspire to competence in *all* phases of the ancient Egyptian language.

But Junker's search for new worlds to conquer propelled him not forward in time into the more classic periods of Egyptian culture-history, but backward, past the Archaic (ca. 3100–2700 B.C.), past even the times of Petrie's Naqada Culture (ca. 4000–3100 B.C.), back to the days of the earliest farming peoples to inhabit the Nile Valley in the late sixth or early fifth millennium B.C.

In the winter of 1927–28, Albert Rothbart of New York financed a preliminary survey by the Vienna Academy's expedition into the western Delta of Lower Egypt. The motivations for Junker's undertaking such a project, so far afield from his own specialty, remain unclear. Certainly, contemporary discoveries of early Predynastic or Neolithic remains by Brunton and Caton-Thompson at Badari and Hemamieh and by Caton-Thompson and Elinor Gardner in the nearby Fayum raised the question of why nothing of comparable antiquity had been found in the Delta. And then, too, there was the convenient financial support of Mr. Rothbart as well as the prestige of finding the first Neolithic site in Lower

Egypt and one-upping the British, who had effectively dominated late prehistoric archaeology for a generation.

And so, probably for a variety of good reasons, the Vienna Academy sponsored an archaeological survey of the northwestern Delta. As a result of their labors two sites were found which offered prospects of success—a microlithic locality and a large Neolithic village near Merimde beni-Salame. Modern archaeologists would be appalled at a professional survey that did not explicitly consider the relevance and relationship of a given site to other sites in its immediate area. In Junker's day, however, it was still necessary to impress the public and the scientific communities with big sites and artistically attractive spoils for museums, while the philosophy of controlled sampling was unknown to most archaeologists. Indeed, it was quite an accomplishment to get anyone even to agree to finance a prehistoric excavation until the 1920's, and then most excavators were expected to produce startling finds and relate these to the popular, colonial image of primitive peoples promoted by early anthropologists like Sir James George Frazer, author of the twelve-volume tour de force, *The Golden Bough*. The urge to treat prehistoric peoples as ancient curiosity pieces led to a stilted and occasionally ridiculous reconstruction of their social life and customs and ultimately detracted from the more positive aspects of Junker's work at Merimde.

The site of Merimde beni-Salame lies just 37 miles northwest of Cairo on the far western border of the Nile, straddling the high ground of the desert. Junker's surveyors were first attracted there by its great size. Covering over 44 acres and rising over 6½ feet above the surrounding countryside, Merimde equals or exceeds the dimensions of all known prehistoric sites in Egypt, with the exception of Hierakonpolis. If the entire settlement had been occupied at one time—and this is extremely unlikely—the population could have exceeded 16,000 individuals. If we draw an analogy to modern traditional towns in Egypt and carefully reevaluate Junker's excavation reports, however, this figure can be reduced substantially to about 5,000. Even so, the settlement must have been a giant in its time. Carbon-14 dating of the different occupation layers in the mound at Merimde done a generation ago when the method was still in its infancy (and over a decade after excavations had ceased) yielded a disappointingly recent range of dates, between 4130 and 3530 B.C. When these estimates are adjusted according to modern correction factors, however, they reveal that Merimde is clearly the earliest known farming village in Lower Egypt, being initially settled around 4880 B.C. and occupied for approximately 650 years. This estimate compares favorably with the new thermoluminescent dates of 5580 ± 420 B.C. to 4360 ± 355 B.C. for the Badarian levels of Hemamieh in Upper Egypt.

When villagers roamed Merimde's curving lands, the Rosetta branch of the Nile flowed but a short distance to the east and the inhabitants could look down on the rich alluvial bottomlands on one side and the desert pasturelands on the other. The site was originally settled by a people intimately familiar with the mixed herding and crop-raising techniques that had dominated the Middle Eastern and Levantine worlds for 2,000 years. As we shall see in Chapter 16, the coming of regular rains to Saharan Africa after 7000 B.C. opened a variety of new environments to such village farming peoples—environments that they gradually filled by a series of still unknown processes. We might imagine that Merimde was first spotted by a mobile outpost of a more settled community to the north or east. The shepherds or herdsmen quickly realized the potentials of the locality and soon a thriving settlement arose as they moved their kinsmen and friends to the new promised land. These first tentative attempts to settle Merimde are reflected in the lowest levels of the site, by a few scattered hearths and 15 burials. The earliest settlers apparently did not have time to build solid dwellings before a sheet flood covered the meager traces of their settlement, providing archaeologists with a unique example of the interrelation between the life-giving rains of the Neolithic Subpluvial and the new farming and herding way of life that was finding its way into the Nile Valley.

From the location of sites like Merimde we can reconstruct something of the rhythm and pattern of settlement of early farming cultures in Lower Egypt. Compact hamlets or towns were located on the main branches of the Nile, taking advantage of the rich food sources that spawned in the river, the ease of transportation afforded by its flow and the rich black soil that it miraculously deposited on the land. To avoid flooding during the annual inundation, settlements were built on natural rises and their elevations rose as the towns grew on their own debris and garbage. Beyond the typical Delta village in all directions stretched empty land: fields for crops and pasturage for the flocks. Unlike their Upper Egyptian neighbors whose towns, villages, and hamlets were strung out like evenly spaced beads on a necklace, parallel to the Nile or along the main desert water courses, the people of Lower Egypt grew up in a world where boundaries were, of necessity, drawn more by social and political convention than by nature. Their villages, surrounded on all sides by expanses of open space, dotted the landscape like knots in a net rather than beads on a necklace—and this pattern has persisted from the pharaohs to the present. For the archaeologist, this has caused problems. In Lower Egypt, not only are many ancient sites buried beneath modern successors, but they have often been robbed for building materials, or pushed farther down into marshy subsoil by the overburden and the alluvial deposit of millennia.

Happily for archaeologists, Merimde's location was at least partially based on an attraction that has long since become a liability—closeness to the desert. As we have seen, 9,000 years ago the aridity of the Sahara had been moderated by rainfall and its wastes transformed into pastures and marginal farmlands. When it was founded, Merimde was ideally situated to take advantage of both the bounty of the semiarid pasture lands outside the Delta and the promise of the rich Nile alluvium. The encroaching desert and the increasing aridity that have discouraged permanent settlements over the last 5,000 years preserved for Hermann Junker and his crew a hermetically sealed early farming community that reflects in its houses, streets, tools, and burials the texture of Neolithic Lower Egyptian society to a degree unknown in most Upper Egyptian sites of comparable antiquity.

Junker's brilliant series of preliminary reports on Merimde (he never completed a final one) show that he recognized the importance of the site immediately. The finds a few years earlier of large Neolithic settlements on the shores of the ancient Fayum Lake by Caton-Thompson and Gardner as well as the excavations at Hemamieh had initiated a whole new era in Predynastic archaeology, one that placed great emphasis on settlement sites. But at Brunton's Badarian village localities, stratigraphy was virtually nonexistent and only the small site of Hemamieh possessed any buried deposits. The layer-cakelike succession of cultures so prized by Middle Eastern archaeologists was totally lacking in the great surface finds of the Fayum. At Merimde, however, 2 meters of debris and several superimposed living surfaces revealed a new chapter in prehistory in Egypt and, for the first time, threw light on the origin of the traditional Egyptian distinctions between the Two Lands of Upper and Lower Egypt.

Although it fell far short of the standards set by Caton-Thompson at Hemamieh, Junker's work at Merimde was quite respectable for its time and exceedingly well organized. Whereas the primitive state and sanitation of Petrie's field camp has become legendary—even notorious—all over the East, Junker provided modern, comfortable quarters for his staff. It is an interesting comment on the differences between the individualistic Petrie and the diplomatic, corporate Junker that while Petrie boasted of the Spartan conditions and rough-and-ready state of his camps, Junker devoted pages of his reports to detailed discussions of the systematic layout of expedition headquarters. He even went so far as to include photographs and plans of his temporary field quarters and the permanent building which succeeded it in following seasons. Surely nothing could dramatize the differences between the old and new generations of archaeologists so eloquently.

In his first season of work, Junker cleared a small area, but subsequently introduced a regular grid system based on the 10 meter square to systematize recording and mapping of his finds. Although Junker did attempt to record his material by level and horizontal placement, he dug in large, one-meter levels and was most interested in clearly defined "living floors." Unfortunately, in a site like Merimde, which had grown irregularly over hundreds of years, the kinds of differences that might be important to archaeologists are often registered in levels much thinner

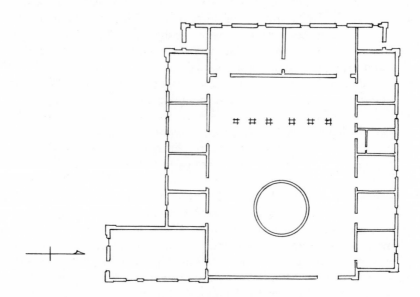

47   The logistics of systematic planning: Junker's expedition house at Merimde
      beni-Salame

than one meter; and the existence of obvious living floors except in
connection with houses, hearths, or similar features is not as common
or obvious as might be expected. Thus, by digging in large vertical units,
Junker probably lumped together the debris of many different occupations, of many generations of Merimdens. Despite his failings, however,
he must be praised for the promptness of his reporting and the com-
prehensiveness of his preliminary publications. He was especially lavish
in illustrating his material and in this aspect his work really surpassed
that of his English contemporaries. It is a telling comment on the state
of Lower Egyptian prehistory that the high quality of Junker's preliminary reports far surpasses the spotty accounts of other Predynastic
Lower Egyptian sites dug many years later.

Every excavator, no matter how methodical and scientific, injects some
of his personal preferences into his work, especially in deciding which
aspects to emphasize and how certain problems should be interpreted.
Hermann Junker was trained as a priest and already had spent a decade
excavating in the necropolis of Giza—a place where the interplay of
ancient Egyptian religious beliefs and the cult of the dead found their
classic expression in the astonishing art and architecture of the Old
Kingdom. When Junker began digging at Merimde, Predynastic research
was still naturally dominated by the opinions of Petrie and his associates

—views formed through the excavations of thousands of graves. Therefore, even had Junker desired to ignore his prior interests in Egyptian funeral practices (he was working in a field where the archaeological evidence was dominated by the cemeteries of the dead rather than the villages of the living), it seemed as if one might understand the nuances of Predynastic culture in terms of the objects buried with the dead. This view was further strengthened by the known Dynastic Egyptian fascination with life after death. In the same way that modern writers like Evelyn Waugh and Jessica Mitford have found a strong theme of contemporary American culture expressed in "the American way of death," so too Egyptologists and archaeologists have stressed the Egyptian fascination with burials, tombs, and mummification as a key to understanding ancient mentality and culture. It is not surprising, therefore, that Junker should display a fascination for Merimden graves and their broader cultural significance.

From the beginning it was clear that the people of Merimde differed radically from both the Predynastic peoples of Upper Egypt and the Dynastic Egyptians. Merimdens were interred inside the settlement in shallow oval pits and laid on their sides in a contracted position. Startlingly, they were almost never accompanied by grave offerings, and in this and other ways recall the earlier burial habits of the Qadan peoples of Palaeolithic times. Most of the 125 individuals found were women and children. Junker, understandably intrigued by the rarity of adult men, proposed that many men had perished away from home on hunting or raiding expeditions and were promptly buried where they fell. Since Junker's day, research by physical anthropologists and paleodemographers has shown that high death rates for women and children, far from being the exception, are the rule in village farming societies where infants and prepubescents are prey to numerous diseases and periodic malnutrition and their mothers, weakened by continuous pregnancy and frequent births, often die young. Such a situation contrasts strikingly to both modern urban industrial society and older hunter-gatherer cultures where smaller nuclear families are common. Junker's belief that the high proportion of women and children could not reflect the true make-up of Merimden society reminds me of the views of an amateur North American archaeologist I once encountered. On walking onto a large village site he had just excavated with mechanical equipment and no grid system, I was quickly informed that the high proportion of young children and infants (about 50 percent) was strikingly unusual and must be explained by an outbreak of disease or some other extraordinary agency. What the excavator failed to realize was that, whereas in both urban industrial and hunting and gathering societies, excess children are undesirable and uneconomical, simple farming economies create a strong market for large families because children can perform the simple, almost mindless tasks of farming and herding at a younger age and with less training than they could effectively hunt or operate complex mechanical equipment. The demands for increased childbearing created by farming also raised adult female mortality and, in all probability, it was these factors that accounted for the peculiar composition of Merimde's burial population.

Only a small portion of the skeletons dug up at Merimde have been studied, so that our impression of the physical appearance of the ancient people is fairly subjective and we cannot, reliably, attempt to trace their origins. What little work was done portrays Merimdens as a slightly built, round-headed folk whose men averaged 5 feet 6 inches in height and women 5 feet 2 inches. Abscesses were a common malady, in contrast to contemporary Nubians, a situation that probably reflects a combination of the new agricultural diet, genetic predisposition, and local water chemistry.

What bothered Junker and most of his contemporaries even more than the high proportion of women and children in Merimden graves was the very "un-Egyptian" habit of including no grave offerings with the dead. With the exception of an occasional bead or amulet or reed mat (i.e., limited personal possessions), Merimden graves contained none of the goods thought essential to the insurance of a properly comfortable life after death by both Predynastic Upper Egyptians and their Dynastic successors. As I have mentioned already, the fact that we have so long accepted the cult of the dead as a dominant theme in ancient Egyptian culture places us in an awkward position in explaining Merimden funerary customs, especially because they contrast so sharply with their Upper Egyptian counterparts and later Dynastic practices. At Merimde there were no masses of personal ornaments, piles of storage jars, or clusters of stone tools. Junker tried to explain this problem in an imaginative way. He felt that instead of grave goods, the relatives of recently deceased Merimdens had offered food and drink to their departed kinsmen around the hearths of the dead person's household. He reached this interesting conclusion by proposing that the dead were buried facing their hearths. Ordinarily, this seems a rather simple archaeological observation. Either a skeleton does or does not face a given feature like a hearth. The only difficulty is proving association between a given hearth and a particular burial. Unfortunately, Junker's excavation techniques did not provide sufficient control over vertical and horizontal associations to test his hypothesis. This mistake, by a fine scholar, should serve as a lesson not only to professional archaeologists but to that growing clique of paraprofessional "social theorists" who freely offer explanations of ancient societies without carefully examining the hard archaeological evidence upon which their theories and hypotheses are ultimately based. In Junker's case, the failure to relate grave pits and adjacent hearths by carefully observing and cleaning each living floor and directly demonstrating the contemporaneity of adjacent features has left us with outstanding questions that can only really be answered by further excavations. Until such work is carried out, we cannot be sure whether burials were contemporary with nearby hearths and houses or made long after the dwellings had been abandoned and their owners moved to other areas of the village.

Another problem arose at Merimde concerning the lack of a cemetery. Junker believed that one of the most important contrasts between Merimde and Petrie's Naqadan sites to the south was the fact that Merimdens buried their dead within the settlement while Predynastic Upper Egyptians were placed in separate cemeteries outside their villages. Superficially, at least, such a contrast suggests a major ideological difference between the belief systems of Predynastic Upper and Lower Egypt—a difference that some experts believe anticipates the ritual and symbolic distinctions between the Two Lands in pharaonic times. Recently, however, this contrast has been questioned by Egyptologist Barry Kemp, who pointed out that the archaeological evidence is not as clear as Junker believed, for two reasons: first, based on the published reports, it cannot be proved whether the Merimdens were actually buried inside the settlement *while* it was occupied, or merely placed in an abandoned area of the town where the high elevation, good drainage, and soft soil recommended the locality. Second, the evidence from Upper Egypt is not as consistent as Junker argued. There are apparently instances in which adults were buried in settlements, but since the sites were dug two or three generations ago when techniques were relatively primitive it is impossible to determine if the settlements and graves were contemporary.

In the larger setting of Egyptian prehistory, Junker's excavation of Merimde is most valuable not for its graves but for the knowledge it has provided of everyday life in Predynastic Lower Egypt—of the workings, architecture, diet, and social organization of a prehistoric Egyptian town of the fifth millennium B.C. The earliest remains of permanent dwellings were discovered in the middle layers of the site. Although it is difficult to draw any exact conclusions about the internal arrangement of houses due to the relatively small portion of the site actually excavated, the earliest structures were apparently dispersed in a random manner, but toward the end of occupation clustered along a winding lane. The basic Merimde house was oval or horseshoe-shaped and built of posts, mud, and wickerwork. Dwellings were small by our standards —from about 1.6 to 3 meters across—and their floors dug into the ground about 40 centimeters and surrounded by aboveground walls over a meter high, built of straw-tempered mud and mud clods, a method still used in some areas of the Middle East. Doorways usually faced southeast, away from the prevailing westerly winds. In the earlier periods, houses generally boasted a single center pole, indicating a conical roof, while later on two such internal supports—one at each end of the oval building—betoken a double pitched roof. Sometimes houses were partitioned inside by a line of posts across the center, suggesting a separation of eating and sleeping quarters or of living and stable areas. A variety of domestic activities are reflected by hearths, grinding stones, sunken water jars and pot basins (holes left by pots whose bases were once driven into the softened floor of the dwelling), and large oval or circular baskets used for storing grain. The dry sands and arid climate of Merimde have preserved these baskets so that we can see just how they were woven and determine that they were made from locally grown rushes and wheat straw. In the upper levels of Merimde, storage baskets were coated on the outside with mud and placed in pits outdoors for use as grain silos. Other storage facilities, like mud-lined pits and huge jars, were plentiful around dwellings, reminding us of the importance of storage in village farming societies and suggesting that the distribution of grain surpluses at this time was the responsibility of individual households and not of a central authority as in Dynastic times.

Also located in the vicinity of huts were smaller, more lightly built structures of posts, wickerwork, and mud—presumably refuges from the hot summer sun that enabled a person to work in a shaded spot. The aspect of small conical or double-pitched roofed houses nestled inside reed fences (some of which were found nearly intact by Merimde's excavators), surrounded by their granaries, grinding stones, and hearths suggests that Merimdens lived in single family units and that each family was, more or less, economically independent. The open settlements of early Predynastic Lower Egypt are so reminiscent of those of the rest of the Middle East and eastern Mediterranean and so unlike what little we know of Upper Egyptian settlements that many prehistorians prefer to use the word Neolithic to characterize the early farming cultures of northern Egypt. Certainly, from a purely impressionistic view, Merimde is not significantly different from contemporary villages in Palestine, Cyprus, and Mesopotamia and shows none of the distinctively Egyptian characteristics of Badarian peoples who were introducing village farming culture to Upper Egypt in the late sixth and fifth millennia B.C. In its general aspects, Merimde seems more like a village of sturdy yeoman farmers than a collection of peasants subject to the whims, avarice, and authority of a powerful man or government, although some cooperative activities (if not centralization of food-producing tasks) are recalled by large threshing floors up to 13 feet in diameter.

The foodstuffs that formed the backbone of the people's diet were all new to Egypt in the early sixth millennium B.C. and had been brought into the Delta either by migrants or by the diffusion of ideas from the rest of the Middle Eastern and circum-Mediterranean worlds. The dietary mainstays were the familiar Middle Eastern domesticates emmer wheat, fodder vetch (*Vicia sativa augustifolia*), pigs, longhorned cattle, sheep, and possibly goats. The bounty of the Nile—the heritage of a much

earlier Palaeolithic and Epipalaeolithic tradition—remained important
and included numerous species of fish and shellfish, turtle, and an occasional hippopotamus and crocodile—reminders that the river could still
be a dangerous place. As we mentioned earlier, in addition to the undoubted food value of the hippo, Merimdens were fond of employing
its massive leg bones (tibias, to be exact) as doorsteps in their homes,
a practice possibly fraught with ritual implications to ward off these
beasts, which were the personification of danger in Dynastic times.
Finally, antelope and possibly polecat were hunted by the men of the
town on the desert grasslands.

The Merimden tool kit was as efficient as it was plain. Chipped stone
axes were common, testifying to the comparative abundance of trees,
and manufactured from a bewildering variety of rock, including flint,
quartzite, granite, nephrite (a type of jade), basalt, red jasper, chal-
cedony, schist, and limestone. Two varieties of axes were popular—a
long, cylindrical type with round cross-section and a smaller edition with
a wider bit and better polish. The possibility of the latter type being at
least partly ceremonial is suggested by the occasional use of an attractive
but utterly useless material like hematite, although differences in economic activities are also possible: small axes being used for root-grubbing
and similar women's work in contemporary societies in New Guinea. Flint
saw-edged sickle blades, many bearing the characteristic sheen deposited
in cutting grasses, were common, as were a number of large bifacial and
unifacial saws—possibly used in woodcutting or fish-scaling. Well-made
stone points, probably arrowheads, were abundant, including the familiar hollow-based variety, although triangular and stemmed types were
also found. Perhaps this variety reflects a number of different jobs and
indicates different stylistic preferences or even different cultural affilia-
tions, since similar artifacts are known from Upper Egyptian sites as
well. Other well-worked bifacial stone tools include knife blades (tanged
and untanged), awls, and scrapers. A few crude hand-axlike implements,
cleavers, scrapers, and boring tools recall Palaeolithic tools, although the
resemblance is certainly fortuitous and does not indicate a direct cultural
link. The bifacial chipped stone technology of the Merimden people
contrasts so strikingly with the earlier Egyptian microblade tradition of
Epipalaeolithic times that many prehistorians take this as evidence that
these farming peoples were recent arrivals in the Delta. As we will see
in Chapter 16, new evidence from the Sahara has shown that plant and
animal domestication and a settled Neolithic way of life not unlike
Merimde's was already present in the deserts west of Egypt by 6000 B.C.

In Egypt, groundstone artifacts became widespread only with the
dawn of an effective farming economy, although grinding stones were
known from Palaeolithic times. Aside from the ubiquitous axes, characteristic artifacts include pear-shaped or spheroid maceheads (also

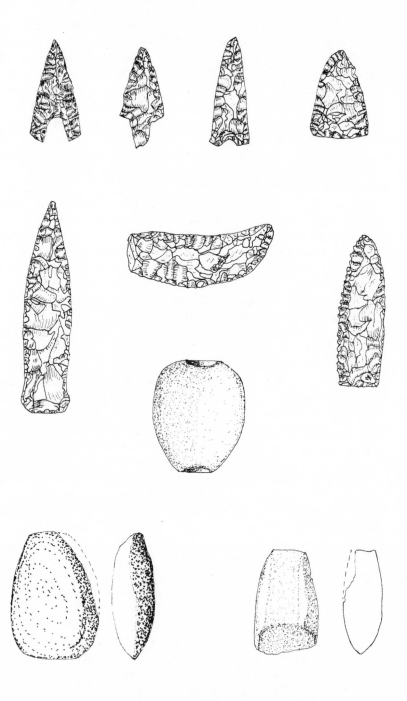

48   Stone artifacts from Merimde beni-Salame. Top row: chipped stone
     projectile points. Second row: chipped stone projectile points and knife
     blade. Third row: groundstone macehead. Fourth row: groundstone celts

found in Upper Egypt), spindle whorls used in weaving, sling stones, hammerstones, manos and metates of basalt and granite, small alabaster palettes for grinding body pigment and a few small stone vases. Although the vases were ground from mottled diorite—a very hard stone—

49 Stone axes from Merimde beni-Salame. Top: groundstone celt. Bottom: chipped stone specimen

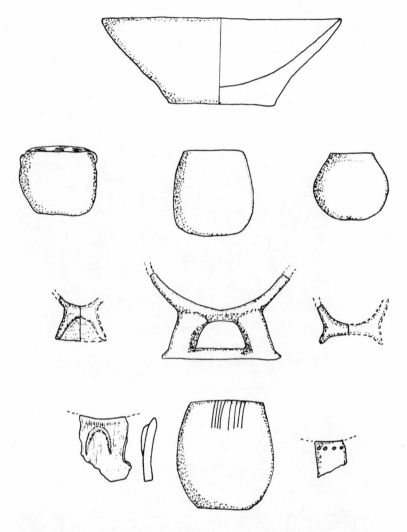

50   Pottery from Merimde beni-Salame. Note the footed forms in center

they reflect a low level of technical competence, especially when compared with the somewhat later products of Naqadan manufacture in
Upper Egypt.

Between 200 and 300 bone, ivory, and horn implements were unearthed at Merimde during Junker's decade there. Most seem to have
been used for dressing and sewing skins. Artifact forms include knife-
like objects, scrapers resembling modern leather-dressing knives, an as-
sortment of needles and awls, bone harpoons, and barbless fish hooks.

A huge quantity of pottery, among the earliest yet known in the Nile Valley, littered the houses, yards, streets, and dumps of the town— 60,000 sherds and 41 whole vessels being found between 1928 and 1932 alone. Pottery, like the bifacial stone industry, shows no prior history of development in Egypt and appears, full-blown, at Merimde with the village farmers in the late sixth millennium B.C. Over a thousand years earlier, as we shall see in Chapter 16, a completely different type of pottery decorated with dots and incisions was spreading across the Sahara as farming and herding peoples moved into the newly greened wastelands around 6000 B.C.

Vessel shapes are usually simple, confined to flat- and concave-bottom dishes and bowls and jars. What little plastic elaboration was done was confined to the creation of footed appendages to support vessels and in the case of some jars and bowls, these were rendered in imitation of human feet—perhaps the earliest example of feet of clay! Other ceramic forms include spouted vessels, carinated vases, conical beakers, chalices, oval and boat-shaped bowls, ring stands for round-bottom jars, ladles, spoons, scoops, and even miniature pots. All pottery at Merimde was made by hand (wheel-made wares did not appear until Archaic times— ca. 3100–2700 B.C.) and all but the finest wares were straw (or chaff) tempered. A very limited number of surface treatments were employed, such as polishing, hand smoothing, coarse and red slipping, and the finest wares were fired a consistent gray and then red slipped. The plainness of Merimde's pottery is yet another variant of an underlying theme that permeates all aspects of its material culture—a theme that sets apart this and later Delta sites from the ornament-ridden and display-oriented culture of Upper Egypt.

Paradoxically, it was Hermann Junker, the Egyptologist and philologist, who laid the groundwork for an archaeological understanding of these two prehistoric life-styles that foreshadow the later historic division between the Two Lands of Upper and Lower Egypt. If Junker was not a trained prehistorian, if he often concerned himself with obscure matters of interpretation and if he never published a final report, his outstanding achievement still must be that he was not only willing to go beyond his own specialty but that he often surpassed the achievements of avowed prehistorians and has left a lasting record of the earliest agricultural settlers in the Nile Valley. It is appropriate that his work has stood for so many generations and that now it is being placed within its proper context by new discoveries of more ancient farming cultures on the desert margins west of the Nile Valley. Such discoveries, which are revolutionizing Egyptian Predynastic archaeology, as we shall see in Chapter 16, owe much of their human ecological orientation to the pioneering research that Gertrude Caton-Thompson initiated in the Fayum two years before Junker began digging Merimde beni-Salame.

13

FEUDS AND FARMERS
IN THE FAYUM

ALTHOUGH MERIMDE is the most important early farming
site in northern Egypt, it was not the first to be recognized. Like so many
other honors in Egyptian archaeology, the credit for that discovery belongs to Gertrude Caton-Thompson. Almost immediately after finishing
Hemamieh, she and her geologist colleague, Elinor Gardner, spent the
winters of 1924–25 and 1925–26 surveying on the northern shore of the
ancient Lake Moeris in the Fayum basin. Today known as the Birket el
Qarun, the lake, which covers an area of about 90 square miles and
attains a maximum depth of 17 feet, lies 60 miles south of Merimde as
the crow flies and 15 miles west of the Nile and is all that remains of a
once great body of water that filled the Fayum in prehistoric times. The
Fayum basin itself is about 147 feet below modern sea level and must be
reckoned one of the more unique pockets of ecological diversity in Egypt.
It encompasses an area of about 680 square miles and was originally
created by a combination of wind erosion, earth movement, and water
action. In recent years the area has made the news as the former home
of a number of important fossil apes dating to late Oligocene times
(about 35 million years ago), one of which, *Aegyptopithecus*, is believed
by paleontologist Elwin Simmons to be a possible precursor of the human
line. The ancestor of today's shallow, swampy Birket el Qarun was
created by a combination of factors between about 7000 and 5000 B.C.,
including an inflow of Nile water through the Hawara Channel and local
runoff caused by the rains of the Neolithic Subpluvial. Over time, the
rains ceased and the Nile gradually cut down through its bed, leaving the
lake high and dry. The Birket el Qarun received a temporary reprieve
from its fate in the nineteenth century B.C. when Pharaoh Amenemhat
III (1842–1797 B.C.) cleared the Hawara Channel and converted the
Fayum into a lushly productive area—a status that it retained down
through Ptolemaic times (305–31 B.C.).

In their first two seasons in the Fayum, Caton-Thompson and Gardner
found abundant evidence of what they took to be Neolithic or farming

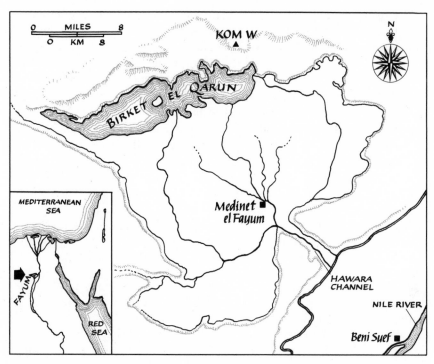

51   Map of the Fayum showing the location of Caton-Thompson's Neolithic
site, Kom "W"

villages along the ancient fossil beaches of the lake. Although, as we
shall see shortly, some of their conclusions have proved incorrect, their
initial reporting of their finds was prompt and exemplary. They were
unable to return to the Fayum for the 1926–27 season but anticipated
resuming their work the following year. But, in Caton-Thompson's own
words:

> Our temporary absence led to disquieting circumstances, so seriously
> affecting, as it turned out, the work ahead that reference to it cannot
> be altogether omitted.
>
> Tranquil in the tradition which forbids appropriation of another
> person's work without inquiry as to their intentions to continue it, I
> found to my dismay, when applying in the spring of 1927 for renewal
> of concession, that, owing to alleged sensational discoveries (a great
> prehistoric cemetery; shelter with breccia ranging from Acheulean
> to Campigny; rows of dolmens; pile dwellings, etc.) by Count de
> Prorok, working unauthorized in our vacated area from the University
> of Michigan Expedition's base, an American expedition had secretly
> applied for, and been virtually accorded the N. Fayum concession.

Prolonged negotiations with the Dept. of Antiquities, so devoid of pre-historians as to be unable to verify the authenticity of the Fayum dis-coveries, resulted in acknowledgement of our moral right to continue the work in which we had led the way, but left undefined the area to be assigned to us. The positions of the sites coveted by the Oriental Institute of Chicago were widespread: no attempt was made from that quarter to alleviate our position; and on arrival in Egypt in November we found ourselves re-alloted a restricted concession within the area we had already exhausted both prehistorically and geologically, sandwiched in between Chicago's western concession near Qasr-el-Sagha, containing the "Palaeolithic cave," and their eastern one near Kom Ashim, containing the "prehistoric cemetery" and "dolmens." . . . In view of the grave inadequacy of this concession, I applied at once for a second one, covering the very difficult ground at the west-end of the lake: this was granted in January.

(Caton-Thompson 1928: 109-110)

Such scholarly chicanery continues to plague archaeology in all areas of the world and it is to Caton-Thompson's credit that she countered it in the most effective way possible—by continuing with her own, careful and scientific work. In the end, she was able to relish her victory, as the inflated claims of the interlopers were proved, one by one, to be totally inaccurate:

My attention has been called to some confusion as to the identity of site arising from allusion to a gypsum-vase factory in the Fayum, in a letter to *The Times* of 13th April from Professor Breasted, describing the Oriental Institute's work there. This place, excavated in January by Mr. Brunton and Dr. K. S. Sandford for the Oriental Institute, is none other than the famous "Palaeolithic" shelter! Situated near Kasr-el-Sagha, some 15 miles from the great Umm es Sewan site, an isolated gypsum worker carried on his trade beneath a sheltering cliff, on a little platform about 10 feet square. The early Old Kingdom date of the little place had been known to me since November, when I was shown in Cairo specimens of the "Acheulean" and "Campignian" flints brought from it by Prorok and Bovier-Lapierre, and recognized them as hand-picks and grinders of early dynastic date, and the "breccia" as consolidated gypsum *debris*. As their Palaeolithic au-thenticity was accepted in Egypt, I sent a private report on the place to the Royal Anthropological Institute. Knowledge of this affair, and of the even more comic "prehistoric cemetery," consisting of entirely natural mounds known to us, make but slight amends for frustration of our prehistoric research. *(Caton-Thompson 1928: 111)*

Notwithstanding her temporary trouble with would-be rivals in the Fayum, the greatest difficulty facing Caton-Thompson had to do with dating her new Neolithic sites. Dating in prehistory is always a hazardous process. We have seen the startling change wrought by carbon-14 dating on our view of the Aterian. Ten years ago new estimates on the two archaeological cultures found by Caton-Thompson in the Fayum had a similarly unexpected result: the chronological order of the periods (Fayum A and Fayum B) was reversed. Fayum A, originally thought to be the parent of Fayum B, suddenly became its descendant. Although the reasons for such a turnabout and its significance may seem initially puzzling, the mistaken dating and interpretation of Fayum A and B were almost inevitable considering the peculiar geological nature of the Fayum basin and the dating techniques available to Caton-Thompson 50 years ago. A final complication arose out of the fact that, in the middle 1920's, no one knew what an early farming culture in northern Egypt should look like. Junker's discoveries at Merimde were still several years in the future and most archaeologists expected to find something closely resembling Petrie's Naqada culture; but this was not to be the case.

The Fayum B sites that Caton-Thompson mistakenly believed to be the latest in her Neolithic series were generally small and lacked ceramics. Their stone tool technology was microlithic in character and old Palaeolithic techniques like backing and truncation persisted. Chipped stone axes were common, suggesting a heavier tree cover than today and hoe-like bifaces were once thought to have been used in agricultural activities, although they would have been equally valuable for digging roots or house or storage pits. What have been called bifacial sickle blades were also found in Fayum B camps, but their use as agricultural implements, in the absence of domesticated plant remains, is highly debatable. Well-made, hollow-base arrowheads provide a link with both Fayum A, Merimden, and Upper Egyptian Predynastic industries.

Fayum A has often been compared to Merimde and presents a striking contrast to the rich Predynastic sites of Upper Egypt. The pottery especially is plain by comparison with the southern wares. It was, of course, all handmade without benefit of the wheel, and constructed from a coarse, straw-tempered paste. Simple shapes such as deep bowls, wide-mouthed jars, footed cups, and rectangular basins were the order of the day. Nowhere do we find the spectacular decorative or technical skill of slightly later Badarian or Amratian ceramicists although some attempts at decoration were made, including burnishing and self slipping or washing—a process that involved slurring the surface of the clay before it was fired in order to produce a creamy, leak-resistant surface. The only other surface modification of note was found on two sherds which bore small, raised studs on their outer faces—motifs common on early Neolithic pottery found in the Sahara. As we shall see shortly, there are hints of other contacts between Fayumis and contemporary desert peoples at this time. Since at least one theory of agricultural/pastoral origins in Egypt sees these economic innovations as introductions from the Sahara, the possibility that the Fayum, itself a kind of oasis, received early stimulation from this quarter cannot be ignored and will be examined more closely in Chapter 16.

Unlike Fayum B sites where no domesticates have yet been found, Fayum A strikes us as a fully agricultural society. Grains of emmer wheat and six row barley filled many of the sunken silos that clustered on the high ground overlooking the small villages. Both of these plants are Middle Eastern domesticates and their presence in fully developed form in Fayum A underscores the speed with which Neolithic economy moved into Egypt during the middle of the Neolithic Subpluvial (ca. 5000 B.C.). Not only Middle Eastern plants, but domesticated animals abounded in Fayum A sites, including sheep or goat, cattle and pig. Despite the influx of essentially foreign domesticates, many elements of the older Epipalaeolithic life-style (see Chapter 6) persisted and a wide variety of animals that abounded in the still unspoiled lacustrine environment were hunted and snared, including fish, hippo, crocodile, elephant, and unidentified carnivores.

The dual agricultural/pastoral and hunting-fishing-gathering economy was reflected in the stone tool industry of Fayum A sites. The fine, hollow-base arrowheads and well-made, translucent groundstone points echo the survival of hunting ways, although microlithic implements were fast going out of fashion. Chipped stone axes with ground bits or cutting edges remained in use, although we cannot actually say whether they were used for woodcutting or as hoes or weapons. Based on the great numbers of wild game present, however, it does seem likely that at least a light forest cover of tamarisk trees and lesser undergrowth continued to thrive around the lake's perimeter, providing the Fayum A peoples with a source of firewood to warm them in winter, cook their food, and bake their pottery. Most of the groundstone implements found in Fayum A sites reflect the agricultural and craft components of the society and include milling stones for grinding grain, mortars, hammerstones, burnishers for polishing pottery, and disc-shaped spindle whorls for weaving the flax that was already grown in the area. Ornamentation, although sparse by Upper Egyptian standards, is reflected by small pigment palettes and stone beads, while a few fragmented stone bowls suggest the beginning of this craft in northern Egypt. Unfortunately, no graves or building remains were discovered in either A or B sites by Caton-Thompson.

She originally believed that she could date the prehistoric material from around the Birket el Qarun by its relative position above modern lake level. She reasoned correctly that at some time in the past water from the Nile had breached the Hawara Channel and caused the lake to raise its level considerably. Then, she believed, the waters gradually receded until they reached today's level. Following this line of reasoning, cultural remains associated with high fossil beaches (as she called the old

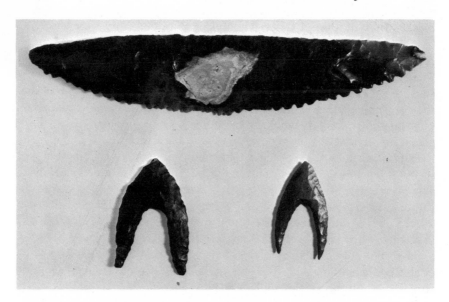

52   Serrated sickle (top) and hollow-base points, typical tools of Caton-
     Thompson's Fayum A Neolithic culture

beach lines left by the ancient lake) were earlier than remains on lower
beaches.

From the beginning, not everyone agreed with this interpretation of
the geologic history of Fayum Lake. In 1926, Sir Flinders Petrie cited
convincing historical evidence that the lake had risen and fallen on a
number of different occasions, a fact that seemed to contradict the basic
assumption of continuous decline upon which Caton-Thompson's scheme
of relative dating was based. Petrie cautioned that

> both physically and historically it seems clear that there is evidence
> for a lake rising with the Nile rise. The interpretation of geological
> evidence for the opposite course can hardly be weighed until full con-
> sideration has been given to the traces likely to remain for variable
> lake-levels. *(Petrie 1926: 327)*

Ironically, Petrie's warning, which was generally unheeded in the light
of his precipitous withdrawal from Egyptian archaeology in the same
year, was to be substantiated by carbon-14 dates forty years later. But
at the time the research was conducted, Caton-Thompson's conclusions
about the relative ages of her A and B cultures seemed eminently logical
and were widely accepted.

Fayum A was located above the 33 foot beach, while Fayum B, by contrast, was scattered between the 33 foot and 13 foot beaches and reached
as low as the 7 foot beach. As we have seen already, Fayum B sites
were often smaller than Fayum A localities and lacked pottery; for these

reasons they impressed Caton-Thompson as rather "impoverished." Although some archaeologists suggested that Fayum B was a logical predecessor of Fayum A, she rejected this interpretation because of her belief that association with fossil beaches was the best criterion for dating the relative ages of her sites. What Caton-Thompson did not know was that the rise of the Birket el Qarun was neither a sudden nor a single event, but apparently took as much as 2,000 years to accomplish. Thus, the B peoples preceded the A peoples and gradually moved their camps up the shores of the growing lake rather than following a declining body of water down toward the bottom of the basin as she originally believed. The proof of this interpretation has been provided by a series of carbon-14 dates that place Fayum B between 6150 ± 130 and 5190 ± 120 B.C., while the earliest date for Fayum A, so far, is 4441 ± 115 B.C. (a reading which, if "corrected," can be extended back to about 5000 B.C.).

Based not only on its new dates, but on its tools and the nature of its eroded settlements, Fayum B seems quite similar to other Epipalaeolithic sites in the Egyptian and Sudanese Nile Valley, like El Kab, with its predominantly microlithic stone industry, lack of pottery, and small settlements—just what we should expect for a fishing, hunting, and gathering group. Nevertheless, there are elements in the tool industry that foreshadow the A culture, including so-called bifacial sickle blades and the beautiful tanged and winged hollow-based arrowheads characteristic of early Predynastic cultures in both Upper and Lower Egypt (i.e., Badarian and Merimden). The presence of such links, however weak, raises the possibility that the development of agricultural society, in the Fayum at least, was an indigenous affair in which essentially Middle Eastern domesticates (wheat, barley, sheep, goats, pigs, and cattle) were adopted by the Fayum A descendants of the Epipalaeolithic Fayum B peoples (what Wendorf calls Qarunian) some time shortly after 5000 B.C. What relation, if any, the development of agriculture in the Fayum had to do with its appearance at about the same time at Merimde in the Delta is still an unanswerable question.

By contrast, the widespread distribution of hollow-base arrowheads throughout Egypt between about 5000 and 4000 B.C. might suggest that this invention was somehow linked to the Neolithic Subpluvial and the changing cultural conditions that followed quickly in its wake. We can speculate that these distinctive points perhaps originated at the very end of the Epipalaeolithic (ca. 7000–6000 B.C.) as hunting and gathering peoples repopulated much of the Sahara. They appear in the Fayum in Caton-Thompson's B sites and in the oasis of Kharga where the name Bedouin microlithic has been applied. As we shall see in Chapter 16 there is now some evidence that their way of life was altered within the space of perhaps 300 to 500 years by the spread of developed pastoral/agricultural economy throughout northeastern Africa after 6000 B.C.

On the surface, at least, the Fayum A peoples and the Merimdens shared much in common, but since most of these similarities involve areas of economy and technology linked to village farming, we should not attribute too much significance to them. If I were to guess, I would say that there is a fairly good chance that the Merimdens were immigrants from a nearby area where village farming was well established (either southern Palestine or the Libyan coast), while the Fayum A peoples were indigenes who learned and adapted to the new ways of what prehistorian V. Gordon Childe called the Neolithic Revolution. Unfortunately, when we reduce the argument over the origins of Egyptian agriculture to its most basic components, we must admit that, at this time, given the evidence available, we are not able to solve this problem and in fact it may never be soluble by archaeologists. Regardless of their origins and differences, the communities of Merimde and Fayum A are united in their common lack of stress upon the ornamental—a basic theme that differentiates them already from the Badarians to the south (ca. 5500–4000 B.C.). In this sense, the Predynastic Fayumis belong more to the world of the north, of the Delta and the lands of the Mediterranean, than to the cultures of Upper Egypt. Contacts with other lands are attested by objects like pierced marine shells from both the Mediterranean and Red Seas and by attractive beads of green amazonite that possibly came from either the Eastern Desert or from the faraway Tibesti Massif—deep in the heart of the Sahara. These latter goods indicate ties with desert peoples, ties that will bear watching. They also suggest something of the complex internal nature of Fayumi society. In addition to such imported ornaments, Fayum A sites have yielded an impressive number of locally obtained ostrich eggshell and stone beads. These goods taken together stand out in a material culture, like Merimde's, otherwise unnoted for ornamentation or display. Although it is traditional for archaeologists to interpret such goods as trade items or ornaments, there is a wider frame of social reference within which they might have been used, namely as important items in social networks of exchange. The use of seashells as important gifts used in interregional trade and even as a kind of early money is well attested among small, traditional societies all over the world; the famous kula ring—a quasi-ritual trading circuit in Melanesia; the highly prized and hoarded dentalia shells of the Yoruk Indians of northern California: the shells used in the wampum of the Indians of eastern North America; and the finely graded shell money of the Kapauku Papuans of modern New Guinea. If the contact among the three Predynastic traditions of Egypt (Upper Egypt, the Delta, and the desert) was an important force in the emergence of a national Egyptian culture with the first dynasties, then it is absolutely essential that we understand the social and economic context of goods like beads—goods that point toward social exchange and the whole body of ideas, relationships, and even myths that often accompany exchange.

If future archaeologists are ever able to approach such sociological questions, it is clear that they will have to avoid the temptation to conduct limited vertical tests or "sondages" and clear and accurately record large horizontal areas of sites. Such an approach was begun by Caton-Thompson 50 years ago when she carefully excavated Fayum A settlements like Kom W with its 300 hearths and grain silos replete with plant remains and, in one case, an intact wooden sickle inset with flint blades. As at Hemamieh, the groundwork toward a fuller contextual understanding of the past was firmly laid by intelligent fieldwork.

> The mound was first planned to a 1-ft. V.I. (Vertical Interval), and fixed bases were established. On this framework excavation proceeded on a latitude and longitude system, my ten men clearing shoulder to shoulder methodically across the mound, in measured strips 160 ft. long and 20 ft. wide, pegged out at 5-ft. intervals, with checks on the general contours by dumpy-level readings on the pegs. Each strip was worked in layers until true bottom was reached. Each object was given a section letter, latitude and longitude figure and vertical depth, and its position recorded on squared paper, and in field book. When each section was stripped, the bottom was levelled and a north to south section across the mound made for every 20 ft. of longitude. Objects may thus be considered in their relative position *above the bottom*, which, rather than relative *depth from the top*, has always seemed to me the desideratum in stratigraphical work.
>
> *(Caton-Thompson 1926: 311)*

When more prehistoric settlements in the Fayum have been excavated with the same care, and when today's sophisticated analytical techniques are applied to problems like the nature of the transition from food gathering to food producing—from Fayum B to Fayum A—we will have answered one of the most important questions in Egyptian prehistory. For now it seems clear that the Fayum, although a special and distinctive ecosystem, could possibly hold the key to the nature of this crucial transition since it lies midway between the desert and the valley, being at once an oasis and a lake which was occasionally linked to the Nile. Thus, the opportunity for the mixing of adaptive responses (i.e., of hunting-gathering-fishing and food producing) during the earlier part of the Neolithic Subpluvial (ca. 7000–5000 B.C.) was great and the probability of hybridized economic systems, if not entire cultures, is likely.

14

EL OMARI: THE ROOTS
OF LOCAL TRADITION

THE PLEASANT Egyptian winter had just given way to the heat and sandstorms of the annual *khamsin* when the International Congress of Geography and Ethnology convened its eleventh session in Cairo in April 1925. For the young Egyptian nation, struggling to free itself of British control and establish its reputation as a respected member of the world community, it was an important occasion. King Fuad I originally had proposed that the conference be held in Cairo to commemorate the founding of the Royal Geographical Society of Egypt in 1875 by his father, Khedive Ismail, the same ruler who had triggered the British occupation through his financial misadventures. After the First World War, Egypt managed to pry a large measure of independence from Britain and its king was anxious to play the role of an enlightened, modern constitutional monarch. It took three years to plan the congress and invite scholars from all over the world. At the time the congress was held, both the president and vice-president of the Egyptian Royal Geographical Society—George Foucart and Pierre Lacau—were archaeologists.

Father R. P. Paul Bovier-Lapierre, who presented two important papers on his prehistoric researches near Cairo, was particularly generous in his praise of Pierre Lacau, Director General of the Antiquities Service. According to Bovier-Lapierre, Lacau contrasted to most of his predecessors since de Morgan for the interest he displayed in Egyptian prehistory, and his friendship had greatly facilitated prehistoric surveys and excavations around Cairo. Father Bovier-Lapierre, who, as we have seen earlier, earned a rebuke from Caton-Thompson in 1928 for his mistaken identification of early Dynastic Fayumi flints as Palaeolithic, had conducted work around Cairo since 1918. Unlike Caton-Thompson or Junker, who often engaged in long-term excavations at key sites, such as Hemamieh and Merimde, Bovier-Lapierre favored short surveys and small test excavations and seldom if ever published thorough accounts of his fieldwork. Nevertheless, thanks to his excursions a number of important Neolithic and Palaeolithic sites were discovered in the suburbs of Cairo.

In exploring the area around Helwan, a town about 23 kilometers south of Cairo, Bovier-Lapierre was introduced to a young Egyptian mineralogist, Amin el Omari, who had just returned from school in Europe. El Omari proved to be an enthusiastic student of archaeology and Bovier-Lapierre seems to have had high hopes that he would go on to establish himself as a leading professional archaeologist in his own country. During the spring of 1924 el Omari discovered a large Neolithic site just northeast of his native town and intended to begin excavations there the following season. Then tragedy struck. Amin el Omari became ill and died.

In the winter of 1925 Bovier-Lapierre himself resumed work at the site, which he named in honor of his young protégé. Coming as it did fully two years before Junker's discovery of Merimde and at roughly the same time Caton-Thompson and Gardner were exploring the Fayum, Bovier-Lapierre's preliminary sounding in the settlements and graves of El Omari marks one of the first attempts to discover a Lower Egyptian counterpart to the Predynastic cultures of Upper Egypt. Regrettably, the fifteen days spent at the site and his two brief published accounts fall far short of the standards set by Junker. Twenty years after Bovier-Lapierre abandoned the site, Fernand Debono reopened excavations in the middle of the Second World War. In 1943 conditions were less than optimal: according to Debono, the indirect effects of the war had menaced the site with total destruction. Under such adverse circumstances it is little wonder that Debono's excavation techniques suffered from haste, but his failure to publish more than the briefest accounts of his work has left many aspects of Omari a mystery. Debono spent three seasons in the field—six months in 1943–1944, four months in 1948, and a brief season in 1952. The site is, or rather was, one of the most important late prehistoric localities in Lower Egypt and parallels Merimde and Fayum A in many respects, reinforcing the view that the north possessed its own distinctive cultural tradition throughout Predynastic times. Sadly, the lack of published information on excavation techniques, artifacts, houses, and graves prevents a detailed comparison with Merimde. Even Debono's longest preliminary report is substantially shorter than the shortest account given by Junker of Merimde. One can imagine the ghost of Sir Flinders Petrie railing from his grave against French excavation techniques.

Properly speaking, El Omari is not one site but an archaeological locality consisting of three settlements and two separate but related cemeteries, all of which are located near the town of Helwan at the foot of the mountain of Gebel Tura, famed in pharaonic times as a source for the fine limestone in which the pyramids were encased. In a way, the location of the main settlement, Omari A, recalls that of the so-called

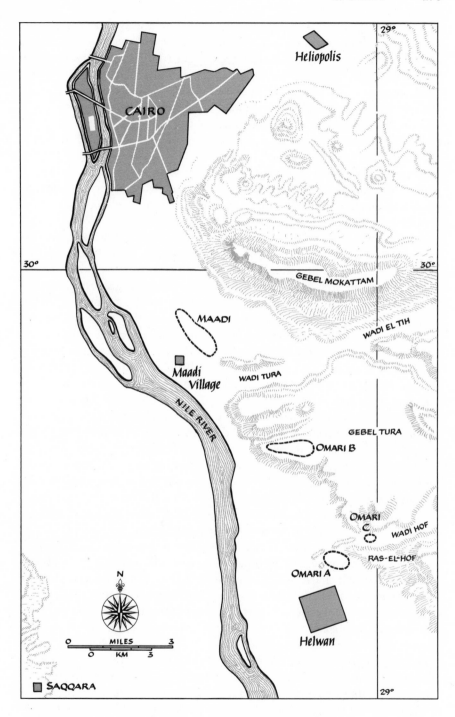

53 Map showing the distribution of Predynastic ("Neolithic") sites around Cairo

Predynastic town site at Hierakonpolis; it lies on a gravel terrace along a major local drainage system (the Wadi Hof) at the southwest (upriver) corner of the wadi's mouth near a rocky spur (the Ras-el-Hof). Omari B lies north of the mouth of the wadi on a 300-foot-high terrace of the Gebel Hof, while a third, badly eroded and obviously late settlement with two accompanying cemeteries is situated in a side branch of the wadi's mouth. For the sake of convenience, I will call this site Omari C.

Because these sites were excavated at separate times by different archaeologists and because they were recorded and published incompletely, it is nearly impossible to date them accurately, let alone reconstruct their original plan and extent. Without exaggeration it may be said that most of the problems raised by El Omari were created by its excavators.

Even Omari's dates are hotly debated. Elise Baumgartel, ever the champion of Upper Egyptian cultural priority, took the extreme position that all the sites might actually date as late as early Dynastic times. Although it is true that there were apparently Dynastic graves and buildings on the El Omari sites, the balance of evidence supports Debono's original claim that the area was first occupied around 4000 B.C. in Naqada I or Amratian times, Debono initially based his conclusion on certain ceramic and lithic styles as well as a hunch that Omari was a slightly more developed form of Merimden and Fayumi Neolithic cultures. In the early days of radiocarbon dating, his conclusions seemed dashed by a single, unexpectedly late date from Omari A of 3305 $\pm$ 230 B.C. This date, in turn, led to all sorts of speculation that the Omaris were culturally retarded folk who somehow managed to remain unaffected by the social, political, and economic developments of late Predynastic times. The fact that some late material was found on many of the sites and that the recording had left much to be desired contributed to the general confusion over the place and importance of El Omari. The recent revolution in carbon-14 dating has, ironically, done much to vindicate Debono's original opinion, since a revised version of the old date comes out to around 4000 B.C. This date makes it possible to envision Omari A as a successor to Merimde and Fayum A, as originally claimed by Debono, while the stylistic characteristics of the Omari B artifacts suggest that the site is roughly contemporary with the Early Gerzean (Naqada II) culture of Upper Egypt. Both the artifacts of Omari C and the fact that its cemeteries are separated from the settlement proper suggest that this community dates from the Late Gerzean or Protodynastic epoch (ca. 3300–3100 B.C.) and remained occupied into Archaic times (ca. 3100–2700 B.C.). The three settlements taken together give an insight into the fortunes of the same group of people over a thousand years, providing a rare look at the evolution of a regional subculture, and at the same time present a useful contrast to contemporary Amratian and Gerzean cultures to the south. If you look at a map it is easy to get the impression that the inhabitants of the three Omari settlements were exploiting the large alluvial embayment of which Helwan is today the chief town. Although the three sites may overlap somewhat in time, it is most likely that each peaked in succeeding periods as the focus of local population shifted in response to environmental, economic, and political pressures.

The village of Omari A covered a large area (just how large is, unfortunately, not known) and yielded remains of more than 100 circular and oval huts with sunken or semisubterranean floors reminiscent of those found by Junker at Merimde. When Debono removed the fill from these dwellings he found their floors covered with a heavy, woven matting covered, in turn, by a coating of clay. Although it is generally believed that this situation reflects an intentional practice of building a prepared clay floor over a heavy mat foundation, the possibility that the clay covering simply accumulated as the wattle and daub walls of the superstructure disintegrated cannot be overlooked. In order to interpret properly such archaeological minutiae, however, we would need to have detailed ground plans and cross-section drawings of the huts—information not provided in the published reports. Around the sides of the house pits the excavators occasionally found remains of the wooden posts used to support the superstructures of the buildings. As at Merimde and Fayum A sites, smaller clay and basket-lined pits were used for storing grain and other household items. The arrangement of houses within Omari A recalls that of Merimde and suggests an open or barnyard pattern of settlement. In some cases the well-preserved remains of reed fences, virtually indistinguishable from *zeribas* found in contemporary rural Egyptian villages, emphasize the ways in which the people of Omari A defined their social space. The small size of Omari houses and their distinctive separation from one another and the degree to which economic activities were self-contained within one's own yard, suggest a pattern of residence that revolved about the small, nuclear family (father, mother, and offspring), and reflect the basically egalitarian way of life of Predynastic Lower Egyptians that sets them apart from their more political and status-oriented neighbors to the south. Omari A seems to have flourished for a long time, probably for several hundred years, and experienced settlement drift. This factor, linked with the rather loose control exerted by the site's excavator, makes it virtually impossible to determine if Debono was correct in reconstructing two distinct periods of occupation.

The fact that the people of Omari A apparently buried their dead within the village (the contemporaneity of graves and settlement has been disputed) echoes the custom at Merimde and serves as yet another reminder of the major differences between Lower and Upper Egyptian Predynastic traditions in the fourth millennium B.C. Individuals of all ages were placed in round pits at Omari A, wrapped in mats, animal skins, or fabrics—perhaps according to their age, sex, or occupation—and sometimes protected by an extra covering of branches and mats. The dead were laid out in a contracted position on their left sides with their heads to the south and faces west—the traditional Dynastic Egyptian Land of the Dead. This orientation was common in Upper Egypt at the time but was not yet evident in earlier Merimden society, and may indicate a diffusion of ideas connected with the mortuary cult from south to north or, perhaps, merely reflects the closer proximity of Omari A to the valley proper.

Grave offerings were scarce and usually amounted to a single jar, although one person had a small clay box and another held in his hand a carved wooden staff that V. Gordon Childe believes marked him as a local ruler. Although it is hard to agree that this man was a dead king, the symbolism of the staff of authority (common in later Dynastic and even modern rural contexts) as well as the presence of greater numbers of imported ornaments like stone and shell beads contrasts with Merimde and Fayum A and suggests the beginnings of those social differences that would later become a hallmark of the highly class-conscious Egyptian society. Nevertheless, by comparison with contemporary Upper Egyptian Amratian and Early Gerzean society, social and economic stratification was still poorly developed in the north.

The staple crops of Omari, well preserved in the arid soil, included emmer wheat; an evolved type of barley (Hordeum vulgare); and, for the domesticated animals, fodder vetch (Vicia sativa). The finding of a possible grain of club wheat (Triticum compactum) not known in Egypt until Classical times once stirred a storm of controversy; but it is now believed to be a later contaminant. Edible fruits including sycamore figs and dates (Phoenix dactylifera) and wild sugar (Saccharum spontaneum) probably satisfied the sweet tooth of Omaris and indicate that the ancient Egyptian fondness for fresh fruit precedes the pharaohs by at least a thousand years. Flax (Linum usitatissimum) was present and almost certainly woven, foreshadowing one of the great industries of Dynastic Egypt. One bunch of flowers found in a grave (a custom echoed 2,500 years later in Tutankhamon's tomb) has been identified as Pulicaria undulata, and numerous specimens of tamarisk wood were found scattered about the village, as in Amratian Locality 14 at Hierakonpolis, indicating one use to which the ubiquitous axes were put. As in Fayum A and Merimde, domestic animals included pig, goat, cow, and possibly dog, suggesting both a barnyard and local pastoral pattern of animal domestication was being followed. In fact, judging from the abundant garbage, the pigs must have fared rather well in the yards of the ancient Omari. By contrast, grazing animals like cattle and goats would probably have been taken out daily to areas where pasturage was available, at least after the winter rains when the desert margins bloomed. During more arid periods of the year, these animals would either have been kept closer to home and fed on fodder vetch or grazed in the abundant grasslands of the nearby Delta. Goats, being more thorough browsers than sheep or cattle, could have ranged a bit more freely. We can imagine that the timing of such activities resembled that known from contemporary Middle Eastern villages where it reflects seasonably available pasturages.

Although primarily agriculturalists and herders, the people of Omari hunted and trapped ducks, ostriches, crocodiles, hippos, and antelopes and obtained large quantities of fish (especially the old Palaeolithic favorites *Claria* and *Synodant*) from the Nile. The presence of antelope and fish emphasizes once more the degree to which the Neolithic peoples took advantage of a variety of different ecological niches and suggests an economic continuity with older Epipalaeolithic traditions which, judging from Bovier-Lapierre's reports, must have flourished in the region. From a cultural point of view the seasonality of Omari economy would have brought the people into periodic contact with pastoral nomads in the Red Sea Hills and exposed them to different ideas and dangers.

Direct evidence for such contact is reflected by a variety of imported ornamental objects—usually pendants and beads of Red Sea gastropods and hard, attractive stones. Local products were also used for ornamentation and possibly for exchange as well: objects like ostrich eggshell discs, cut bone, fish spines, mother of pearl, and even unusually shaped fossils. Bits of ocher found inside Omari A huts were probably used for pigment as in Upper Egypt, where fancy slate grinding palettes were a hallmark of Predynastic culture.

Another characteristic that leads some prehistorians to see Omari ties to Palestine is a shift away from heavy reliance on bifacial techniques back to the simpler flake and blade traditions. Flaked stone axes with ground bits, similar to those in Fayum A, were still common, as were serrated sickle blades and the ubiquitous hollow base and triangular projectile points and a few tanged specimens. When we consider the high percentage of points overall, the frequency of hunting and/or conflict must have been marked. Groundstone implements included the familiar hammerstones, manos, metates, spindle whorls, grooved "fishnet" weights and a single polished ax of serpentine. A number of bone tools, especially eyed needles, echo the emphasis on weaving and sewing seen in the various skins, mats, lengths of cord and string and flax seeds found in the settlement and graves. Fish hooks of shell and horn abounded at Omari and show that fish were taken with solitary methods as well as in nets and wires. Mollusk shells doubled as scoops and spoons while whole ostrich eggs, pierced at one end, probably served as portable water canteens for journeys into the nearby desert.

The pottery of Omari A fits well within the general Deltaic ceramic tradition seen at Merimde and Fayum, except that it is technically somewhat superior. Colors run to red, brown, and black and surfaces were smoothed and occasionally burnished to produce lustrous surfaces—a possible Upper Egyptian influence. Deliberate ornamentation was absent. Omari pottery shows sufficient regularity of form and consistency of shape to suggest to some that it might have been turned on a hand turnette or slow wheel. Even if this were so, however, we should not imagine that pottery production was as systematized or as professionalized as in later Dynastic times when introduction of the true potter's wheel turned this home-oriented craft into a full-time specialty. A variety of vessels, reflecting the wide range of functions now performed by ceramics, were discovered at Omari, including ovoid vases, narrow-mouthed vases, goblets, cylindrical containers, pans with flaring and concave sides, two- and three-footed bowls and vases (a link to earlier Deltaic ceramics), pots with lug handles for ease of transportation, large storage jars and a large number of coarse ware forms for more workaday jobs.

The site of Omari B was quite similar to Omari A though even less extensively investigated and reported. There is, however, one outstanding difference in its location that serves to point up the dependence of these later prehistoric Lower Egyptians on an assured water supply. The site was located on a high terrace 300 feet above the floor of the Wadi Hof, just north of Omari A. Apparently the vital factor influencing the location of the B settlement was the proximity of two natural catchment basins which, at the time of exploration in the early 1920's, still contained water year-round. Such catchments would have provided ready and dependable supplies of water away from the river and attracted plant and animal life—functioning as kinds of mini-oases. Their use in Omari B times (perhaps the middle fourth millennium B.C.) might indicate an adaptation to diminishing rainfall, a defensive measure, or simply a desire to exploit every possible environmental niche since proximity to these basins provided proof against failure of rainfall while permitting access to desert animals like the antelope and gazelle, which, like man, were attracted by a relatively permanent water supply.

The locality I am calling Omari C is the least well reported and probably the latest of the lot. Properly speaking, this is a settlement that has been heavily eroded but which has shown signs of oval post and wicker-work houses and storage pits and two or more cemeteries separate from the village. The settlement yielded carbonized wheat and barley and a stone tool assemblage consisting of small blade tools, knives, scrapers and chisel-shaped arrowheads. These latter artifacts are known from reliefs from the Archaic and Old Kingdom period and, along with the separate cemeteries, give an impression that Omari C is late—perhaps even early Dynastic. Its location in the Wadi Hof itself further reinforces this date, since it indicates that rainfall and the sudden freshets it once brought were no longer important factors governing site placement.

The cemeteries themselves lay to the south and west of the village. The graves were shallow, round pits topped by roughly circular mounds of small stones. The dead were buried in a crouched or flexed position with their hands before their faces, but were not oriented in any particular direction as at Omari A. Bodies were wrapped in mats or cloth and occasionally accompanied by a pottery jar, mussel or snail shells, microblades, decayed organic matter (perhaps leather) and, in one case, an agate bead necklace. The presence of hearths and small circles of stones on top of several graves reminds us of the ceremonies that were performed on behalf of the dead—and the living—on top of the freshly closed grave: the ritual of feeding the dead. While Omari C graves might, as some have argued, be early Dynastic, if they are this late they hint at a tremendous Lower Egyptian conservatism and continuity and suggest that from a cultural standpoint the unification of the Two Lands was not a sudden event but rather a long process and that regional populations like those around Helwan survived intact throughout much of the prehistoric period on into historic times. Perhaps it was this very continuity that gave the nomes or provinces of historic Egypt their sense of unity and tradition as separate groupings within the Dynastic state.

15

COPPER, CATTLE,
AND STORAGE CELLARS:
THE MERCHANTS OF MAADI

FOR MORE THAN a thousand years, between 4000 and 3000 B.C., the people of the Omari district passed their lives in small towns of domed huts, tended their fields of wheat and barley and bred sheep, goats, cattle, and pigs—in short, lived a life but little changed from that of their Neolithic predecessors at Merimde and in the Fayum. Through the centuries the changes that did occur were gradual—almost imperceptible—as new ideas about wealth, power, and the afterlife slowly filtered into their society. To the south, the Gerzean people of Upper Egypt built fancier tombs, manufactured and accumulated more wealth and, eventually, launched a successful invasion of the north; but such events seem to have mattered little to the people of El Omari. Although they apparently borrowed the custom of burial in separate cemeteries from their Upper Egyptian neighbors, the people of Omari resisted change and managed to remain outside the cultural mainstream of the new pharaonic order for as much as a century or two after the unification of Egypt around 3100 B.C. Because Omari was apparently so conservative, it is difficult if not impossible to generalize from what was happening there to all of Lower Egypt—a land of surprising geographical and cultural contrasts—in the last five centuries before the emergence of Egyptian civilization.

The site of Maadi, located only 10 kilometers north of El Omari on a low, narrow ridge in the mouth of the Wadi el Tih, although roughly contemporary with the later B and C occupations of Omari, represents a different and vastly more dynamic adaptation to life in Lower Egypt in the late fourth millennium B.C. On the surface it displays many of the typical characteristics of a Lower Egyptian Predynastic farming village, but the evidence unearthed there by Oswald Menghin and Mustafa Amer, between 1930 and 1935, reveals an emphasis on trade, metallurgy, and foreign contacts unknown in other northern sites like El Omari. In a way, it is a real pity that Menghin and Amer never published a definitive report on Maadi and that their interpretations have been so open to criticism. Much like Omari, Maadi has suffered from the lack of concise reporting and problems of recording that cast doubt on the dating of many finds.

Between approximately 3600 and 3000 B.C. a number of innovations appeared at Maadi that heralded Egypt's entry into a greater world *oecumene* or cultural sphere that stretched from the far-off lands of the western Mediterranean to the eastern marches of the Indus Valley. In a way, Maadi is unique among the known Predynastic sites of Egypt; its life was dominated by trade as no site in Egypt before, and few since. Its location along the Wadi el Tih, the principal historic route to the copper mines of Sinai, as well as the presence of foreign house types and pottery, domesticated donkeys, elaborate storage facilities, and a well-developed copper industry all attest the new importance of trade and exchange in late Predynastic Egyptian society.

Although the impact of foreign trade hit both Lower and Upper Egypt about the same time (just after 3600 B.C.), its effect was far from uniform, especially in the north. There, because of the greater distances that separated settlements than in Upper Egypt and because Lower Egyptian towns and villages were not linked by a single channel of the Nile but widely dispersed along the fan-shaped Delta tributaries, access to routes of communication was unequal. Thus, while some communities like Maadi felt the effects of foreign trade strongly, others like El Omari seem to have been little affected. By contrast, in Upper Egypt, although some communities doubtless had better access to trade than others, this problem was not geographical since most Gerzean towns were close to the main channel of the Nile River; rather it was sociological and political.

In Maadi's case, there can be little doubt that the site enjoyed a highly favorable geographical position with access not only to the mainstream of the Nile just south of where it branches into the Delta, but to the coast of the Mediterranean and to the desert frontiers to the east through the Wadi el Tih. Conversely, it might have been the very prosperity of Maadi that isolated the Omari district and which accounts for its apparent poverty and conservatism. Later, Maadi's favored position at the apex of the Delta was successfully imitated by capitals of Egypt from ancient Memphis to modern Cairo.

One of the most striking examples of foreign contacts at Maadi is a house type apparently imported from southern Palestine. Although most of the dwellings in the 45-acre settlement were of the usual Lower Egyptian variety—oval in shape with post walls and frames of mud-daubed wickerwork—Maadi is unique among the villages of prehistoric Egypt in possessing true underground houses. Since such structures are present at several sites around Beersheba in southern Palestine but otherwise foreign to Egypt, archaeologists believe them to be imports and perhaps even the actual houses of aliens resident at Maadi. The struc-

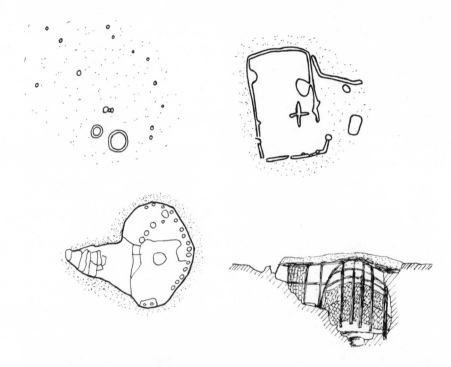

54   Selected houses from Maadi. Top row: post pattern, wall trench structure
(possible corral). Bottom row: subterranean structure with author's
reconstruction of interior

tures were dug 2 to 3 meters into subsoil and attained dimensions as
great as 3 by 4.8 meters. Entrance was gained through a slanting passage-
way whose steps were sometimes faced with stone. Around the interior
of the pit, posts were driven into the floor to support a roof that must
have been constructed of light materials like woven mats, the remains
of which were found inside some of the buildings. In their centers, these
subterranean dwellings contained sunken hearths, and plenty of living
debris was found during excavations supporting the claim of Menghin
and Amer that these buildings were actual houses and not, as some have
argued, ceremonial structures akin to the *kivas* of the Pueblo Indians of
the American Southwest.

But it was not just in the presence of underground houses that the
settlement pattern of Maadi displayed evidence of foreign contacts. The
ancient inhabitants of the site were unusually concerned about the storage of goods. At earlier Lower Egyptian sites (with the single exception
of Fayum A localities) storage pits and jars were associated with individual households and although such residential storage bins also existed
at Maadi, there were also two specialized storage zones located at oppo-

site ends of the site. On the southern border were large, underground storage cellars while on the northern fringe stood rows of great storage jars (known by the Greek name, *pithoi*), which were buried up to their rims in the subsoil.

The storage cellars were 1 to 2 meters deep and attained a maximum length of almost 4 meters. Large *pithoi* covered with stone lids were occasionally sunk into the floors, and there was evidence that some cellars at least had formerly been roofed over with light timbers. The use of a crudely built stone retaining wall in one cellar is one of the earliest instances of stone employed as a building material. Some cellars were linked together, suggesting the growing wealth of their former owners; and, although many had been disturbed or filled with trash in later times, some fortunately still contained portions of their original contents—a valuable clue to the types of goods in which the entrepreneurs of Maadi once dealt. Sometimes the sunken storage jars contained grain, and in several cases as many as 12 pots were still lying in place. One cellar that was still sealed contained a number of well-made stone jars and vases, carnelian beads, and a decayed, unidentifiable white substance. The presence of well-made stone jars at Maadi indicates that at least some sites in Lower Egypt had finally attained the technical competence in stone grinding that had since Amratian times (ca. 4000–3500 B.C.) been a hallmark of Upper Egyptian culture. The Maadi products were both well made and attractive and manufactured from a variety of stones, including granite, gneiss, diorite, imported Fayumi basalt, limestone, and alabaster. The most common shapes were elongated cylinders with flat rims, small handles and flaring, ringlike bases. Without doubt, many of the fancy stone vessels stored in Maadi's cellars were capital investments intended to back an elaborate system of exchange. For more workaday tasks, local limestone was roughly shaped into dishes, bowls, cups, and lamps.

The carnelian beads that were found in the same sealed cellar were almost certainly made from imported materials—possibly from the Eastern Desert—and might well have been manufactured abroad and brought into the site by nomads in the course of their seasonal wanderings. The attractive red-orange, translucent color of carnelian caused it to become a highly sought-after material in the ancient Middle East and South Asia during the fourth and third millennia B.C., and it enjoyed the additional advantage of being easily transportable and relatively scarce. For such reasons, it may well have served as a type of primitive currency.

Even more useful than stone bowls and carnelian beads in illustrating Maadi's foreign connections is the so-called Palestinian pottery found there. As an item that is plentiful and easily shaped and decorated, pottery frequently is studied by archaeologists for evidence of ethnically or regionally distinctive cultural patterns. Thirty-five years ago Dr. Helene

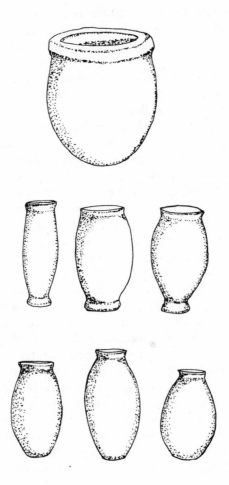

55   Stone and ceramic vessels from Maadi South. Top: alabaster vase. Middle:
ring-based red ware pots. Bottom: black ware pots

Kantor of the Oriental Institute of the University of Chicago examined
the pottery from Maadi in an attempt to trace the site's foreign relations. Although her analysis was carried out in an era before the development of modern techniques of radiochemical testing of clay and
mineral sources and although statistical techniques could not be employed because of the way Maadi had been excavated, Kantor's study
has shed important light on the role of trade in late Predynastic Lower
Egypt. The pots and sherds that she identified as imports included the
familiar black-topped red ware of Upper Egypt, hardly a surprise considering El Gerzeh, the type site for the Gerzean period (ca. 3600–3100
B.C.) lies only 30 kilometers south of Maadi. In addition to the expected

southern imports like pottery and the ubiquitous slate pigment palettes, however, Maadi contained several ceramic types that, like its underground houses, have precedents in the Beersheba area of southern Palestine. These include ledge-handled jars, round-body lug-handled pots and loop-handled pots with light bodies. The presence of narrow, bottle-like necks and of handles and lugs on these apparent imports is extremely interesting because it suggests that only easily portable wares were being brought into Egypt from abroad. Today in the Middle East, jars of analogous shape are strapped on the backs of donkeys or camels by nomads (not to mention urban salesmen) and transported with ease over long distances.

The fact that Maadi has produced some of the earliest domesticated donkey remains known in prehistoric Egypt goes a long way to explaining how these containers might have been brought to Egypt from southern Palestine. Regarding the contents of the imported pots—the ultimate reason for their long journey—many prehistorians have speculated that they were filled with scented oil or fat, since Petrie had found such substances in his famous wavy-handled jars at Naqada as early as 1894. A possible explanation for the large number of pots of local manufacture found in the cellars is that they were meant to be filled with supplies like wheat and barley that were stored in the larger *pithoi* that were set permanently into the cellar floors. Such dry goods would have been in demand among the pastoral peoples who plied the route across the Sinai between the Nile Valley and southern Palestine.

At this point one may well ask where would such nomadic peoples have originated and what would have attracted them to Maadi. It will be remembered that sometime after 7000 to 6000 B.C. (Chapters 6 to 11) rich grasslands sprang up over the desert borders of the Sahara and even well out into the heart of that forbidding waste, accompanying a new rainy period (the Neolithic Subpluvial). When such grasslands were close and easily accessible to the Nile Valley, as along the Great Wadi of Hierakonpolis, they were exploited by Predynastic Naqadan peoples. But between about 6000 and 3100 B.C. (or perhaps even 500 years later) there was enough grass on vast stretches of the deserts west and east of the Nile Valley to support a thriving pastoral economy. In Chapters 16 and 17 we will examine the evidence for and the importance of the mysterious "peoples of the frontiers" who populated these vast spaces. For now all we need remember is that the evidence for their pastoral way of life abounds in rock pictures all over the deserts of northeastern Africa. Their life-style was mobile and cattle were their principal domesticate, much like modern Nilotes such as the Nuer. In light of their interest in cattle, reflected both in their rock drawings and in Egyptian wall paintings of the Old Kingdom, the existence of a type of structure at Maadi which archaeologists like Hermann Junker have interpreted as a corral is of especial interest. One such feature measured about 3 by 5 meters and consisted of four shallow, mud-filled wall trenches into which posts had been sunk. A windscreen protected the entrance and the entire structure recalls the post and wall trench building of Protodynastic date found at Hierakonpolis. For this reason, it is difficult to determine its true function: it could have been a dwelling, temple or, as Junker believed, a corral.

As we will see in following chapters, the Saharan cattle nomads are important because like their modern counterparts in the Middle East and Africa, they probably dealt in mobile wealth which, in addition to meat and dairy products, must have included easily portable items like leather and skins, jewelry, spices, and oils, valued by settled peoples— the very goods that appear in the storage cellars of Maadi. Today, it is a well-known fact that nomads favor such items because they are portable, easy to hide from the prying eyes of government tax collectors, and readily convertible into other kinds of wealth (not the least of which are husbands and wives and political alliances). In return for such goods, the nomads probably sought summer pasturage for their herds in the rich fields of the Delta and valley, as well as sweet dates, grapes, vegetables, wheat, and barley. Finished products too must have attracted their attention, items like linen cloth, ceramic jars, small, portable stone vessels (especially lamps), and stone and metal tools. Despite the fact that many recent nomads in the Middle East have acquired a reputation as raiders and warriors and were regarded as more of a curse than a blessing by settled peoples, it is unlikely that such was the case in late Predynastic times before the horse and camel were domesticated. Nevertheless, after about 3100 B.C. the mobility of the nomads was eventually seen as a threat by the earliest pharaohs who had themselves just conquered the Delta. As we shall see in some detail in Chapters 16 and 20, once Egypt became a unified state, its rulers sought to control and exclude these nomads who had once enriched Lower Egyptian sites like Maadi and brought with them into the country a host of new ideas.

Direct evidence of the abundant produce that probably attracted nomads to Maadi is conveniently provided by the contents of the great *pithoi* that clustered on the northern edge of the village. These contained large amounts of emmer wheat and barley as well as cooked mutton, animal and fish bone and shellfish. Other nonfood items included small pots (possibly used as scoops), flints, spindle whorls, and jar stoppers. The juxtaposition at opposite ends of the village of storage cellars containing mostly luxury goods (for capital investment?) and *pithoi* filled mostly with foodstuffs suggests a rather well-organized, community-based system of storage and exchange at Maadi that contrasts markedly to the later historical pattern in Egypt in which kings, nobles, and priests managed storage and redistributive systems through temples and private estates—a system that probably originated in Upper Egypt shortly before

3100 B.C. and spread thereafter to the north, quickly eroding the basis of Maadi's mercantile existence after Menes's conquest.

If the architectural features and artifacts found at Maadi furnish direct evidence for trade, we still lack a convincing *raison d'être* for the site. Some years ago Elise Baumgartel proposed that "a budding copper industry caused by the first exploitation of the Sinai mines could well have been the reason for Maadi's existence" (cited in Hayes 1965: 122). Although no prehistoric copper mines have yet been found in the region of the later Dynastic mines at the Gebel Ataqa in Sinai, there are several bits of indirect evidence that support Baumgartel's claim, including pre-processed copper bars (ingots?), bits of unprocessed copper, the miscast head of an ax, and a possible smelting area (a feature originally identified by the excavators as a pottery kiln). If Baumgartel's interpretation is correct, then it goes a long way to answering the question of why Maadi was able to maintain long-term relationships with foreign areas and how it developed an important surplus by acting as a processor of ore received from the desert which it could resell as finished products to many of the very people who mined it—a system reminiscent of British industrial and mercantile imperialism of the last century.

But it is one thing to discuss the role of trade and metallurgy in the modern, industrial world, or even in ancient historic Egypt where documentary sources are available and where the world functioned within a context of nation-states, and quite another matter to speculate on the beginnings of metallurgy in Egypt and its effect on late Predynastic society at Maadi. As we have already noted in Chapters 7 to 11, copper tools are known from both Badarian and Amratian sites in Upper Egypt (ca. 5500–3600 B.C.), but these implements are generally small and simple (punches, pins, drills and beads) and most experts believe that they were hammered from natural copper, rather than smelted and cast from ore. Around 3500 B.C. true smelted and cast copper tools including ax heads, daggers, and adzes appeared for the first time in Egypt at both Gerzean sites in the south and at Maadi at the apex of the Delta. Like agriculture 2,000 years before, metallurgy had developed first in other regions like the Mediterranean and Iranian Plateau, and spread into Egypt via trade with foreign lands. Therefore, it is impossible to discuss the importance of metallurgy to Egyptian prehistory without considering also the role of trade. Nowhere is this fact better demonstrated than at Maadi—a mercantile community which invested its surplus wealth in metallurgy, transportation, and storage while its Upper Egyptian neighbors engaged in status-oriented conspicuous consumption of their wealth.

In evaluating the impact of metallurgy on prehistoric Egypt in general and on the inhabitants of Maadi in particular, we need to appreciate the difference between simply working raw copper and actually smelting the ore and casting tools from molten metal. The type of organization of labor required to recover and fashion raw copper—that is, copper that occurs naturally in a metallic state—need not be significantly different from that involved in obtaining flint and chipping it into a desired tool. Both processes involve the *reduction* of a parent material to a finished product and both processes require that tools be produced one by one, by hand. Fashioning artifacts from natural copper, therefore, is a process that can be carried out with relatively simple techniques like cold hammering and annealing, as long as the raw material is available. Naturally, as in stone working, the procurement of such raw material might require a trade system and the maintenance of appropriate exchange relationships between individuals and special groups. There is usually no need, however, to invest in various types of support technologies like those needed to mine, store, ship, smelt, refine, and cast copper tools. Although in some complex societies like those of the Aztecs and early Dynastic Egypt, the manufacture of stone tools did become a well organized, full-time craft, such organization was not implicit in the technology as it was in true metallurgy and developed only because other productive systems in those societies were becoming more highly centralized and organized. As long as copper was worked into tools directly from its metallic state its use was much like that of stone in prestate societies and there was no need to develop a complicated support technology. For example, in the Great Lakes area of the United States, the prehistoric Indians of Wisconsin and Michigan developed a sophisticated repertoire of tools made from hand-hammered natural copper as early as 5000 B.C., but this Old Copper culture did not require a complex technological, economic, or social system to maintain it. It was essentially the product of a food-collecting and hunting people who transferred their knowledge of stone working to another readily available and highly malleable resource that was close at hand. The prehistoric Eskimos did the same thing, though to a lesser degree, with meteoric iron.

By contrast, true metallurgy developed around the production of cast copper tools refined from a nonmetallic ore and involved a kind of social transformation that was intimately related to the rise of early states like Dynastic Egypt. At first, the implications of true metallurgy took some time to be realized, much like farming and herding two millennia before. Although true metallurgy was not a necessary precondition to the emergence of civilization, it did contribute to the establishment of foreign relations that brought into Egypt during the second half of the fourth millennium B.C. a host of new ideas that ultimately contributed to the growth of wealth, military expansion, and the final centralization of political power under southern rulers like the legendary Menes who built the new national capital only 10 kilometers north of Maadi at Memphis.

Although the new wealth and ideas that flowed into Egypt during the five centuries before the founding of the First Dynasty around 3100 B.C.

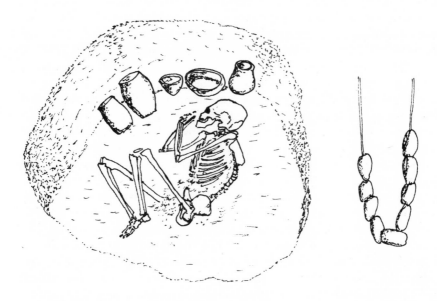

56   Grave and grave goods from Maadi South

found most fertile ground for expression in the status-symbol-oriented cultures of Gerzean Upper Egypt, increasing wealth did have its effect in the north, although the more sober merchants at sites like Maadi, as we have seen, preferred to invest most of their extra wealth in trade, storage, and metallurgy rather than in fancy tombs and luxury goods. Nevertheless, on a much smaller scale than their southern neighbors, they too were caught up in the quest for prestige. Just around the time that foreign contacts accelerated about 3600 B.C., the people of Lower Egypt adopted their southern neighbors' burial customs. We have seen that at Omari, the cemeteries became separated from the settlement in Upper Egyptian fashion, and the same is true at Maadi. It is possible that the shift in burial customs represents a major social change. However, based on the properly reported evidence presently available, we cannot be sure. In fact, the casual recording of the three cemeteries of possible prehistoric date associated with Maadi has caused so much confusion that we cannot be confident of their relative dates. Of the three cemeteries—in the Wadi el Tih, Maadi North, and Maadi South—the first two are probably Protodynastic or Archaic (ca. 3100–2700 B.C.) since they often had rectangular or cubical superstructures over the graves while burials were frequently accompanied by pottery normally dated to later, Archaic times.

The best reported cemetery from the Maadi group and the site most likely to have been used by the townspeople of the late prehistoric settlement is the so-called Maadi South graveyard, located a kilometer southeast of the town on a low rise in the mouth of the Wadi Digla. A total of 468 burials were uncovered there between 1952 and 1953 by Mustafa Amer and Ibrahim Rizkana, distributed over little more than an acre of land. In addition to the human occupants, the Wadi Digla cemetery contained the remains of one dog and 13 gazelles, at least one of which had had its throat cut in an apparent sacrificial rite. As in the Wadi el Tih and Maadi North cemeteries, the graves in the Wadi Digla were shallow circular or oval pits, some of which were covered by limestone blocks. Unfortunately, no proper anthropological analysis of the abundant skeletal material has ever been published and yet another valuable and direct clue to the demographic composition of a prehistoric Egyptian population has been wasted. Although Maadi South was originally believed to be later than Maadi North and Wadi el Tih, the reverse is probably true, as Egyptologist W. C. Hayes noted when he argued that both Maadi South and a similar cemetery containing 50 human and 9 animal burials found by Fernand Debono in 1950 at Heliopolis were probably the oldest in the series. A clearly prehistoric date for Maadi South is supported by the contents of its graves—artifacts that closely resemble those excavated in the settlement by Menghin and Amer. These included a number of pots of the familiar oval, ring-base variety on smooth red and polished black wares; stone vases of alabaster, basalt, and limestone; flake and blade tools; trapezoidal and rhomboidal palettes with beveled edges similar to Upper Egyptian Naqadan types; shell pigment containers and combs; bracelets and combs. Other ornamental objects included a number of carnelian and colored stone beads and traces of manganese and malachite—materials probably used as pigment. Conspicuous consumption, although pale by Upper Egyptian standards, had arrived in the north. The absence of copper artifacts from the Maadi South cemetery reinforces the impression that this material might have been deemed inappropriate to waste on the dead when it could be amassed and traded by the up-and-coming merchants in the town.

Although the social and economic differences evident at Maadi South are minimal by comparison to those in contemporary Gerzean society to the south, they are attested to clearly for the first time in Lower Egypt not only by differences in grave goods but by the segregation of the poorest graves at the western end of the site—the same area where the 14 animal burials occur. Although it is tempting to regard the association of the poorest human burials with those of gazelles and a dog as reflecting low status, a number of other explanations can be posed. Since animals were often accorded special religious importance in historic Egyptian religion, it might be that the humans buried in the western end of the cemetery (a geographical direction later to be associated with the Land of the Dead) were religious specialists. Alternately, they might have been members of a special occupational or ethnic group, like hunters or nomads, or perhaps even some of those foreign traders we have speculated about. One thing is certain, however: the world of Lower Egypt was changing more slowly than that of the south, and, very soon, both cultures would be locked in a struggle for the dominion of the entire Nile Valley.

Having traced the development of farming cultures in Lower Egypt from Junker's work at Merimde through the excavations of Menghin and Amer at Maadi and having already reviewed the great discoveries of Petrie and his colleagues in Upper Egypt, we are almost prepared to consider the findings of those archaeologists who studied the third and most elusive tradition that shaped Egyptian society in the 2,000 years preceding the founding of the First Dynasty—the culture of the desert frontiers. I say "almost prepared" because, having come so far down the road that leads to what historians call ancient Egyptian civilization, having traced the roots of two major traditions that would form the backbone of that culture, I believe we need to offer some preliminary conclusions— some controlled speculations—about the similarities that linked and the differences that divided the developing societies of Upper and Lower Egypt between about 5500 and 3100 B.C. Viewed from the historian's point of view, the beginning of that literate, complex society known as Egyptian civilization was essentially a political act accomplished by a series of Upper Egyptian rulers (like the traditional Menes) who marched forth from the south and subdued the north. As we have seen in the preceding chapters, Lower Egypt had developed a strikingly different culture from Upper Egypt and, as we shall see in Chapters 16 and 17, the cultures of sites like Maadi were not the only ones that would seem strange and outlandish to the triumphant descendants of Petrie's Naqada culture as they attempted first to conquer and then to rule the Delta and the desert frontiers. The deserts too were alive with a host of different peoples and cultures. Yet within the space of a few centuries, between about 3300 and 3100 B.C., the diverse regions of the Delta and the desert frontiers were subdued by the peoples of Upper Egypt and the values and life-styles of these Gerzeans became those of the new Egyptian state and ultimately of Egyptian civilization itself for the next 3,000 years. Looking at this scene, across a gulf of nearly 6,000 years, we are quite at a loss to explain the extent and nature of the many values that separated the cultures of Predynastic Upper and Lower Egypt at the moment that the Nile Valley stood at the threshold of statehood during the latter part of the fourth millennium B.C. I believe that to get a feeling for the depth and extent of the differences that separated the two cultural provinces at this time we must abstract ourselves momentarily from the silent archaeological evidence and from the cautious language of science and controlled inference and speculate on the basic issues— the core values—that animated the peoples of Lower and Upper Egypt in the middle of the fourth millennium B.C.

From a materialistic point of view, the closest contrast between Upper and Lower Egypt at this time lay between a growing mercantilism in the north and a conspicuously consuming, politically oriented society to the south. In Lower Egypt, trade and metallurgy set the tone at strategically located sites like Maadi, while in Upper Egypt social status, burial, public ritual, and display dominated the Naqadan world view. In our journey through the villages, towns, and cemeteries of Predynastic times, we have already glimpsed the richness and complexity of Upper Egyptian Predynastic life and death at sites like Naqada, Badari, and Hierakonpolis, while Maadi has underlined the role of commerce and foreign relations in the cultures of Lower Egypt. To better appreciate the substance of these differences between late Predynastic Upper and Lower Egyptians, I believe that a useful analogy may be drawn to a situation in our own recent history—the contrasts that existed between the northern and southern British colonies in North America during the eighteenth century. Here, as in Egypt of the late fourth millennium B.C., two very different subcultures grew out of a similar but varied ethnic foundation and each came to hold different attitudes toward the outward manifestations of wealth, social class, fashion, and values. In New England, merchants grew rich but preferred to invest their excess wealth in their businesses: in more goods, better factories, and storage depots and improved transportation facilities. In the southern colonies, planters also grew rich, but the source of their wealth was largely agricultural—in great plantations—and they preferred to invest their surplus earnings in their country seats: in bigger and better mansions and in fancy furniture and clothing that would set them off publicly from their poorer compatriots. Although a great northern merchant might build a mansion, it would usually be located in a great commercial center where the action was, and it would almost invariably be inferior in size if not quality to the manor house of his southern counterpart.

For the most part, with the single and only partial exception of the College of William and Mary, the great southern landowners preferred to educate their sons abroad, whereas the merchants of New England built universities at home, like Harvard and Yale. In the South family solidarity, marriage and alliance systems and a highly ritualized and display-oriented system of entertaining and hospitality formed the backbone of society. New England, on the other hand, and the North in general, was a society more open to foreign trade, to rapid movement and social mobility. Even its traditional values, rooted in the religious protest movements of seventeenth-century England, placed hard work and community solidarity above kith and kin. The southern, labor-intensive agricultural economy, based on slavery, social privilege, and territorial expansion, developed a semiprofessional military caste which, like its own counterpart in seventeenth-century Cavalier, royalist England, made certain to combine the interests of the landed gentry with those of the military by simply co-opting leadership roles in militia-type organizations. The South focused its growth inward, developing symbols of its elitist and semifeudal attitudes that emphasized the strong security and stability of an essentially agrarian society ruled by a church-state type of arrangement which aggrandized the economic, intellectual, and military skills of outstanding members of its own elite. People like Washington, Jefferson, and later Lee would have statues erected to them and whole historical cults develop about their careers, cults largely fed by the interests of a southern intelligentsia. In New England and most of the other northern colonies, the symbols of class and power were blurred by a set of traditionally inherited, semiegalitarian religious values, and effectively controlled by the growth of trade and industry and a constant influx of new men which created a dynamic—almost frenetic—society, whose heroes (Sam Adams, John Hancock, Alexander Hamilton) exemplified new capitalistic values. It would be difficult to build statues to these individuals, although the association of one with a large, modern insurance company seems, somehow, completely appropriate. In a world in which wealth and power depended on mobility and innovation, it was difficult for the northern elite to develop time-honored symbols of authority like great country seats, military heroes, and home-grown and -bred intellectuals. While descendants of colonial southern elites still exercise considerable authority in their homeland, nothing comparable survived the early nineteenth-century economic revolution that occurred in the former northern colonies.

Although it would be absurd to draw a one-to-one parallel between the history of colonial America and late prehistoric Egypt, the contrasts that we have just reviewed do serve as useful models for understanding the social and economic significance of the silent artifacts that archaeologists dig from prehistoric sites like Maadi. This site, 5,000 years removed from colonial America, takes on a different meaning from that argued by its apparent workaday and lackluster material culture when viewed in light of the values and life-style of a trading and commercial people. In this sense, the prehistoric Maadians are most reminiscent of our own colonial New Englanders, while the Gerzean peoples to the south remind us more of the subculture of the southern colonies.

Finally, in summarizing and evaluating the contributions of Maadi to the rise of the Egyptian civilization, we are faced with an apparent paradox that this vital society and its commercial style of life were ultimately doomed by the rise of the pharaohs. As we have seen, during the second half of the fourth millennium geography had given the peoples of Maadi a natural advantage over their immediate neighbors at places like Omari, and they drew on this favored position to lay the foundations of a successful commercial culture. Unluckily, their way of life had little place in the monopolistic state economy established around 3100 B.C. by conquering kings from Upper Egypt. Some archaeologists believe that Maadi met a violent end as witnessed by widespread ash and human bones scattered over the settlement. If so, then perhaps this was the "final solution" arranged for the heterogeneous society of Maadi by the victorious kings of the First Dynasty. From the start, Maadi had charted a course to civilization more similar to that taken by contemporary societies in Mesopotamia and on the Iranian Plateau than that which would soon be characteristic of Dynastic Egypt. The spirit of commercialism as exemplified in the storage cellars, foreign imports, draft animals, and copper industry was not destined to set the tone for Egyptian civilization, however, and the god kings of Upper Egypt, whose ancestors were already buried in fancy tombs at Naqada and Hierakonpolis when the prehistoric inhabitants of Maadi were building their commercial empire, and not the merchants of Lower Egypt were destined to establish political hegemony over the Two Lands at the end of the fourth millennium B.C. and reject forever the outward-looking attitudes of the people and cultures of the Delta.

PART V

PEOPLES
OF THE FRONTIERS:
THE DESERT TRADITION,
ca. 6000–3100 B.C.

16

THE RED LAND:
EGYPT'S DESERT FRONTIERS

Prelude: Nubians, Sand-Dwellers, and Nabta

AROUND 2650 B.C., Pharaoh Snefru, father of Khufu and founder of the Fourth Dynasty (ca. 2650–2500 B.C.), launched a military expedition

Hacking up the land of the Negro.
Bringing of 7,000 living prisoners, and 200,000 large and small cattle.
(Breasted 1906 I: 66)

Although scholars have disputed the extent of this raid, it is fairly certain, even allowing for the usual royal hyperbole, that Snefru despoiled a prosperous pastoral people whose homeland included both the oases and remnant grasslands of the Western Desert and a portion of the Lower Nubian Nile Valley.

Four hundred years later, around 2250 B.C., Count Weni, Governor of Upper Egypt, Warden of Nekhen, Chief of Nekheb and Sole Companion, carved his proud autobiography in his tomb chapel at Abydos. In it he relates a career of long service under the first three monarchs of the Sixth Dynasty (ca. 2350–2180 B.C.) and includes an account of a military expedition against the land of the Sand-dwellers.

> *This army returned in safety,*
> *It had ravaged the Sand-dwellers' land.*
> *This army returned in safety,*
> *It had flattened the Sand-dwellers' land.*
> *This army returned in safety,*
> *It had sacked its strongholds.*
> *This army returned in safety,*
> *It had cut down its figs, its vines.*
> *This army returned in safety,*
> *It had thrown fire on all its (mansions)*

> This army returned in safety,
>   It had slain its troops by many ten-thousands.
> This army returned in safety,
>   (It had carried) off many (troops) as captives.
>   (Trans. Lichtheim 1973 I: 20)

Like Snefru's earlier account, Weni's tale leaves us with the distinct impression that the peoples of the deserts were anything but poor, but at the same time the patronizing tone taken by such early Egyptian texts is calculated to create an image of frontier peoples as cultural inferiors. Ironically, ancient Egyptian propaganda has been so effective that modern historians and prehistorians have long ignored the significant role played by the Sand-dwellers in shaping Egyptian civilization. As exploration of the Western Desert (also known as the Libyan Desert, or, more generally, the Sahara) proceeds at an ever-quickening pace, it is now apparent that the despised foreigners of Egypt's desert frontiers comprised a major areal tradition roughly comparable to those of Upper and Lower Egypt. Paradoxically, it was this desert tradition and not those of the Nile Valley that contributed to prehistoric Egypt those critical innovations like farming, cattle pastoralism, and long-distance trade that laid the groundwork for her precocious civilization.

Nowhere is the excitement of a new archaeological frontier so strong as on the deserts west of the Nile. In Chapters 4 to 6 I spoke of the revolutionary discoveries in Palaeolithic prehistory made by Fred Wendorf, Romuald Schild, and their associates. Now, most recently, has come the announcement of a find that demonstrates conclusively the importance of the desert peoples in the later prehistory of northeastern Africa, between about 7000 and 4000 B.C.

At Nabta Playa, 100 kilometers west of Abu Simbel and 180 kilometers east-southeast of the important Palaeolithic areas of Bir Sahara and Bir Terfawi, a series of terminal Palaeolithic and early Neolithic sites have been discovered which date to between about 7300 and 4000 B.C. Today, fossil dunes, heavy clays, and silicified root casts bear witness to the effects of the Neolithic Subpluvial as its rains reopened the Sahara to extensive human occupation for the first time in 30,000 years. Although the finds are so new that they are difficult to evaluate, it seems that terminal Palaeolithic peoples moved into Nabta Playa around 7300 B.C. and remained there until at least 6600 B.C., hunting gazelle and hare. Their way of life must have resembled that of the so-called desert culture of the American Southwest which flourished at approximately the same time, or of the recent Shoshoni Indian tribes of the Great Basin who snared rabbits in great, communal drives and hunted the elusive antelope. Unlike the desert cultures of North America, however, the terminal Palaeolithic hunting and gathering way of life of Nabta soon gave way to a Neolithic farming and herding economy based on the cultivation of

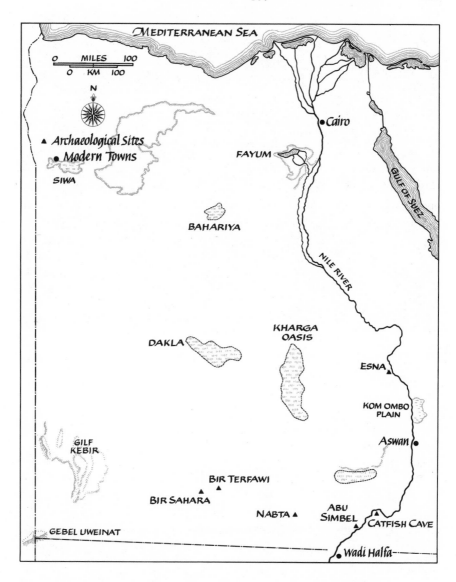

57   Map showing location of important prehistoric desert tradition sites

barley and the domestication of sheep, goat, and cattle. This change took place around 6000 B.C. Despite variations in rainfall during the Neolithic, settlement persisted at isolated spots like Nabta for at least 2,000 years. The earliest Neolithic cultures used a type of wavy-lined pottery similar to the early Khartoum ware discovered many years ago by the prehistorian A. J. Arkell near the city of Khartoum, 800 kilometers to the

58 House floor and hearth at Nabta Playa, Site E-75-6 (dark area below figure
indicates floor outline)

THE PREHISTORIC SITES AT NABTA PLAYA

59 Nabta Playa: View of Site E-75-6 along fossil beach at contact between
playa silts on right and dune sand with artifacts on left

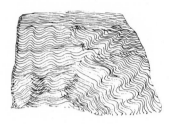

60 Khartoum pottery

south. The fact that the pottery of the latest Neolithic occupation is burnished may even show a connection to the Predynastic sites of the Nile Valley.

All of these newly discovered and tantalizing clues echo an age before Egyptian civilization was formed, before Snefru, Weni, and others created a no-man's land on their desert frontiers in order to secure plunder and safety for the farmers of the Nile Valley. The story of the later prehistory of the red land, as Egyptians called their desert borderlands, that is now unfolding is the result of fifty years of geographical and archaeological research which began in the early 1920's in an era of romantic expeditioneering set against a background of international colonial rivalry and diplomatic maneuvering.

The Lure of the Desert: Of Explorers, Princes, and Counts

The film *The Sheik* appeared in 1922 and starred Rudolph Valentino. It is now regarded as a classic by some movie critics, but it is more relevant for the cultural stereotype and the interest in desert exploration it helped to create. The strong, handsome prince of the desert portrayed by Valentino became a byword for a generation that sought in the Bedouins of the Sahara the vestiges of a mounted nobility whose last European remnants had vanished in the mechanized slaughter of the Great War. Predictably, the 1926 remake, *Son of the Sheik*, was an even bigger box-office smash than its parent and kept filmgoers standing in line for hours just to glimpse Hollywood's latest version of the heroic Bedouin. Only two years later, in 1928, Sigmund Romberg produced the musical *The Desert Song*, a melodrama about a heroic Arab sheik who uses trickery, bravery, and disguise to thwart the unwelcome French rulers of his desert homeland. Ironically, at the moment these popular

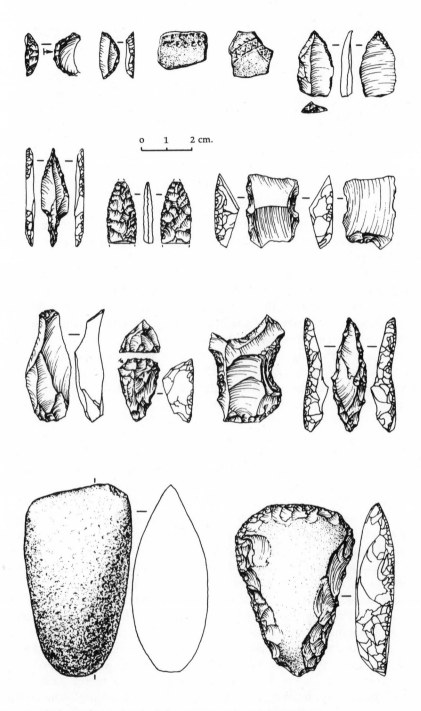

o   1   2 cm.

61   Tools from the early Neolithic Site E-75-8 at Nabta Playa

dramatizations were beguiling an American and European public, the last vestiges of political independence were being stripped from the desert tribes of the Sahara by French colonial forces. The pacification of the desert tribes, begun by the French shortly before the turn of the century, and temporarily interrupted by the First World War, was resumed in earnest after Germany's defeat. Within a few years, the introduction of the airplane enabled France to break the centuries-old dominion of the great trading and raiding confederations like the Tuareg and ensure at least comparative safety to and control over the camel caravans that crisscrossed the desert vastness of the Sahara.

During the 1920's a number of scientists and explorers in both French and Anglo-Egyptian territory benefited from this pax Sahara, visiting and mapping heretofore remote and unknown areas of the North African interior. Although camels were used at first, the automobile increasingly became the main method of transport, and the airplane was converted from its military role to photograph some of the least accessible reaches of the desert. If this activity seemed far removed from the romantic exploits of a Rudolph Valentino, there was still plenty of glamour attached to desert exploration. Partly because of the recent military pacification of the Sahara, partly because of the economic and strategic importance of the area and partly because of the romantic lure of the unknown, many of the outstanding names in desert exploration in the 1920's belonged to soldiers, diplomats, and titled nobility. In the next decade, the scientists made their debut, but it was amid a spirit of free-wheeling adventure and glamorous expeditioneering that the first discoveries of the prehistoric cultures of the Libyan Desert took place.

The Gebel Uweinat deep in the Libyan Desert was first explored by Ahmed Mohammed Hassanein Bey in 1923. To look at the photograph of Hassanein Bey reproduced in his 1925 book *The Lost Oases* is to see a real-life personification of Valentino's character. Dressed in flowing white Bedouin garb and wearing a *kafiya* with a rifle slung over his back and a staff in his hand, Hassanein Bey looked more like a Bedouin sheik than a cultivated diplomat, accomplished fencer and graduate of Balliol College, Oxford. It was still romantic to be an explorer and geographer and Hassanein Bey was simply playing the part. But he was a competent geographer and a good leader, too, and the work he did laid the ground-work for numerous expeditions that followed in his wake. He also uncovered an archaeological mystery whose solution is only now coming within our grasp. Before arriving at Uweinat he had heard stories of strange rock drawings that traveling tribesmen regarded as the work of jinns or genies. Following the accounts he had heard, Hassanein Bey decided to try to locate these drawings once he reached the Uweinat.

They were in a valley at the part where it drew in, curving slightly with a suggestion of the wagging tail. We found them on the rock at ground level. I was told there were other similar inscriptions at half a day's journey, but as it was growing late and I did not want to excite suspicion, I did not go to them.

There was nothing beyond the drawings of animals, no inscriptions. It seemed to me as though they were drawn by somebody who was trying to compose a scene. Although primitive in character, they betrayed an artistic hand. The man who drew these figures of animals had a decorative sense. On their wall of rock these pictures were rudely, but not unskillfully carved. There were lions, giraffes and ostriches, all kinds of gazelles, and perhaps cows, though many of these figures were effaced by time. The carving is from a quarter to half an inch in depth, and the edges of the lines are weathered until in some parts they can be scraped off easily with the finger.

(Hassanein Bey 1925: 228-229)

Hassanein Bey rightly concluded that these pictures were extremely ancient and from a climatic epoch considerably moister than the present. Since the camel was not found in any of the Uweinat drawings, he guessed that they dated before the introduction of that beast of burden to the area around 500 B.C. (Hassanein Bey 1925: 229). How long before 500 B.C. he could not have guessed! As it turns out, these were the first prehistoric rock drawings ever found in Egypt's deserts.

The initial report of Hassanein Bey's discoveries in a 1923 *National Geographic* article ensured his popularity and in a world that worshipped heroes and lionized desert sheiks his findings had an even greater impact than one might normally expect. Another factor that indirectly helped Hassanein Bey was the magnificent find one year earlier of the tomb of Tutankhamon by Howard Carter and Lord Carnarvon. For several years after Tutankhamon anything in Egyptian archaeology was big news. Although far less impressive than the tomb of Tutankhamon, the desert rock drawings of the lost oases of Uweinat attracted sufficient attention and seemed of sufficient merit to arouse the interest of no less a figure than His Royal Highness Prince Kemal el Din Hussein, who mounted a full-scale expedition to the Libyan Desert in 1925.

Prince Kemal el Din could have been king of Egypt. On December 19, 1914, his aged father, Prince Husain Kemal, was proclaimed sultan of Egypt by Britain in a diplomatic maneuver to depose the pro-Turkish (and pro-German) Khedive Abbas Hilmi. Egypt was now completely independent of the Turkish Porte. But Husain was old and the succession had to be assured. The High Commissioner, Sir Reginald Wingate, approached Husain's son, Prince Kemal el Din, and offered him the throne. The prince refused and the British turned to Fuad, a younger son of the same Khedive Ismail who had presided over the opening of the Suez Canal and the economic ruination of his country half a century before.

62   Aerial view of the southern Gilf Kebir Plateau taken by Apollo VII in
     1968. The edges of the central massif are etched by root-like wadis,
     weathering products of recurring rainy periods

Much like England's Edward VIII, Kemal ei Din chose to follow his own
star.

That star led him to pioneer the use of motor vehicles in the exploration of the southern Libyan Desert in 1925, only two years after Hassanein Bey had made a similar journey with camels accompanied by
armed Bedouins—the twentieth century was coming to the Sahara. On
Kemal el Din's journey from Kharga Oasis to the Gebel Uweinat, he
discovered the Gilf Kebir, a large barren plateau that was later to yield
prehistoric rock drawings similar to those at Uweinat. Kemal el Din
returned to Uweinat in 1926 and within two years had published the
first scholarly accounts of the mysterious rock engravings. The fact that

the prince was able to interest the great French expert on cave art, Abbé Henri Breuil, in jointly authoring one of the articles on the Uweinat rock drawings is a good indicator of the international prestige these new and unexpected archaeological finds had acquired.

The fascination of the desert for members of the European and Egyptian nobility—the jet set of their day—is understandable when we recall that these men were either rich, well-educated semiprofessionals with infinite means at their disposal, like Prince Kemal el Din, or diplomats and soldiers (officers, naturally) whose professional inclinations were to explore the unknown so that it could be mapped, understood and, ultimately, ruled. Such men as Hassanein Bey, Major R. A. Bagnold, Count L. de Almasy, Count L. di Caporiacco, and Lieutenant Commander Roundell fall into this latter category.

Ever since their occupation of the Turkish provinces of Cyrenaica and Tripolitania in 1911, the Italians had pursued colonial ambitions in North Africa. Although the coastal areas were subdued rather easily, the desert presented a much more difficult problem. Led by the Senussi religious order, the Arabs of the interior carried on an effective guerrilla war that persisted until the Italians were beaten in North Africa by the British in 1941. In 1933, the Count de Almasy, who, a year before, had flown the first aerial reconnaissance of the Gilf Kebir in a small two-man Gypsy I Moth plane, met an Italian detachment in the Gebel Uweinat. He told their commander, the Count di Caporiacco, about some cave paintings and within a year di Caporiacco and a colleague, P. Graziosi, had published accounts of these striking prehistoric representations. But by the 1930's, the rock drawings of the Libyan Desert were known to the world and a host of expeditions to the area regularly included accounts of them.

The two best archaeological studies of the paintings and carvings in the Libyan Desert prior to the outbreak of the Second World War were made by a German expedition in 1933 and 1934–35 led by the self-taught and incredibly energetic scholar Leo Frobenius and by Major R. A. Bagnold in 1938. Frobenius recorded a number of sites in the Gilf Kebir, Uweinat, and northern Sudan, but sadly, most of the artifacts he collected perished in the Allied bombings of Germany during the war. Happily, Hans Rhotert's account of the drawings was published in 1952 and remains a useful record for scholars. Equally valuable are the accounts left by the Swiss art historian Hans Winkler and the British prehistorian Oliver H. Myers of their findings on Bagnold's last expedition to Uweinat and Gilf Kebir in 1938. Major Bagnold first ventured into the Libyan Desert in 1929 and became interested in studying the mechanics of wind-blown sand. Even today, his accounts of the complicated ways in which sand moves, deposits, and erodes is a geological classic. In 1932 Bagnold took Karl Sandford into the desert to handle the geology for his expedition—the same Sandford who had undertaken the prehistoric survey of the Nile Valley with W. J. Arkell. By 1937 Bagnold realized the potential importance of the Saharan rock drawings in regard to the ancient climate of the desert area and turned to the eminent British philanthropist and amateur archaeologist Sir Robert Mond for financial assistance. Mond, who was then sponsoring avant-garde excavations at the Predynastic site of Armant for three years, responded by releasing his two best prehistoric scholars, Myers and Winkler, who had just made some important discoveries of their own relating to the prehistory of the desert frontiers.

Interlude: The Riddle of Armant

In the middle 1930's, the site of Armant on the west bank of the Nile 30 kilometers south of Naqada unexpectedly revealed a link between the Predynastic cultures of the valley and the prehistoric rock drawings of the Libyan Desert. The site's excavator, Oliver Myers, found microlithic tools and incised and combed pottery that he attributed to a nomadic, desert society which he called the Saharan culture. Had it not been for the foresight and organizational ability of the Armant expedition's backer, Sir Robert Mond, however, Myers and his art historian colleague Hans Winkler would never have had the opportunity to study the puzzling similarities shared by Armant's Predynastic inhabitants and the faraway prehistoric peoples of the Gebel Uweinat and Gilf Kebir. Myers and Winkler were both important elements in Mond's Armant expedition; Myers was chief archaeologist in charge of excavating the Predynastic settlement and cemetery while Winkler conducted a detailed survey of the rock art in the barren hills and wadis of southern Upper Egypt. Mond, as financier, orchestrated the entire Armant production to perfection.

Archaeological excavations have been compared to many things but seldom to theatrical productions. But in the complexity of tasks, variety of personnel, individuality of personalities and, above all, in their financial needs, successful excavations require both competent directors and financial angels to provide the funds to mount and sustain a major effort. Backing today is usually provided by governments, universities, museums, or, in some cases, by international agencies; but in the late nineteenth and early twentieth centuries wealthy individuals like the legendary Lord Carnarvon bore the major burden of financial support. Among the wealthy patrons who favored Egyptian archaeology, Sir Robert Mond was perhaps the most enlightened and least recognized. In his sensitive obituary of Walter Emery, the Egyptologist H. S. Smith relates the following story about Sir Robert Mond, Emery's first patron:

The quality and style of Mond's generosity is illustrated in Emery's story of going to report to him in Luxor the winding up of the camp and his own departure home at the end of his first season; Mond, after advising him to visit the Egyptological collections in the Museums of Europe on his way home, said good-bye, then turning added, 'Oh, I expect you'll need some lolly' and thrusting his hand into his pocket pushed a large wad of notes into Emery's hands and departed without a word. *(Smith and Dawson 1971: 192)*

By the time he began to indulge his interests in Egyptian archaeology in 1926, however, the age of great discoveries had passed; and when Mond initiated major prehistoric investigations at Armant in 1935 his field director, Oliver H. Myers, could write:

The cream has been skimmed off Egyptology and it is almost useless to start an excavation with the idea of discovering easily a mass of information about the lives of people or a hoard of treasure suitable for museums. Such things can occasionally be found with luck, but the conscientious excavator must (to continue the metaphor) extract from the skim the proteins and albumins. That this skimming has left much of great value undiscovered no one can doubt who examines the blanks in our knowledge, but to extract the information from everyday finds requires a new technique.

(Mond and Myers 1937 I: vii)

That these words echo the sentiments of Petrie a generation earlier in *Naqada and Ballas* is not purely accidental. When Mond and Myers began excavating at Armant they found it necessary to reorient the previous work of the Mond expedition which had been digging at a classic temple site—the Bucheum, a spot sacred to the Buchis bull. The multidisciplinary approach pioneered on the Bucheum served as an ideal training ground for the more exacting skills required by a prehistoric site. It was here that the hand of Flinders Petrie was most apparent. The man chosen as chief foreman or *Reis* at Armant, Ali Mohammed es Suefi, had been Sir Flinders's "best lad" at the pioneering prehistoric Naqada excavations forty years before (Petrie and Quibell 1896: viii). Even Myers's account of the excavations has a familiar ring to it:

The excavation of ordinary *baladi* cemeteries has a charm all its own. It is true that no very startling results are to be expected, nothing that will make a nine days' wonder in the Press, or bring the tourists flocking to the site, but almost every day has its small rewards and prizes. The digger never knows what he may find next. Tombs are often in the most surprising juxtaposition, and even where a cemetery is uniform in date, some new fact about the daily life of an ancient people, bringing them closer to us, is constantly appearing.

(Mond and Myers 1937 I: viii)

Unquestionably, Sir Robert Mond believed in obtaining the best talent available for his expedition. The roster of contributors to the Armant report is impressive: forty-six individuals worked on the two volumes, including seven professors and nine Ph.D.'s and M.D.'s. Their interests and skills ranged through ceramic identification, mineralogy, metallurgy, botany, entomology, petrology, pathology, paleontology, zoology, epigraphy, osteology, spectrography, and drafting.

The excavations were ably directed by Oliver H. Myers, who stressed careful recording, analysis, and publication of all the material, no matter how apparently insignificant. One of his major contributions was his attempt to revise and update Petrie's Predynastic pottery corpus, and to systematize ceramic typology. Myers wrote:

> If Egyptology is to become an exact science, it can do so only by the fullest application of the basic idea of *corpora* introduced by Petrie into Egyptology. However long it be delayed by national and personal rivalries, the time must come when reproductions of *all* objects found in Egypt no matter of what date or aesthetic worth, no matter who the finder, will be arranged in type series in a set of uniform volumes, to which the excavator, research worker, or student can turn and find what he wants in as many seconds as it may now take him months.
> *(Mond and Myers 1937 I: 49)*

That same compulsion that drove Petrie to ignore no clue, to overlook nothing as insignificant, motivated Oliver Myers and led him to an unusual discovery of great importance to the study of prehistoric connections between the Nile Valley and the desert frontiers in Predynastic times.

> During the building of Bucheum House, and the excavation of cemeteries 700–900, a number of incised sherds was found just beneath the desert surface. With the sherds from the cemetery area some microlithic agate flakes were discovered.
> *(Mond and Myers 1937 I: 267)*

After searching the archaeological literature of surrounding areas for a clue to the origin of this strange pottery (whose accidental discovery recalls Brunton's first experience with Badarian rippled pottery) and having satisfied himself that it was not of Egyptian origin, Myers proposed that

> the true connections of this culture are to be found in the Sahara, and the Nubian resemblances must be attributed to infiltration from that area. *(Mond and Myers 1937 I: 268)*

Today, thanks to the work of French archaeologists in North Africa, Myers's views have been at least partially substantiated. In 1937 he could only suspect that the several undated surface finds from the Sahara were the remnants of peoples who had flourished far in the past at a time when the climate was wetter and vegetation more abundant. Today, this is common knowledge. Despite the fact that Myers wished to date the end of wet conditions in the Sahara too early and attribute to the desiccation of the area the origin of Predynastic culture, he did grasp a critical factor. The appearance of what he called a Saharan culture characterized by incised and combed pottery and microlithic tools was intimately connected to the arrival of the rains of the Neolithic Sub-pluvial and the changes it wrought across the face of all of northern Africa. Thanks to Bagnold's expedition Myers was able to test his ideas in some of the most forbidding and isolated regions of the Libyan or eastern Sahara only a few years after his initial discovery at Armant.

Return to the Desert: The Bagnold Expedition

In the winter of 1937–38, Major R. A. Bagnold, accompanied by geographer R. F. Peel, Oliver Myers, and Hans Winkler, set out for the Gebel Uweinat and Gilf Kebir region of the southern Libyan Desert. Unlike Hassanein Bey, who made the trek on camels accompanied only by stalwart Bedouin guides and two Egyptian servants, Bagnold's small group of scientists rode in specially adapted automobiles. But if some of the air of romanticism had gone from desert exploration, the scientific excitement had reached a higher pitch. Oliver Myers, armed with his findings at Armant, fully expected to find remnants of his shadowy desert culture associated with the famous rock drawings of the Gebel Uweinat and Gilf Kebir. His hopes were founded on a handful of sherds brought back from the Gilf Kebir a few years earlier by W. B. K. Shaw (Mond and Myers 1937 I: 270).

Although Myers lived to publish only the briefest account of his findings at Gilf Kebir, he did keep copious notes and recovered substantial collections of artifacts. Thirty years after the Bagnold expedition these were resurrected by Dr. William McHugh, who has recently published and reinterpreted the results of Myers's discoveries.

Initially, Myers sought "to see if traces could be found of a Saharan culture which invaded the Armant district in the VIth Dynasty" (Myers, in McHugh 1971: 57). Myers was aided in his explorations of the south-eastern portion of the Gilf Kebir by a selected contingent of Guftis whom he had trained at Armant—descendants of Petrie's original Naqada workmen. His conclusions about Palaeolithic climate and settlement patterns and careful field methods anticipated by thirty years the recent work of Wendorf in the Western Desert.

From the large Acheulian site, Myers had the non-artificial material removed from the surface and then, impressed by the heavy abrasion (due to sand blasting) on the northern edges and surfaces of the hand axes, Myers carefully marked each hand axe with an arrow pointing to magnetic north. He had hoped that an analysis of the relative amounts of abrasion caused by wind carried sand would provide a means of reconstructing past wind regimes. The site was photographed and Myers put a small trench into the site which enabled him to determine that the cultural materials were found entirely on the surface or only slightly embedded in the soil. After the surface materials were collected, the upper several centimeters of soil were sieved to recover the smaller debitage. *(McHugh 1971: 57)*

To ensure that his collections were statistically comparable, Myers even took the modern precaution of digging and collecting from the same-sized areas (of 64 square meters) in many of his sites.

Some of Myers's most important finds were made along two wadis on the eastern edge of the southern Gilf Kebir plateau—the Wadi el Bakht and the Wadi Ard el Akhdar. In the narrow, upper reaches of these dry water courses large sand dunes had once choked the channels. Later, during the Neolithic Subpluvial, lakes formed behind these natural dams and settlers were attracted to their shores, a process vaguely reminiscent of the contemporary settlement of the Fayum depression. Although we know that Myers was able to collect from and even excavate some of these lakeside settlements, none of this material has been published and were it not for the exhaustive detective work of Professor McHugh (1971), they would still be lost to the world. The Neolithic sites Myers located around the ancient lakes contained a number of chipped stone implements, primarily of local silicified ferrocrete sandstone material, milling stones for preparing vegetable foods (perhaps even grain) and pottery—the original source of Myers's interest in the Libyan Desert. There were also several stone circles along the Wadi Ard el Akhdar fossil lake like ancient tent rings of similar date to those found by Hester and Hoebler in Dungul Oasis—dwellings that echo far more ancient Palaeolithic sites found by Chmielewski in Nubia. It is a real pity that no plan of these apparent nomadic structures could be found among Myers's notes, since they are probably the first ancient nomad dwellings excavated by an archaeologist anywhere in the Middle East. To know the exact size, numbers, and arrangement of such dwellings in a site would provide a valuable clue to the reconstruction of the types of social groups which occupied the Libyan Desert in later prehistoric times.

To unravel the mystery of Myers's Neolithic sites, McHugh not only studied his notes and carefully examined Peel's photographs taken on the

1938–39 Bagnold expedition, but eventually traveled to Paris to observe firsthand and draw Myers's collections. These are housed at the Musée de l'Homme and their analysis represents a final tribute to Myers as well as a comment on the number of archaeological sites that still lie "unexcavated" and unpublished in museum vaults. Sadly, very little remains from the Wadi Ard el Akhdar sites, even though Myers reported finding substantial amounts of chipped stone, pottery, milling stones, and stone circles. But artifacts from four Neolithic sites in the Wadi el Bakht have survived the vicissitudes of time and thrown some light on the material culture of the late prehistoric inhabitants of the Libyan Desert. Even though the collections are comparatively small, totaling 782 pieces of chipped stone from four sites and 697 pottery sherds from two sites and despite the fact that they were taken from 8 rather than 64 square meter sampling areas, they suggest a wide range of human activity, including storage, transport, light woodworking and even, perhaps, agriculture. The milling stones, reaping knives and chaff(?) impressions on pottery all recall the farming tools of contemporary agricultural peoples in the Middle East, even though there is still disagreement as to whether or not the remains from the Wadi el Bakht and other Saharan sites constitute sufficient evidence for agriculture. Certainly with increased rainfall small crops of wheat or drought-resistant barley could have been raised along the desert wadis as they were at Predynastic Hierakonpolis, although we still lack direct evidence in the form of preserved vegetable remains or pollen that the agricultural implements were actually used for agricultural purposes. Some archaeologists have argued that such tools could have been borrowed from other, truly agricultural societies and simply employed in a hunting and gathering economy.

The major significance of Myers's Neolithic sites for Egyptian prehistory is twofold: (1) they provide direct evidence of climatic change and population increase in a previously empty quarter of the Libyan Desert, and (2) they raise the possibility that economic changes like herding and maybe farming reached the Sahara before the Nile Valley. As always, the solution to the second problem hinges on chronology, and to date we lack radiocarbon estimates for Myers's sites. Based on recent discoveries by Wendorf and associates in the Libyan Desert and by Gerard Bailloud and Paul Huard in Ennedi and Tibesti, eastern Chad, the Neolithic sites in the Gilf Kebir probably date between 6000 and 4000 B.C. An even more difficult problem involves the use of the term Neolithic itself. Although the word usually implies both agriculture and animal husbandry, as I have noted, there is as yet little clear evidence for the cultivation of grain at the so-called Neolithic sites in the deserts of northern Africa. Nevertheless, the primary mainstay of the new desert economy, the factor that differentiated it from an older Epipalaeolithic pattern, was cattle pastoralism. Despite the careful work of Myers in the Wadi Ard el Akhdar and until the most recent discoveries of Neolithic villages at

Nabta by Wendorf and Schild, our best evidence for the cultural changes that took place on the deserts of northern Africa between about 7000 and 4000 B.C. are not provided by stone tools and potsherds but by the spectacular rock art of the Sahara which suggests a slow transition from hunting to cattle pastoralism between about 7000 and 6000 B.C.

Hans Winkler's Rock Drawings: Ethnography on the Rocks

Ever since Hassanein Bey's discovery of the rock drawings at Uweinat, prehistorians have tried to use the rock art of the Libyan Desert to flesh out the bare bones of the archaeological record. Especially in circumstances where no plant or animal remains have been preserved, the pictures on the rocks offer unique insights into the lives and customs of ancient prehistoric peoples. It is the analysis of this rock art that gives the late prehistoric archaeology of the desert frontier much of its distinction and charm and, incidentally, often sets the archaeologist and art historian at each other's scholarly throats.

It will be remembered that in 1938–39 Bagnold brought along not only Oliver Myers but his colleague Hans Winkler, a man who had come to know the desert art of Egypt intimately in his years of work for Sir Robert Mond. At the moment Winkler was traversing the Libyan Desert with Bagnold and Myers, the first volume of his monumental book on the *Rock Drawings of Southern Upper Egypt* was appearing at Mond's personal expense, providing the world with its first systematic, scholarly account and analysis of the rock art of the desert borderlands of the Nile Valley. Winkler's work was much more than a picture book.

> These researches are especially connected with prehistory. Rock-drawings replace in some degree written records. We may not only learn from them different artistic conceptions, but we may also obtain rich information about dress, weapons, hunting, shipping, wild and domestic animals; sometimes we can even draw conclusions as to religious beliefs and social institutions of the authors of such drawings.
> *(Winkler 1938: 1)*

Winkler's explicit purpose was

> to explore one very limited area thoroughly, so as to get as clear an insight as possible into the chronological sequence of the different styles in such an area, and to create in this way a basis for future researches. *(Winkler 1938: 2)*

With rock drawings it is seldom possible to use stock-in-trade archaeological dating methods. Seldom, if ever, are pictures buried and very infrequently are they even indirectly associated with artifacts. Even in cases where rock overhangs contain both pictures and artifacts, these seldom can be linked with any degree of assurance. Rather, the dating of archaeological rock drawings depends on a number of clues and cues: (1) the internal composition of the picture—are extinct animals or datable artifacts shown?, (2) the presence of dated inscriptions—useful on historical sites, (3) the overlapping and cross-cutting relationships of different styles or themes—does one type of representation definitely and consistently overlie another?, and (4) general stylistic trends and patterns of artistic development—is there a consistent trend toward the stylization of motifs?

In the work he did in the deserts just east and west of Armant, Winkler collected and classified rock drawings from 40 different sites. These he broke down into three categories: inscriptions, signs, and pictures, the last group being by far the most important as far as prehistoric cultures are concerned. Winkler next subdivided his categories according to period and, in many cases, attempted to connect particular art styles with particular peoples. For example, pictures were dated to one of five periods: (1) Arab, (2) Greco-Roman-Coptic, (3) Dynastic, (4) Undatable Early Predynastic and Prehistoric Pictures in the Eastern Desert and (5) Undatable Early Predynastic and Prehistoric Pictures in the Western Desert. Categories (4) and (5) were further broken down according to the art of four prehistoric groups: (a) Autochthonous Mountain Dwellers, (b) Early Nile–Valley Dwellers, (c) Eastern Invaders and (d) Earliest Hunters. In an attempt to breathe life into his subjects, Winkler described each group in terms of its major cultural characteristics, such as fauna, weapons, hunting practices, shipping, social life, and religion. He even went so far as to propose ethnic divisions based on costume and comparisons with modern peoples in the same area. Unfortunately, by modern anthropological standards his ethnographic analogies were not adequately controlled and he almost certainly pushed interpretation beyond the evidence at hand. Nevertheless, he did uncover some real differences in the prehistoric rock art of the desert, differences that indicated that the Predynastic–late prehistoric climate supported an abundant fauna, including giraffe, elephant, cattle, ibex, antelope, wild ass, gazelle, and ostrich. Furthermore, not all of these animals flourished at the same time. The elephant especially required a relatively lush environment and was probably most plentiful at the beginning of the Neolithic Subpluvial (around 7000 to 6000 B.C.) when the human inhabitants of the Sahara were still hunters and gatherers.

The most ancient rock-drawings are quite distinct from anything later. Animals, footprints of game, traps, geometrical designs occupy the minds of these men; they have little interest in the portrayal of human beings. In the moment of the first discovery of these drawings and again after having studied them week after week, I feel that they are the expression of quite a foreign mentality. It is the same mentality, the same genius, which inspired artists of other primitive hunters, in Australia as in Northern America: animals, footprints, and geometrical designs are the result. Our earliest hunters lived in close contact with the Nile—the crocodile suggests it (which other prehistorians believe might actually have been a lizard). They had the bow and the dog. *(Winkler 1938: 40)*

Winkler believed his earliest hunters were succeeded by cattle pastoralists (perhaps about 6000–5500 B.C.). The fact that Winkler used the strange term Autochthonous Mountain Dwellers to designate his cattle pastoralists is particularly unfortunate and quite confusing. The word autochthonous in a literal sense means "sprung from the earth," or "native." Since Winkler also believed his cattle-raising Autochthonous Mountain Dwellers were early speakers of the ancestral Hamitic language (a forerunner of ancient Egyptian and modern Berber) and that they immigrated out onto the deserts east and west of the Nile during the Neolithic Subpluvial, they can hardly be classified as native to the desert. Such pseudoethnic terms are generally avoided by modern archaeologists and anthropologists. Although the rock drawings suggested to Winkler that his Autochthonous Mountain Dwellers (i.e., cattle pastoralists) still hunted wild animals like the ass, ibex, antelope, and ostrich, he thought that the most commonly depicted animals—longhorned cattle—were now thoroughly domesticated as demonstrated by

(1) artificial deformation of the horns, (2) by care applied to the representation of the udder, indicating that the draughtsman appreciated the milk. The udder is drawn at the natural place, not, as elsewhere, behind the hind legs. Some drawings show cattle with one, two, or three little strokes hanging down from the neck, probably amulets. Generally cattle pictures excell in the care applied to them. This means that the animal was particularly important. The dappling of cattle is occasionally drawn in. Sometimes men are shown catching a bull or cow by lassoing its horns. Once people are hunting cattle with bow and arrow; this is proof that there existed also wild cattle.

(Winkler 1938: 20)

Later, while exploring Uweinat with Bagnold and Myers, Winkler found paintings of domed huts reminiscent of contemporary dwellings of East African cattle pastoralists. "In each of them pots hang down from the roof. The inside of these pots painted white suggests milk" (Winkler 1939: 23). As I mentioned earlier, the similarity of these shelters to the archaeological remains of Neolithic stone rings found by Myers in the Uweinat, by Hester and Hoebler at Dungul Oasis and by Wendorf and

Schild at Nabta is striking and provides an all too rare insight into the ways archaeology, art history, and ethnohistory can be brought to bear on a single problem.

In addition to his earliest hunters and Autochthonous Mountain Dwellers Winkler thought that he had found evidence of other late prehistoric peoples who inhabited the Eastern and Western Deserts near to the Nile Valley. For the moment, however, we will postpone their story and consider the hunters and herders who dwelt beyond the immediate vicinity of the Nile, far out in the Libyan Desert. When Winkler and Myers accompanied Bagnold to the Gebel Uweinat and Gilf Kebir in 1938–39, each was coming fresh from his own project in the Armant area. Myers had just completed several successful seasons of Predynastic excavations at Armant and Winkler had published the first volume of his pioneering study and analysis of the rock drawings of southern Upper Egypt. Each man, therefore, viewed the archaeological remains of the far-flung lost oases of the Libyan Desert in terms of his own recent experience in and around the Nile Valley. Myers's work at Uweinat and in the Gilf Kebir involved archaeological survey and test excavation and was motivated in large part by his search for a desert culture. Winkler, on the other hand, studied the now famous rock drawings of the area, but when he was confronted by the same two artistic themes he had just seen in the prehistoric art of the desert borders of the Nile Valley—hunting and cattle pastoralism—he inexplicably reversed his earlier position and said that the "paintings and engravings are made by the same people" (Winkler 1939: 25). The paintings, which were concerned almost exclusively with cattle, he thought to be the work of women, while the rock engravings with their stress on hunting and wild animals, were executed by men. This is a strange interpretation indeed, and one that is inconsistent not only with the content of the rock drawings and Winkler's previous findings around Armant, but with what anthropologists know of the sexual division of labor among contemporary cattle pastoral peoples of Africa like the Nuer of the Sudan where men, more especially the young, unmarried youths—and not the women—herd the cattle.

In criticizing Winkler's conclusions on the prehistoric rock art of the Gilf Kebir and Gebel Uweinat, McHugh (1971: 173) pointed out:

> The hypothesis of a sexual division between the painters and the engravers flies in the face of the overwhelming preponderance of male's representations in both forms of rock art. Were women alone responsible for the paintings, surely their activities would have been more prominently displayed. Yet domestic and social scenes involving women are quite rare.

A comparison of the frequency of animals depicted in paintings with those shown in engravings from the Gilf Kebir and Gebel Uweinat and archaeological sites in other areas of the Sahara and near Armant has led

McHugh (1971: 174-175) to conclude that engraved hunting art clearly preceded the painted pastoral scenes. In his analysis, he stresses

> that the paintings and engravings tabulated by Winkler are significantly different in the species represented. Although cattle are most abundant in both categories, they comprise almost 98% of the animals depicted in Winkler's series of painted scenes as compared with only 32% in his series of engravings. On the other hand, wild animals (dogs excluded because their domestic status is uncertain) comprise 62% of all animals in the engraved scenes but only 2% of those in the painted scenes. If the engravings and paintings were made by the same people, the former by men, the latter by women, one must ask where are all the man-made engravings which should accompany the woman-made paintings of Ain Doua? Engravings are less likely to weather away than are paintings, so this is no explanation. It seems likely that only paintings were made . . . because the period of engraving had already passed or had yet to come.

McHugh's conclusions are supported by findings in eastern Chad where engraved hunting scenes also precede painted pastoral motifs in both the Ennedi and Tibesti Massifs (McHugh 1971: 177; Bailloud 1960: 187). By around 5000 B.C. in the Tibesti Mountains, Ennedi, and the southwestern Libyan Desert, McHugh believes that the rock art mirrors a slow transition from hunting to cattle pastoralism, possibly indicating that domestication developed independently in at least some areas of North Africa rather than simply diffusing from the Middle East as older researchers believed.

Thanks in part to new radiocarbon dates from many North African sites, it is now clear that the pastoral way of life with its denser populations, greater mobility, and ultimately more militaristic style of social and political organization replaced big game hunting soon after the Sahara was reopened to extensive human settlement by the Neolithic Subpluvial. Even if the initial impetus for the new pastoral way of life came from the Middle East, it soon caught on throughout North Africa, moving swiftly across the grassy savannas, and being adopted by native peoples who, only a few centuries before, had wandered as hunters into this land. How could such a major change from big game hunting to cattle pastoralism occur so quickly without wreaking havoc among the changing societies or without requiring an influx of new peoples? Perhaps the best answer is that the big hunters themselves were recent colonists of the Sahara. The country was a frontier and they were pioneers. Those who left their homes in the great oases and possibly even in the Sudanese Nile Valley for the new promised land could not have been the most timorous or the most tradition-bound members of their terminal Palaeolithic societies. Perhaps they were not even the best hunters. Almost certainly they came from a variety of late Palaeolithic racial and ethnic groups which inhabited the southeastern fringes of the Sahara in what is now Chad and the Sudan. The fact that they did move, for whatever reason, set them apart from those who remained behind, set them adrift in a new world in which innovation rather than custom, flexibility rather than rigidity determined survival. Their tool traditions were diverse, their art reflects cultural differences; but shortly after their successful conquest of the Saharan grasslands they faced a common dilemma —the elephants and possibly the giraffes vanished. Cattle were now the biggest and most efficient source of protein remaining to these former aficionados of big game. For a reason or series of reasons still unknown, the Saharan hunters quickly became herders with a speed and thoroughness reminiscent of the switch from farming to horse and gun nomadism made by the Indians of the North American Great Plains in the late eighteenth and early nineteenth centuries. Perhaps the Saharans found pastoralism the best strategy for clinging to their old dietary staples; maybe they had heard of new ideas about food producing originating in the Middle East, or perhaps they invented pastoralism on their own, independently of their eastern neighbors. Whatever the causes, what Professor Chester Chard has called the great transformation from hunting and foraging to pastoralism and cultivation took place on the grassy steppes of the Sahara at places like Nabta, while the peoples of the Nile Valley continued to fish, hunt, and gather wild plant foods at sites like El Kab in the manner of their ancestors, since their own late Palaeolithic experiment in food producing had collapsed 5,000 years before (see Chapter 6).

The recent discoveries by Saharan archaeologists portray Egypt from a far different perspective than normally drawn by her own ancient chroniclers or even modern Egyptologists and archaeologists. In the past, our interpretation of Egypt's Predynastic prehistory, say after 5500 B.C., has been dominated by the traditional ancient Egyptian symbolic dichotomy between the red land of the desert frontiers and the fertile black land of the Nile Valley. Traditionally, for a literate ancient Egyptian, at least, the red land housed nomadic barbarians who were held culturally inferior to the settled, highly organized valley dwellers. According to ancient Egyptian records, the valley people usually maintained effective political dominion over their desert neighbors. No one knows what the picture looked like from the nomads' viewpoint, since they did not write down their impressions. For instance, the British conquest of the nonliterate Zulu, or the American defeat of the Cheyenne and Sioux confederation a century ago takes on an entirely different meaning when viewed from the oral accounts given by the native victors of Isandluana and Little Big Horn. But oral history had not been thought of when pastoral nomads roamed the Sahara. Even when the Egyptians developed writing, not long before the effective collapse of the Saharan culture, it was highly restricted in subject matter and an explicit tool of royal propaganda.

An insight into the way Dynastic Egyptian history or ethnography worked is provided by the account left by Rameses II of a battle he fought with the Hittites in Palestine in the early thirteenth century B.C. at the town of Kadesh. At the time of the battle the Egyptians had possessed writing for nearly 2,000 years. They were, along with the Mesopotamians, the oldest literate culture in the world. And yet their official account of what happened at Kadesh turned a clear defeat into a resounding personal victory for the all-conquering pharaoh. Were it not for embarrassing internal contradictions in the Egyptian account and references in the Hittite archives, we should be tempted to view Kadesh as a major triumph for Egyptian arms. Unlike the Hittites, the despised desert dwellers did not write down accounts of their encounters with their Nilotic neighbors. If they had, then surely the history of northern Africa might be quite different. If the pen is mightier than the sword, it is also far mightier than silence.

Only now are archaeologists working in the vast wastes of the Sahara beginning to piece together the story of the real cultural relationships between the red land and the black land. For now at least, it seems as if the food-producing revolution occurred in the red land many centuries, if not a full millennium before it penetrated the fertile Nile bottomlands. So the priorities of progress have been reversed and the barbarians were once the wave of the future. The desert herdsmen whose descendants were so vilified by ancient Egyptian scribes seem, ironically, to have brought the Neolithic revolution to Africa and perhaps indirectly to have laid the foundations of Egyptian civilization—the world, in the words of the old British march, has indeed "turned upside down."

Nomads, Nilotes, and Middlemen: The Problem of Contact Between the Sahara and the Nile

It took Hassanein Bey seven months to make the 2,200-mile trek from Sollum on the Mediterranean coast to El Obeid in the Sudan in 1923 with camels. Prince Kemal el Din Hussein drove directly from the Nile to Uweinat two years later. In late prehistoric times, neither camel nor motorcar was available to Saharan pastoralists. Distances were formidable, even in the relatively lush conditions that prevailed during the Neolithic Subpluvial. It is about 500 miles as the crow flies from the Uweinat to the Sudanese Nile Valley and over 700 miles from the Tibesti Mountains. To seek the neighbors of the Predynastic Egyptians in these spots seems to stretch credulity. If we look closely at a map, however, we will see that even today, during a period of almost unprecedented hyperaridity, a string of oases and watering places exists in between the mountain massifs and plateaus of the Saharan and Libyan Deserts and the borderlands of the Nile Valley. Slightly farther to the south, Kharga and Dungul Oases complete the chain. Unfortunately, this string of oases, like that farther to the west, runs from north to south and today very few permanent water holes are found between the massifs of the deep desert (like Haggar, Tibesti, Uweinat, and Gilf Kebir) and the line of oases that flanks the Nile Valley 50 to 200 miles out into the Western Desert.

Until quite recently most archaeologists believed that this gap actually prevented, or at least severely limited contact between the Sahara and the Nile Valley in late prehistoric times (ca. 7000–3000 B.C.). For instance, McHugh (1971: 19) once argued:

> In the vast area in between the Nile River and the Gilf-Uweinat-Ennedi axis south to about 18° N. Latitude, the elevated formations which could have served as major dry season refuges for the cattle pastoralists are completely lacking.

McHugh felt that in order for Saharan pastoral peoples to engage in regular contact with Nile Valley dwellers they must have been able to find permanent water holes during the dry season that would have been fairly close to the river. Otherwise, they would have been obliged to retreat farther into the desert to more well-watered spots like Uweinat, Gilf Kebir, Tibesti, and Haggar.

Based on the information available until quite recently, notably from Dungul and Kharga Oases, there was no evidence that cattle pastoralists had ventured even within 50 to 200 miles of the Nile. Based on Hester and Hoebler's work at Dungul in the early and mid-1960's and Caton-Thompson and Gardner's explorations in Kharga in the 1930's, the arrival of either cattle raising or farming seemed quite late. In Dungul, dozens of sites of late prehistoric date (i.e., post 7000 B.C.) were attributed to hunter-gatherers oriented to the water-bearing playa environment (McHugh 1971: 19) (called by Hester and Hoebler Dungul C), while at Kharga Caton-Thompson placed her Peasant Neolithic and Bedouin Microlithic sites (too conservatively, as it turns out) after 4000 B.C. None of these late prehistoric sites—in either Dungul or Kharga—show clear connections with the artists of the Sahara or the Predynastic peoples of the Nile Valley. A slightly different pattern occurs 300 kilometers south of Kharga and 175 kilometers southwest of Dungul at Nabta where, according to McHugh, the rains of the Neolithic Subpluvial were apparently more intense (see Chapter 6). At Nabta, where something like a complete and well-dated sequence of sites spans the period between about 7000 and 4000 B.C., Wendorf and Schild (1977) see some Nilotic influence in the burnished pottery of the latest Neolithic occupation (ca. 5000–4000 B.C.), but before this time there are neither Nilotic contacts nor

Saharan rock drawings; and although the presence of domesticated cattle is virtually certain, few of their bones are ever found in Neolithic villages.

In short, the evidence from the isolated oases and dried-up playas of the Libyan (eastern Sahara) Desert is extremely complicated and difficult to fit together at this time. Part of the reason for this doubtless lies in the uneven history of research and publication of Saharan sites, but I believe the main culprit is in the very nature of oasis societies. Regardless of whether they are hunters and gatherers or farmers, the inhabitants of oases, like islanders, live in a tightly defined living space or biosphere. Their contacts with the outside world are limited and prescribed by the availability of water and local landform. Just as island navigators have their defined routes, so too oasis peoples move along narrow and perilous land corridors across virtually lifeless wastes. In such societies, the opportunity to develop local eccentricities in their material cultures in response to finely graded but crucial ecological differences is great. Although innovations like pastoralism, agriculture, and pottery might spread rapidly across a world of grasslands and oases, once adopted by any social group they will be tuned to the cultural ecology of any given locale. Thus arose the stylistic and economic differences that produced a veritable mosaic of cultures in the newly greened Sahara between about 7000 and 3000 B.C. It is no wonder that it is hard to relate the oasis cultures of Dungul, Kharga, and Nabta to each other, let alone to those of Uweinat and the Gilf Kebir.

Nevertheless, one of the purposes of this book is to offer speculations and generalizations based on currently available evidence. Without some broader view, the culture-history of Egypt and the continuity between its prehistory and history will ever elude us. In offering such a summary view and in pursuing the question of possible contacts between the Saharan and Nilotic peoples, we need to return to the internal nature of the late prehistoric Saharan societies and the cultural ecology of modern pastoral peoples who inhabit that area of the world.

Following the repopulation of the Sahara around 7000 B.C. we have seen that the rock art shows a general tendency for pastoral themes to replace hunting themes. So far this change has not been documented in the archaeological evidence, although Nabta shows a shift from early hunting and gathering to farming, and a reinterpretation of Caton-Thompson's Kharga material suggests that her Bedouin Microlithic actually preceded rather than followed her Peasant Neolithic.

Based on the preliminary finds at Nabta and considering the content of the pastoral rock drawings there were two adaptive economic strategies pursued in varying degrees by Saharan peoples during the Neolithic Subpluvial—cultivation of barley and dates, and grazing of sheep, goats, and cattle. In the central and northern Sudan where the rainfall was greater than in Upper Egypt, a relatively continuous blanket of savanna vegetation—grasses and drought-resistant tamarisk trees—stretched from the Nile west into the heart of the desert, to Uweinat, Gilf Kebir, Tibesti, and Haggar. In such country the free-ranging cattle pastoralism still typical of the Sudan and eastern Africa flourished and cattle were doubtless always relatively more important than agricultural cultigens like barley. Such is the case among the modern Nuer and Dinka. In this area movement was always great and contact with the Nile may have been established between 6000 and 5000 B.C. producing early pottery-using Abkan sites along the Sudanese Nile. We must anticipate great difficulty in dealing with and relating the different types of archaeological habitation sites of such southern pastoral peoples if the example of the Nuer is any indication. The pastoral cultures of eastern Africa and the Sudan today are organized into a series of age grades, each of which performs a different task. The job of herding usually falls to the young men between about fourteen and twenty-two years of age. If anything resembling this type of organization prevailed in the area during the Neolithic Subpluvial when cattle pastoralism originated in Africa, then it could produce strikingly different sites depending on whether we were dealing with a herding camp inhabited mainly by young men or a village inhabited by older members of the society living in relatively permanent dwellings like those just uncovered by Wendorf and Schild at Nabta.

Toward the southern border of modern Egypt and then northward into Upper Egypt proper the vegetative cover on the desert must have grown more spotty and consequently the contacts between Saharan and Nilotic peoples been even more infrequent than in the south. At Kharga, for instance, there is no similarity between the pottery of the Peasant Neolithic and that of Predynastic sites along the Nile, although Caton-Thompson detected some resemblance between the Peasant Neolithic and Armant lithic industries. Unfortunately, stone tools are notoriously poor indicators of cultural relationships, because the material itself greatly limits the forms that finished tools can assume, and similar functions often produce similar forms. Hence, with all but the most specialized of chipped stone artifacts, similarities may be explained by like function or the operation of chance, rather than by the possession of a common technological tradition, especially in the absence of large, statistically valid samples.

So for the time being, our evidence for direct contacts between the Egyptian Nile Valley and the Sahara remains weak, even though the new finds to the south by Wendorf and Schild have raised hopes and demonstrated the presence of sophisticated agricultural and pastoral life-styles in the desert before Egypt ever embarked on her course toward village life.

Perhaps, in the final analysis, the question as to whether or not there was ever extensive contact between the Sahara and the Nile Valley during the Neolithic Subpluvial hinges on a heretofore neglected facet of Egyptian and Nubian prehistory: the question of draft animals. If the

Neolithic Saharans and Predynastic Egyptians already were using the donkey (as we have suggested in discussing Maadi in Chapter 15) then the practical means existed whereby contact could have been established and maintained, albeit on a small scale compared to the great donkey caravans sent forth by Old Kingdom monarchs under command of nobles like Weni and Harkhuf. Not only were donkeys efficient beasts of burden for treks across the desert (especially during the rainy season when pasturage and drinking water were most abundant) but they could be used effectively by one or two men. Hermann Kees, an Egyptologist who devoted a lifetime to the careful study of Egypt's cultural geography, cites an account given in the classic Middle Kingdom tale of the eloquent peasant, of a poor man who transported goods from the Wadi Natrun, west of the Delta, to the capital city of Heracleopolis:

> He took with him on his ass all kinds of plants, wooden articles including rods from the Land of the Cow (i.e., the Oasis of Farafra), skins, furs and minerals which he hoped to barter for food.
>
> *(Kees 1961: 131)*

Even if, as Kees claims, "this enumeration of products which are typical of most oases is surely excessively optimistic when applied to the Wadi Natrun," it is likely that richer oases like Kharga, especially during the Neolithic Subpluvial, actually did produce such perishable exports. In terms of future archaeological research, much hinges on whether the historic accounts of trade can be projected back into the Neolithic Subpluvial (ca. 7000–2500 B.C.), since without effective draft animals like the donkey for transport any regular contact between Saharan and Nilotic peoples would have been sporadic and limited to areas in the Sudan where pastoralists could range with relative ease between desert and river.

In the Red Sea Hills: What's in a Boat, a Diffusionary Dilemma

To date, the best evidence of contact between desert and Nilotic peoples during the Predynastic period is the rock art described by Winkler from the Eastern Desert of southern Upper Egypt. In his careful studies in the Armant area, Winkler discovered that although rock drawings extend only 12 miles into the Western Desert, abundant pictographs are found on the east bank of the Nile up to 65 miles from the river, well into the heart of the Red Sea Hills, almost halfway to the Red Sea itself. The abundance of boats in many Predynastic rock drawings fascinated Winkler. On the basis of their likeness to examples painted on Gerzean pots, he felt that some boats clearly belonged to "Early Nile Dwellers" (Predynastic peoples) while he attributed others to mysterious "Eastern Invaders" whose pictures were "all over the Eastern Desert" and who "came from the Red Sea" but still showed "connexions with the Mountain-dwellers (use of the same game-trap, kilt) and with the Nile-Valley dwellers (intermediate forms of boats)" (Winkler 1938: 26-28).

63   Winkler's boat types (by column, from top to bottom). Left column: sickle boat; incurved sickle boat; square boat, derivation A; square boat, derivation C. Center column: square boat, derivation D; square boat, derivation F. Right column: incurved square boat; square boat; square boat, derivation B; square boat, derivation E

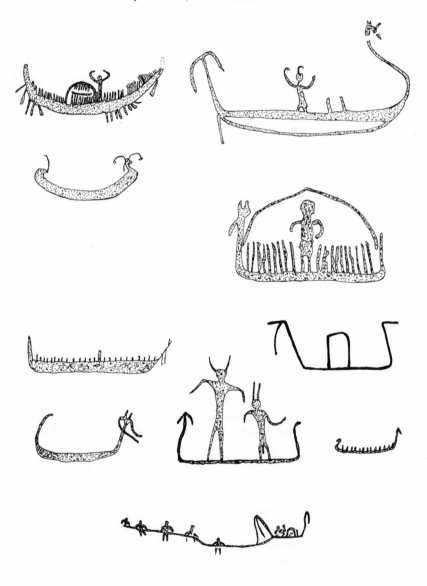

The Early Nile Dwellers used three types of boats: sickle-shaped, incurved sickle-shaped, and incurved square. By contrast, the vessels of the Eastern Invaders were of a form "foreign to Egypt" (Winkler 1938: 27).

> The hull is straight; hull and stern are bent upwards in a rectangle. The multitude of boat-pictures enables one to distinguish different developments of this "square boat" type. Of particular importance is the fact that one of these derived forms is in use among the Early Nile Dwellers ("the incurved square boat"), suggesting an intercommunication between the two peoples. *(Winkler 1938: 27)*

At the heart of Winkler's interest in boat typology was his conviction that the "type of boat with tall vertical prow and stern is, among other evidence, proof of a Mesopotamian influence in Egypt" (Winkler 1938: 26). One might retort that had such boats been found first in Egypt rather than Mesopotamia, the connection probably would have been the other way around. The other evidence of Mesopotamian influence mentioned by Winkler was listed by the great Egyptologist Henri Frankfort and includes high-prowed boats, cylinder seals, the animal master motif, the standing winged griffin, serpent-necked panthers, figures wearing head-dresses and long robes, and niched mud-brick architecture.

Exciting as we find Winkler's ideas about Eastern Invaders, there are serious flaws in his arguments that prevent acceptance of his "diffusionist" approach to later Egyptian prehistory. First, if we really examine closely his excellent drawings of the different types of prehistoric boats his distinctions fade. Both boat size and the curvature of the prows and sterns seem to vary independently of one another. Second, although Winkler's initial survey showed the Eastern Invaders confined to the mountainous Eastern Desert, he later found their drawings on the western bank of the Nile. Third, Winkler believed the people who rowed these vessels came up the Red Sea and through the mountains of the Eastern Desert to the river. To be sure, such a journey would not have been difficult, since the higher land of the Eastern Desert has always attracted more rainfall than the Western Desert so that even today several of its wadis abound in life and during Dynastic and Classical times Egypt maintained ports on the Red Sea on a regular basis. Unfortunately, there are no known drawings made by Winkler's Eastern Invaders along or even near the Red Sea coast. The closest is over 50 miles inland and all are in valleys that drain directly into the Nile and not the Red Sea.

Even though we cannot accept Winkler's Eastern Invaders (in the imprecise way that he originally described them), the themes and artifacts shown in all later prehistoric rock art near the Nile Valley raise a number of questions that eventually must be answered if we are to explain the emergence of Dynastic culture in Egypt. Although Predynastic peoples seem not to have penetrated regularly more than a day's journey from the Nile into the Western Desert (about 10 to 12 miles at most), they were all over the Red Sea Hills east of the river. Now it is difficult to accept the idea that people living up to 65 miles from the Nile and well aware of the use of ships were analogous to the Bedouins who still inhabit the valleys of the Eastern Desert. And yet when many Egyptologists interpret the records of early Dynastic rulers who subdued their eastern neighbors, they use the term Bedouin. The problems created by such a translation are nicely illustrated by an ivory label belonging to King Den (Udimu), fifth king of the First Dynasty (ca. 3000 B.C.), on which the monarch smites the "East" in traditional fashion, with mace upraised in his right hand while his left hand somewhat improbably grasps both a spear and the long hair of his kneeling opponent (Aldred 1965: 64, Illustration 65). Examination of the seal shows that the "Easterner" appears to be coming out of the mountains. His standard is surmounted by one of Winkler's straight-hulled Eastern boats on top of which stands the "Set" animal—guardian of the desert and ritual opponent of Horus, whose image surmounts pharaoh's own cartouche. Behind Den is a sickle-shaped boat (one of Winkler's Nilotic types). The fact that this same boat was classified by Frankfort as Mesopotamian illustrates some of the sticky problems one runs into in discussing cultural relationships.

In contrast to the traditional interpretations of King Den's label, I believe that another story can be read in its highly stylized imagery and symbolism. In the scene, the Easterner is dressed much like the pharaoh. He lacks both the skins and long, garishly decorated robes used later in official Egyptian iconography to represent hunters and herders respectively. Instead, he wears a good Egyptian-type kilt, and wears his long hair in Egyptian fashion. Unlike all contemporary Egyptians with the exception of the pharaoh, he has a beard. He stands with his back to the steep escarpment of a mountain (almost certainly the Red Sea Hills). The whole scene (perhaps a stylized representation from even earlier times) looks more like a fight for control over access to the Nile

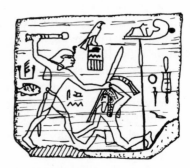

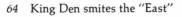

64   King Den smites the "East"

than a pharaonic invasion of the East, since the Easterner himself stands on flat ground and contends there with pharaoh. When we now reconsider the facts that the Red Sea Hills are covered with late prehistoric rock art, that many ship motifs include (but are not limited to) straight-hulled boats and that the Neolithic Subpluvial would have converted the Red Sea Hills into a zone capable of supporting a population considerably denser than that harbored in the well-watered mountain massifs of the far Western Desert, the Easterners assume a more prominent role. No longer are they simple Bedouin (whatever that means), but herders, farmers, and watermen. We do not know if they actually plied their ships on the Red Sea or whether they simply sought to maintain control of transport and markets along the Nile. What they had to exchange we also do not know, although the increasingly critical resource copper was probably one important item. Meat and dairy products also, to be traded for grain, might have been involved in their transactions as well as many of the exotic shells from the Red Sea favored by Predynastic Egyptians and buried in their tombs.

The nature of their relations with Nilotic Egyptians is even more problematic. We suspect that ethnic differences have been overemphasized. They were, to be sure, mountain people and outsiders as far as the valley people were concerned, but they were probably linked to them by networks of reciprocal exchange, by trading partnerships and even ritual systems. The thousands of imported shell beads, many of which came from the Red Sea, which Petrie and Brunton unearthed from Predynastic graves, represent one of the most important aspects of the exchange network that has been preserved for us.

A comparison to the kula ring of Melanesia is enlightening as to the possible mechanics of trade in this period. As we mentioned in Chapter 4, in Melanesia over a vast area, a system of exchange has been studied by anthropologists that serves real economic and social functions but, at the same time, is encased in ritual. The kula ring promotes communication and even acts as a sort of quasi-political device by which production of goods, like pottery or stone axes or even seagoing boats, is centralized and rationally distributed at certain locations throughout the trading sphere. In one way, Winkler was probably right. The Easterners, although probably not invaders in the classic sense, were transshippers—middlemen—in an exchange system that, by the middle to late fourth millennium B.C., was linking various economies of the ancient Middle East in a vast superexchange network that revolved around symbolically prestigious, exotic goods increasingly in demand by the emergent social and political elite from Egypt to India. Viewed in this light, it is easy to see why, after achieving political unification, Egypt felt jealous of and threatened by the Easterners. They were neither simple Bedouin nor invaders; they were more akin to carpetbaggers: middlemen in a trade network that stretched both north across Sinai into Palestine and Mesopotamia and south along the Red Sea and South Arabian coasts to the east. The price they demanded to carry on their work successfully was unhampered mobility—the freedom to travel at will from the river up into the hills and possibly to the sea or possibly into Sinai and beyond. But such mobility must have been incompatible with the newly centralized Egyptian state which wished to draw boundaries, maintain them against outsiders, and eventually expand their compass—a game that all states play. It was probably the clashes between Nilotic and Eastern Egyptians following the political unification of the valley around 3100 B.C. which led to the rapid cessation of Middle Eastern influence soon after the beginning of the First Dynasty, clashes similar to the one depicted on the label of Den. Ironically, the pharaohs, by protecting their own interests, isolated Egypt from the rest of the Middle Eastern world by seizing control over a growing long-range exchange network and, as we have seen in Chapter 15, ruining Lower Egyptian trading centers like Maadi. No longer the finely tuned circuit of exchange characteristic of kula-ring economics, but rather a highly centralized storage-redistributive system centered on one man and his relatives, clients, and descendants dominated the quest for foreign goods. It was no longer necessary or even desirable to trust the importation of exotic or necessary goods to a relatively egalitarian and decentralized exchange system. Pharaoh commanded the resources to go straight to the source or to locate new sources of power closer to home, and from now on, most Eygptian contact with other lands would be through the watchful eyes of the royal administration.

So, by the close of the fourth millennium before Christ a definite pattern had emerged with respect to the diverse late prehistoric traditions of northeastern Africa. First, in Lower Egypt at sites like Maadi, then on the desert frontiers to the east and west of the Nile River, and finally in Nubia to the south of the First Cataract at Aswan the expansion of an Upper Egyptian state spelled the end for independent courses toward civilization among the peoples of the Delta, the Sahara, and the southern Nile Valley. Lower Egypt was incorporated into the new state as a theoretically equal partner. The nomads who roamed the deserts with their herds of cattle and traded with foreign lands were isolated from the river. And Nubia—the Land of Kush—bore the full brunt of Egyptian economic and military exploitation, with nearly disastrous results for the developing civilization in the northern Sudan.

17
NUBIA:
GEORGE ANDREW REISNER
AND THE LAND OF KUSH

GEORGE ANDREW REISNER, the most successful and skilled field archaeologist of his day, died in the summer of 1942 at seventy-four, within six weeks of the eighty-nine-year-old Petrie. Both men were pioneers and giants in Egyptian archaeology, and both worked on a wide variety of sites spanning the historic and prehistoric periods. Although Reisner's principal scholarly triumphs lay in his study of the Dynastic cemeteries of Naga-ed-Der and Giza, he also made a lasting contribution to the study of Nubian prehistory. Nubia, known to the ancient Egyptians as the Land of Kush, is that relatively poor stretch of the Nile Valley south of Aswan. Like Petrie's research at Naqada, Reisner's work in Nubia was concerned principally with graves and cemeteries and, like Petrie in Egypt, he devised a scheme of relative dating that still dominates the historic and prehistoric archaeology of Nubia.

The parallels between Reisner and Petrie are quite revealing, in a personal as well as a professional sense. Both owed their success to a driving personality and a desire for perfection. Both were self-taught in the field, possessed boundless energy and dedication and were impatient with incompetence. But Reisner, as the son of wealthy parents, had received formal training in ancient Oriental languages and Egyptology and possessed a more tactful if hardly less competitive personality than Petrie. Reisner earned his A.B. from Harvard in 1891 and his Ph.D. in Semitic languages two years later. Like many of his American contemporaries, he was attracted by Adolf Erman and became so closely identified with the Berlin school of Egyptology that he even served as an assistant at the Berlin Museum in 1895.

After holding a number of scholarly and scientific positions, the dapper Reisner managed to interest Mrs. Phoebe Apperson Hearst, a wealthy widow, in backing an expedition to Egypt. As lecturer in Egyptology at the University of California and Director of the Hearst Expedition to Egypt, Reisner embarked on his first venture into field archaeology in

1899. This was only five years after Petrie had opened Naqada and literally at the very moment that he was demonstrating the value of prehistoric graves and cemeteries through the application of his revolutionary method of sequence dating to the newly discovered Predynastic material (Petrie 1901). Reisner, at thirty-one, was totally inexperienced at fieldwork yet, within a space of four years, he managed to evolve a systematic approach to excavation that surpassed Petrie's and set the standard for his work in Nubia eight years later. At the beginning, he was dependent on "old Egypt hands" to introduce him to the terrain and help him locate archaeological problems worthy of 'the Hearst Expedition's attention:

> With the help and advice of Dr. Ludwig Borchardt and especially of Mr. J. E. Quibell, the plan of work for the first year was formed; and I determined to look for the cemetery of Coptos (Keft) in the desert of that place. Mr. J. E. Quibell (who had just become Inspector of Antiquities) went on a trip of inspection with me to Keft, Der-el-Ballas, Ballas, El-Kab, Kom-el-Ahmar, Matana, Esneh, Edfu and other sites in September 1899. Absolutely inexperienced as I was in camp life, Mr. Quibell and his sister, Miss Kate Quibell, were of the greatest assistance to us in the organization of a rational camp life at the start.
>
> *(Reisner in Mace 1909: VI)*

Reisner made the wise decision of hiring F. W. Green, who had just finished up at Hierakonpolis in March 1899, to act as a field director, and also took on one of his own former students from Harvard, A. M. Lythgoe. Whereas a modern archaeological expedition generally works within a tightly defined geographic region and generally employs a statistically based, problem-oriented strategy for selecting archaeological sites to excavate, the Hearst Expedition lacked focus in its first year.

> In December 1899 and January 1900, we searched the desert at Keft and finally found the cemetery inaccessible in the cultivation between the village of Kellahin and the village of 'Awedat. In the meantime a predynastic flint camp was found and excavated; and a plundered predynastic cemetery at Shurafa was examined. In February, the whole expedition moved to Der-el-Ballas, where in the spring, February-July, 1900, and November-December, 1900, two 18th dynasty cemeteries, a number of houses, and two mud-brick palaces were excavated.
>
> In May 1900, having been informed by Sobhi Effendi, Inspector of the Department of Antiquities, that plundering was going on in a predynastic cemetery at El-Ahaiwah, opposite Menshiah, I obtained permission from the Department of Antiquities to excavate that site. During May-August, I worked at El-Ahaiwah on a predynastic ceme-

tery and a town of the late New Empire, and a fort which showed signs of occupation from the Middle Empire to the late New Empire.

In November-December, 1900, work was resumed on the palaces at Der-el-Ballas. In December, Mr. Lythgoe was sent with a gang of men to search the desert to the south as far as a predynastic cemetery which Quibell and I had seen in 1899, which I now wished to excavate. In the meantime Mr. Quibell had informed us that the site of Naga-ed-Der opposite Girga and about five miles south of El-Ahaiwah, was being plundered. Having obtained permission from the Department of Antiquities, I went to Naga-ed-Der on February 1st, 1901, leaving Mr. Lythgoe to finish up at Ballas and at Der-el-Ballas.

(Reisner in Mace 1909: VI)

For Reisner, Naga-ed-Der was to be a turning point, a training ground on which he would test and quickly perfect a systematic approach to field archaeology that would make his work the envy of other Near Eastern excavators for the next 40 years and prepare him for his work in Nubia.

Despite the fact that Mrs. Hearst's support was withdrawn from his expedition in 1905, Reisner and his colleagues managed to publish a massive three-volume account of their work. Although the last volume by Reisner himself did not appear until 1932, 27 years after the completion of excavations at Naga-ed-Der, and a final volume on the Predynastic cemeteries by Dows Dunham was not published until 1965, the quality of work done at Naga-ed-Der set a new tone for archaeological research in Egypt and the world. Reisner enunciated five basic principles that guided his expedition and laid the groundwork for all his later work:

1. It is necessary to have an organized staff of Europeans and of workmen trained in all branches of the work, and following careful methods of excavation and recording *as a habit*.

2. It is necessary to excavate whole sites and whole cemeteries. The excavation of individual tombs, while interesting and at times valuable, does not provide that sufficiency of continuous material which is necessary to justify conclusions on the development of a civilization such as we have in Egypt. The discovery of beautiful objects is, of course, greatly to be desired; but the search for museum specimens is an offence against historical and archaeological research which is utterly unworthy of any institution which pretends to be devoted to the advancement of knowledge.

3. Every cemetery and every building represents a series of deposits which ought, so far as practicable, to be taken off layer by layer in the inverse chronological order and recorded layer by layer.

4. It is necessary to make a complete record by drawings, notes and *photographs*, of every stage of the work. . . .

5. It is necessary to publish these records so far as practicable, *tomb by tomb*, and at the same time to give a careful systematized consideration of the material they contain. The hasty and incomplete publication, year by year, of the season's work, with the temporary working hypothesis of the hour, satisfies the curiosity of those who have a less direct interest in the work, but tends to deprive the systematic archaeologist of a large mass of useful material.

(Reisner in Mace 1909: VIII)

Across the gulf of time that separates us from the forty-one-year-old author of these words is a barrier that transforms, mitigates, dilutes the impact of Reisner's statements. Only if we try to put ourselves in the context of his time can we fully appreciate what he was saying and why it was so important and controversial for the developing science of Egyptian archaeology. For Reisner in 1909 to charge that the "discovery of beautiful objects . . . for museum specimens" was "an offence . . . unworthy of any institution which pretends to be devoted to the advancement of knowledge" was not only a slap at the irresponsible search for objets d'art by men like Amélineau but a comment on the dissolution of the Hearst Expedition and the subsequent bitterness between members of its staff over the loss of funding. Perhaps Reisner felt that the sponsoring institution had not done its part in trying to save the situation. We cannot be sure today. Whatever did happen, "feelings were hurt," as Professor John Wilson has put it (Wilson 1964: 145) and Reisner "rowed with many of his old cronies."

Reisner was also emphatic in his insistence on completely recording and publishing every single tomb. When we recall that his friend Quibell had taken *no* systematic notes a decade earlier at Hierakonpolis and that the renowned Professor Petrie was famous for scores of "hasty and incomplete" annual publications, Reisner's statements must have sounded like a declaration of war. The idea of actually publishing every tomb, no matter how insignificant, was a major step forward in archaeological ethics and laid the groundwork for the prehistory of Nubia. Since our work ultimately destroys the record of the past, we not only incur the responsibility of preserving that record in our excavation notes, but of reproducing our information for the interested public. Considering that Petrie himself published only one-fifteenth of the Naqada burials and that many writers would later scoff at Reisner's approach as needlessly fact-oriented, his method constituted a revolution in and of itself. His insistence on proper and complete recording enables us to *measure* the results of his work and compare it with that of his contemporaries. On that criterion alone, on the basis of objective and careful recovery and publication of all the facts, Reisner was better than *any* of his contemporaries and even far surpassed Petrie. In fact, after Reisner, Egypt would be a land of remembered triumphs for the brilliant but truculent and unchanging Sir Flinders. Reisner, by sheer force of competence, forced other archaeologists and Egyptologists to acknowledge the propriety of his exacting methods.

When the Egyptian government decided to raise the height of the Aswan Dam in 1907 and flood an additional 250 kilometers of the Upper Nubian Nile Valley, they turned to Reisner to direct a systematic archaeological survey of the threatened area. As mentioned earlier, this was probably the first example of large-scale multidisciplinary salvage archaeology and reflects the growing concern for the destruction of the record of the past that has accompanied rapid technological growth and industrial development as well as the growing interest in multidisciplinary research. Reisner's assignment would have daunted many of his contemporaries and a less organized excavator.

> The whole reach was to be surveyed, and all evidence of former human habitation was to be collected and recorded in order to preserve as accurate and complete an account of the existing vestiges of early life and culture, which must inevitably perish when submerged. . . . Dr. Reisner's intimate acquaintance with early Egyptian art and civilization was especially valuable in the study of this new region, for it enabled him to date each interment, and thereby provide a firm basis for anthropological studies; for a thorough study of such a region involved not only the collection of objects and the reconstruction of the culture of the people who had once inhabited the valley, but also the determination of their race and ethnological affinities.
>
> *(Lyons in Reisner 1910: III and IV)*

When these ambitious goals are viewed in light of the new archaeology of the last 15 years, they hold up remarkably well. Even though, as William Y. Adams has noted in *Nubia: Corridor to Africa* (1977), Reisner's work would result in a decidedly Egyptian interpretation of Nubian history and prehistory, his exacting fieldwork and broad anthropological orientation produced a wealth of new information about the northern Sudan. Ironically, most of these data suggest that Nubia (the stretch of the Nile between the First and Fifth Cataracts) was frequently a satellite of Egypt in historic and even prehistoric times. As we shall see shortly, Reisner's view that much of Nubia's later prehistory (what he called its Predynastic and A-group phase) was a pale reflection of developments to the north bears on a broader ethnological argument about the possible African origins of Egyptian kingship.

To accomplish his immediate task of salvaging Nubia's antiquities in 1907–8, Reisner's first concern was the accurate location of sites in the vast survey area. He employed two principal methods: surface survey by teams of workmen and trenching and test-pitting of ground surfaces that were either virgin or disturbed. In the first instance,

A gang of about 12 trusted and experienced men were sent out to cover a particular stretch of territory. They were divided into two parties and walked along the bank parallel to each other, looking for exterior signs. On the return journey they changed places, and each party covered the ground previously gone over by the other. On their return, they reported to me; and I then went over the ground with the gang leader. *(Reisner 1910: 8)*

But when the surface yielded no obvious signs of occupation or was disturbed, Reisner insisted on further testing to determine the nature of the underlying archaeological strata, if any. Such a method, which emphasized the importance of boundaries between sites and hidden sites, has not been widely used by most archaeologists until the last 15 years and underlines the extent to which Reisner's insistence on careful, reliable testing of all areas was far ahead of its time. In testing apparently sterile or disturbed ground

two methods were used: trenches and small trial pits. The trench method is the surest, and consists in driving parallel trenches about 30 to 60 cm. wide into any area from the edge. These trenches are cut through the surface debris into the underlying geological stratum. As the trench progresses, any pit or grave made in the underlying stratum is detected by the change in colour and consistency of the soil. . . . This system is necessary where the surface debris is very deep. The trial pit method consists in making small pits 20 to 50 cm. in diameter through the surface debris to the underlying stratum. These pits are placed in parallel lines about 50 to 100 cm. apart, and reveal at once any change in the colour or consistency of the substratum. When such difference in consistency is noticed, the pit is enlarged in all directions until it can be determined whether the change in consistency is accidental, or due to the presence of a tomb. The trial pit method is perfectly sufficient over large uniform areas where the surface debris is light. *(Reisner 1910: 8)*

Because of severe erosion and the diggings of *sebakhin*, very few settlement sites survived when Reisner arrived in the survey area. For the most part, only tombs, dug deep into the subsoil, remained. Needless to say, he handled the problem brilliantly and was able to propose a chronological framework for Lower Nubia that illuminated the later prehistory and ancient history of that region for the first time. His success was due to the same systematic rigor and organizational genius that had guided his work as director of the Hearst Egypt Expedition and is summarized in the four operating principles he laid down for the Nubian project:

1. Sites were excavated as a whole, except that to avoid reduplication of material, certain late cemeteries were excavated "in skeleton."

2. Each community was completely cleared and the debris carried outside.

3. Each grave was carefully excavated, and no object moved except by direct order, or by a member of the scientific staff.

4. The work was carried out by an organized permanent gang of workmen who carried out these principles as a matter of habit.

(Reisner 1910: 11)

When dealing with such a vast area and large number of subordinates, Reisner realized the necessity of a uniform, systematic, and methodical approach to excavation and recording. To meet this challenge and avoid the pitfalls of uneven reporting and incomplete publication which plagued Petrie and his school, he developed a system for detailed mapping and photography of all the material unearthed based upon the premise that the ordinary, unremarkable finds, when taken together, would contribute more to our understanding of the past than the isolated spectacular find.

The archaeological evidence from which Reisner reconstructed both the later prehistory and history of Lower Nubia came from 58 cemeteries dug during the first year of his campaign. Most of these sites (55 out of 58) were almost completely excavated and well recorded and, like any true monument of science, Reisner's analysis of these tombs has withstood the test of time and today forms the basis of our knowledge of later Nubian prehistory. The earliest sites found by Reisner were virtually identical to the Predynastic cemeteries uncovered by Petrie and his young associates in Upper Egypt (Chapter 7). Reflecting on this similarity, Reisner assigned the terms early Predynastic to material similar to Petrie's Naqada I or Amratian assemblages and middle Predynastic to the Naqada II or Gerzean culture. The Badarian epoch, as yet unrecognized in Upper Egypt, was apparently absent from Lower Nubia, suggesting that this early farming culture must have originated somewhere north of Aswan and that the center of earliest Predynastic development was in Egypt proper.

Succeeding the middle Predynastic were a number of archaeological groups. Reisner used the concept of *group* as a tool for relative dating much the way Petrie used Naqada I and II. The A Group, originally called the late Predynastic, coincided with the Egyptian Protodynastic and early Dynastic periods; B Group (now no longer accepted by archaeologists) spanned the Old Kingdom; and C Group was contemporary with the First Intermediate Period and the Middle Kingdom (ca. 2180–1560 B.C.). D Group was so similar to Egyptian New Kingdom culture that it was seen as a direct Egyptian colonization. Between the New Kingdom and the Greco-Roman period was a gap in the archaeological record which came to an end with the Romano-Hellenistic W Group. Next came an intrusive X Group, and finally the Nubian Christian Meroitic Y Group held sway from the sixth through the twelfth centuries A.D.

Although Reisner believed that the courses of late prehistoric cultural development in Lower Nubia and Upper Egypt were roughly similar during the early and middle Predynastic periods (from about 4000 to 3400 B.C.), he discovered that Lower Nubia began to lag behind Egypt by late prehistoric times, as evidenced by the survival of Predynastic type pottery in tombs containing early Dynastic style wares. Therefore, in Lower Nubia there was slow and rather uneven change in ceramic technology from about 3400 to 2800 B.C. at a time when Egypt herself underwent radical change and development.

Beyond mere technological differences in ceramic styles lies a growing cultural division between Egypt and the region immediately south of Aswan, for some time late in the fourth millennium B.C. arose those differences in wealth and political, social, and economic organization that distinguished the two neighbors for thousands of years. From Predynastic times down to the New Kingdom when Egypt actually occupied the land, Lower Nubia remained a region of few social and economic distinctions and comparatively low population density. The reason for her tendency to lag behind her rich northern neighbor has sometimes been explained in terms of racial inferiority. But in physical affinity the peoples of this region cannot be differentiated consistently from those of southern Upper Egypt. An environmental explanation is more accurate, since Lower Nubia possessed only limited amounts of tillable land. But the biggest single factor inhibiting political and economic growth was, ironically, the precocious development of Egypt which, in achieving first regional and then national political unity, managed to control effectively the Nile and access to the markets that it served.

The Egyptian domination isolated Lower Nubia not only from the towns of Egypt but ultimately from the Mediterranean world itself. By the late fourth millennium B.C. Egypt had become the permanent middleman to Africa. When this development is seen in light of the gradual depopulation of the surrounding desert borderlands at the end of the Neolithic Subpluvial, the isolation of Lower Nubia and her inability to compete politically or economically for markets on the lower Nile is understandable. The final, ironic blow, however, was that Nubia and her southern neighbors contained certain riches like copper, ebony, ivory, and oils that were of use to a strong, centralized state like Egypt, whose rulers could exchange these goods for other prestigious materials like Lebanese timber with the distant lands of the Mediterranean littoral. Once again as at Maadi and on the desert frontiers, the rise of the Egyptian state around 3100 B.C. doomed Nubia to a position of economic satellite before she was able to develop her own strong political institutions. It was the apparent absence of one such institution—kingship— that has led to a long-standing controversy which has sought to explain the role of Egypt in the prehistory of sub-Saharan Africa.

Nubia, Egypt, and the Origins of Egyptian Kingship

So far, our review of the later or Predynastic phase of Egyptian pre-history has focused mainly on tangible aspects of ancient societies—their artifacts, settlement patterns, economies. But as we move closer and closer to the emergence of complex society or civilization in Egypt around 3100 B.C. it is hard to avoid the more intangible features of culture which historians tell us helped make Egypt unique among the states of the ancient world. Perhaps the single most distinctive trait of ancient Egyptian civilization was the concept of divine kingship. It was the ideological glue that held the early state together and, as we shall see later, there is considerable evidence that it developed out of a pre-historic antecedent. There can be little question of the importance of divine kingship to the process by which Egypt passed from prehistory to history. Nevertheless, there are a number of important disputes about the origin of divine kingship in Egypt as well as its possible institutional descendants among the tribal states of modern sub-Saharan Africa.

One of the most persuasive arguments about the origins of Egyptian kingship was raised some years ago by the noted Egyptologist and orientalist, Henri Frankfort, who proposed in his classic book *Kingship and the Gods* that many elements in ancient Egyptian culture could be traced to an "African substratum." Particularly enticing has been the long-noted association of many seemingly Egyptian customs and cere-monial regalia with the institution of sub-Saharan African kingship. Late nineteenth- and early twentieth-century ethnologists sought to ex-plain some of these apparent coincidences in terms of anthropological theories about the workings of culture change.

Around the turn of the century two men in particular, Sir James George Frazer, author of *The Golden Bough,* and Charles Seligman, be-came fascinated with the custom of the ritual death of kings. Frazer wrote some of the most famous pieces of anthropological prose ever penned, compiling evidence from all over the world, from many different time periods, to show that the death of the king was a custom typical of cultures operating on a certain level of social evolutionary complexity. Unfortunately, much of Frazer's information was of questionable validity and his tendency to see all customs as evidence of earlier and general evolutionary stages led to his scientific downfall.

Seligman was interested in custom and social behavior and also at-tracted to Egypt. In the early part of this century, he wrote one of the better summaries of Egyptian Palaeolithic prehistory and in 1909 he was appointed by the government of the Sudan to conduct an ethnographic survey. He also pioneered the study of psychotherapy among non-Western societies. It was this multifaceted genius who first pointed out the striking similarity between ritual conceptions of kingship among the southern (or upper Nubian) Sudanese Shilluk tribe and primitive Egyptian ideas about the divine king, in his 1934 book *Egypt and Negro Africa: A Study in Divine Kingship*. Seligman and some earlier social anthropologists/ethnographers collected information about traditional Shilluk kingship that indicated that a king who outlived his ritual usefulness was periodically and ceremonially put to death. The apparent reason for this behavior was the belief that the king was also the rainmaker. In order for him to be effective, he must be vital and active. Any inability to perform his duties might result in disaster in the semiarid environment of the Shilluk. Since the Shilluk were primarily pastoralists, much of their ritual symbolism recalled the fertilizing powers of the bull and represented his horns. Seligman and many of his contemporaries saw in the bull symbolism and formal regalia and customs of Shilluk kingship much that was reminiscent of Egyptian kingship.

When Henri Frankfort wrote *Kingship and the Gods*, he returned to Seligman's arguments and added much archaeological data from early Dynastic Egypt. He, like Seligman, talked of the Heb-Sed festival, performed by an aging Egyptian king to renew his vitality, and saw in its origins a way in which an aging monarch, faced with ritual execution, might evade his fate and renew the vigor of his body and of the land he ruled. This was a convincing argument, especially when it was reinforced with examples from many African kingdoms in which certain ritual objects were amazingly similar to those employed in Dynastic Egypt (e.g., Yoruba, Dagomba, Shamba, Igara, Songhay, Katsena, Daura, Gobir Hausa, Shilluk, Baganda, and Jukun (Diop 1974: 139, Meek 1931, Seligman 1934)). In posing these similarities, Frankfort also recognized the problem that several thousands of years separated the nineteenth-century Shilluk and sub-Saharan African kingdoms from ancient Egypt. He therefore fell back on the general notion that Egyptian kingship was derived from a broader African substratum of ritual divine kingship that contrasted sharply with notions that evolved in the rest of the Middle East.

Other scholars were not as careful or conservative as Frankfort. The man who was originally employed by Reisner to identify and study the skeletal remains from Nubia, Dr. Grafton Elliot Smith, soon became enamored of ancient Egyptian culture and, through his exposure to the Nubian and African materials, argued that Egypt was the source of much of the entire world's high culture. He and his colleagues, like W. H. R. Rivers and W. J. Perry, were called heliocentrists because they argued that, among other things, a cult of the sun god Re had spread knowledge and high culture around the world through the medium of Phoenician traders. The extremes to which they went to find an ancient Egyptian under every stone foreshadowed the more extreme and ridiculous diffusionist claims of recent years in which beings from outer space are supposed to have brought all high culture and learning to a world living in benighted savagery. But, despite their often absurd and overblown claims, Elliot Smith and his school did raise some valid questions about the relation of Egypt and sub-Saharan Africa that are diametrically opposed to the position taken by Frankfort—questions that can now be resolved through analysis of the carefully excavated and reported facts unearthed by men like Reisner.

Simply put, Frankfort's position can be reduced to a claim that many of the most distinctive attributes of the Egyptian concept of divine kingship are not native or restricted to Egypt, but belong to a larger pan-African context. On the other hand, Elliot Smith and the extreme heliocentric diffusionists would argue that divine kingship and its distinctive ritual attributes originated in Egypt and spread or diffused from there. We shall ignore the more extreme claims of the Smith school in order to focus on the problem and nature of Egypt's southern frontier and shed light on the peculiar changes that were occurring in Egypt at the end of the prehistoric era. Arguments of cultural context and diffusion ultimately have to do with the way cultures change or do not change— they deal with time. If Frankfort is right, then we should expect to find archaeological, ethnographic, and historic evidence for divine kingship distributed over large areas of Africa as far back as the institution of kingship itself. But if the diffusionists are right, then kingship and the archaeological evidence for its presence should be clearly oldest in one area or region and successively more recent in other areas of the continent to which it has spread.

Now what must an archaeologist look for if he is investigating this argument? One thinks immediately of large monuments, of wealthy tombs and of ceremonial regalia. But in many instances the regalia will not be preserved or will have been robbed as they have been from all but a handful of Egyptian royal tombs. Inscriptions and artistic representations are useful, especially in reflecting the context of such regalia, but again, here Egypt will always have precedence since her representational art and literary accounts go back thousands of years, while her neighbors remain silent. Ultimately, we are reduced to the archaeological evidence for socially stratified societies, for the types of cultures that could have supported kings and paramount chiefs. Here we are on firmer ground and are able to compare similar classes of evidence. Early on in the Predynastic era, as we have seen, status and death rites were closely associated. Thus, important people were buried in bigger tombs with more grave goods. At both Naqada and Hierakonpolis there is clear evidence for major differences in wealth and status and even in Lower Egypt where grave goods were not commonly buried with the dead, an individual at Omari was interred with what appears to have been a scepter of office. The trend toward the development of a power elite who buried themselves in splendor reflects directly the growth of a social order that was a direct predecessor to that of Dynastic Egypt.

In Lower Nubia, however, this social order did not emerge. The society remained more or less egalitarian until the impact of Egypt was felt directly. For example, Reisner's successor in Nubia, C. M. Firth, excavated what appears to be the earliest examples of a "chiefly" grave in Lower Nubia in late Gerzean or Protodynastic times (ca. 3300–3100 B.C.). At cemetery 137 Firth discovered a group of rectangular graves roofed by large sandstone slabs. Many appear to have served as family tombs, since a number of burials were found inside. One grave in particular was comparatively rich, boasting many heavy copper axes, chisels, and bar ingots; several stone vases, a dipper of banded slate, a lion's head of rose quartz covered with green faience glaze, a mica mirror, two maces with gold-plated handles and two large double-bird shaped palettes (Firth 1927: 206, and Trigger 1965: 75). Judging from the style of animals on one of the mace handles and the round-topped variety of adz, the grave can be dated to the early part of the First Dynasty—the very moment when Egypt was undergoing political unification. But compared to contemporary graves in Egypt, this tomb is poor indeed and a late expression of emerging social-economic class distinctions; and there is clearly an attempt to import the ritual paraphernalia already associated with emergent Egyptian kingship (e.g., the maceheads and palette). Professor Bruce Trigger, an archaeologist who has recently restudied the culture history of Nubia, has summed up the limited horizons of chieftainship in Lower Nubia in Protodynastic times:

> There were no opportunities for land to acquire special value, which in turn would reinforce the development of a public authority and of the state. The Nubian chiefs probably controlled much of the trade with Egypt, or at least were collecting tolls on the goods that passed through their territory as they did in Harkhuf's time, and hence stood at the apex of small redistributive systems in their own country. Some of these men may have been skillful politicians who were able to collect tribute or taxes along the river and use this revenue in turn to support their own retainers. Others probably functioned as the village *omdahs* do today, namely as the first among equals. In any case the power which any of these chiefs had must have been severely limited both in terms of area and of authority. *(Trigger 1965: 75)*

Only two or three centuries before these early Lower Nubian chiefs were laid to rest in cemetery 137 (around 3300–3400 B.C.), the farming peoples of the central Sudan, 500 miles to the south as the crow flies, lived a mixed farming, hunting, herding existence in villages that showed no signs of social stratification or developing elites. A. J. Arkell who, as stated in Chapter 16, has excavated two major Neolithic sites at Khartoum and Esh Shaheinab, sees the indigenous people of this region developing a food-producing culture out of previous microlithic Khartoum Mesolithic hunting-gathering and fishing cultures native to the southern

Sudan and analogous to the El Kabian of Upper Egypt—a view supported by recent finds by Wendorf and Schild at Nabta. Although there may have been indirect contact between Predynastic peoples in Upper Egypt and the Khartoum Neolithic peoples of Upper Nubia, by way of the desert pastoralists, there is no evidence of any complex societies developing in the southern region until well after Egypt had penetrated Lower and Middle Nubia in the New Kingdom (ca. 1550–1080 B.C.). If the institution of divine kingship had indeed evolved from a more general African context, then we should be able to trace its more or less parallel emergence among many fourth millennium B.C. farming and herding societies along the Nile. Instead, we find a slow diffusion of Egyptian influence up the Nile beginning in Late Gerzean times (ca. 3300–3100 B.C.) and a concomitant copying of some of the attributes and paraphernalia of Egyptian kingship by frontier and client groups over the next 2,000 years.

During the Old Kingdom, for example, we now know that the Egyptians established a major outpost at Buhen near modern Wadi Halfa in Lower Nubia for the purpose of exploiting local copper resources and controlling trade with the south. This fortified town, which may have been founded as early as the Second Dynasty (ca. 2950 B.C.), flourished through the Fifth Dynasty (ca. 2350 B.C.). In the Sixth Dynasty, around 2250 B.C., Harkhuf, governor of Upper Egypt under pharaohs Merenre and Pepi II, left an account of a journey to the Land of Yam, apparently near the Third Cataract. By this date there was a powerful local ruler who controlled a large territory. During the Middle Kingdom, especially the Twelfth Dynasty (ca. 1980–1798 B.C.), the Egyptians garrisoned Lower Nubia but were forced to abandon the area during the politically unstable times of the Second Intermediate Period. At this time, a series of local magnates were able to establish a powerful center of influence at Kerma, near the Third Cataract. Their graves, the earliest truly monumental tombs known south of Aswan, were excavated by Reisner, who initially believed them to be the burial places of the Egyptian governor-generals of the Twelfth Dynasty. More recent analysis of the tombs and their contents reveal them as graves of native princes, which measure up to 90 meters in diameter and contain between 50 and 400 sacrificed retainers. Although many of the grave goods were of Egyptian origin or inspiration, the burial rites of the rulers of Kerma retained a decidedly non-Egyptian flavor. As we shall see in Chapter 18, massive human sacrifice appears to have achieved a brief period of popularity in Egypt at the beginning of the Dynastic epoch and then died out. Such practices seem to be most typical of newly emerging states, such as Archaic Egypt, early Dynastic Sumer and Shang China, but quickly disappear when the elite realizes that it is consuming its most useful and skilled henchmen. Whatever the case, the rulers of Kerma probably thought they were copying the most essential elements of Egyptian royal burial ritual and saw no contradiction in using a custom that had gone out of fashion in Egypt 1,200 years before; and their tomb furnishings clearly illustrate the diffusion of Egyptian political symbolism up the Nile.

By the New Kingdom (ca. 1550–1080 B.C.), Egypt occupied much of Nubia and extended her influence all the way up to the Fifth Cataract, 400 miles upriver from Harkhuf's home at Aswan. After Egyptian rule once more collapsed at the end of the New Kingdom, a powerful native state grew up at Napata in Upper Nubia and eventually launched a successful invasion of Egypt in the eighth century B.C., resulting in the establishment of the Twenty-fifth or Ethiopian Dynasty on the throne of the pharaohs. The records show these Nubians to have been thoroughly acculturated Egyptians who portrayed themselves in traditional fashion and worshipped traditional gods, especially Amon-Re, whose priests, transplanted to the sacred mountain of Gebel Barkal in the New Kingdom, continued to exert a strong influence on the Nubian sovereigns. When these rulers were forced out of Egypt by the Assyrians in the early seventh century B.C., they retreated to their capital at Napata just below the Fourth Cataract near Gebel Barkal. After the destruction of Napata by an Egyptian army in 591 B.C., the capital was moved south of Khartoum to Meroe on the White Nile.

Throughout the Napatan and Meroitic periods, till the triumph of Christianity in the fourth century A.D., Nubian kings continued to imitate Egyptian royal customs. The kings of Napata and Meroe still styled themselves pharaohs of Upper and Lower Egypt centuries after their expulsion from Egypt. They continued to write official decrees in the Egyptian language and to use hieroglyphs until the third century B.C. and, most anachronistically, they had themselves buried in pyramids until the fourth century A.D. Obviously, the Napatan-Meroitic version of Egyptian kingship was peculiarly antiquated and modified heavily by local custom. The practice of royal pyramid burial had been abandoned for almost a thousand years in Egypt before being revived in Nubia, although small pyramidal superstructures were built above tombs or incorporated into tomb chapels by the middle and lower classes throughout the New Kingdom. Other customs, like the importance of the queen mother and the tendency of the throne to pass from older to younger brother, are probably local practices dating back to the Kerma period or before. There is even some suggestion that the Nubians practiced ritual murder of their king, reminding us of Frazer's discussion of the dying king and Seligman's belief that this custom persisted until recent times among the Shilluk. These customs, like the ritual *sati*, or sacrifice of the king's retainers, never seem to have been important or typical aspects of early Egyptian monarchy but rather assert themselves under the later Nubian kingdoms of the upper Sudanese Nile Valley. In fact, the only parallel in Egyptian history that even hints at the importance of the queen mother or the practice of fraternal inheritance occurs during the late Seventeenth and early Eighteenth Dynasties when the rulers of Thebes were reuniting Egypt and leading the war of liberation that led to the establishment of the New Kingdom. In this instance, it is

65 Continuity and tradition in African symbols of the state. Top: The Ogoga of Ikere (in Yorubaland) receives the first British Administrator in A.D. 1895. Middle: King Narmer reviews his captives. Bottom: An Archaic king (ca. 3100–2700 B.C.) portrayed on a miniature ivory statue found at Abydos

hard to decide whether we are seeing a practice that was common to some southern Egyptian families influenced by Nubian custom or merely the result of the vicissitudes of war in which maternal alliances counted for more, and in which the strength and political sagacity of royal wives was given freer rein in a situation in which kings fought hard and died young, often without direct issue.

The fact that the later Napatan-Meroitic kings chose to pose as the last legitimate heirs of the pharaohs does not obscure the archaeological and historical fact that the symbols and the economic and social context of centralized kingship evolved first in the Egyptian Nile Valley during late prehistoric and protohistoric times and only later spread south. As these customs spread up the Nile into the heart of Nubia and Africa they assumed very different forms, forms that were passed on and imitated by emergent states and chiefdoms throughout African history down to the dawn of the European conquest. That such anachronisms exist should not cause undue alarm about racial superiority nor should it impel us on a search for a missionary cult of Egyptian priests that made it its business to carry civilization to the hinterlands. If social usages survive for a long time or are borrowed, albeit in greatly modified form, it is for a reason. Custom does not float in a social vacuum. The ritual and symbolic paraphernalia of Egyptian kingship served as a constant model, a source of tradition to which emergent and ambitious political rulers could appeal in attempting to validate their claims to prestige and authority.

Modern states employ similar anachronisms or survivals to enhance the mystery, majesty, and authority of their rule. Long ago the French social philosopher Émile Durkheim stressed the importance of ritual as a public act through which society's integration might be expressed and reinforced. In a historical sense, the symbols of Egyptian kingship and their ritual manipulation persisted and spread through Nilotic and sub-Saharan Africa for a very good social and economic reason. As chiefdoms and states consolidated, their rulers consciously sought props for their regimes. Drawing on the available pool of tradition, either oral or written, they utilized a tried and true Egyptian formula which had passed through many filters as it spread up the Nile and across the savannas of Africa, eventually becoming a sort of mythical substratum or, one might say, a pool of ideas available to emerging states throughout the continent. Returning to Henri Frankfort's proposition, we can see, archaeologically, historically, and socially, that the social and economic underpinnings of African kingship can be traced to late Predynastic and Early Dynastic Egypt, and were not present even in Lower Nubia before about 3300 B.C. at the earliest. The institution of divine kingship, therefore, was an Egyptian (specifically, Upper Egyptian) invention and need not be relegated to a general ahistorical limbo or substratum.

PART VI

FROM PREHISTORY TO HISTORY, ca. 3100–2700 B.C.

18

THE ROYAL TOMBS:
AN END AND A BEGINNING

Scandal at Abydos—Affaire Amélineau

ALTHOUGH the search for a clearly African ancestry for the divine kingship of Egypt has proved illusory, it cannot be denied that that peculiar institution was a crucial social, political, and economic bridge between history and prehistory. Even if Henri Frankfort over-stressed the idea that the institution was a deliberate political creation of the first pharaohs, there is no doubt that the king became both a real and a symbolic focal point for the process of national unification—for the process of civilization.

Archaeologically speaking, our most impressive evidence for the role divine kingship played in transforming Egypt into a single, national society is the great royal tombs of the First and Second Dynasties, built between about 3100 and 2700 B.C. Located at Abydos in Upper Egypt and at Saqqara at the apex of the Delta just outside the new royal capital of Memphis, these tombs are less well known than the pyramids but were, nevertheless, forerunners of those magnificent piles. Their function, which I will explore at greater length in Chapter 19, was to memorialize the acts of the king as ideal expressions of national unity, prosperity, and cultural achievement. The royal tombs were not only burial places for the king and his immediate entourage but were delib-erate statements of propaganda. They at once advertised and embodied the objectives of the new state. They were consciously created symbols of a break with the disunited prehistoric past, and yet they also con-tinued long-established Predynastic customs of memorializing local "big men" by burying them in large tombs, chock-full of rich offerings. Even some of the attributes of the new god kings, notably their identification with bulls and the use of bulls' horns as decorative features around the Archaic tombs at Saqqara, echo associations already present at the late Palaeolithic graveyard at Jebel Sahaba (Chapter 6).

Tombs not only played a critical role in the political transition from

Predynastic chiefdoms to a centralized state ruled by a divine king, but they also constitute our principal source of information for the nature of this change in Egypt. The story of the exploration of the early royal tombs at Abydos and Saqqara and of the fascinating problems they raised is intimately involved with the goals and aspirations of three very different archaeologists—Amélineau, Petrie, and Emery.

The discovery and excavation of the great royal tombs of the First and Second Dynasties at Abydos by E. Amélineau between 1894 and 1898 caused a public uproar. Some Egyptologists labeled the incident the *"affaire Amélineau."* Sir Flinders Petrie, never a man to mince words, called it "scandalous":

> The pottery jars were smashed, avowedly to prevent any one else obtaining them. The stone vases, broken anciently by fanatics, are referred to thus, "ceux qui etaient brises et que *j'ai reduits en miettes*" ("those that were broken, I reduced to smithereens") (Amélineau, *Fouilles*, 1897, p. 33), and we indeed found them stamped to chips; the stacks of great jars which are recorded as having been found in the tomb of Zer . . . were entirely destroyed; the jars of ointment were burnt, as we read, "Les matieres grasses brulent pendant des journees entiers comme j'en ai fait l'experience" ("I burned the fatty material for many days") (*Fouilles*, 1896, p. 18): The most interesting remains of the wooden chamber of Zer, a carbonized mass 28 feet by 3 feet, studded with copper fasterings, have entirely disappeared, and of another tomb we read "j'y rencontrai environ deux cents kilos de charbon de bois" ("I found about two hundred kilos of carbonized wood") (*Fouilles*, 1896, p. 15), which has been all removed. The ebony tablets of Narmer and Mena—the most priceless historical monuments—were all broken up in 1896 and tossed aside in the rubbish, whence we had rescued them. . . . In every direction we can but apply to the destroyer his own words concerning the Copts who left the remains, "tous brises de la maniere la plus sauvage" ("all broken in the most savage manner"). (*Petrie 1901: 2*)

As soon as Amélineau and his crew had decamped, Petrie rushed to Abydos ". . . to rescue for historical study . . ." what was left. "It might have seemed a fruitless task," he tells us, "to work at Abydos after it has been ransacked by Mariette, and been for the last four years in the hands of the *Mission Amélineau*. . . . My only reason was that the extreme importance of results from there led to a wish to ascertain everything possible about them after they were done with by others, and to search for even fragments of the pottery" (Petrie 1900: 3). And so Petrie went to rescue fragments, while Amélineau smashed whole specimens in order to increase the value of surviving objets d'art for the collectors who had financed him. There can be no doubt that Abydos was a scientific triumph for Petrie. For twenty years he had labored long and hard to rescue Egypt's history from the earth. Just before coming to Abydos he had discovered thousands of Predynastic graves and ingeniously arranged them in chronological order by his new technique of sequence dating. His latest sequence dates carried Predynastic culture to the very threshold of history, to the times of the legendary Menes. Now Abydos presented him the unique opportunity to combine scientific discovery with personal triumph. From the wreckage left by Amélineau he reaped

> . . . a rich harvest of history . . . from the site which was said to be exhausted; and in place of the disordered confusion of names without any historical connection, which was all that was known from the *Mission Amélineau*, we now have the complete sequence of kings from the middle of the dynasty before Mena to probably the close of the IInd Dynasty, and we can trace in detail the fluctuations of art throughout these reigns. *(Petrie 1901: 2)*

What Petrie rescued from the debris heaps of the avaricious art collector was a treasure immeasurably more valuable than the baubles prized by Amélineau's backers. Half a millennium of history, heretofore confined to the realm of myth, was suddenly brought to light. History had been joined to prehistory and our entire perspective of Egyptian civilization changed. Walter Emery, who, before his death in 1971, was perhaps the greatest student of this Archaic period, paid tribute to the historical importance of Petrie's work:

> Before 1895, our knowledge of Egypt's history did not extend back beyond the reign of the Pharaoh Snefru, first king of the Fourth Dynasty (2680 B.C.), and to the historian of that day even he was somewhat of a shadowy figure. It is true that we had the records of the Classical writers giving long lists of kings with what was considered the most important events of their reigns. We also had Egyptian lists of the kings back to the legendary Menes, the first monarch of the First Dynasty and the founder of united Egypt. But these records, both Classical and Egyptian, were too fragmentary to give the scholar any sure foundation for historical research, and indeed many authorities regarded these kings as largely mythological. Certainly no one had any conception of the highly civilized state which existed in the Nile Valley hundreds of years before the Pyramid Age. *(Emery 1961: 21)*

Abydos today is one of the most fertile and agriculturally productive regions of Upper Egypt. There the flat Nile bottomlands reach miles into a great embayment coming unusually close to the towering 800-foot-high cliffs of the Western Desert. At the base of these cliffs, on an old alluvial fan or terrace known locally as the Umm el-Qa'ab (the mother of pots), lie the tombs of the first pharaohs and what some archaeologists, including Petrie himself, believe to be the graves of their immediate prehistoric ancestors. Petrie cleared and mapped 11 royal tombs including the grave of the Protodynastic Pharaoh Narmer (ca. 3100 B.C), eight First Dynasty tombs (see Table XI), including one belonging to a queen, and two burial places of Second Dynasty monarchs. Although the tombs became larger and more elaborate with time, they all consisted basically of large open pits dug deep in the ground around the edges of which were constructed thick mud-brick retaining walls. The interiors of the brick-lined pits were partitioned around the edges into a number of small chambers with mud-brick dividing walls, while the central portion of the tomb was reserved for the royal burial chamber. This was built of costly imported timber and the entire pit roofed

TABLE XI LIST AND COMPARATIVE SIZES OF ROYAL TOMBS FOUND BY PETRIE AT ABYDOS

*Ruler's Horus[1] (Throne) Name	Principal Variants of Name	Petrie's Tomb Designation	Dynasty	Total Floor Area (sq. m.) (After Reisner 1936)
Narmer	Narmer	B-10	O	103.4
Aha	Aha-Mena,[1]	B-19	I	110.0
	Aha Menes,[2]		I	
	Hor-aha[3]		I	
Djer	Zer[1]	O		311.1 (or 313.0)
	(Queen) Merneit,[1]	Y		229.0
	Merneith,[2]			
	Meryet-nit[3]		I	
Wadji	Zet,[1] Uadji,[3] Djet[4]	Z	I	158.7
De(we)n	Den,[1] Wedymuw,[2] Udimu[3]	T		341.6 (or 346.0)
Anedjib	Azab,[1] Az-ib,[2] Enezib-Merbapen[3]	X	I	109.0
Semerkhet	Mersekha[1]	U	I	209.0
Qaa	Qa,[1] Qay'a,[2] Ka'a[3]	Q	I	385.9 (or 369.0)
Peribsen	Perabsen-Sekhemib[3]	P	II	270.0
Khasekhemwy (Khasekhem)	Khasekhemwy (Khasekhem)	V	II	1001.88

KEY   * Information provided by Prof. Klaus Baer
    [1] After Petrie 1900, 1901
    [2] After Reisner 1936
    [3] After Emery 1961
    [4] After Kemp 1966

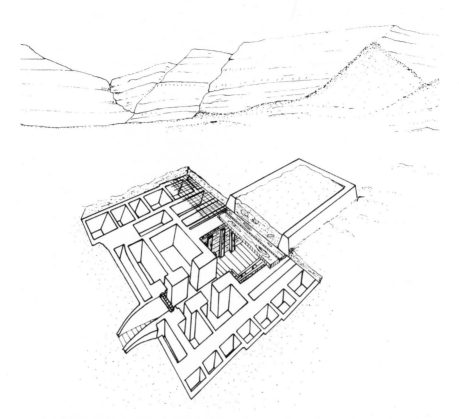

66 Hypothetical reconstruction of the Tomb of Ka'a at Abydos

by means of wooden planks supported by vertical timber joists and keyed into the tops of the retaining walls. The roofs and most of the superstructures of the royal tombs of Abydos had long since disappeared by Petrie's day, but it seems as if the retaining walls were continued upward for a short space and the hollow area over the timber and brush roof filled with rubble, gravel, mud-brick or packed mud (or a combination of these materials) to create the effect of a low, benchlike building or *mastaba*. To judge from the fragmentary superstructure of the tomb of Wadji, the exterior faces sloped slightly inward from bottom to top and were smooth, plastered, and unadorned, in contrast to large tombs of the same date at Saqqara near Cairo, where aboveground mud-brick walls were elaborately niched and painted in brightly colored, geometric patterns to imitate palace façades.

Table XI compares the dimensions of the royal tombs found by Petrie at Abydos and lists the Horus or throne names of their builders. Since, in some cases, the readings of the royal names are uncertain and, in others, various spellings still in print reflect the peculiarities of different European languages, the principal variants have been noted along with the generally acknowledged scientific spellings currently in vogue. Since the ancient Egyptians did not write vowels, these have been supplied for the ease of the reader.

The earliest royal tombs of Narmer, Hor-aha, and their queens were simple rectangular affairs divided into two compartments. Beginning with Djer, multiple chamber tombs were introduced and finally, in the reign of Den (fifth king of the First Dynasty), a long, sloping stairway was incorporated into the design. Theoretically, this improvement enabled the superstructure of the tomb to be completed and even stocked during the lifetime of the ruling pharaoh. Whether or not this actually occurred is not known, but the use of the tomb before a king's death as a storehouse for vast quantities of surplus goods would have had the effect of banking such commodities in a safe place, since at least one of the official royal residences probably stood within clear view of the necropolis. Around many of the tombs were clustered smaller, subsidiary graves, often arranged in neat rows. As we shall see shortly, these have given rise to heated debates over the question of human sacrifice in Archaic Egypt.

It is clear from Petrie's and Amélineau's finds that even after millennia of looting and neglect, the storerooms of the royal tombs contained great quantities of goods. Petrie even found chambers in the tombs of Meryet-nit and Ka'a that remained intact. Enough was left in the 40 chambers of Ka'a's tomb to indicate that separate rooms were reserved for different types of offerings, for example, wine storage jars, ivory, grain, oxen meat, and so on. The variety of food, drink, weapons, tools, furniture, containers, ornaments, and games stored originally in the tombs must have been vast so that it is small wonder that tomb robbery flourished even at this early date.

It is believed by experts that much of the cedar wood used to line the royal burial chamber was imported by boat all the way from Lebanon while other luxury materials, like ivory, ebony, carnelian, gold, turquoise, and lapis lazuli also came from foreign lands. Perhaps the most astounding individual find was the mummified arm of Djer's queen. Inside its wrappings, still in place after nearly 5,000 years, were four bracelets of gold and precious stones. The treasure had been spared by an accident of fate that prompted an ancient robber to shove the arm into a hole in the wall.

It is usually an axiom of archaeology that treasure means trouble, and this was especially true in Petrie's day when thieves and looters vied openly with archaeologists for salable art objects. To avoid robbery, Petrie believed that one could only work safely with trained and honest workmen who trusted the archaeologist. Regarding the queen's arm, he remarks:

67   Jewelry from the Tomb of Djer at Abydos

Nothing but obtaining the complete confidence of the workmen, and paying them for all they find, could ever make them deal with valuables in this careful manner. On seeing it, Mr. Mace told them to bring it to our huts intact, and I received it quite undisturbed. In the evening the most intelligent of the party was summoned up as a witness of the opening of the wrappings, so that there should be no suspicion that I had not dealt fairly with the men. I then cut open the linen bandages, and found, to our great surprise, the four bracelets of gold and jewelry. . . . When recorded, the gold was put in the scales and weighed against sovereigns before the workman, who saw everything. Rather more than the value of gold was given to the men, and thus we ensured their goodwill and honesty for the future.

(Petrie 1901: 16)

Petrie's description of the jewelry communicates not only the excitement of the find, but the skill and labor required to produce such objects and the degree to which a class of craftsmen already fully dependent on royal patronage and long-distance exchange networks had evolved by the First Dynasty.

Such is this extraordinary group of the oldest jewelry known. . . . Here, at the crystallizing point of Egyptian art, we see the unlimited variety and fertility of design. Excepting the plain gold balls, there is not a single bead in any one bracelet which would be interchange-able with those in another bracelet . . . the purest handwork, the most ready designing, and not a suspicion of merely mechanical polish and glitter. The technical perfection of the soldering has never been ex-celled, as the joints show no difference of colour, and no trace of excess.

Also from the tomb of Djer came an attractive pin of gold alloy, sur-mounted by a round head. Small ivory labels were found in most of the tombs and were usually incised with the king's name and provided with a hole for fastening to objects to indicate ownership. Fragments of thou-sands of finely made stone vases and bowls of alabaster, marble, diorite, slate, schist, breccia, volcanic ash, gray limestone, and even rock crystal attest to the high development of the stonecutter's art and the demand for his products among the prestige-conscious ruling elite. Even after being despoiled on a number of separate occasions, the tomb of Khasekhemui yielded enough wealth to hint at the vast drain on technology and pro-ductivity that the construction and stocking of a royal tomb involved: a scepter of sard and gold, gold bracelets, copper bowls and ewers, numerous model tools of copper including drill bits and adzes and ele-gant small white marble vases tightly sealed with golden lids. In all the tombs Petrie found fragments of finely carved and inlaid wood and ivory artifacts, including bull's-hoof furniture legs and ivory, ebony and horn tubes decorated in favorite geometric designs.

Petrie and his colleagues continued to dig at Abydos until the out-break of the First World War, and although no more royal tombs came to light, three rectangular groupings of long burial trenches were found in the desert just below the Umm el-Qa'ab near Abydos. Petrie believed these tombs once belonged to Archaic courtiers although it is now fairly certain that they housed lesser functionaries, perhaps funerary priests. They consisted of long, narrow trenches lined with mud-brick walls and subdivided into a number of separate compartments and recall the sub-sidiary graves that surround many of the First Dynasty tombs on the Umm el-Qa'ab. The grouping of the trenches in great hollow rectangles suggested to Petrie and many modern Egyptologists that the courtiers' graves must have been arranged around great walled enclosures. T. Eric Peet, one of Petrie's most competent and thorough assistants at Abydos, even discovered a portion of a large mud-brick wall in 1913 inside the circuit of burial trenches, lending tangible support to the opinion that the graves surrounded valley temples or funerary shrines of the Archaic monarchs. Although some archaeologists still doubt the existence of such shrines, their existence is comforting to Egyptologists who point out that traditional royal mortuary practice in ancient Egypt involved two important aspects: (1) burial of the king himself, and (2) adequate provision for the continued sustenance of the king's soul or Ka. During the Old and Middle Kingdoms, it was usual for the mortuary temple to be attached to the tomb of its builder. In the New Kingdom, this arrangement was altered for security reasons. The royal tomb was built in a supposedly secret place and the mortuary temple located in the floodplain close to the palace and major centers of population as well as within easy access of the Nile—the major artery of transportation.

The pharaohs buried at Abydos seem to have followed a custom more analogous to that which prevailed in the New Kingdom. Presumably because usable space was highly restricted on the optimal burial spot— the Umm el-Qa'ab—the Archaic kings situated their mortuary temples on the gravelly plain below. The ruins of some of their surviving temples still stand today, in the immediate vicinity of the graves of the courtiers. For years known as forts, these huge structures are located so close to one another as to negate their military value, while they cannot be shown to command any really strategic position. Ironically, the best-preserved enclosure, the so-called Shunet ez Zebid, has never been excavated. Most Egyptologists agree with Petrie's original notion that the grave trenches originally surrounded similar fortlike mortuary temples that would have served as massive storage centers for the royal cult and provided prestigious last resting places for the priests who served those cults.

A Question of Human Sacrifice

It may be asserted, without hesitation, that *no* event is so terribly well adapted to inspire the supremeness of bodily and mental distress, as is burial before death. The unendurable oppression of the lungs— the stifling fumes of the damp earth—the clinging to the death garments—the rigid embrace of the narrow house—the blackness of the absolute Night—the silence like a sea that overwhelms—the unseen but palpable presence of the Conqueror Worm—these things, with thoughts of the air and grass above, with memory of dear friends who would fly to save us if but informed of our fate, and with consciousness that of this fate they can *never* be informed—that our portion is that of the really dead—these considerations, I say, carry into the heart, which still palpitates, a degree of appalling and intolerable horror from which the most daring imagination must recoil. (*From "The Premature Burial"* in Edgar Allan Poe's Tales of Mystery and Imagination, *Padraic Colum, ed., Everyman's Library, 1908, pp. 273-274*)

As we have already noted, many of the great tombs on the Umm el-Qa'ab were surrounded by large numbers of subsidiary graves (see Table XII). In the case of King Djer, these reached a total of 317 burials, not counting those around the so-called valley temple, or the occasional individuals, like Djer's queen, entombed within the royal sepulcher itself. The discovery of these hundreds of subsidiary burials immediately raised the question of ritual human sacrifice or *sati*. Such practices are well known archaeologically and most often associated with societies undergoing transitions to state-type political systems, such as early Dynastic Ur or Shang China. Unfortunately, the situation at Abydos is much less obviously a case of ritual human sacrifice than the so-called death pits of Ur and Anyang. In no instance is an individual lying in a contorted posture, suggesting his last, desperate death throes. Also, whereas both Ur and Anyang were undisturbed when discovered and excavated by professional archaeologists, Abydos had been plundered by ancient tomb robbers, religious fanatics and Amélineau before Petrie arrived on the scene. In fact, very few bodies were left in the subsidiary graves. Another possible source of information, the extensive Egyptian religious texts, are primarily ritualistic rather than historic and offer no clear hint of the practice of *sati* in early times. All that we know for sure is that it was not a prominent feature of royal mortuary practice in the better-known phases of Dynastic culture. Ultimately, then, the analysis of the meaning of the subsidiary graves rests with the archaeologist and the inferences he can draw from the remains. In the absence of clear skeletal

TABLE XII   FREQUENCY OF *SATI* IN THE ROYAL TOMBS OF ABYDOS

Ruler	No. of Subsidiary Graves	Probable Cases of *Sati*		Possible Cases of *Sati*		Max. Total of *Sati*	
		#	%	#	%	#	%
Narmer	34	0	0	0	0	0	0
Hor-aha	1?	0	0	0	0	0	0
Djer	317	63	19.87	99	31.23	162	51.10
Meryet-nit	41	33	80.49	0	0	33	80.49
Uadji	174	14	8.05	99	56.90	113	64.95
Udimu (Den)	133	40	30.07	83	62.41	123	92.48
Enezib	64	0	0	14	21.88	14	21.88
Semerkhet	68	68	100.00	0	0	68	100.00
Ka'a	26	26	100.00	0	0	26	100.00
Peribsen	0	*	100.00	0	0	*	100.00
Khasekhemui	0	2†	100.00	0	0	2†	100.00

KEY   * A small but undeterminable number of individuals were all buried inside Peribsen's tomb.
† Between 10 and 15 individuals were probably buried inside Khasekhemui's tomb. Only 2 were found.

or textual evidence for *sati*, the best clue to multiple human sacrifice lies in the architecture of the subsidiary graves and what it tells about the numbers of individuals whose graves were roofed over and sealed at the same time.

To date the most reliable analysis of the evidence for *sati* in the royal tombs of Abydos was presented by George Andrew Reisner in 1936, in his definitive book, *The Development of the Egyptian Tomb Down to the Accession of Cheops*. Summarizing all the then-available information on the evolution of the Egyptian tomb from Predynastic times through the early Fourth Dynasty (ca. 5000–2600 B.C.), Reisner's work was a tour de force. In reviewing Petrie's finds at Abydos, he systematically analyzed and critically evaluated the evidence for *sati* on a tomb-by-tomb basis. The task was not easy and was rendered more difficult by the aura of sensationalism that surrounds human sacrifice. Many authorities before and since Reisner's time have taken the mere presence of subsidiary graves around royal tombs or monuments as proof positive of human sacrifice, invoking parallels from early Dynastic Sumer and Shang China to support their case. Although a tempting comparison, the evidence supporting wholesale *sati* in Archaic Egypt is not nearly as clear-cut as that from Sumeria and China.

Reisner was able to appreciate the problems raised by the subsidiary graves as no other Egyptian archaeologist because he viewed Egyptian funerary customs in a broad comparative context and, most important, because he himself had excavated one of the most striking examples of *sati* ever found. The following excerpt, taken from his account of the burial pits of Kerma in Lower Nubia, reads like an archaeological version of Edgar Allan Poe:

The location and various attitudes of the bodies show that they must have entered the grave alive on their own feet and taken their positions as they could find place. . . . the movements exhibited are largely those of emotion at the prospect of death by burial under earth. The most common thing was for the person to bury the face in the hands. It was also not unusual for one hand to be over the face and the other pressed between the thighs. But most of the better preserved graves presented a case or two of unusual attitudes. In K XX, three bodies have one arm passed around the breast clasping the back of the neck from the opposite side. . . . In K X B, the very well preserved body AC has the head bent down into the crook of the elbows in a manner most enlightening as an indication of her state of mind at the moment of being covered. Near the body is another lettered PB, which lies on the right side, head west, but with the shoulder turned on the back, while the right hand clutches and presses an ostrich-feather fan against the face which is bent down toward the breast; the left arm passes across the breast so that the left hand holds the right forearm. In

K 444, the two bodies, G and H, lie with their foreheads pressed against each other as if for comfort. In K 1026, body B has the fingers of the right hand clenched in the strands of the bead head-circlet. . . . Another most instructive example is body B in K 1047, a woman lying at the foot of the grave and under a hide; she has turned slightly on her back with the right hand against the right leg and clutches the thorax with the left hand as if in agony. But it is unnecessary to multiply these gruesome evidences further. No one of normal mentality who will read the detailed evidence in the descriptions will escape the conviction that these extra bodies are the remains of persons who died in the places where we found their bones, and who had been in fact buried alive. *(Reisner 1923, cited in Heizer 1959: 108-110)*

Unlike these examples from Kerma and others found at Ur and Anyang, the so-called Egyptian *sati* burials did not occur in massive, communal death pits but, for the most part, in individual graves. Moreover, few if any Egyptian burials display the gross distortions characteristic of persons buried alive. It seems that they were dead well before being sealed in their tombs. The single most important clue to their fate—the initial reason archaeologists believed the people in the subsidiary graves were true victims of *sati*—was the subordinate manner in which their humble tombs clustered around the great royal sepulchers. Unfortunately, as Reisner was well aware, there was another common Egyptian burial custom that could create the same effect.

In his forty years of work at Giza, he had traced the development of royal burial practices through the Fourth Dynasty. At that time it became common for important nobles and their families and dependents to be buried in systematically laid-out *mastaba* tombs clustered around the pyramid of their chief. The pyramid of Khufu, for example, is flanked on its eastern and western sides by a veritable village of the dead. The tombs and tomb chapels of his own and later, Fifth Dynasty, high officials arranged neatly about the burial place of Khufu reflect, in reality, the extreme degree of political and religious centralization reached by the mature Old Kingdom state, when even the rewards of eternal life depended on continued association with the person of the king—a doctrine that Louis XIV would have envied. Although this practice produced row on row of neat, subsidiary tombs huddled around the king's pyramid, in no case is it argued that any of Khufu's officials either voluntarily or forcibly committed suicide to accompany their master. On this, at least, the archaeological evidence seems clear. Thus, when we try to understand what actually happened at Abydos at the dawn of Egyptian history, the analogy of later Old Kingdom practice of dependent burial poses a real challenge to the idea of *sati*.

Proceeding, as always, in a methodological fashion, Reisner pointed out that the subsidiary tombs of Abydos were not directly analogous to those of the Fourth and Fifth Dynasties. The graves at Abydos did not belong to the great provincial court nobility but rather to lower-ranking court functionaries. By a comparison of the relative sizes of the subsidiary tombs, he ingeniously suggested the presence of a number of social categories, including officers and members of the harem, servants, bodyguards, household officials, and service personnel (Reisner 1936: 111). Although his categories are surely conjectural, they do represent an original attempt to employ archaeological evidence carefully and systematically in social reconstruction—an approach independently rediscovered by a number of contemporary archaeologists. In extending his analogy to the subsidiary valley tombs, he suggested that these belonged to priests of the royal mortuary cults and were thus not examples of *sati*.

Returning to the question of *sati* on the Umm el-Qa'ab, Reisner decided that the only archaeological proof of the custom would be an indication that groups of individuals had been roofed over in their last resting places at the same time. But in many instances the roofs and their supports had been sufficiently destroyed so that no logical decision could be made, and in other cases the evidence was highly circumstantial. Only in instances where subsidiary burials were clearly sealed under the superstructure of the main tomb could Reisner be sure that *sati* had occurred. For instance, Djer's bejeweled queen or princess clearly was interred with her master (unless the tomb was reopened and resealed—an unlikely alternative in the case of Egyptian royal burial). Reisner's analysis of the frequency of *sati* in the royal tombs at Abydos is summarized in Table XII.

The fact that *sati* acquired a brief period of popularity under the first two dynasties (ca. 3100–2700 B.C.), is best explained by the social and political innovations that accompanied the emergence of the state. In Egypt, the god king sponsored a number of experiments at this time in writing, religion, art, and architecture, all calculated to legitimize and augment his political power as head of a newly unified state—the first of its kind. Most of the experiments were phenomenally successful. In the case of death monuments and the cult of the dead king (see also Chapter 19), the monarchy developed a theme that dominated Egyptian world view for the next two or three millennia. Yet some experiments did not work so well! Human sacrifice never attained the scale reached in Shang China, early Dynastic Ur, or Napatan Kerma, where early kings also experimented with the limits of power, and the custom of *sati* passed quickly from practice with the end of Egypt's period of experimentation about 2700 B.C. It was a symbol of the transitionary process from prehistory to history, from small-scale chiefdom to a unified, totalitarian state. It was an aberration of power at a time when power was becoming the game everyone played. As such, it quickly fell into disuse once the rules of the game were firmly established after the passing of Khasekhemui and the Second Dynasty around 2700 B.C.

Walter Emery at Saqqara: Where Are the Royal Tombs?

When Reisner published his monumental work on the development of the Egyptian tomb in 1936, archaeologists believed that most of the royal tombs were at Abydos. Even though large First Dynasty *mastaba* tombs were known from Naqada and Giza and fairly substantial examples from Tarkhan and Saqqara, these posed no real problem of interpretation. It was generally agreed that the gigantic structure at Naqada, excavated by de Morgan in 1897, belonged to Queen Neith-hotep, consort of Hor-aha (Menes). Neith-hotep's tomb consisted of a large aboveground *mastaba* with complicated niched *serekh* façade in imitation of a royal palace, surrounded by an enclosure wall. Strangely, the burial chamber was aboveground as well, in the middle room of a five-chambered rectangular structure centered within the niched façade, and the grave of the queen was thought to lie in a circular hole in the burial chamber. That a queen should be buried 80 miles from her spouse, the unifier of Upper and Lower Egypt, may seem odd, but it is thought that, as daughter and heiress of a powerful southern chief, she merited her own sepulcher. Perhaps it was through her hand that Hor-aha consolidated the country and perhaps throughout her lifetime she maintained some kind of formal authority over a section of the valley—much in the way that after her marriage to Ferdinand of Aragon, Isabella I of Spain continued to reign as monarch of Castile and Leon.

The *mastaba* tomb known as Giza V is more puzzling. It was surrounded by 56 graves of retainers and was dated by its excavator Petrie to the reign of Zet (Uadji). Like the tomb of Neith-hotep, Giza V was a large, rectangular *mastaba* with a niched façade, surrounded by an enclosure wall. In the center of the complex stood the tomb proper: a rectangular pit lined with thick mud-brick walls and partitioned into five compartments. As in the tomb of Neith-hotep, the burial chamber stood in the center surrounded by storage magazines. Giza V differs from the earlier structure at Naqada and resembles the Abydos tombs in the sense that its central portion is completely subterranean and that the burial chamber was lined with wood.

Unfortunately, no one knows who was buried in the Giza tomb. At present, an educated guess would be that it belonged to a royal queen or perhaps a crown prince. There is even an outside possibility that it might have been a cenotaph for King Uadji—a kind of burial monument in the form of a tomb. The question of cenotaphs is a very important one and ultimately lies at the bottom of one of the greatest historical and cultural mysteries of Archaic and Old Kingdom Egypt—the relationship of mortuary custom to the role of kingship. It was this problem that was raised only a year after Reisner had published his definitive study of the Egyptian tomb by an archaeologist who challenged the long-accepted primacy of Abydos.

Walter Brian Emery was something of a prodigy as far as Egyptian archaeology was concerned. Born in England in 1903, he was destined by his family to pursue a career in marine engineering. Although he apprenticed in this profession and learned drafting and architectural skills that would stand him in good stead in his future years in Egypt, he never cared for the calling that had been so arbitrarily chosen for him. In 1921, at the age of eighteen, his fascination with Egyptology led him to attend classes at the Institute of Archaeology of the University of Liverpool under T. Eric Peet. In 1923, Emery went to Egypt for the first time as an assistant of the Egypt Exploration Society's Tell el Amarna expedition. There, working in the city of the heretic King Akhnaton, he met young archaeologists like J. D. S. Pendlebury, who would soon revolutionize Minoan archaeology, and the Egyptologist Stephen Glanville, with whom he struck up a lifetime friendship. His career took a dramatic turn in 1924 when he met Sir Robert Mond, the wealthy and enlightened patron of archaeological excavations in Egypt, who later financed prehistoric research at Armant and who invited Emery to dig the tomb of Ramose. The tomb, built at the height of the Eighteenth Dynasty by a vizier of Thutmose III, is one of the most spectacular private graves at Thebes and contains much important historical and artistic information. At the time he was digging there, Walter Emery was the youngest archaeologist to head a major project in Egypt. His love for the monumental and flamboyant aspects of Egyptian archaeology, nurtured at Amarna and the tomb of Ramose, and his ability to sense an important find classes him with the older school of archaeologists who worked in the Near East. His old friend and close associate at Saqqara, H. S. Smith, wrote:

> In some ways he may be considered the last of a long and famous line of "monumental" archaeologists, in that his *forte* was the excavation of the major remains of ancient civilization, not the detailed dissection and analysis of living debris by modern methods. But he had made himself a master of the work he really understood, the presentation and interpretation of ancient architecture, and his methods were largely appropriate to the sites he dug and their physical condition. *(Smith 1971: 200)*

Between 1929 and 1934 Walter Emery directed the second archaeological survey of Nubia, surveying and excavating a 90-mile stretch along both sides of the Lower Nubian Nile between Wadi es Sebua and Ballana, extending and refining Reisner's earlier work there. His life's work really began in 1935, however, when he was asked to take over the work started by C. M. Firth in 1930 on the Archaic necropolis of north Saqqara and halted prematurely by the excavator's death in 1931. Emery's career at Saqqara saw one success follow another, and eventually led him to the conviction that Saqqara and not Abydos was the real burial place of Egypt's Archaic kings.

In his very first season at Saqqara, in the course of completing the clearance of Tomb 3035 begun by Firth, it occurred to him that he should investigate the internal fill of the *mastaba* superstructure, hitherto regarded as solid. He was rewarded by the discovery of forty-five intact magazines containing a magnificent funerary provision, including some remarkable inlaid alabaster discs, now among the treasures of the Cairo Museum. The next year he discovered a great *mastaba* tomb (No. 3357) belonging to the reign of Hor-aha, the earliest in the necropolis. In the following seasons (1936–39), he discovered further remarkable tombs of the First Dynasty. No. 3471 of the reign of the Horus Djer contained a unique and magnificent "copper treasure" now in Cairo, which radically changed our knowledge of First Dynasty craftsmanship. No. 3111 was unique in preserving intact the skeleton of a First Dynasty noble *in situ*, probably the "district administrator Sabu." In No. 3038, of the reign of Anedib, the burial chamber was surmounted by an unparalleled stepped structure of brick which Emery was later to see as a precursor of the Step Pyramid. These tombs were published with others in a series of volumes (*The Tomb of Hemaka*, 1938; *Hor-aha*, 1939; *Great Tombs of the First Dynasty*, Vol. I, 1949), which set a new standard in the presentation and reconstruction of the mud-brick architecture of ancient Egypt. (*Smith 1971: 194*)

The publication of Volumes II and III of *Great Tombs* in 1954 and 1958 brought to light the remarkable bull's-head bench of Tomb No. 3504, the boat grave of No. 3503, and a model estate of the reign of Hor-aha as well as a wealth of items that illustrate vividly the sophistication of the material culture of Egypt's early ruling class. The objects found at Saqqara round out the picture of the Archaic period first sketched by Petrie at Abydos. Unlike Abydos, however, Saqqara had never been subjected to the heavy hand of Amélineau, and by Emery's day archaeological techniques had reached a generally high standard, especially in the realms of recording and publication of architectural remains.

The tombs found by Emery were similar to Giza V; they consisted of underground burial chambers covered by large rectangular *mastabas* decorated with niched façades and surrounded by plain mud-brick enclosure walls. Inside the *mastaba*, above the burial chamber, the whole structure was subdivided into numerous magazines, some of which were still packed with their original contents. For instance, Tomb No. 3504 boasted about 1,500 stone and 2,500 pottery vessels even after several of the storage compartments had been robbed repeatedly. Often pottery jars were still sealed with their conical mud caps and bore the stamp of the ruling monarch or an important noble, making it possible for Emery to date the tombs accurately and study their architectural evolution. One of the most useful characteristics of the tombs proved to be the style of their niching. As a general rule, the niching of the earlier tombs was most complex. By the Second Dynasty niches were simplified but appear in their earlier form again in the lesser tombs of the Third Dynasty. Aside from its decorative value and political association with the royal palace, the niche and associated false door in Old Kingdom times was incorporated into most tombs of consequence as the spot where offerings to the dead were made. Inside the tombs' magazines, in addition to the thousands of stone and pottery jars and dishes, were finely wrought, large stone knives and flint end scrapers of amazing uniformity. Personal ornaments abounded, including bracelets of schist, onyx, ivory and flint, while inlaid ivory, bone and wood gaming boards and gaming pieces reflect the early fascination for intellectual games of skill and chance admired by ancient Egyptians of all ages. Wood-lined tomb chambers and delicately carved and joined wooden furniture with the ubiquitous bull's footrests illustrate both the skill of the carpenter's art and the volume of trade in precious woods which existed at this early date with both Lebanon to the north and Africa to the south. Baskets and leather goods, including arrow quivers and sandals, items rarely found in archaeological sites, were well preserved by the dry Egyptian desert, while cereal grains and animal bones remind us of the agricultural and pastoral surpluses which ultimately supported the magnificence of upper-class life. In one case, in the tomb of a lady of the lesser nobility dating to the Second Dynasty, Emery found

. . . a complete meal, lying entirely undisturbed by the side of her coffin. Such was the state of its preservation that each dish was easily recognizable and the only knowledge that we lack is the order in which it was eaten. Some of the food was served on rough pottery platters and some on beautiful plates and bowls of alabaster and diorite. This gives us an indication of which dish was eaten hot, because, of course, a stone vessel is useless for heating purposes. The menu of this elaborate meal was as follows:

   1. A form of porridge made from ground barley
   2. A cooked quail, cleaned and dressed with the head tucked under the wing
   3. Two cooked kidneys
   4. A pigeon stew
   5. A cooked fish, cleaned and dressed with the head removed
   6. Ribs of beef
   7. Small triangular loaves of bread made from emmer wheat
   8. Small circular cakes
   9. Stewed fruit, possibly figs
   10. Fresh nabk berries from the sidder tree—rather like cherries . . .

With this meal were small jars containing some form of cheese and large pottery vessels for wine and perhaps beer. *(Emery 1961: 243-246)*

Such remains constituted the ritual meal for the dead.

In addition to the rich offerings interred with the occupants of the great tombs of north Saqqara, several *mastabas* were surrounded by smaller graves of retainers. Although in no instance does the number of these subsidiary graves approach that found at Abydos, Emery argued that the minor graves reflect the custom of *sati* and therefore support the idea that the main structures were indeed royal tombs. In fact, many of the so-called *sati* burials at Saqqara could have been interred after (or even before) the death of their lord. Probably the most telling argument for royal ownership of the great Archaic tombs at north Saqqara, however, is their comparative size and luxury and the nature of their location. There is no doubt that Emery's tombs are larger than those identified by Petrie and Amélineau as royal sepulchers at Abydos. The Saqqara tombs are also capable of holding many more goods than the royal tombs of Abydos. Their appearance must have been more impressive than the low mud-brick tumuli of Abydos, decorated as they were by intricate niching, plastered and painted in richly colored geometric patterns. Finally, the tombs at Saqqara are near to the site of ancient Memphis, the traditional Archaic capital of Egypt. That the individuals buried at north Saqqara were not ordinary nobles or court functionaries is proved by the presence four and a half miles across the Nile to the east of a rich cemetery at Helwan. Here the Egyptian archaeologist Zaki Saad unearthed 10,258 tombs in twelve seasons between 1942 and 1954. It seems clear that these graves belonged to the lesser nobility of the Memphite court, while all this concentration of wealth at Helwan only serves to emphasize the disproportionate wealth of the gigantic *mastaba* tombs of north Saqqara. Emery believed that the monuments he found must have been the real sepulchers of the rulers of the first two dynasties, while the tombs dug by Amélineau and Petrie were simply cenotaphs. Certainly there is ample precedent for the custom in ancient Egypt, especially in Third and Fourth Dynasty times. The extent to which the Egyptians carried the illusion of royal burial in a false tomb is nowhere better shown than in the Third Dynasty step pyramid of King Sekhemkhet at Saqqara. Discovered by the archaeologist Zakaria Goneim in 1950, the tomb held great promise of revealing for the first time the sealed burial of an Old Kingdom monarch. On penetrating the burial chamber in 1955 Goneim's excitement increased when he found a strange rectangular alabaster sarcophagus still sealed at one end by a vertically sliding door and covered by the decayed remnants of a funeral wreath of flowers. On opening the coffin, Goneim found that it was, and always had been, empty. Emery pointed out that several royal cenotaphs were built at Abydos because of the area's association with Osiris, including the well-known temple of Seti I (ca. 1300 B.C.), which has been called a regular antique gallery by some Egyptologists because of the old-fashioned representations piously carved on its walls. Finally, there is a resemblance between the topography of both the Abydos and Saqqara Archaic tombs. Both lie on gravelly plateaus on the western bank of the Nile and both were located on sacred ground.

Despite Walter Emery's most vigorous efforts to win a place in the sun for his tombs at Saqqara, the balance of professional opinion still favors the idea that most of the Archaic kings were buried at Abydos. The strongest argument for Abydos revolves about the critical factor of tomb size. Although Emery was right in pointing out that the Saqqara tombs are larger and capable of holding more offerings than their Abydos counterparts, he did not include the so-called valley temples of Abydos in his calculations. These were apparently huge and have no known counterparts at Saqqara. Then, too, the large number of subsidiary tombs at Abydos suggests the presence of the king himself, while the presence of the arm of Djer's queen or favorite attests that high-status people (possibly royalty) were actually buried at Abydos. And there is the question of the private seals. Emery initially identified his first great find as the tomb of Hemaka (No. 3035), since a number of seals bearing that name were found inside, and only later decided that it belonged to Udimu himself. Since we know almost nothing of the process by which goods came to rest in a tomb (was it through slow accumulation or a one-time tax levy?) and our knowledge of Archaic writing is more rudimentary than the script itself, it is hard to assess the meaning of so-called private seals in these great tombs.

Emery found the seals of four different great nobles in four different tombs at Saqqara—Hemaka, Ankhka, Nebitka, and Sekhemka. If we assume that these are not royal names or titles and belong rather to great nobles or court officials, their presence in supposedly royal *mastabas* raises problems of ownership. Emery believed:

> In the tomb of a king or his consort, it would not be strange to find objects bearing the seal or name of his seal-bearer. Taking Hemaka as an example—because of the frequent appearance of his name on jar sealings, etc.—we came to the conclusion perhaps too hastily, that No. 3035 belonged to him. But on this evidence we might with equal reason believe that Tomb T at Abydos was also his burial place; for the same jar sealings in conjunction with the name of the king, Udimu, were found in it, as in No. 3035 at Saqqara. It is therefore possible that both Abydos T and Saqqara 3035 are actually monuments of King Udimu; and the fact that the name of his senior official appears with equal frequency amid the wreckage of both structures is what we might expect, particularly if the servant survived his master.
>
> (Emery 1954: 3)

The fact that the tomb next to No. 3035, No. 3036, also contained seals of King Udimu but this time linked to one Ankhka, is believed by Emery's critics to prove that both Hemaka and Ankhka were officials who lived, died, and were buried during the reign of Udimu. If this were not the case, they argue, how can we reasonably interpret two neighboring and architecturally unlinked tombs to the same monarch? Emery, admitting this problem, countered with the suggestion that the smaller structure, No. 3036, belonged to a consort of Udimu, to whom Ankhka rather than Hemaka was the principal servant.

Although on linguistic grounds the ownership of the great tombs at north Saqqara is admittedly tenuous, Emery's persistent claim that these substantial structures were built by the Archaic kings carries a logical appeal. It is difficult to imagine the kings of a newly united Egypt erecting a capital at Memphis, gathering about them the nobility of the land and then permitting themselves to be outshone by great nobles and court officials whose tombs outstripped in sophistication and size anything in the vicinity. Even the scanty information that history and archaeology and tradition have preserved about these shadowy monarchs suggests that they were not the types of individuals to permit the kingship to be flouted. Every aspect of Archaic art and iconography emphasizes the superhuman qualities of the king. When Narmer conquers the north, he is depicted on the famous Hierakonpolis palette as towering in stature above his allies and enemies alike—a convention that persisted throughout Egyptian history and came into use throughout much of the Middle East. Behind the official symbolism of public iconography, of public propaganda, lay the political and social fact of the king's role. It does not require a good deal of political savvy to realize that the greatest potential threats to royal power are the great nobles. It strikes me as illogical that the military monarchs of the First Dynasty should on the one hand go to a good deal of trouble to publicly tout their roles as unifiers and at the same time permit themselves to be outshone in such a critical area as public tomb architecture practically in front of their new court. Memphis had been raised as a monument to the new order. Its tombs mirrored its social and political structure and organization to an amazing degree. To the ancient Egyptians who had been concerned with the ritual of death and the symbolic reflections of status in their tombs since Predynastic times, the meaning of the great *mastabas* of north Saqqara was clearly *royal* writ large. Situated on a holy spot and displaying their owner's power and magnificence for all the court to see, the great Archaic tombs of Saqqara must have had some kingly associations. Yet this does not solve the riddle of where the king was actually buried. I think that we might justifiably modify Emery's intriguing argument that the *mastabas* of north Saqqara were the true burial places of the First Dynasty kings, while the monuments of Abydos were merely their cenotaphs. As I have already shown, it is hard to completely refute Emery's idea that the north Saqqara tombs belonged to royalty. On the other hand, the balance of scholarly opinion still favors Abydos, deep in the traditional homeland of the Archaic kings, as the real place of royal interment. A solution to the problem might be just the reverse of what Emery originally argued; the tombs at Saqqara are really royal cenotaphs erected outside the new court town of Memphis, while the tombs and valley temples of Abydos were the last resting places of the kings of this era. For the time being, however, no solution is in sight.

Whatever viewpoint we adopt in trying to unravel the mystery of the earliest royal tombs, eventually we return to two themes that we have encountered again and again throughout this book: first, the inherent problems raised by differences in preservation and the quality of the archaeological evidence, and second, the usefulness of active scientific debate in questioning, clarifying, and refining our knowledge of the past. Nowhere are these issues better illustrated than in the controversy that has raged about the royal tombs of the first two dynasties and their interpretation, and nowhere is the contribution of the modern archaeologist better summed up than in H. S. Smith's parting tribute to Walter Emery:

> . . . he expressed in print a view which had long built up in his mind that the large *mastaba* tombs of North Saqqara were in fact the true burial places of the First Dynasty kings of Egypt. This provoked a mass of scholarly comment, mostly adverse, much of which Emery did not trouble to read, for he was not really concerned whether his view triumphed or not, but only that new evidence should be garnered and objectively presented. *(Smith 1971: 199)*

Having reviewed the great finds and controversies connected with the royal tombs (or cenotaphs) of Abydos and Saqqara we are ready to move from the realm of archaeology into that of history and anthropology. Although we will by no means abandon specific artifacts and sites, we have reached the point where prehistory encounters history, where the silent and material meets the vocal and symbolic. The great royal tombs, like the first two dynasties themselves, stand with their foundations in the prehistoric past and their superstructures in the historic future. They contain short, barely decipherable inscriptions that formally qualify them as historic but these, like most of the other objects in the tombs of Abydos and Saqqara, are not yet typical of the classic culture of ancient Egypt as it developed from the Third Dynasty onward (i.e., from about 2700 B.C.) and as it persisted for the next 2,000 to 3,000 years. The Archaic period (the first two dynasties, ca. 3100–2700 B.C.) is not wholly the realm of any one group of scholars in the way that prehistoric Egypt belongs to the archaeologist and Dynastic Egypt to the Egyptologist.

In relating prehistory and history, one of the main goals of this book, we must seek metaphors from the culture of Archaic times to describe, to explain all that went before, and all that was to come. The information on which I will draw in fashioning an explanation of the cultural processes that shaped Egypt's destiny in the late fourth and early third millennia B.C. is broad and varied and includes both the physical manifestations of social change—writing, art, and wealth—and the great, overarching cultural dimensions of population, human ecology, technology, subsistence, social stratification, burial and belief, exchange and conflict.

19

IN SEARCH OF MENES

A **The King's Egyptian: The Inscriptions of Abydos**

C C O R D I N G to ancient Egyptian tradition, it was Menes, king of Upper Egypt, who founded the First Dynasty and built Memphis, thereby becoming the first ruler of a united Egyptian nation. Regrettably, this event, which probably occurred around 3100 B.C., is not recorded on any contemporary written document, unless the pictographic evidence on the Narmer Palette is accepted at its face value. Written accounts of Menes's unification of Egypt come from hundreds if not thousands of years after the alleged event, by which time Menes (if he ever really existed) had been transformed into a culture-hero whose life and accomplishments were embroidered with semimythical anecdotes. According to one of these stories, he is supposed to have perished after a long reign by being carried off and devoured by a crocodile while hunting in the river—a fitting end for a son of the Nile! Without contemporary written records, we are somewhat ironically reduced to discussing the quasi-historical figure of Menes and his activities in terms of a highly ambiguous body of archaeological data, information best used to interpret cultural changes strung out over generations or even millennia and not the accomplishments of individuals.

Nevertheless, the search for Menes or his real equivalent has deep relevance for the broader theme of the relationship between history and prehistory. In a sense, Menes is the first person in Egyptian history, or almost. In fact, the Palermo Stone (the Fifth Dynasty king list compiled about 2400 B.C. and discussed in Chapter 2) does mention several enigmatic characters believed by James Henry Breasted to represent real Predynastic kings of Upper Egypt. Unfortunately, since the Palermo Stone was inscribed approximately 700 years after the unification, the authenticity of names like "Seka, Khayu, Teyew, Thesh, Neheb, Wazenz and Mekh" (Breasted 1906 I:57) cannot be proved. The very fact that they were recorded, however, suggests that the ancient Egyptians themselves perceived a clear link with their own prehistory—a link that is supported by the archaeological evidence of large, Late Gerzean tombs at Naqada and Hierakonpolis dating as much as 200 years before the time of Menes and tombs at Abydos belonging to kings like Sma and Ka assigned by Petrie to the last generation or two before the final unification of Egypt (ca. 3200–3100 B.C.). Since many of the attempts to link the personalities of history with the broad social trends of prehistory hinge on the earliest inscriptional evidence, and since that evidence, meager as it is, is primarily associated with the royal tombs at Abydos and Saqqara, it is fitting that we begin the search for Menes with the Egyptian, hieroglyphic system of writing.

Almost universally, the presence of writing is taken as a sign that a society has made or is making the transition from prehistory to history. With the single exception of Peru, all the civilizations of antiquity possessed a system of writing. The skill, like so many other developed arts and crafts, was linked intimately to the appearance of new elites—a fact demonstrated graphically by Petrie's discoveries at Abydos.

In 1900 the prominent paleographer Francis Llewellyn Griffith could write of the new finds at Abydos:

> . . . Professor Petrie has far more than doubled the materials available for studying the earliest known period of writing in Egypt.
>
> (Griffith in Petrie 1900: 34)

What was especially exciting to the trained eye of an epigrapher like Griffith was the existence of an already developed, cursive writing as early as the First Dynasty.

> Another fact which is interesting to observe is that, with one exception, all the essential features of the Egyptian system of writing appear well developed at this remote period.
>
> (Griffith in Petrie 1900: 34)

Despite such high praise, Archaic Egyptian, as Egyptologists call the earliest written language of the ancient Egyptians, has proven very difficult to decipher. The main problem is that inscriptions are short and, at this early date, rules of spelling and grammar were unformed or, at best, vague. For example, the same proper name may be read differently by two different translators. An example of the confusion that results from this state of the art is illustrated in Table XI, which lists some of the principal variants used over the years by archaeologists and Egyptologists to designate Archaic rulers. Under such circumstances, it is not easy to project back to Archaic times (ca. 3100–2700 B.C.) what we know about the classic Middle Egyptian of the Middle Kingdom (ca. 2130–1785 B.C.).

The language spoken by the first pharaohs was clearly Egyptian and is today classified by linguists as a member of the Afro-Asian or Hamito-

Semitic family, a group that also includes Semitic, Berber, Cushitic, and Chadic (Hausa). The fact that all these languages are, more or less, geographically contiguous suggests to some scholars that, far back in time, they must have diffused from a single center in the Near East or North Africa. It is still logically impossible to identify the language of a prehistoric group, although it seems highly probable that the Predynastic peoples spoke Egyptian. Nevertheless, it is possible for a people to change their language without radically altering their material culture —an obstacle that archaeologists and historical linguists often forget.

Like many Egyptologists, Walter Emery was puzzled by the apparently precocious development of writing in Egypt where, unlike Mesopotamia, it seems to have gone through no formative phase; but he felt that

> . . . the pick of the excavator is yearly providing fresh material, and already evidence has been obtained which shows that the written language was by no means in its infancy, even at the beginning of the First Dynasty. *(Emery 1961: 192)*

One of the scraps of evidence that suggests writing was in more widespread use than heretofore believed during the First Dynasty came from Emery's excavations at Saqqara, where

> two rolls of papyrus were found in a small box, dated to the reign of Udimu, and although they had not been written on, there is little doubt that this was the purpose for which they had been made.
> *(Emery 1961: 235)*

Although early First Dynasty inscriptions are generally short, they do appear in a wide variety of contexts—on stone grave markers, jar sealings, wooden and ivory labels and plaques, and ceramic and stone vessels. Some archaeologists believe that another type of sign—pot marks—apparently unconnected with hieroglyphs, but somewhat standardized in Archaic times, might also represent a link to an early stage of writing history in Egypt. Pot marks were incised with sharp instruments on ceramic vessels before they were fired, presumably to indicate either their manufacturer or function. Regardless of their purpose, pot marks do have a long history in Egypt, extending well back into Predynastic times. Petrie and a number of other Egyptian archaeologists have conscientiously collected and published these scratchings but, to date, we have been unable to link them to the Egyptian system of writing. In some instances, however, there are tantalizing suggestions that more careful investigation might even yet link early Egyptian writing to a Predynastic forerunner.

In 1969, while surveying Predynastic sites along the Great Wadi at Hierakonpolis, I picked up a large rim sherd of a broken storage vessel. The fact that the vessel was extremely large (having a reconstructed

68   Large Late Gerzean jar with graffito,
found in Predynastic grave at
Hierakonpolis in 1978

mouth diameter of almost one meter) indicates that it was a household
feature, native to the site where it was found, while its distinctive style
and temper also suggest a Predynastic date. On the outside of this surface, badly eroded by wind and sand, was the upper portion of a potter's
mark which resembles one of several known hieroglyphs. Although a
slim strand of evidence, this find, along with Emery's papyrus box and
Petrie's pot marks, does remind us that the search for the origins of
Egyptian writing is far from over. As more Predynastic settlement sites
are excavated, we might expect more information to come to light.

There is, however, another point of view about the origins of Egyptian writing, one that has momentous implications for the identity of
Menes and the reasons for Egypt's rapid leap into the arena of history.
Professor John Wilson, in reviewing the evidence for early Egyptian
hieroglyphic writing, rejected the suggestion that the earliest stages of
development of the script have been lost to us because people wrote on
perishable materials like wood or hide (not to mention papyrus), preferring another explanation, one that

would greatly shorten that period of infancy, the theory that the
principles of picture writing, including the rebus-principle, had been
borrowed from Mesopotamia at the time of the other borrowings in

the late predynastic. None of the Mesopotamian pictures was taken over, only the two ideas that a standardized picture may be used as a symbol to convey a specific word and that words which cannot easily be pictured may be conveyed phonetically by the rebus-principle. If Egypt did thus borrow the idea of writing from Babylonia, it brought her abruptly into literacy and was a powerful factor in the construction of history. *(Wilson 1951: 38)*

We have encountered ideas about Mesopotamian influence earlier, in dealing with Winkler's rock drawings (Chapter 16) and the Painted Tomb at Hierakonpolis (Chapter 7); and now, at the dawn of history, we face the issue squarely, because it is at this moment that the spate of foreign influences identified by Henri Frankfort appear in the Egyptian record. In trying to unravel the puzzle of Menes, we encounter the diffusionist position at every turn. Sometimes it is stated in capital letters and labeled "Dynastic race" as in Walter Emery's recent revival of Petrie's and Elliot Smith's old theory of a conquering master race, and sometimes it is clad in much more sophisticated clothing, as in Wilson's and Frankfort's notions of "borrowings" and indirect or "stimulus" diffusion.

For the time being, given the somewhat older and continuous development of writing in Mesopotamia, the possibility of Eastern influence raised by Wilson is very real, but it is hard to deal with notions like diffusion, given the imprecise dating methods at archaeologists' disposal.

Then, too, there is a more serious objection to diffusion explanations as illustrated by the problem of stimulus diffusion. This concept, first proposed by the noted cultural anthropologist Alfred Kroeber, was originally meant to explain apparently synchronous but independent inventions (like that of calculus by both Newton and Leibnitz or the principle of natural selection by Darwin and Wallace) by explaining them in light of the general context of their times. Thus, these ideas were current or at least they were logical in terms of the intellectual climate of the day. When you think about it, though, the problem with stimulus diffusion is that it is virtually indistinguishable from independent invention. In fact, the problem with the whole viewpoint that separates the processes of history and prehistory into diffusion versus independent invention is that it ignores both the social function of artifacts and the real degree of contact between premodern peoples. For example, modern archaeological research is now showing that across a large portion of the Old World from about 4000 B.C. on, there were subtle linkages—forms of exchange—that involved societies from the Balkans to the Hindu Kush in what an American archaeologist, Dr. Stewart Streuver, called an "interaction sphere." The lapis lazuli that we find in Predynastic graves probably came from Badakshan 3,000 miles (about 4,800 kilometers) away in northeastern Afghanistan; and there are many other examples of such luxury goods traveling long distances.

Such items do not travel in a vacuum. They are passed on for a reason. Whatever the specific mechanisms of exchange that distributed exotic luxury goods over Eurasia during the fourth and third millennia B.C., it is clear that they were in demand because they conferred prestige on their possessors; and prestige was intimately linked to the acquisition and maintenance of power. Exotic goods which helped legitimate someone's status and rank might even be called "powerfacts" rather than "artifacts" because they were so useful to the emerging elites of the civilizations of the Middle East. Writing was one of the most important powerfacts because of the things that it enabled people like Menes to do: to communicate in a new way, to label goods that could be stored and redistributed to clients, to keep records of one's possessions, to delight in the esoterics of a new art form and, above all, to live eternally. To the ancient Egyptians, perhaps more than any other people, written words were real. Just reading the name of a deceased person on his tomb wall was a powerful kind of honor and as long as one's name persisted, carved in stone, then the spirit lived on. Words could also be dangerous; thus we have seen the avoidance of certain potentially harmful animal hieroglyphs or an attempt to bind these forms both linguistically and symbolically in order to protect the spirit of the dead from attack. The fact that hieroglyphs came into vogue with the state, then, should be no surprise. Writing was a tool of the elite. Its function was both economic and political. It assumed positions of prominence on tablets and memorial plaques, like the Narmer Palette, indicating that its purpose was to preserve forever the official record of the king's accomplishments.

Returning to Abydos, Griffith noted that, with the translation of the royal names:

> There can no longer be a shadow of a doubt that the bulk of them belong to the earliest kings in the Abydos list of Sety I [ca. 1300 B.C.], corresponding to the 1st Dynasty of Manetho.
> *(Griffith in Petrie 1900: 35)*

One reason that it was so easy to determine that particular names belonged to kings was that they were marked by many of the same familiar hieroglyphic devices used in later Dynastic times, showing the tremendous continuity in the actual symbols of kingship and emphasizing the primary function of writing in Egyptian civilization. Since early literature was clearly a royal tool meant to designate ownership and record political achievements, we should not be too surprised that the earliest inscriptions seem already well developed. After all, rank, title, and ownership were the overweening concerns of Egyptian writing until about 2000 B.C. and even when dealing with a late New Kingdom monarch like Rameses II (ca. 1250 B.C.) there was little reason to alter the core iconography of the language that enabled the elite to glorify itself.

By the end of the Old Kingdom, the king bore five official names, at least three of which date back to the First Dynasty and are found at Abydos. These include the Horus name, shown inside a rectangle surmounted by a falcon (Horus). The bottom portion of the rectangle is often divided into vertical panels imitating the niched *serekh* façade of the royal palace. The *Nbty* (*nebti*) name was represented by combining the vulture (Nekhbet) of the south with the cobra of the north (Wadjet) and denoted the king as ruler of Upper and Lower Egypt. The third or *nesu-bit* name again emphasized the dual aspect of Egyptian kingship by combining the sedge of Upper Egypt with the bee of Lower Egypt. The last two names, which came into use later, were the Horus of Gold name and the Re name.

The association of the early pharaohs with the falcon Horus is particularly close, and their henchmen were even called Followers of Horus on the Palermo Stone. As we have seen, Egyptologists like Walter Emery have tried to see in this title proof of a foreign master race but it is more likely that Horus was either a regional or, more probably, a heraldic device employed by the followers of the kings who unified Egypt. More will be said on this question shortly.

In continuing the search for Menes, two of the labels found by Petrie at Abydos have special significance and illustrate nicely the prob-

69   Two incised Predynastic sherds from Hierakonpolis. Molded clay object in center may be incense tray

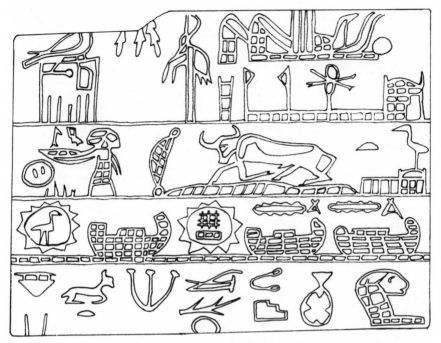

70   The Abydos Label. Top register: name of King Aha (left); post and reed
temple dedicated to the goddess Neit (right bottom); boat-shaped shrine
(right top). Second register: figure holding vessel of precious metal and
offering libations (left); bull that appears to be trapped in an enclosure
(center); temple similar to that in top register (right). Third register: boats
sailing past towns and islands on the Nile. Bottom register: unreadable
early hieroglyphs

lems Egyptologists encounter in trying to interpret the earliest inscriptions. Both labels are of ebony, rectangular in shape, and they bear
identical inscriptions. They have been drilled at the upper right-hand
corner to permit them to be affixed to another object, presumably to
indicate ownership. It is also possible, however, that they were badges
of office borne by special henchmen of the king as marks of rank and
favor. The inscriptions are divided into four registers, running the length
of the label:

In the top line after the name of Aha, with the title, "born of Amiut,"
there are two sacred barks, and a shrine and temenos of Neit. . . .
In the next line is a man making an offering, with two signs above,
possibly *uaau,* "alone." Behind him is a bull running over wavy ground
into a net stretched between two poles, exactly the same position of
the net as seen on the far later Vapheio gold cups. At the end is a
crane or stork standing on a throne. . . . The third line shows three
boats on a canal or river passing between certain places. It is tempt-

ing to see in these place names *Biu*, a district of Memphis. . . . Pa She, the "dwelling of the lake," capital of the Fayum, and the canal of *Mer* or Bahr Yusuf . . . divided in two, above and below the Fayum. In the fourth line is a continuous line of hieroglyphs, the first of such that is known. *(Petrie 1901: 21)*

71   Protodynastic and Archaic iconography. From left to right and top to bottom: ivory plaque from Hierakonpolis. Bottom register exemplifies the so-called Eastern influenced style of the period (Quibell and Green 1902); cylinder seal; ivory label of Queen Neith-hotep from Helwan (redrawn from Saad 1969); fragments of clay jar sealings from Abydos showing the Gaming Board Glyph "Men" alternating with the name of Narmer (after Petrie 1901)

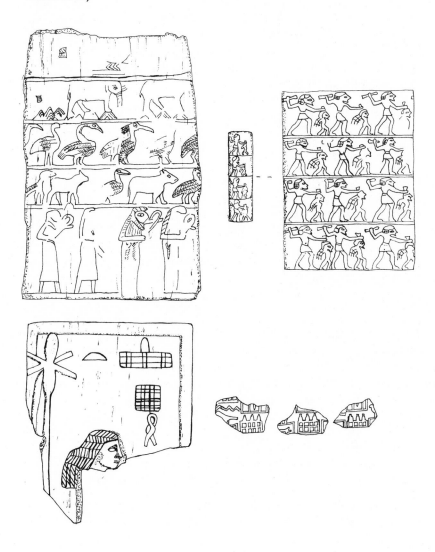

Both labels have painted signs on their reverse faces: a spindle on one and a gaming board on the more fragmented specimen. Since the phonetic equivalent of the gaming board is "men," many historians take this as proof that Hor-aha was Menes. Unfortunately, there are also jar-sealings that Petrie found at Abydos (Petrie 1901: 93, Plate XIII) which associate the same "men" glyph with the king Narmer. One argument, for example, sees the association of Narmer's name (in a *serekh* rectangle) and "Meni" in an unenclosed space as indicating the ruling king and his son and heir. Accordingly, Aha would be the real Menes. Needless to say, such delicate problems of interpretation have merely fueled the fires of linguistic debate over the identity of Menes. Although the niceties of Archaic paleography are clearly beyond the scope of this book, the interested reader will find the linguistic arguments summarized by Walter Emery in *Archaic Egypt*, while the more stout-hearted student of ancient writing systems might consult P. Kaplony's *Die Inschriften der ägyptischen Frühzeit* (*The Inscriptions of the Egyptian Early Period*) for a relatively complete collection of all the early inscriptional evidence.

The King's Art: Symbols of Power

We at last realised that we had found a great heap of archaic objects, not distributed in separate chambers, as Amélineau's finds in the royal tombs made us expect, but carelessly thrown together.

The heap was approached from every side till its boundaries were known, and the objects were gradually removed. This was a month's work, and for more than half this time we were working with penknife and steel ruler, instead of adze and basket, extricating the delicate objects from the sandy clay in which they were embedded.
(Quibell and Green 1902: 29)

The Hierakonpolis ivories, many of which date to the time of Menes (ca. 3100 B.C.), were discovered under extremely adverse circumstances, and it is really a wonder that anything at all was salvaged. Such works of art, although less imposing than the Narmer Palette and the Scorpion Macehead, are important clues to the type of political, social, economic, and ideological transformations which Egypt was experiencing at the close of the fourth millennium B.C. Especially when one recalls Amélineau's wanton plundering of Abydos a few years before, Quibell's words reflect the disappointment and frustration of an archaeologist who is unable to wholly save an important find, despite his best efforts:

Day after day we sat in this hole, scraping away the earth, and trying to disentangle the objects one from another; for they lay in every

possible position, each piece in contact with five or six others, inter-
locking as a handful of matches will, when shaken together and
thrown down upon a table.

Had the site been drier, scores of ivory statuettes of fine workman-
ship, and dating from the earliest periods, would have enriched our
museums. *(Quibell and Green 1902: 30)*

The fate of the Hierakonpolis ivories raises another problem in the
search for the identity of Menes: the historical significance of Protodynastic Egyptian art. At or just before the dawn of Egyptian history,
in those two or three protohistoric generations preceding the ultimate
unification of the country under a single ruler, Menes and his forerunners transformed themselves from bellicose, Upper Egyptian chieftains into paternalistic national kings. Even kings, however, need to
translate power into authority—raw force into willing submission—if
they wish their accomplishments to last. The doctrine of divine kingship
was one means to this end; art was another and related means. Today,
5,000 years after Menes's achievement, the artistic symbols of power
generated as political propaganda remain our principal sources of information about the transition from prehistory to history.

Beyond their obvious role as devices of political propaganda and items
of wealth and prestige calculated to legitimize the political authority of
the king, art objects like the Narmer Palette, the Scorpion Macehead
(see Chapter 20), and the Hierakonpolis ivories were products of a
distinctive type of social and economic organization that developed in
tandem with the state during the late fourth millennium B.C. There is
little doubt that the careers of artists and craftsmen were linked closely
to those of the rising political elite of Upper Egypt throughout Gerzean
times (ca. 3600–3100 B.C.). It was no accident that most of the products
of these early artistic specialists were manufactured or brought in to
Upper Egypt during the Gerzean period, since this was the one area
(contrasted to the Delta and the desert) where a display- and status-
oriented society was developing a political, social, and economic organization capable of centralized administration, military expansion, and
large-scale ideological motivation. Painted pottery, murals, well-made
ceramic and stone vessels, fancy slate palettes, ripple-flaked knives with
carved ivory and bone handles, plentiful personal jewelry, and large
tombs all appear in Upper Egypt by at least Gerzean times, if not earlier.
By contrast, the Lower Egypt of Maadi and Omari, as we saw in Chapters 14 and 15, developed a different life-style based on large, self-
contained, and politically independent villages, prosperous agriculture
and herding, and active foreign trade. In the Delta there is no evidence
of political centralization such as happened in Upper Egypt during the
second half of the fourth millennium B.C., nor, interestingly enough, is
there any development of a politically oriented, representational art. The

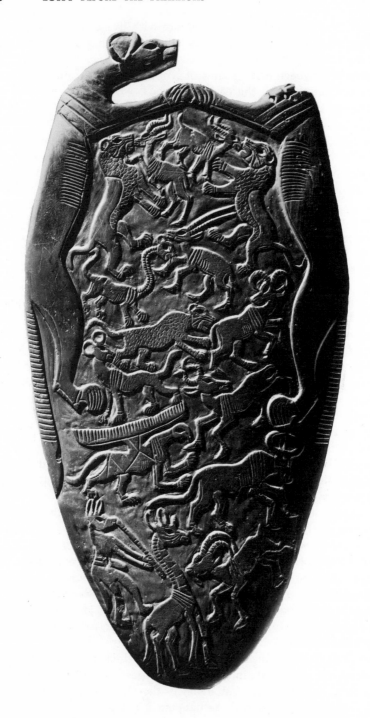

72   The two-dog palette from Hierakonpolis executed in the so-called
Mesopotamian style

invention of the Egyptian state and its distinctive iconography was largely an Upper Egyptian affair.

It is appropriate, therefore, that the bulk of our good artistic evidence for the emerging state should come from the south, or, after the actual unification, from the area of the new capital at Memphis and its necropolises, Saqqara and Helwan. For archaeologists, one of the greatest problems is that we simply do not know the proper context of many of the art objects from the Gerzean and Archaic periods that today decorate the world's museums or grace the vaults of private collections. Thanks to excavators like Amélineau and a brisk international trade in illegal antiquities, the same artifacts that imparted prestige to early pharaohs and their immediate predecessors now fulfill the same function for wealthy and clandestine collectors of ancient art. Another problem is that even when we do know the source of a particular find, like the Narmer Palette for example, it was often excavated three-quarters of a century ago under less than optimal conditions with relatively crude techniques. Such is the case with most of the material from Abydos and Hierakonpolis. After 75 or 80 years, moreover, many of the artifacts and much of the relevant information collected along with them in the field have been dispersed to a variety of museums throughout the world before being properly cleaned, catalogued, drawn, photographed, and published. Only once in a great while, as in the case of the "London box" discussed in Chapter 7, is a collection of notes or artifacts recovered that throws additional and unexpected light on the original finds. An example of this occurred only a few years ago when another important rediscovery of Predynastic and Archaic materials took place at University College, London.

Barbara Adams, a museum assistant at University College, began to catalogue many of the artifacts from Hierakonpolis in the Petrie collection in 1970 and in the course of her work encountered many of the badly decayed ivories recovered by Quibell and Green more than 70 years before. With the advice of the Research Laboratory of the British Museum, Mrs. Adams was able painstakingly to clean them of the wax and mud that still adhered from Quibell's attempt at conservation. He had first attempted to remove the salt and lime encrustations with vinegar and dilute hydrochloric acid

> and then some of the pieces of ivory were soaked in gelatine, melted stearine or beeswax. But most of the consolidation was done subsequently by soaking in boiling wax in London.
>
> *(Quibell and Green 1902: 30)*

These processes had hidden much of the surface detail carved into the plaques and figurines so that when Barbara Adams finished cleaning the objects she was able to comment:

It would be true to say that there is virtually nothing to compare
with them from excavations of other early sites in Egypt.

(Adams 1974: xvi)

Although the provenience of the ivories at University College is uncertain because most lack labels, it is highly likely that they came from
the Main Deposit. Some of the objects, like a particularly striking, slender
female figurine, are difficult to date stylistically and may well be Old or
Middle Kingdom; but some of the plaques, "wands," and gaming pieces
are of undoubted Protodynastic or early Archaic date (ca. 3150–2900 B.C.).
The characteristically stylized animals typical of the famous Hunter's
Palette also from the Main Deposit belong to that period when Egypt
was being unified and supposedly foreign artistic influences were penetrating the land. Typical of these is a small rectangular ivory plaque
about 17.3 by 12.5 centimeters, which is divided across its width into
five registers (after Quibell 1900: XVI). The bottom register shows four
anthropomorphic figures—apparently female—carrying the hieroglyph
ankh (life) before them. As mentioned earlier, much of the applied art
of this period seems to bear a strong resemblance to that of contemporary Mesopotamia and Susa, although Eastern motifs appear hand in
hand with Egyptian decorative themes, suggesting that the objects were
made in Egypt, probably by Egyptian craftsmen, to suit an Egyptian
demand. This demand was for fancy, exotic art objects to shore up the
prestige and help validate the economic and social dominance of the
new ruling class, which was leading the land quickly toward political
centralization.

In addition to the ivories, Barbara Adams has published or republished
a number of different objects from Petrie's Hierakonpolis collection that
probably date to the Protodynastic era or First Dynasty (ca. 3150–2900
B.C.). There was a large number of animal figurines, both stone and
ceramic, including many representations of the scorpion. Since the
famous ceremonial macehead of the Protodynastic King Scorpion was
found in the same deposit, it is tempting to see these obnoxious creatures
as tokens of his cult or that of his patroness, the goddess Selket, or even
his political personality. A large number of uninscribed stone (mostly
limestone), pear-shaped maceheads recall the military expeditions of
Narmer. Recently, Mrs. J. Crowfoot Payne, Egyptian Curator of the
Ashmolean Museum, has speculated that the kings of Hierakonpolis
called in all the maceheads from newly conquered regions to deprive
local chiefs of one important emblem of their authority, thus explaining
the large number of maceheads in the Great Deposit.

The abundance of these implements is also a clue to the weaponry
and type of combat favored by the fighting unifiers of the early Egyptian
state. They emphasize the interpersonal nature of Protodynastic combat
in which important people could engage one another on the field of

battle in an aristocratic fashion, vaguely foreshadowing the chariot-borne aristocracy of Homer's *Iliad*. A secondary function of such mace-heads was undoubtedly that of dispatching wounded warriors on the field of battle: a favorite pharaonic theme. The importance that later Egyptian iconography attached to the ideal of pharaoh bashing his wounded opponent with such an implement suggests that there may well have been a certain amount of honor attached to the act of actually touching an enemy (wounded or not) similar to the American Plains Indian custom of counting coup. In this instance, the pear-shaped mace-head is another one of those powerfacts that took on a loaded meaning in the throes of state formation around the time of Menes—one that became inextricably linked to the successful king's role as bold warrior, or, as the Egyptians of the early First Dynasty put it, "Fighting Hawk."

Barbara Adams also has published a number of specialized flint tools of apparent early Old Kingdom date (ca. 2700–2500 B.C.) associated with the manufacture of stone beads and, probably, other fine ground-stone artifacts. Increasingly during late Predynastic times in Upper Egypt, there was a shift away from finely made pottery to beautiful stone vases of hard materials. Undoubtedly this shift reflected both a technological innovation (the invention of an efficient stone-weighted drill for grinding stone in a controlled and rapid fashion) and a shift in the direction of consumer demand. As we have seen, the rise of the elite placed a positive value on exotic luxury goods which could symbolize the increasing gulf of power that separated members of the decision-making class from their fellows. The idea of stone vases as imperishable items also undoubtedly enhanced their favor among other-worldly-minded elite who wished to take as much as possible with them to the next world.

The tool kits found at Hierakonpolis recall those reported by Karl Butzer from just a few hundred meters away in the so-called Predynastic town and remind us of the close relationship between the social changes that were leading Egypt down the road to statehood and the techno-logical changes that archaeologists and scholars like Barbara Adams have labored so hard to rescue from decay.

An Embarrassment of Riches:
Professor Renfrew's "Multiplier Effect"

In light of the invention of writing and the expansion in arts and crafts, many prominent historians, Egyptologists, and archaeologists have argued that the only way to explain the explosion of wealth and material culture in Egypt with the rise of Menes's state is to posit an invasion of civilizing conquerors or the diffusion of fresh ideas from the East. We might, somewhat facetiously, characterize the first type of explanation as the Four Horsemen model of cultural change, relying as it does on apocalyptic events like invasions, deluges, or droughts. This is not to say that such events could not occur. Indeed, as we have seen, there is good reason to credit environmental change with some role in the rise of Egyptian civilization. Unfortunately, apocalyptic models of cultural change often restrict themselves to a single, oversimplified view, like Emery's master race or some of the climatic or immigration explanations offered by Palaeolithic archaeologists.

Another old standby for explaining the type of change in Protodynastic times is the diffusion model of culture change, best exemplified in the various suggestions of cultural influence or an influx of fresh ideas from the East. One paleobotanist, E. S. Higgs, has characterized a similar viewpoint in his field as "the Garden of Eden approach." Although there is undoubtedly a good deal of truth in many of the traditional explanations, the great difficulty is that they are not broadly based theories. They do not reach deep into the roots of Egyptian prehistory and consider the wide variety of archaeological and paleoenvironmental evidence that has accumulated over the last century or so, nor do they consider the effects of change on the internal organization of prehistoric Egyptian culture.

At least some respite from the all-or-nothing explanations usually proposed for the rise of Menes's state has been provided by Professor Colin Renfrew of Sheffield University, England. In 1972 he published a truly massive tome called *The Emergence of Civilisation: The Cyclades and the Aegean in the Third Millennium B.C.* Although dealing primarily with a different place and a different time, Professor Renfrew's book is one of those rare works which have taken a theoretical approach to the birth and growth of civilization—an approach that finds a useful application in Egypt. Central to Professor Renfrew's approach is what he calls the multiplier effect:

> Changes or innovations occurring in one field of human activity (in one subsystem of a culture) sometimes act so as to favour changes in other fields (in other subsystems). The multiplier effect is said to operate when these induced changes in one or more subsystems themselves act so as to enhance the original changes in the first subsystem.
> (Renfrew 1972: 37)

Renfrew, drawing heavily on economic and systems theory, attempts to picture culture as a series of functionally interrelated parts. A change in one part or subsystem, therefore, will produce a change in the other parts of culture. Although this observation seems logically self-evident, it is quite revolutionary for civilizational studies, where causes and explanations have been offered as more or less self-contained and exclusive factors external to a cultural system.

Renfrew begins his argument by stressing that most cultures are conservative by nature. Their rules and the traditional values that underlie them favor little or no change. When we observe a major change, as in the rise of civilization in the Nile Valley, the question becomes, What happened to encourage change throughout the various sectors of contemporary Egyptian society? Simply saying that increased trade with the East was the cause is inadequate because it does not deal with the Eastern innovations in terms of their effects on and function within Protodynastic culture. Likewise, a conquering elite does not constitute a sufficient explanation; because even if a foreign military elite did establish itself in Egypt, it had to initiate change within a thoroughly Egyptian context and to deal with traditional Egyptian values and cultural systems.

The immediate archaeological problem in explaining the cultural identity of Menes and his state is to account for the sudden embarrassment of riches that characterizes the material culture of Egypt between the Late Gerzean (ca. 3300 B.C.) and Archaic period (ca. 3100–2700 B.C.) in terms of a sophisticated, multifaceted explanation. Professor Renfrew borrows the term "take-off point" from the economist Walter Rostow to characterize the rise of civilization and the proliferation of certain types of artifacts. Over the years a number of propensities develop within a social system which predispose it to a really major transformation. When that transformation does occur, it is so thorough as to convey the impression of crossing a critical threshold. The rise of Menes's state and Dynastic culture can, I believe, be understood through such an analogy and, in Renfrew's words (p. 39), "To investigate this threshold is essentially to seek the circumstances which bring the multiplier effect into active operation."

Since it has been my aim in this book to demonstrate the continuity in Egyptian prehistory and history through discussion of the excavators and discoveries that have led us to such a major reconsideration of Menes and his new state, I think that the most appropriate way of illustrating the multiplier effect at work is through considering the artifacts of the unification. In letting the archaeological remains of this epoch tell their own story, I will employ a particular artifact as symbolic of an entire cultural subsystem. Although an almost infinite number of such subsystems might be imagined in contemplating the rise of Egyptian civilization, as I stated in Chapter 18, I have chosen to restrict myself to eight, partly because they seem to touch on major themes and partly because they are represented by the archaeological evidence. These are population, environment, technology, subsistence base, social stratification, burial and religion (the two are virtually inseparable in Egypt), exchange, and conflict.

20

THE EMERGENCE OF EGYPT

Demography, Settlement, and a Civilization Without Cities: Wilson's Riddle

FOR ARCHAEOLOGISTS, the study of population has two main aspects: demography and settlement patterns. We have already encountered a number of specific cases in which Egyptian prehistorians have offered interpretations based on this type of information. Now we are concerned with the general role of demography and settlement in the rise of Egyptian civilization. In Renfrew's terms, we want to know whether the archaeological and historical records indicate any possible deviations or amplifications between the Late Gerzean and Archaic periods due to increasing uncertainty and change in the population system of Egypt (ca. 3300–2700 B.C.).

Although approximately 15,000 Predynastic graves have been unearthed and great numbers of Protodynastic and Archaic burials recovered, there is, sadly, almost no usable demographic information available at this time. We cannot, therefore, compare the relative sizes, life expectancies, and patterns of mortality among local late prehistoric and early historic Egyptian populations. Perhaps in the future, when modern physical anthropologists and human biologists have reexamined many of the skeletal remains from older excavations and carefully compiled paleodemographic statistics, we will know more of the relation between demographic changes and the rise of the state. For now, all must remain guesswork.

In the realm of settlement patterns, our information is somewhat more reliable. Despite the regrettable lack of excavated settlement sites in Upper Egypt, finds at Hierakonpolis plus some inferential studies based on historically derived statistics permit us to offer some intelligent guesses about the types of changes that were occurring in the villages and towns of Egypt at the time of the unification.

In Chapter 12, I discussed the recent work in the Hierakonpolis area and its implications for settlement archaeology. To recapitulate briefly, the region from the alluvium into the low desert for perhaps 5 or 6 kilometers was occupied by farming and herding villages during the Predynastic period. Sometime in the late Predynastic (probably during the Late Gerzean) the entire site of the settlements along the Great Wadi was abandoned and the population moved back toward the alluvium, settling either in the vicinity of the already occupied Predynastic town or on the alluvium itself around the traditional site of Hierakonpolis (what archaeologists once called the Kom el Ahmar). The most likely reason for this shift was a deterioration of the climate.

Although still tentative, the archaeological remains at Hierakonpolis further suggest that one attraction of the Kom el Ahmar was the presence there of a shrine or temple. The earliest temples and shrines clearly date to at least the Protodynastic period and it is logical to infer that these provided a point of attraction for footloose immigrants as well as an arena in which a population accumulated of sufficient size to be of potential use of an up-and-coming politician. That such local big men existed at Hierakonpolis at this very moment is attested to by the Painted Tomb and several of its companions (Chapter 8).

It is at this point that we are able to use hypotheses borrowed from recent studies of historical Egyptian settlement patterns and the interrelationships between towns and temples to flesh out the picture of population-related change during the Protodynastic period. Karl Butzer, whose study of hydraulic civilization in Egypt has already been mentioned, tentatively reconstructed the population density of the Hierakonpolis region as one of the highest in all of Egypt at this time. He relates this high density primarily to ecological and technological factors—the high proportion of river frontage to alluvium and the effectiveness of basin irrigation under such circumstances—and the abundant archaeological remains seem to support his historically derived figures.

Also working with inscriptional and archaeological data from Dynastic times, Egyptologist Barry Kemp has proposed a general model to describe the workings of Egyptian towns and their intimate relationship to the institution of the temple, a model that has implications for late prehistoric settlements. In New Kingdom times (ca. 1550–1080 B.C.) he concludes that Egyptian towns and cities

> would appear to have had as their principal characteristic a two-tier economic structure based on farm centres, the temple—an adjunct of the state—being a major one, with below it others represented by private landholders. . . . This pattern was necessary because the nature of economic transactions required farm produce close at hand all the time. (*Kemp in Ucko, Tringham, and Dimbleby 1972: 676*)

Although many Egyptologists and prehistorians still balk at the idea of extending such a model back into late Predynastic or Protodynastic times, the evidence at Hierakonpolis at least suggests that the sacred precinct there was of prehistoric vintage; and, although the large, organized priesthoods of the New Kingdom might well have been a late historical development, the principle of the temple as a central point linked to a settlement seems well attested.

In a recent and massive study of the origins and character of the Chinese city, Professor Paul Wheatley has reviewed the evidence for the earliest urban forms and claimed:

> Whenever, in any of the seven regions of primary urban generation . . . we trace back the characteristic urban form to its beginnings we arrive not at a settlement that is dominated by commercial relations, a primordial market, or at one that is focused on a citadel, an archetypical fortress, but rather at a ceremonial complex.
>
> *(Wheatley 1971: 225)*

While reserving judgment on the universal priority and apparent exclusivity of early ceremonial centers, we can see in Wheatley's reconstruction the ideological element that animated the world's first civilizations. As an archaeologist familiar with the vicissitudes of fieldwork, I would say that it is probably impossible in most instances to decide even in a well and extensively excavated settlement the priorities of religious over commercial or subsistence remains. When one considers that most sites were dug many years ago or by archaeologists unfamiliar with controlled, horizontal excavation techniques, the archaeological task of determining the priority of religious over secular occupation is virtually impossible. Besides being archaeologically untenable, a solution that relies on a single reason—ceremonial centers—ignores the functionally complex nature of all village farming settlements. Even in cases where Classical authors assert that such-and-such a Greek colony was founded for religious motives, the reasons were actually quite complicated and included commercial, military, political, and environmental considerations.

Wheatley's argument also points out another problem in establishing the nature and original function of Protodynastic Egyptian settlements. He implies that each of the seven "regions of primary urban generation" which he examined had its own, distinctive history of urbanization. This is a necessary distinction, particularly in a land like Egypt where the eminent Egyptologist, Professor John Wilson, characterized the nation as a "civilization without cities" (Wilson in Kraeling and Adams 1960: 124-164). By claiming that ancient Egypt, at least until the New Kingdom, had no cities, Wilson really meant that it had no cities comparable either in style or extent to those well-known examples in Mesopotamia (Uruk, Ur, Babylon). The archaeological evidence, although still quite weak on this point, does suggest that Wilson was partially right. Large, dense clusters of population, surrounded by walls and separated from their neighbors by relatively empty stretches of countryside, were not characteristic at least of Upper Egypt. But this does not mean that the overall population density of Egypt was inferior to that of Mesopotamia or any other civilization with great urban centers. The population, within certain districts at least, was almost certainly better distributed over the arable land than in Mesopotamia, where periodic salinization sterilized great chunks of territory and forced recurrent abandonment of man-made wastelands.

The question for Wheatley, as for other students of early civilizations, was not whether Mesopotamia had cities and Egypt did not, any more than it is any longer a matter of deriving Egyptian civilization from Mesopotamian by stimulus diffusion. The problem is to see population and settlement as interrelated factors modifying and being modified by other cultural and physical-environmental systems.

> Certainly the differentiation and development of urban political, social, economic, and religious institutions did not proceed symmetrically . . . nor was the relationship between those institutions and their material expression as direct as . . . might be held to imply.
> (Wheatley in Ucko, Tringham, and Dimbleby 1972: 622)

Seen in this light, it was the concentration of a population, possibly around a ceremonial center, triggered by environmental events that provided a group of people of sufficient permanence and size for the emerging political elite to organize.

Thus, population concentration (if not actual growth) played a crucial role in the rise of civilization. Such information has important implications for contemporary economic theory. In 1965 an economist, Ester Boserup, wrote a book called *The Conditions of Agricultural Growth*, in which she explored anew the relationship between food supply and population growth and came to a surprising conclusion (p. 11) which interpreted population growth "as an independent variable which in its turn is a major factor in determining agricultural developments." Her conclusion was controversial because economists for the last two centuries since Malthus's time have viewed population growth as a potentially limiting rather than an enhancing factor in economic growth since "food supply grows arithmetically while population grows geometrically." The Malthusian approach stresses the disastrous effects of a runaway population growth, implications we know all too well in a world whose very existence is threatened by uncontrolled human fertility. Boserup's view, however, may force us to modify Malthusian principles, especially in regard to early states where population growth (or concentration) might have led to the development of new social, economic, and political strategies and, eventually, to the state itself.

Examining Boserup's proposition carefully, there is really not as much conflict with Malthusian principles as meets the eye. In the long run, say several hundreds or thousands of years, food supply will of course limit population growth. No technology or technological system is eternally elastic. However, in the short run, Boserup has often been proved correct. An increase in population (or its concentration) as seems to have occurred in Late Gerzean Upper Egypt between about 3300 and 3100 B.C. in areas like Hierakonpolis probably did trigger internal forces in Predynastic society that led to increased competition and productivity, which in turn led to growth. Of course, very soon a new stability was reached by Old Kingdom times (ca. 2700–2180 B.C.) when the force of social and economic innovation had been spent and Malthusian factors returned to limit the growth potential of the population until further technological and sociological innovations in the Middle and New Kingdoms (ca. 2130–1080 B.C.), coupled with favorable environmental conditions, again allowed population growth.

In summary, although it is impossible to approach the problem of ancient demography by utilizing the poorly analyzed skeletal material, the other archaeological evidence does suggest steady population growth throughout the Predynastic (ca. 5500–3100 B.C.), with a sudden concentration of population in certain areas in Upper Egypt during the two or three centuries preceding 3100 B.C. Such conditions, I believe, provided the demographic boost called for by Boserup's theory and ultimately served to knock the component subsystems of Predynastic society out of balance. Once this occurred, Renfrew's multiplier effect came into play.

Nile Floods, the Palermo Stone, and Environmental Change

Two important environmental changes took place in Egypt between about 3300 and 3000 B.C. The first, which I have already discussed at some length in Chapters 11 and 16, saw the decline of rainfall from the Neolithic Subpluvial. This was certainly not a sudden event, nor was its impact felt everywhere at the same time in northern Africa. In the Hierakonpolis region it seems to have spelled the end of the wadi-based component of the local subsistence economy between about 3300 and 3100 B.C. However, until further work is done there and excavators in other areas publish their data, we will have to remain fuzzy about the timing of this event. The primary results of the increasing desiccation were not disastrous, but simply involved the resettlement of a sector of the regional population, producing an increase in population density around the Kom el Ahmar and boosting the size of the available labor force. This, in turn, created a climate in which local big men or power-brokers could gain more importance through doing the things leaders are supposed to—providing judgment in cases of disputed land, water, and dower rights; providing technical expertise to clear additional land and construct irrigation basins; providing transportation on the Nile to customers; acting as intermediaries in systems of local exchange geared to the supply of exotic materials for ornaments and grave goods; and, finally, providing leadership and resources to construct temples and wage war. To what degree these functions were originally distributed among a variety of individuals is unknown. The tendency for such power-related tasks to be increasingly concentrated in the hands of one or two people (to diversify, in the slang of modern, multinational corporations) is evident and will be reviewed in discussing the changing system of social stratification. In addition to its sociological consequences, the desiccation also affected directly the subsistence economy of Upper Egypt by gradually eliminating the pasturages of the Sahara and thereby rendering more attractive to Upper Egyptians the fields of the Delta, creating an inducement to military expansion.

The second major environmental change took place between Proto-dynastic and Archaic times (ca. 3100–2700 B.C.) and involved a decline in the average heights of the annual Nile inundation. Although this change is often treated as more or less contemporaneous with the desiccation of the Sahara, there is some evidence now to suggest that the processes were separated by an interval of 200 to 600 years. Their effects on the emerging Egyptian state should, therefore, be considered as a distinct episode in a sequence of cultural change that began in Late Gerzean times and only culminated with the beginning of the Third Dynasty and the establishment of the Old Kingdom.

Ever since its first and most famous fragment was described shortly after the turn of the century, the Palermo Stone has occupied a position of distinction. In the sense that it includes a chronology of the earliest kings and a chronicle of the most important events of their reigns by year, it is the world's oldest history book. The stone, as I mentioned in Chapter 3, today exists only in badly damaged form, with fragments distributed in many different museums. It was divided by its authors into a number of horizontal registers or year boxes separated by the hieroglyph for year, corresponding to the length of a king's reign in which the principal events of his reign were recorded. At the bottom of most of these columns were numbers, which most Egyptologists now believe to be records of the height of the annual Nile inundation (see Bell 1970). The fact that some columns have been left blank indicates the accuracy of the copyists who originally compiled the Palermo Stone and who were apparently loathe to fill in information where no records existed (a caveat many modern scientists might do well to remember).

In 1970 Dr. Barbara Bell analyzed these ancient records by first adjusting them to a common value in meters and then plotting their frequency on a graph. Although there are gaps in the record, we have the unprecedented good luck of having information that goes all the way back to the rein of Djer (ca. 3050 B.C.), second king of the First Dynasty. It is indeed a shame that no heights are recorded for the reign of Hor-aha or the Predynastic rulers, although these latter are probably of semi-mythical status anyway. What Bell was able to conclude from these records is fraught with implications for the early history of the Egyptian state:

> . . . it is clear that the height of the inundation, and thus the amount of summer monsoon rainfall over East Africa, averaged less from Dynasty II onward than in Dynasty I. The difference between the average floodheight for Dynasty I and for Dynasties II-V is 0.7 meters, under the assumption of a zero-point that rose at a uniform rate with the alluvium. Under the assumption of a fixed zero for the Nilometer, the decline in flood height is greater, and is also progressive with time.
> (Bell 1970: 569–573)

More recently, Bell has extended her research into later periods of Egyptian history and shown a definite relationship between periods of historical prosperity and collapse and the heights and consistencies of Nile inundations. This echoes Fekri Hassan's hypothesis that pins the collapse of late Palaeolithic food-producing experiments to a period of disastrously high floods and has prompted Professor Karl Butzer to observe:

> . . . it has become difficult to ignore the possibility that major segments of ancient Egyptian history may be unintelligible without recourse to an ecological perspective. (Butzer 1976: 56)

Although the drop in Nile inundations after the First Dynasty might be related to the apparent political disturbances of the next dynasty (see Chapter 21), it is difficult to see a link to the initial consolidation of the Egyptian state. Without a knowledge of the flood heights immediately preceding Hor-aha, we might only speculate that they assumed increased importance to the emerging elite. It might well be that, with the increased stress laid on floodplain agriculture with the collapse of the desert ecosystem, those individuals familiar with the hydraulic regime of the lowlands were able to parlay their knowledge into increased power through the medium of their organizational ability. The presence of irrigation projects during the Protodynastic and early First Dynasty and their importance to the rising elite at least suggests this as a possibility and provides the occasion for a direct consideration of the technological system and its role in the multiplier effect.

The Scorpion Macehead and Butzer's Hydraulic Hypothesis

During the Tenth Dynasty, shortly before 2100 B.C., Kheti I, monarch of the Lycopolite province, boasted of a new canal he had built:

I brought a gift for this city, in which there were no families of the Northland, no people of Middle Egypt (sm); making a monument in ____. I substituted a channel of ten cubits (17 feet). I excavated for it upon the arable land. I equipped a gate (for) its ____ it in the ground of (____) in one building, free from (____) (____) ____. (I sustained) the life of the city. I made the (____) with grain-food, to give water at (mid) day, to (____) ____. (I supplied water) in the highland district, I made a water supply for this city of Middle Egypt in the (mountains) which had not seen water. I secured the borders ____ ____ ____ (____). I made the elevated land a swamp. I caused the water of the Nile to flood over the ancient (landmarks). I made the arable land ____ ____ water. Every neighbor was (supplied with water and every citizen had) Nile water to his heart's desire; I gave waters to his neighbors, and he was content with them.

(Breasted 1906 I: 188–189)

There is currently on display in the Metropolitan Museum of Art in New York City a large, green slate dish dated to the early First Dynasty. It bears a short inscription commemorating "The Opening of the Lake called 'The Striding of the Gods' in Memphis." The lake is possibly an artificial irrigation basin or lake created to water the fields around the new capital of Memphis.

One of the most spectacular discoveries in the Great Deposit at Hierakonpolis was a large white limestone ceremonial macehead belonging to the Protodynastic king Scorpion—the probable predecessor of Narmer. The king is shown wearing the white crown of Upper Egypt, ritually digging or breaking open a canal while his courtiers look on. Nearby a bearer squats with a large basket ready, apparently, to receive a load of dirt as a token of royal participation. It is not hard to imagine the Metropolitan bowl as a somewhat glorified descendant of the humble basket, specially prepared for a similar ceremony.

Although certainly not the only area of Egyptian technology where the multiplier effect is seen at work during the transition to the state, irrigation seems to be one of the most critical subsystems, related as it was to subsistence economy, the production of storable surpluses that could be traded for goods and services, the periodic organization of labor and the performance of pious acts of public beneficence through which powerful individuals validated their right to just authority, or *maat*. It is especially important therefore that we have a record of a Protodynastic king engaging in such an activity—that he chose to depict this as one of the important accomplishments of his reign.

The role of irrigation in the genesis of civilizations has been a hotly debated topic for forty years, even since Karl Wittfogel proposed that it was through such technological changes in hydrology that "oriental despotism" first arose in the empires and states of antiquity. The prob-

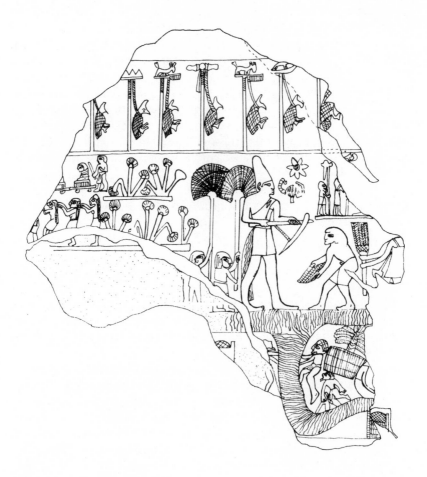

73, 74   The Scorpion Macehead

lem with Wittfogel's hypothesis is that it was initially overstated and that subsequent research by archaeologists in Mesopotamia, for example, suggests that irrigation originated long before the state. In applying Wittfogel's ideas to Egypt we encounter a second problem. Egyptian irrigation technology was never as extensive or as complex as that of Mesopotamia or China, revolving mainly about basins that evened out the effects of the annual inundation. As Butzer has pointed out in his recent restudy of the role of irrigation in Egyptian civilization, hydraulic networks in Egypt were localized, not rambling linear affairs like their Mesopotamian counterparts; hence any political ramifications that irrigation had would have been restricted to a small geographical area. This fact doubtless helps account for the origin of nomes (later

historical provinces), but the knowledge that Egyptian irrigation technology was comparatively simple next to its Mesopotamian counterpart
has for many years discouraged speculation on the possible role that
hydraulic technology might have played in the rise of Egyptian civilization. Although, as Butzer has pointed out, there is no direct evidence of
centralized administration of irrigation networks in Dynastic times until
the Middle Kingdom (Butzer 1976: 110), there is strong documentary
evidence in autobiographies like that of Kheti I that the establishment
and maintenance of local irrigation networks were the duty of anyone
aspiring to legitimate regional political hegemony and did involve the
application of special technical and administrative expertise. If we go
back to the Late Gerzean and Protodynastic period when Upper Egypt

was apparently divided into a number of regional political units and consider the symbolic importance attached to irrigation and hydraulic projects by monarchs like Scorpion and later First Dynasty pharaohs (Menes allegedly built a dike to divert waters from Memphis), then it is logical to suppose that the manipulation of irrigation technology, at least, required the patronage of a big man on a local level and the skills he or his clients possessed. This person would have possessed the knowledge and managerial and juridical expertise to make the decisions that even a simplified irrigation system required. As a good politician he certainly would have appreciated the debts and obligations he acquired from his clients by sponsoring an irrigation project—debts and obligations that would have involved those clients increasingly in his service and made them more willing to support him in conflict with other, neighboring rulers. Patronage of such an activity, in addition to its network of rights, duties, and obligations, had the effect of training aspiring rulers in group leadership and of providing them with a cut of the produce derived from their projects. By diverting this tax or a portion thereof to the establishment or maintenance of a local shrine, their participation also would have augmented the public image of the big man as a pious person and ritual leader. In Egypt, where the principle of divine kingship would become central to the institution and ethos of the state, the spiritual prestige that would accrue from such acts of public piety would have been of considerable value to an up-and-coming ruler and even would have served to justify his increasing separation from the multitudes. Thus, although Butzer's warning against accepting an oversimplified "linear causality model of stress $\longrightarrow$ irrigation $\longrightarrow$ managerial bureaucracy $\longrightarrow$ despotic control" (Butzer 1976: 111) is well taken, we also cannot ignore the direct evidence that the Protodynastic elite deemed participation in irrigation ceremonies almost as important as warfare and that, when viewed as part of a larger functionally interrelated system, irrigation technology was one of the areas most sensitive to manipulation in the game of power politics as well as a focal point of community sentiment and organization.

Indirectly, the Scorpion Macehead illustrates another important area of technology that was subjected to the multiplier effect during Protodynastic times. As an object, the Scorpion Macehead was a powerfact—an artifact with obvious symbolic linkages to the ideal role and personification of kingship. It was a commemorative object of unusual size, probably meant to be borne by the monarch or displayed in a public place like a temple. It was also a product of some craftsman's long and productive labors. In an era when such representational art, especially on stone, was a relatively new thing, the individual who executed the Scorpion Macehead was obviously several cuts above the average producer of stone war clubs. As such, his time and skill were valued and had to be paid for, presumably by Scorpion. The easiest form of payment would have been provision of room and board near the royal lodgings. Such provision assumed that quarters were available in the king's architectural complex and quite possibly tools and a workshop space as well. If the craftsman did not reside in the royal presence, he nevertheless had to be remunerated for his services in kind. Given the economic structure of Egyptian towns, temples, and palaces in Dynastic times, it is likely that craftsmen were maintained on the estate or estates of the ruler (much as in later Mycenaean Greek society or in recent East African kingdoms), reflecting Kemp's two-tiered economic system. Although the archaeological evidence is not extensive, we do have remains of numerous storerooms and well-planned complexes of workshops for metal working, butchering and stone vase manufacture in the Archaic and Old Kingdom town of Nekhen (Hierakonpolis) dating between about 2800 and 2200 B.C. as well as a model estate of Aha's reign (ca. 3080 B.C.) at Saqqara. Given the massive amounts of status-indicative artifacts that are found in tombs from the beginning of the First Dynasty on, it is plausible that the search for power produced a need for material symbols (like the Scorpion Macehead, the Narmer Palette, and the jewelry of Djer's queen) that could be displayed in public and, after the death of the ruler, either placed in one of his temples or buried with him. Thus, in the best tradition of Renfrew's multiplier effect, demand for wealth items produced increasing supply which, in turn, fueled the fires of class consciousness by providing a graded series of items whose possession was a direct reflection of their owner's rank. Although some wealth items, like Lebanese timber, were imported, these were usually reserved for the king. Many more "goodies" were manufactured in the king's workshops to be used, as the need arose, as payoffs for faithful clients, who in turn took them to their graves as guarantees of exalted status in the afterlife. The commitment of a sizable portion of the productive sector to the manufacture of such powerfacts was an eminently logical activity from an ancient Egyptian point of view since it was through such goods that one "maximized" eternity. I will consider the complicated and all-pervasive role played by Egyptian beliefs about death, status, and early kingship later in this chapter in dealing with the Egyptian way of death.

The Subsistence Base: The Granaries of Egypt

Amid all the pomp and circumstance and the spectacular new products that herald the dawn of Egyptian civilization, it is easy to lose track of the simple fact that Egypt was, to an even greater extent than other early civilizations of the ancient world, an agricultural country. At Saqqara Emery discovered two sophisticated types of Archaic granaries and I have already mentioned the stocks of grain Petrie found in the tomb of Ka'a at Abydos. Egyptian paintings of all periods depict granaries and food processing and storage as one of their central themes. Predynastic sites have yielded large jars and pits filled with grain. Without question, the Egyptian economy by Predynastic times was quite capable of producing abundant surpluses for at least a segment of the population.

One of the favorite arguments of historians and social evolutionists has been that such surpluses were themselves primary stimulants to the growth of states and civilizations; that agriculture and animal domestication produced surpluses of food which, in turn, permitted more and more specialists in areas like crafts, religion, and politics. These specialists, who themselves did not produce, exchanged their services for food and gradually came to dominate society. Such a view implies that an agricultural economy is almost bound to lead to higher levels of organization—states and civilizations—and assumes that surpluses are desirable things to produce. More recent research has shown this not to be the case. Many food-producing societies never developed into states and still lack or reject the notion that large stored surpluses are necessary. The basic impulse seems to be to follow the principle of least effort and keep just enough seed to propagate next season's crop and provide a small margin of safety.

For the acquisition and storage of surplus food to be a going concern requires a shift in attitudes, an investment in the technology of food storage and redistribution, and a certain degree of centralized decision-making. In Dynastic Egypt, the provision of grain was assumed to be one of the duties of a leader, one of the ways that he legitimated his authority. The butler Merer of Edfu writes in the Eleventh Dynasty:

> When it happened that Upper Egyptian barley was given to the town, I transported it many times. I have a heap of white Upper Egyptian barley and a heap of hmr-barley, and measured out for every man according to his wish. (Trans. Lichtheim 1973: 87)

As an interesting side note to the above translation, Lichtheim (1973: 88, footnote 3) points out that the word heap has also been read as granary by some Egyptologists and, no matter how one reads the word in question, "the content of the granary is meant." An approximate contemporary of Merer, the steward Seneni of Coptus, boasts: "I measured out Upper Egyptian barley as sustenance for this whole town in the gateway of the Count and Chief Priest Djefi, in the painful years of distress" (Lichtheim 1973:90).

Seneni's account of his role during a time of famine echoes the Biblical story of Joseph, in which the slave ingratiated himself with the pharaoh by predicting seven years of bumper crops followed by seven years of drought. The familiar solution was to store the surpluses in granaries against impending bad times. Recent research by Dr. Bell and

Professor Butzer confirms that while Egypt could produce legendary food surpluses, the country was also subject to periodic loss of grain harvests through a series of low floods or high and extremely destructive inundations. Thus, a requirement of any complex social and economic system involves the need to store centrally and redistribute foodstuffs and other goods (such as tools, weapons, baubles, etc.), and provide services like housing. Even in times of comparative plenty, the changes that were taking place in Protodynastic society could be expected to encourage the development of a localized storage-redistributive system in order to ensure the periodic concentrations of large numbers of people to undertake public works, such as tomb construction and the building of town walls and irrigation basins. On a day-to-day basis, a big man in a local community of Protodynastic times, desirous of climbing the social ladder, needed stored surpluses in order simply to maintain his household staff, army, and the growing body of craft specialists that were producing status goods for burial and exchange. All of these factors would have made the technology of food storage and redistribution absolutely vital to the emergence of the state and so, while there need not have been a major technological change in Egypt's subsistence economy, there was a major alteration in the social organization by which that economy was run.

With the rise of a conquest-oriented superelite in late Predynastic and Protodynastic times, the pressure for more effective organization of the subsistence economy increased. At some point early forerunners of Menes, like Scorpion, must have established their right to tax a certain portion of stored food surpluses throughout their kingdom. Evidence for the methods of early tax collection is preserved in the Palermo Stone, where nationwide counts on occasions or royal tours of inspection called Followings of Horus are known from Archaic times and are reminiscent of the royal progresses developed so effectively by the Tudors in England to ensure the loyalty of their nobles by periodically requiring them to foot the not inconsiderable expenses of the royal court during one of its visits. On such occasions, Henry VIII or Elizabeth I would receive the obeisance of their nobles, avoid strain on their own coffers and, if they were pleased by their reception, reward their host with some bauble or title as a token of royal favor. Such methods were doubtless employed by early Protodynastic kings, who after either conquering or otherwise cowing their powerful neighbors, sought to soften the blow by including their new provincial governors in the royal court. Once again, the role of the subsistence economy in the emergence of Egyptian civilization is not a simple one and cannot be divorced from the other cultural systems which were now caught up in what Colin Renfrew has termed a "deviating-amplifying relationship"—a situation in which change literally fed on change.

Neith-hotep's Ivory Label—Rank, Titles, Payoff, and Kinship: What Zaki Saad Found at Helwan

Ere they hewed the sphinx's vissage
Favoritism governed kissage,
Even in those early days,
Who shall doubt the secret hid
Under Cheops' pyramid
Was that the contractor did
        Cheops out of several millions?
Or that Joseph's sudden rise
To Comptroller of Supplies
Was a fraud of monstrous size
        On King Pharaoh's swart civilians?
        (Kipling: "Departmental Ditties: General Summary")

Although the particular style by which an individual pursued his or her star varied in Dynastic Egypt according to one's status and personality as well as the general ethic of the age into which one was born, the quest for upward mobility was a dominant theme in Egyptian life. The Instructions of Ptahhotep, written near the end of the Old Kingdom, emphasize the virtues of right thinking and right behavior in obtaining wealth and rank and have an almost Calvinistic ring:

If you are poor, serve a man of worth,
That all your conduct may be well with the god.
Do not recall if he once was poor,
Don't be arrogant toward him
For knowing his former state;
Respect him for what has accrued to him,
For wealth does not come by itself.
It is their law for him whom they love,
His gain, he gathered it himself;
It is the god who makes him worthy
And protects him while he sleeps.
        (Trans. Lichtheim 1973: 66)

A somewhat different attitude is heard two centuries later, during the unsettled times of the First Intermediate Period, when the rough soldier Qedes of Gebelein boasted:

I was a worthy citizen who acted with his arm, the foremost of his whole troop. I acquired oxen and goats. I acquired granaries of Upper Egyptian barley. I acquired title to a (great) field. I made a boat of 30 cubits and a small boat that ferried the boatless in the inundation season. *(Trans. Lichtheim 1973: 90)*

With the establishment of the monarchy in the First Dynasty, the acquisition of status, rank, and wealth in Egypt became a national pastime instead of a matter of mere local and familial concern. The old Predynastic tendency to express differences in wealth through conspicuous consumption of grave goods was amplified and has very fortunately provided us with whole series of nicely graded tombs which reflect, even mirror, the relative status of their occupant during life.

The establishment of any state requires a large and well-paid clientele. Perhaps, as I suspect, at the heart of this clientele lay an extended kin-based group that provided an organizational core and solved basic problems of leadership recruitment, but in order to conquer and rule a large territory and keep the people happy, even god kings had to consider practical concerns of patronage. Nowhere are the immediate consequences of royal patronage more clearly reflected than in the 10,000-plus tombs of courtiers excavated by Zaki Saad at Helwan. If we estimate that the first two dynasties occupied the throne for about 400 years and divide this figure into 10,000, we arrive at a death rate of middle-class dependents (not provincial nobles) of 25 per annum. This ratio is undoubtedly too low, since some of the 10,258 tombs excavated had multiple burials and we cannot be sure how many more tombs of this date originally existed or still await the excavator's trowel. Nevertheless, if we figure 25 clients died each year and accept Hayes's average of 24.5 years per reign for the 17 kings of the first two dynasties, then we come up with a minimum calculation of 613 retainers per king.

Judging by the amount and high quality of the goods which Saad recovered from Helwan, members of the court had already learned to appreciate royal patronage and the rewards, both tangible and spiritual, it could provide. In one instance, a beautiful rock crystal bowl, 22 centimeters tall and 13.5 centimeters in diameter was found.

> An especially important feature is the inscription of the name of King Semerkhet on the side of the bowl, together with the name of one Semer-sepedou, who was probably the owner of the tomb. The bowl was no doubt a present from the king to Semer-sepedou.
>
> *(Saad 1969: 41-42)*

Although this artifact, as a royal gift, would have been of great use to its owner during his lifetime as a sign of royal patronage and as a treasure in itself, there is an alternative explanation for its presence in Semer-sepedou's tomb. We know that tomb robbery was already well developed by Predynastic times and it doubtless flourished in all ages, forming an alternative system of wealth redistribution. Since royal officials and craftsmen as well as masons, herdsmen, and household menials are known to have conspired in New Kingdom times to pilfer the royal storerooms for their own tombs, it is possible that the rock crystal bowl was acquired surreptitiously. Another possibility would have been that a craftsman inscribed the king's name on the artifact to enhance its prestige and magical potency after death, a means of spiritual upward mobility. Despite these possibilities, the presence in other tombs of massive amounts of wealth and signs of royal favor and the likelihood that the king had to pay off his followers in some fashion, leads one to suspect that Semer-sepedou obtained his precious gift from the hands of a grateful king and that even at this early date, "favoritism governed kissage."

As an example of the quantum leap in the traditional system of rank and status that had occurred in the few short centuries since Menes, we have only to look at one of the larger tombs at Helwan (423 H. 9) in which one intact magazine contained "seventy bowls, vases, cups, and other items of alabaster and slate." As Saad remarks, "When we consider that all these objects were recovered from one small magazine, we can imagine what a rich treasure the tomb originally contained" (Saad 1969: 42).

One of the most important finds at Helwan was made in tomb 728 H. 5 where a broken ivory plaque of Queen Neith-hotep, the wife of Hor-aha or Narmer, was recovered. Not only was this artifact probably a token of royal favor, but it raises a sticky historical and sociological problem. It will be remembered that it was de Morgan's excavation of Neith-hotep's *serekh* façade tomb at Naqada in 1897 that first provided Petrie with the date for his late type of wavy-handled pots. Names of both Hor-aha and Narmer were found in the tomb. It is obvious that Neith-hotep was a very important person and that she was related to two pharaohs. Saad believes she was Hor-aha's bride, while Walter Emery argues that she was the bride of Narmer and mother of Hor-aha, who would have presided at her burial, an argument supported by the Narmer macehead found in the Great Deposit at Hierakonpolis. This artifact depicts an important personage, apparently from the north, being received by Narmer, who wears the crown of Lower Egypt. Emery thinks that the figure is a woman, that the woman is Neith-hotep and "that the conqueror of the North attempted to legitimize his position by taking the Northern princess as his consort" (Emery 1961: 47). Saad (1969: 66) prefers to have Neith-hotep marry Hor-aha and unite the Two Lands officially. Whoever married whom, the importance of Neith-hotep at practically the moment of unification, as already suggested, parallels the historical position of Isabella of Castile and Leon and underlines the role of marriage and alliance systems in state building—a factor pointed out with considerable persistence by social anthropologists and sociologists. What records we do have from ancient Egypt that bear on inheritance indicate what anthropologists call a bilineal tendency—property could be passed on through both mother and father to their offspring. Although we do not know if, as many have claimed, in prehistoric times inheritance was primarily matrilineal, it cannot be doubted

75   The Narmer "Wedding" Macehead from Hierakonpolis

that Neith-hotep was in the right sociological place at the right historical time.

Next we encounter the problem of why a "Northern" queen should be buried in a northern-style *serekh* façade tomb deep in the south at Naqada. One explanation comes to mind that may throw some light on the old problem of just what the Protodynastic Egyptians meant by "Upper and Lower Egypt." It will be remembered from Chapter 7 that, to date, the only prehistoric representation of a typical red crown of Lower Egypt was discovered by Petrie in an Amratian grave at Naqada. Since Narmer and the unifiers apparently came from the extreme south, in the neighborhood of Hierakonpolis, Naqada would have been down-river and hence north. If, indeed, Egypt had coalesced into two contending kingdoms shortly before unification as most traditions staunchly maintain, it is then possible that the northernmost kingdom was based at Naqada and had already subdued an area extending into the Delta, bringing with its dominance the appropriate symbols of kingship. When the bellicose southerners finally achieved the conquest claimed by Narmer on the famous palette from Hierakonpolis, they would have taken over another, larger Upper Egyptian kingdom that included part of the Delta. In the process of political consolidation that accompanied the rules of Scorpion, Narmer, and Aha, it would have been possible to recast Lower Egypt in terms of its geographically most alien component —the Delta.

This interpretation treads a middle ground between two extreme views of the unification. On one side, Henri Frankfort took what might be called a symbolist approach:

> When Pharaoh assumed dualistic titles or called himself "Lord of the Two Lands," he emphasized not the divided origin but the universality of his power. The dualistic forms of Egyptian kingship did not result from historical incidents.
>
> They embody the peculiarly Egyptian thought that a totality comprises opposites. Menes gave political expression to a basic Egyptian mode of thought when he styled his rule over the conquered and unified Nile lands a "kingship over Upper and Lower Egypt."
> *(Frankfort 1948b: 19)*

On the opposite side of the fence stands the literalist, Walter Emery, when he maintains that Archaic Egypt was a real

> dual monarchy and, so soon after the unification, the individuality of two states of the North and the South was more marked than in later times. In fact there appear to have been two separate administrations united only under the throne. Even the elaborate ceremonies of the king's coronation, his "Sed" festival or jubilee and ultimate burial, were twice repeated with the different insignia, architecture, and customs of Upper and Lower Egypt. *(Emery 1961: 105)*

Given the historical documents constituted by the Protodynastic commemorative artifacts, the archaeological evidence and the environmentally based divisions within Egypt, one has to side somewhat more closely with Emery in this argument.

But however interesting arguments are about the nature of things during the rise of the Egyptian state, it is in the minutiae of social organization and the effects upon the internal make-up of society that the most profitable research can be performed. Until we know more of the relationship between the growth of great elites and the comparative size and functions of their clientele, it will be difficult to relate the changes seen in the other cultural and physical-environmental systems to the changing texture of society.

The questions that must be asked about those henchmen buried at Helwan and the larger scene of which they were a part must be geared to defining status and occupational differences and establishing different rankings, based partly upon the archaeological evidence and partly on the physiological evidence itself, with occasional stimulus provided by ethnohistory and social anthropology. Standard social evolutionary theory maintains that, with the rise of the state and civilization, status among the elite at least moves from achieved to ascribed, that kinship becomes less important than territoriality as an organizing principle and that new social categories are generated that are both by their life-style and their own consciousness independent classes, participating in distinct subcultures. These theories have been around a long time and often lead us to ignore the fine tuning of civilizations and cause gross errors. For instance, the idea that states, nations, and civilizations must, perforce, abandon kinship as an organizing principle in favor of territoriality assumes two things: that kinship is universally the basic organizing principle in prestate societies and that kinship and territoriality are necessarily mutually exclusive strategies. In point of fact, early pharaonic administration was almost certainly grounded in a clientele the core of which was kin-based and whose bonds were periodically cemented by strategic marriage alliances.

Since we do not as yet have a very clear picture of Dynastic kinship and how it worked, it is extremely difficult to offer suggestions about the role of social organization in the building of Menes's state. If, as we suspect, the Egyptian system was bilineal or cognatic like our own, that is, if relatives could be traced through a common relative, whether by blood or marriage or through the male or female line, then a strong leader could have easily developed a faction and formed marriage alliances that extended out well beyond the bounds of a particular village or district. Such "kindreds" are flexible and have been compared by anthropologists to personnel pools

> from which groups of individuals coalesce for specific cooperative activities, such as work parties, revenge groups, exchange groups, households, and transition rites. *(Hoebel 1972: 443)*

A slightly more formal type of kin group having another definition than a kindred but still preserving the flexibility of descent reckoning is the *ramage*. The ramage is a group whose members reckon descent from a common ancestor through either the mother's or father's line. Usually its rules of membership are somewhat more well defined than a kindred's, giving it a stronger cooperative quality.

A number of older anthropologists and Egyptologists argued over the possibility of the Egyptian descent system being unilineal, that is, reckoned through one line. At one time, as we have seen, the occurrence of powerful women who even occupied the throne spurred debate that prehistoric Egyptian kinship was matrilineal in nature. This speculation took place two generations ago when it was fashionable to see societies making the transition from village agriculture to state as going through an obligatory transition from matrilineal to patrilineal descent and from matriarchy to patriarchy. Today these notions have fortunately dropped out of fashion, although ideas of similar vintage concerning an evolutionary trend from kin-based groups to territorially-based states persist. In both cases, however, there is insufficient evidence to support claims that either society in general or ancient Egyptian society in particular developed from matrilineal to patrilineal or bilineal any more than we can prove that, in Predynastic times, kinship more than territoriality dictated the form, size, and boundaries of social groups.

It is clear that more research needs to be done in this interesting area, and that social anthropologists who have long held history, archaeology, and physical anthropology in disdain will have to turn to the careful analysis of cemeteries, skeletal remains, and grave goods at rich sites like Helwan which come from a period when Egypt was undergoing a transition to statehood. Only by taking such a multidisciplinary approach can we begin to reconstruct societies from the ground up. And only by attempting to introduce functioning social groups into the drama of the rise of Egyptian civilization can we hope to balance the environmental and materialistic determinism that so often plagues archaeological explanation. For the time being, however, it is premature to make any absolute statements about the role of kinship and descent systems in the rise of Menes's state and we cannot even rule out the possibility that a variety of social forms existed in Protodynastic times which, under stress of the multiplier effect, provided the social solutions to ecological, demographic, and technological problems.

From Jebel Sahaba to Saqqara: The Egyptian Way of Death

For more than two years anthropologist Dr. Peter Metcalf worked in the jungles of Borneo, living with and learning from a people known as the Berawan. In trying to understand their culture, he found that, much like the ancient Egyptians, death and burial are extremely important to the Berawans. His interest kindled by what he found in Borneo, Dr. Metcalf and a colleague, Dr. Richard Huntington, have recently completed a major comparative study of the role of death rituals among different peoples of the world. Unlike earlier anthropologists like Frazer and Elliot Smith, they are not concerned with bizarre customs for their own sake, nor do they attempt to derive everything from ancient Egypt.

Rather, they are trying to understand the broader social significance of death and its rituals. Their work holds a good deal of promise for Egypt, since it proposes a number of general hypotheses that allow us to study the sociological role of the ancient Egyptian death ritual and its relation to the growth and maintenance of Menes's state.

If there is one aspect of Egyptian culture that attracts the public interest and fascinates laymen and professionals alike, it is the unusual, unique concern shown by the ancient Egyptians for death and burial. If a culture can be said to have a symbolic specialty, in the sense that France is known for its fine cuisine and Spain for its bullfights, then ancient Egypt must be remembered for its elaborate and all-pervasive death rituals. These have often taken on a lugubrious flavor to modern Englishmen and Americans schooled in a series of "mummy movies" spawned by Sir Arthur Conan Doyle's short story "The Ring of Thoth." In ancient Egypt, however, the burial ritual was not simply a morbid ballyhoo but one of the key systems through which many of the political, economic, and religious aspects of society were resolved and unified.

Throughout this book we have seen numerous archaeological examples of the Egyptian mortuary cult, beginning with the late Pleistocene burials at Jebel Sahaba, continuing through the increasingly elaborate tombs of the Predynastic era, to the Painted Tomb at Hierakonpolis built just before the unification and culminating in the great royal burial complexes of Abydos and Saqqara. There is always the danger when studying these monuments from an archaeological point of view of becoming completely absorbed in the splendid detail of their artistic or architectural achievement—the tendency to see them as technical and aesthetic products in and of themselves, and to ignore the greater functional significance of death and burial. Particularly during the period of the unification, it is the burial complexes that personify the nature of the new state and its regime. They are microcosms of the way that the new kings conceived the relation of the cosmic and earthly orders, manipulations of space and form calculated to serve the emerging doctrine of divine kingship and integrate a society. Below this philosophical or ideological level the great royal tombs performed a host of more mundane functions: their construction provided occasion to bring together large numbers of people, both specialists and laborers, and organize them to work toward a single, tangible goal; they afforded opportunities for the king and his henchmen to demonstrate their leadership ability; they required efficient planning and accumulation of massive food surpluses to feed and house the workmen; they required large concentrations of wealth, most notably of imported, exotic goods which had to be obtained from distant lands; they afforded king, commoner, and nobleman with a stage on which to participate in the drama of national unity and the rites of passage of the dead god king as he joined his fellow gods and a chance to reemphasize the continuity of the dynasty through the participation of the heir apparent in the funeral of his father.

That all of these separate functions should be united about a single activity emphasizes the degree to which a society's different parts are all functionally interrelated. Since burials and graves were of paramount importance to Egyptian culture and since their archaeological remains are well attested and reliably dated, they are our most important source of evidence for the multiplier effect and the changes that were permeating the Two Lands between late Predynastic and early Dynastic times.

It is one thing to assert that an ancient system worked in such and such a way and quite another thing to prove it. In examining the prominence of the royal death ritual in the role of state building we are fortunate in being able to rely on the recent studies by Metcalf and Huntington of living and historical peoples, which help demonstrate the relation between the sand-covered tombs of an emerging Egyptian elite dead for 5,000 years and contemporary peoples dealing with the everyday concerns of power, status, mobility, public display, and exchange.

Metcalf and Huntington have examined the funerals and funeral monuments of three societies, each of which, for our purpose, can be seen as roughly analogous on an organizational scale to Egypt between the Late Gerzean and Archaic periods (ca. 3300–2700 B.C.). They deal first with the Berawan of Borneo, a village farming people who

> comprise neither a populous centralised state like the Thais, nor a complex of highly stratified and competing realms like the Balinese. By comparison Berawan society is small in scale, relatively egalitarian, and composed of just four autonomous ritual and political units—the separate longhouse communities. Nevertheless, extended death rites play an even more important part in its ongoing political process than in that of the Thai and Balinese states because they affect the survival of the entire community. *(Metcalf and Huntington 1979)*

Hypothetically, the Berawan would resemble most closely the Gerzean people of Upper Egypt. The fact that they also dwell along a river enhances the relevance of the comparison as we shall see later in discussing trade. The Balinese, divided into a number of feudal realms, recall Protodynastic Egypt, prior to the unification, while the highly centralized Thai realm suggests the Archaic state. In no case should these comparisons be taken as definitive, yet they do provide a useful point of departure for examining the broader role of the Egyptian mortuary cult in the rise of civilization and suggest questions that can be tested with archaeological and historical information.

In their overall functions, the funerals of important people among the Thai, Balinese, and Berawan are analogous respectively to death rites in

Archaic, Protodynastic, and Predynastic society. In the Thai Kingdom, as in Archaic Egypt

> . . . it was crucial, even for a resilient and enduring state . . . that the prestige of the royal court be maintained. Any tarnish on its claim to be the most sublime representation of the cosmos immediately translated into a diminished orbit of influence.
>
> *(Metcalf and Huntington 1979)*

Accordingly, Thai royal funeral rites performed three social functions. First, they re-focused attention on the center. Second, "the funeral could be used to express the continuity of kingship" with sumptuous public display at the always-dangerous moment of succession.

> The format of the death rites provided an opportunity to combat this vulnerability. . . . Since the cremation of the old king must await the drying of his bones, the coronation of the new king preceded it. . . .
>
> Third, the secondary treatment of the corpse resulted in the production of royal relics that reinforced the centripetal tendencies of the kingdom. *(Metcalf and Huntington 1979)*

In Bali the fractious political units, like their Protodynastic analogs

> were engaged in constant rivalry to maintain their autonomy and extend their influence. . . . the carefully staged cremations of the kings were a principal weapon by which their successors maintained or advanced their standing. *(Metcalf and Huntington 1979)*

Finally, among the Berawan of Borneo, like the Predynastic chiefdoms of Upper Egypt, the effective political units were small and their coherence closely related to the way local big men were able to mobilize their communities to construct a fancy mausoleum for an often-undistinguished relative. "In honoring them with a mausoleum the leader ennobles himself" (Metcalf and Huntington 1979).

As we have seen already, Predynastic society from the start showed a strong interest in the welfare of the dead and people attempted to take as much to the afterlife as they could afford. This consumer belief or propensity of Predynastic Egyptians is attested to from Badarian times on. From the start, there are indications of social differences and women's graves seem to be among the richest. By Gerzean times these differences become one of kind rather than degree and large, well-built graves begin to appear in different areas of Upper Egypt, almost certainly indicating local political consolidation and increased competition for status within regional polities or chiefdoms.

Although archaeologists like Petrie and Emery preferred to see the increasing evidence of wealth, conflict, and trade at this time as the result of a new population influx, we have seen that the bulk of the

76   A Berawan burial monument in Borneo

evidence reflects internal changes. Judging from the elaborate displays
of wealth apparent in Late Gerzean tombs like the famous Painted
Tomb at Hierakonpolis, local chiefs were manipulating their fortunes
and those of their clients in a manner that foreshadows that practiced by
the Berawan—by using fancy tombs and status-indicative burial goods
to create a political system.

Among the Berawan, as among Egyptians of late Predynastic times, only a powerful leader can muster the resources to build an impressive tomb. Since political leadership among the Berawans is passed on with great difficulty, a man builds a tomb for an unimportant ancestor. It is not the ancestor who is important, but the act of building the burial monument. A version of this explanation has often been offered to explain the pyramids of the Old Kingdom—that they were types of public works projects and in many cases they might never have been intended to afford burial to the king.

Metcalf emphasizes that the great burial monuments constructed by the Berawan require public labor that has to be organized and paid for by the chief. Paying for such monuments requires stocking up enough surplus rice to feed everyone and obtaining the services of craft specialists to do the carving. A major tomb must also be stocked with expensive, status-indicative things—items usually obtained through trade like pottery or brassware. We are reminded of the Painted Tomb which likewise required a number of workers to dig the pit and to make and lay the mud-bricks. A specialist must have been employed to decorate the walls according to the fashion of the day, complete with Mesopotamian motifs. Pottery jars containing grain, unguents, wine or beer and oils as well as a wealth of slate pigment palettes, figurines, carved amulets, beautifully made ripple-flake flint knives, scepters, painted pots and even jars imported from southern Palestine were probably placed in the Painted Tomb, judging by contemporary, unlooted tombs.

There is another facet of tombs that looms as important in their function as powerfacts—their location. Building a large tomb at a given spot often increases the sacred aura of that place, rendering it more attractive than the normal dictates of economy and environment might otherwise suggest. For example, the tomb of Djer at Abydos was believed by later, Dynastic Egyptians to be the tomb of Osiris, god of the afterlife, and attracted thousands of pilgrims. Metcalf's study of a contemporary people, the Berawan, helps throw speculative light on the social-economic complexity of burial and the mortuary cult in the chieftainships of Late Gerzean Egypt (ca. 3300–3100 B.C.) and suggests the need to examine our archaeological data in functional terms. Among the Berawans there is a complex relation between big tombs, important fortified settlements (longhouses) and the ambitions and ability of rising politicians—latter-day Scorpions or Narmers. In Borneo, under precolonial conditions (before about 1888) raiding and warfare were rife. Then, a great longhouse, stoutly constructed, was the only way to ensure protection for the village unit, yet its construction required an unusual amount of self-discipline, leadership, and centralized planning—attributes difficult to come by in the basically egalitarian Berawan society (a factor that would not have existed among the stratified chieftainships of Late Gerzean Egypt).

Among the Berawan, once a powerful man began to establish himself, he usually undertook the construction of a great longhouse but, significantly, he could not have accomplished this task, Metcalf believes, without the death monument.

> The longhouse is itself a monument to the authority of its leaders. But the construction of a new longhouse may take many years. . . . What the new leader requires to cement his position is a demonstration of community solidarity behind him personally.
> The building of mausoleums provides an opportunity for such a demonstration. Funerals have an important integrative function.
> *(Metcalf and Huntington 1979)*

Although we know nothing directly of the particular sociocultural processes by which leaders exerted and legitimized authority in Late Gerzean Egypt, the archaeological remains suggest interesting functional analogies to many of the activities engaged in by Berawan leaders in terms of the methods and motivations (both economic and ideological) by which clienteles were created and mobilized. In the case of Late Gerzean Egypt, however, the leaders had at least two distinct advantages over Berawan big men. First they lived in a society already cross-cut by complex social-economic strata—leadership had stronger roots. Second, large permanent settlements (such as Hierakonpolis) were regular features of the Predynastic landscape. Thus, any leader who wished to manipulate the mortuary cult to his own ends had no trouble in locating a settlement of permanence or a temple with appropriate religious prestige for the site of his (or someone else's?) interment.

I have raised the possibility that demographic change during Late Gerzean times was leading to increased intergroup competition—in short, to warfare. Returning to Metcalf's findings among the Berawan, the existence of such pressures is often an important inducement to follow a big man in the first place and allow him to manipulate one's pattern of settlement through the construction of a great mausoleum. If we recall the success with which this process was used by the earliest pharaohs with their multiple tombs (or cenotaphs) at Abydos and (possibly) Saqqara and consider the archaeological evidence for big, Late Gerzean tombs, developing social stratification and warfare, it is hardly surprising that conflict reinforced the tendency of late prehistoric Upper Egyptians to concentrate in fortified centers. The evidence for these is clear on the Narmer Palette and in Petrie's clay model town from Naqada, while fighting and warfare are common themes in both Late Gerzean and Protodynastic art (e.g., the Gebel el Arak knife, the Narmer Palette, the Hierakonpolis cylinder seal). Such conflict (discussed at length later in this chapter) strengthened the hand of the rising chieftain and abetted the tendency for population to concentrate in response to environmental pressures discussed earlier. The concentrations of large numbers of people in small areas, each of which doubtless had its own shrine like Hierakonpolis, created an effective stage on which important men could manipulate the death ritual to achieve increasingly greater prominence.

Although the long-term continuity of Predynastic population in areas like Badari, Naqada, and Hierakonpolis contrasts with the shifting Berawan settlement pattern, the contrast nevertheless reveals some of the possibilities present in Predynastic Egyptian society that are not found in other (modern or ancient) societies. People in Late Gerzean Egypt dwelt in larger, more permanent settlements than the modern Berawan, and there is a good deal of evidence at sites like Hierakonpolis, for example (see Chapter 8), that these towns were also religious centers. The magnetic effect of local shrines as well as their ability to survive over long periods of time is well attested in many areas of the world like Mexico, where Christian churches and cathedrals stand on the ruins of Aztec pyramids. Similarly, the great temple at Luxor, Egypt, which is at least 3,500 years old, was used successively by pagans (including Egyptians, Greeks, and Romans) and Coptic Christians, and even today shelters the mosque and tomb(!) of the local Moslem saint, Abul Haggag. One wonders how the sight of a ruined Christian church and an active Moslem mosque, both enclosed and overshadowed by an ancient Egyptian temple sacred to (supposedly) long-forgotten gods, would have struck Milton who, never having seen Egypt, wrote in the seventeenth century:

> *The brutish gods of Nile as fast,*
> *Isis and Horus and the dog Anubis hast.*
>> *Nor is Osiris seen*
>> *In Memphian grove or green*
> *Trampling the unshowered grass with lowings loud;*
>> *Nor can he be at rest*
>> *Within his sacred chest;*
> *Nought but profoundest hell can be his shroud.*
>> *In vain with timbrel'd anthems dark*
> *The sable-stoled sorcerers bear his worshipped ark.*
>> *(John Milton: "Hymm on the Nativity" quoted in*
>> *Bulfinch, The Age of Fable: 295–296)*

Many of these ancient temples, like that of Horus of Nekhen at Hierakonpolis, can trace their origin to prehistoric times. The long-term sanctity of geographical spots was reinforced by the construction of great burial monuments; for instance, as I just mentioned, the tomb of Djer at Abydos was apparently believed to belong to the god Osiris. Compared to the Berawan, then, Late Gerzean Upper Egyptian leaders had much more investment in a particular spot and, consequently, the job of building and maintaining a power base that could be passed on to a chosen successor was much easier.

77 Luxor Temple, a long tradition of sanctity. A statue of Rameses II gazes at
the Mosque of Abul Hagga, founded on the ruins of the ancient temple

Along with increasing political centralization came increasing elaboration of the mortuary cult, this time linked closely with the emerging
principle of divine kingship. Both Scorpion and Narmer portray themselves as larger-than-life superbeings on their monuments at Hierakon-

polis with the same artistic conventions used in later Dynastic times to portray the divine king. The tomb of Narmer and other presumed Protodynastic kings at Abydos, although much larger than the Painted Tomb, are built according to the same plan; however, their concentration in one sacred locality suggests that the kings of this era had co-opted a spot of special religious significance or, perhaps by design, built their tombs there to endow the place with their collective aura. The later association of Osiris, god of the afterlife, with Abydos, and legends that depict him as an ancient earthly king who once ruled over a united Egypt in prehistoric times, may derive from a time when the princelings of Abydos were generating about their mortuary cults a kind of national propaganda that would serve them well in the continuing wars of consolidation. The very fact that these wars and the later rise of the Egyptian state were called a unification process suggests that Henri Frankfort was partly right in claiming that the dual monarchy was a political invention. To the extent that the political consolidation of Egypt was euphemistically termed a unification rather than a conquest and that Osirian legend insinuated that Egypt had once been whole, there was an attempt to interject an air of righteousness to the political and military machinations of the kings of the south in their struggle for the hearts, minds, and property of their neighbors. The lasting religious associations of Abydos doubtless stem from this age when the political power and communal leadership symbolized by a big tomb were being translated into religious dogma in which the dead king in his royal tomb was becoming a national god.

In a sense, the evolution of the mortuary temple in the First Dynasty was another step in the process that defined kingship in terms of the death ritual. Here a clientele could continue to serve an individual, even after his death, and the living could continue to pay taxes and less tangible homage to the spirit of the dead king. The mortuary temple and its cult would continue to be an economic force, what Barry Kemp has called "an arm of the state," throughout Egyptian history. With the unification of Egypt, therefore, there emerged about the royal death cult a series of institutions that formed the central core of the state. The first was the mortuary cult, and the second was, apparently, the principle of multiple tombs or memorial cenotaphs. In Chapter 18 we reviewed the many arguments for and against the reasons why huge royal tombs exist both at Abydos and Saqqara. Although we might dismiss one group or the other as not genuine royal tombs, this seems unlikely for reasons discussed earlier. It is safest to assume that the early pharaohs realized full well the potential of the royal mortuary cult as a means of cementing their kingdom ideologically and institutionalizing kingship. They might also have realized that their tombs constituted a sort of outdoor theater in which royal rites of passage might be celebrated.

Whether, like the Thai kings, they yet realized that these theaters might be designed for large audiences and that the performance of the death ritual of a dead king could be linked to the coronation of a successor to ensure the continuity of the state is not known. I suspect that the tombs and funerals of the first two dynasties were fairly private and that public rites were restricted to the large open spaces of the mortuary temples of Abydos. It was not until the reign of Djoser that the principle of constructing an elaborate jubilee court around the tomb was fully developed. Such a court was a dummy intended for the deceased king's jubilee or Sed festival by which he ritually renewed himself. Its size and arrangement, however, recall a real festival court and we might imagine Djoser inviting his nobles to observe the construction of the wonder of the age and delighting in their awe of his new-fangled pyramid tomb, rising slowly, layer by layer above their heads, like a ladder to heaven. The impact of contrived and monumental architecture—the ways it manipulated space and scale—certainly were linked to the social function of the royal mortuary cult itself. As Egypt consolidated from local chieftainships into regional kingdoms, into the world's first national state, it developed the royal tomb as its flag: a symbol of political integration, under god. With the elaboration of the tomb as a national political symbol came the concern for preserving the body of the king. Mummification, which probably dates back to Archaic times in its crudest forms (i.e., wrapping the dead body in linen swathing), required its own specialists and generated its own beliefs. From our brief exposure to the study of known mortuary practices and monuments, we can conclude that the development and function of the royal mortuary cult in late prehistoric and early historic Egypt (between about 3300 and 2700 B.C.) was one of the most socially, economically, and politically sensitive indicators of the rise of the state and was one of the most important reasons why Egyptian civilization emerged when it did and in the fashion that it did.

The Cedars of Lebanon:
Trade and the Makings of a Royal Monopoly

It was Amélineau who thought so little of the vast quantities of imported wood in the royal tombs at Abydos that he incinerated much of the material, earning Petrie's rage and the condemnation of history. It is so seldom that large amounts of normally perishable material are preserved for the archaeologist that our view of human prehistory is often limited to a small remnant of a people's endeavor. This is especially true of commodities that are exchanged. The accounts of Classical Mediterranean antiquity record vast transactions in oils, unguents, furs, grain, cloth, timber, and metals—materials seldom preserved in the archaeological record. Considering the large volume of trade attested to by literary sources from the ancient world and the degree to which it affected the policy of states and empires as well as the prosperity or poverty of local economies, it is hard not to believe that similar systems of exchange must have existed well back into prehistoric times.

The development of new techniques of radio-chemical analysis has permitted archaeologists in the last decade to probe the extent and mechanics of ancient, prehistoric exchange systems and to discover networks covering vast areas of the earth's surface—networks that extend back to the advent of farming and probably well into the late Pleistocene. One of the earliest types of raw material traded was obsidian, a fine, volcanic glass that permitted more efficient chipped stone tools. Obsidian exchange networks are known to have flourished in Anatolia and the Aegean as early as the seventh millennium B.C. In Egypt, we have seen throughout the Predynastic epoch strong evidence that locally exotic goods were exchanged and eventually found their way into the graves of their owners. These materials doubtless served combined func-

78   The Nile as an artery of trade: modern pots from Qene awaiting shipment at Armant

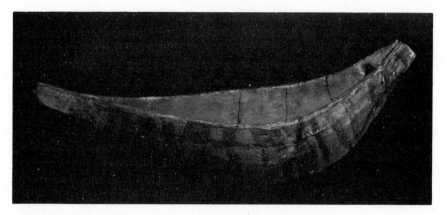

79 A Predynastic boat model from Grave 619 at Naqada

tions as ornaments, status objects, and currency all rolled into one and many had to be obtained from areas several hundred miles away. I have already suggested that the Nile River provided a cheap and efficient means of moving materials from north to south and that donkeys could be relied on to transport commodities overland for substantial distances. The exchange networks that existed in Predynastic times were doubtless more complex than indicated by the archaeological evidence. Few if any perishable imports have been recovered from Predynastic graves that rival the Lebanese timber in the royal tombs of the First Dynasty (Chapter 18). Nevertheless, the list of exchanged goods for which we do have evidence in Predynastic times is impressive: copper, Red Sea and Mediterranean Sea shells, hard and attractive gemstones from the Eastern and Western Deserts, and ceramic vases from Palestine. To this list could doubtless be added local specialties, like the so-called Qena ware pottery, but until more careful scientific tests are made it is premature and inaccurate to make definitive statements about the origins of these products. It is also fairly certain, given the ecological and productive differences between and within Upper and Lower Egypt, that foodstuffs and other perishable materials found their way into the hulls of the Nile boats shown on Gerzean pots. Upper Egyptian grains doubtless attracted Middle and Lower Egyptians in prehistoric times, while the pasturages of Lower Egypt and, to a lesser extent, those of the Sahara supported herds of cattle that were considered valuable booty by Narmer's day and probably a good deal earlier.

But examining the great bulk of the trade material that has been preserved archaeologically from the Late Gerzean through Archaic periods, one major theme emerges. The prime motivation for exchange was the acquisition of exotic powerfacts that could display the status of an individual during life and ensure his prosperity after death—a situation paralleled by Dr. Metcalf's riverine Berawan. The continuing elaboration of the mortuary cult by the growing elite, in the tradition of the multiplier effect, caused a giant leap into open competition for access to the symbols of power and prestige. We have already seen in Chapter 16 how King Den contended with the peoples of the Red Sea Hills, probably for the purpose of controlling trade routes and markets. The presence of a Late Gerzean or Protodynastic gold-handled scepter in a Nubian grave and of Egyptian stone vases in Palestine, Byblos, and Crete suggest what was traded for foreign imports.

As we have already seen, the appearance of Eastern artistic motifs and architectural innovations in Egypt was linked to the growth of the state between the Late Gerzean and First Dynasty. Significantly, the Mesopotamian or Susan motifs are all found on objects or in circumstances where high status and power are being represented and most are linked directly with graves. The *serekh* façade was employed both on the palace of the living king and on his tomb, his eternal home. The Painted Tomb employed several Eastern motifs, as do a number of the animal palettes from this era and weapons used by the elite, like the Gebel el Arak knife. As status became increasingly a concern of the king's and as he sought to monopolize the distribution of rewards to his clientele, the control over foreign markets passed out of the hands of prehistoric local entrepreneurs and middlemen.

In the same way that the king's tomb quickly became the monument of monuments, so trade became a royal business par excellence—the main purpose of which was to provide the tomb of the king and those of his followers with goods appropriate to their new and exalted status. Like the other systems in Egyptian society, trade in luxury goods grew geometrically with the rise of the state, rather than at the slow, arithmetical rate characteristic of the Predynastic era.

To appreciate the magnitude of trade we have only to return to Abydos and consider that the sawed and aged timber of several Lebanese cedars must have been required for each royal tomb. Such a demand required substantial technical and organizational skill. It required large ships such as those shown on the labels of Hor-aha at Abydos to transport the timber from Palestine or at least relay it from the Delta as well as a militarylike organization of trade expeditions and, in some instances where mere force could not be used, it required goods to pay for the precious raw material.

Beyond the remarkable nature of the rare materials lies the whole question of the structure of trading relationships—a problem usually ignored by archaeologists, because we lack the information to talk about trade in terms of the specific mechanics of exchange. In a book called *The Gift*, the French sociologist Marcel Mauss tried to portray the activity of exchange as a major component of social organization and structure. Although principally concerned with simple societies, his distinction between symmetrical (or balanced) and asymmetrical (or one-way) exchange, and his view of marriage and alliance systems as types of exchange, offers the Egyptian prehistorian and historian a number of useful insights that should be applied to the study of trade in ancient Egypt. Particularly in dealing with the possible effect of Eastern contacts on the rise of the state, our explanations have all too often fallen back on oversimplified diffusion or invasion models. It is clear, however, from both the volume and extent of trade in Late Gerzean through Archaic times, that it was linked to the other subsystems of society in many ways so that it cannot be understood without reference to the political, economic, and ideological changes going on within Egypt itself when that nation stood poised on the threshold of statehood and civilization.

The Gebel el Arak Knife: Invasion or Competition?

It is impossible to study the rise of civilization in Egypt and not come to grips with warfare. Many of the most famous monuments and reliefs of the Late Gerzean and First Dynasty (ca. 3300–2900 B.C.) glorify the military exploits of the unifiers, the most famous military monument undoubtedly being the Narmer Palette. Scenes of fighting are also shown in the Painted Tomb, but on a small scale. Nevertheless, the military role in the rise of the state is clear. The earliest kings of Egypt were Followers of Horus. The falcon is one of the deadliest predators known, and the scorpion also is not an animal known for its docility, while other throne names of early kings—Narmer (Catfish), Wadji (Cobra), Djer (Palisade), De(we)n (Spearer), and Aha (Fighter) all echo the sounds of conflict. Many of the numerous war clubs or maceheads found in the Great Deposit at Hierakonpolis must have been employed in battle. But of all the records of fighting and military expeditions from this time, the most puzzling is surely the so-called Gebel el Arak knife.

Consisting of a beautiful ripple-flaked flint blade set into an ivory handle, the knife apparently dates to the Late Gerzean or Protodynastic period. The scenes carved on its handle are done in the Eastern style of the day. On one face the depiction of the "master of animals" is thoroughly Mesopotamian in costume and design; however, it is the opposite side of the handle that attracts the most attention. In the top two registers men are shown engaged in hand-to-hand combat, employing hands, knives, maces, and simple clubs, while below is shown the world's oldest sea battle. Two types of boats appear to contend with one another—one the high-prowed variety and the other the low, crescent-shaped type frequently seen on Gerzean painted pots. Many experts believe that this represents an invasion of Eastern, Mesopotamian

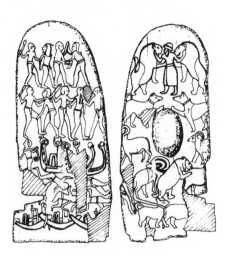

80 The Gebel el Arak knife

81 Gerzean "ripple-flaked" flint knife, the product of a professional flint knapper. The opposite face was ground smooth after flaking

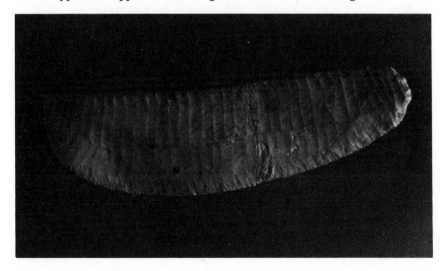

82 Miniature groundstone vase of Archaic date. Stone vase grinding
    developed as a full-time craft during the Gerzean and reached a peak
    under the first two dynasties

peoples, but, as mentioned in Chapter 16, it is impossible to distinguish
the high-prowed boats as non-Egyptian. The boats carry fighting men
and people are seen struggling in the water in a manner that recalls a
scene drawn 2,000 years later at the temple-palace of Medinet Habu to
commemorate a victory of Rameses III over the "people of the seas." It
is not possible to determine where the battle is taking place, but the best
bet is that it occurred on the Nile and reflects an encounter between
contending chieftains. Throughout Egyptian history, the river was the
most efficient means of transport and boats must have been used for
almost any military operation.

The combat scene shown on the Gebel el Arak knife plus the numerous
examples of Predynastic and Protodynastic fortified towns reviewed
earlier, as well as the later Egyptian traditions of the fighting that led
to the unification, all emphasize the role of warfare in the consolidation
of the Egyptian state and raise the question of how this activity related
to the other changes that were remolding Egyptian society at the time.

Today, most experts reject the idea of an outright foreign invasion of
Egypt. The fighting men on the Gebel el Arak knife all look Egyptian
and their weapons and watercraft need not be derived from any other

area. The same is even more true of the scenes of battle depicted on the Narmer Palette from a century or two later. The important question is what factors encouraged the fighting, what role did it play in the political consolidation of the land, and between what political units did this fighting take place?

Anthropologist Robert Carneiro has suggested that conflict and warfare are among the most important factors in the emergence of the state in different societies. He maintains that, given a village farming and pastoral economy similar to that of Predynastic peoples, population growth is quite likely. Under conditions in which resources are unevenly distributed, especially when agricultural land is tightly circumscribed, "it was population pressure that gave the necessary impetus to state formation" (Carneiro in Spooner 1972: 65). Thus, the natural outcome of population growth is seen causing conflict which, in turn, generates the conquest state. In order to test this idea, it is first necessary to know something of the relative population density of Egypt in late prehistoric times. If population density was high and agricultural land or some other critical resource needed by the population as a whole restricted, then the conditions specified by Carneiro would apply. Although we are not able accurately to reconstruct Predynastic or early Dynastic demography, Karl Butzer has guessed that the population was *not* evenly distributed over the Upper Egyptian Nile Valley at this time and that agricultural land was not particularly scarce. It therefore seems unlikely that population pressure was a main stimulant of warfare and the rise of the Egyptian state. However, increased warfare did not have to result from competition for agricultural resources any more than it had to result from foreign invasion.

A resource worth fighting over is a hard thing to define cross-culturally. People need to value something before they will fight over it. And, above all else, Egyptians valued their way of death. Their religion was tied to it, as well as their trading systems and their system of rank and status. Any threat to or encouragement from this particular area of their culture could well have brought on war. I suggest that armed conflict occurred during the late prehistoric and early historic times due largely to the actions of local chiefs and kings, who were trying to monopolize stored goods, services of growing clienteles, and the symbols of power by which their own statuses and those of their followers were defined. If armed aggression was one arm of the extension of the late Predynastic and Protodynastic state, then it was merely an extension of the ambitions and quests for power of elites—their attempts to dominate local and long-range exchange systems and bury themselves in bigger and better tombs—that ultimately brought on conflict. Population growth might have been a factor but, for now at least, it seems that there was enough room to grow without conflict. If there is reason for a demographic explanation, it is to be found in the rearrangement of population forced by increasing desiccation or overuse of the desert margins in Protodynastic times. But this was an indirect stimulus, mitigated through local elites which suddenly found themselves with bigger audiences and more manpower. It may be that the push into the Delta, late in the process of consolidation, was partly prompted by the need for more and better pasturage for Upper Egyptian cattle, but here too the cause would have been ultimately environmental and did not necessarily involve the demands of more mouths to feed.

Whatever the final verdict, it is clear that hypotheses like Carneiro's are valuable in focusing attention on the internal changes in Egyptian society without requiring invading master races. It is still too early to completely reject Carneiro's explanation and, whatever the demography of late Predynastic Egypt, it is clear that no explanation of the rise of Egyptian civilization that ignores the role of internal conflict among the growing chiefdoms and ministates of the late prehistoric will succeed in providing a complete picture of the foundations of Egyptian civilization.

Power and Glory

"My name is Ozymandias, king of kings:
Look on my works, ye Mighty, and despair!"
    —Shelley: "Ozymandias"

So Percy Bysshe Shelley described the gigantic statues of Rameses II that even today lie in ruins around the Ramesseum in the flat bottom-lands of the west bank at ancient Thebes. Across the Nile at Luxor stand the impressive ruins of two millennia of devotion to the god Amon and other great ones of the Middle and New Kingdoms, while behind loom the fire-red cliffs of the Theban Hills, concealing in desolate valleys the tombs of some of Egypt's greatest and most flamboyant rulers.

Above and beyond the megalomaniacal personality of "Ozymandias" Shelley's poem is about power—absolute power—its abuses and style and its peculiar personality

. . . whose frown
And wrinkled lip, and sneer of cold command,
Tell that its sculptor well those passions read
Which yet survive, stamped on these lifeless things,
The hand that mocked them and the heart that fed.

Throughout Western history, beginning with accounts given in Exodus, the name pharaoh has been synonymous with absolute power and with a style of government as philosophically alien from our own as night from day. Perhaps because of that very strangeness, we find ourselves drawn to god-kings like Khufu, Rameses, and even the unimportant Tutankhamon, who caused to be raised in their names some of the oldest and most magnificent monuments ever conceived. The brilliance of this monumental tradition has often obscured the social functions of public architecture and royal tombs and blinded us to the greater continuities in Egyptian cultural history—continuities that we have traced in the preceding chapters from the hand axes of the Lower Palaeolithic through the great royal tombs of Abydos and Saqqara. We have come finally to the time when Egypt became one of the first societies in the world to accomplish the transition to what we sometimes call civilization.

There was a time, not too long ago, when the word civilization carried with it implicit faith in the progressive evolution of human society, but the paths of empire traveled by Quibell and Green in the early days of Egyptian prehistoric archaeology have been obscured by the shifting sands of changing world history. Two world wars and a major economic transformation have shaken much of our previous Victorian self-confidence. Although some historians continue to speak of civilization exclusively in terms of art, literature, and "high culture," most serious students of the past now prefer to avoid the clichés of upward and onward and adopt a more cautious stance. Now the word civilization has come to have a more materialistic meaning, in accordance with the ideals of modern man. Today, when we use the word, archaeologists generally refer to large, internally stratified, and economically diversified societies characterized by dense populations, developing sciences and literatures, impressive public art and architecture and—above all—power.

Power has many definitions, but basically it is the ability to initiate and direct activity, the ability to get things done. A concomitant of power is an elite. As the noted University of Chicago prehistorian Robert McCormick Adams has observed, the urban revolution (or civilization), unlike its Neolithic predecessor, was primarily social and not technological. With the emergence of complex societies we are dealing first and foremost with behavioral and organizational changes. If there is one distinctive characteristic of the transition to complex societies (civilizations) it is the emergence of groups of people able to concentrate vast amounts of power in their own hands. In the end, all the panoply of the state—its temples, religions, public ceremonies, art, trade, architecture, wars, literature, and even its social and economic systems—can be seen as corollary to the centralization of power. At the vortex of centralization, as the very personification of power, inevitably stands an elite. Elites are common to all modern industrial societies (be they capitalist or communist) and most agricultural ones, and the games they play have dominated the later prehistory and history of mankind. In his recent study, *The Emergence of Society*, author John Pfeiffer has written "a prehistory of the establishment" which stresses as its central theme the rise of states and the changes wrought by power elites. Characterizing our special interest in the rise of early elites and the states and civilizations that formed around them, Pfeiffer observes:

> Many elites have come and gone since the founding of the earliest states. But the first elites had a special aura, a special degree of power and divinity, simply because they were the first, and the shock of their passing must also have been something special. Modern society is still very much under the influence of pomp and circumstance and ritual, yet it is difficult to imagine how utterly the early elites and the rest of the populace must have been committed. *(Pfeiffer 1976: 472)*

Elites, especially the early elites, were by definition small. For that reason and because the literature of history that they created is designed to glorify individuals, we often see the emergence of states in strictly personal terms. To ancient Egyptians, Menes, and not economic systems, climatic or geographic factors, caused the Egyptian state. When we ask, Who is Menes?, therefore, we are immediately thrown into a quandary created by the very nature of what we are studying—power is both personal and cultural. It is of course legitimate to search for the causes of the rise of the Egyptian state, or the unification, as it was called by the ancients, in the qualities of an individual, but it can be at times an impossible task and it can obscure some of the broader reasons why Egyptian civilization crystallized at the moment it did. Although power is manipulated by people, by members of an elite, it deals ultimately with *both* impersonal and personal things. It manipulates artifacts—architecture, science, costume, graphic arts, luxury trade, ceremony, religion, literature, production, exchange, and conflict—according to its own self-defined goals. To be sure, the changes wrought by elites derive ultimately from a broader culture whose traditional values have developed through countless millennia of prehistory and to be sure the elites—the early ones at least—were symbols of a collective sentiment, not raw power: kings, popes, flags, parents, and Santa Claus all rolled into one.

> Civilization is a new dimension of human experience. The great idea, moving among many traditions and in newly troubled minds, is now an agent of change, a shaper of the moral order. *(Redfield 1953: 83)*

When the anthropologist Robert Redfield wrote these words, he was attempting broadly to characterize the primitive and the civilized worlds. To him what mattered was the part played by the urban revolution in affecting a "great transformation whereby the minds of men in local communities came to be shaped by reformist ecumenical ideas expressed in written word and preached in far-flung teachings" (Redfield 1953: 83). A quarter of a century after Redfield, we are less sure of the role played by cities in the "great transformation" and the differences between primitive and civilized have been blurred by a fuller appreciation of the accomplishments of so-called primitive peoples and what many believe to be the impending collapse of our own technological order. Our society appears to be racing toward ecological suicide while the cities that once nurtured intellectual revolution stagnate. The world is seen as a more complicated place than Redfield thought and it appears that the roads to civilization were more varied and a good deal more rocky than once believed. Even progress, that deity of nineteenth-century social Darwinism, seems reversible.

In this light, the lesson of Egypt, perceived anew in the light of hundreds of thousands of years of developments, changes, advances and retreats, seems especially timely. The search for the prehistoric foundations of Egyptian civilization has brought us face to face with major contradictions in the standard interpretations and once-accepted principles of history and prehistory. That search has also had both its intensely personal and its broad, theoretical aspects and carried us from the dawn of humanity to the rise of the Egyptian state under Menes and his successors. If we now prefer to avoid the word civilization and substitute complex society, we are nevertheless concerned with the same spectacular transition. We believe, or wish to believe, that our explanations, interpretations, and models are more sophisticated than those of older scholars like Redfield. This is as it should be; 25 years have seen much new evidence unearthed and much more reexamined. Perhaps our stress on the materialistic aspects of civilization is itself an artifact of the age in which we live. Perhaps in another decade or two, emphasis will shift; this is to be expected; but it will not change the substance of the archaeological evidence. With any luck, this will continue to grow. But over and above the differences caused by one's particular theoretical viewpoint, emerge some central themes in Egyptian history and prehistory that create an image of the splendor that was Egypt. Herodotus, our own barbarian ancestor, perceived it 2,500 years ago when he studied and wondered over the power and glory once aspired to by divine kings like Ozymandias, of whom

Nothing beside remains. Round the decay
Of that colossal wreck, boundless and bare
The long and level sands stretch far away.

21

KHASEKHEMUI:
A POSTSCRIPT TO PREHISTORY

KHASEKHEMUI was the last king of his dynasty, the second to rule the Two Lands since their unification 400 years before. A generation after he was laid in his tomb, over 2,700 years before the birth of Christ, King Djoser erected the step pyramid, inaugurating the glorious epoch known to historians as the Old Kingdom, or Pyramid Age. It is this Egypt—the land of Khufu and Khafre, of pyramids and sphinxes, of unbridled royal autocrats whose starkly wrought features still epitomize absolute power and unshakable confidence—that most of us recall when we ponder the origins of Egyptian civilization. But, as we have seen throughout this book, these monuments stand at the end rather than at the beginning of a long sequence of cultural development, a sequence that stretches back through the Archaic period of the first two dynasties, through Predynastic times into the dimmest reaches of the Palaeolithic era. Visitors from Herodotus on have marveled over the wonders of Giza, only to miss the true progenitors of Egyptian civilization: the Archaic peoples and their prehistoric antecedents. It seems appropriate, therefore, after unraveling the many threads that bind history and prehistory, to end this account at that protohistoric point in time when literacy was in its infancy and Egypt in the throes of cultural, political, and economic revolution.

The death of a monarch was an important occasion in Egypt and in the case of Khasekhemui the event assumes a very special meaning. Before his passing, the land he ruled retained much of its prehistoric flavor. The subsistence economy was still basically Neolithic, and stone rather than metal continued to dominate the tool kit as it had done since earliest Palaeolithic times. Writing was little used and architectural and artistic cannons had not yet hardened into their classical Dynastic molds. What little we know of the political organization of the new state suggests that it kept many of its Predynastic trappings, while important and potentially disruptive cultural differences between Upper and Lower Egypt persisted. The concept of divine kingship, essential to the Egyptian political order down through Cleopatra's time (i.e., to 31 B.C.), was still evolving from simpler prehistoric antecedents into the ceremonial absolutism of the impending Pyramid Age.

If the Archaic period (ca. 3100–2700 B.C.) in general acts as a bridge linking history and prehistory, then Khasekhemui himself, as much as Menes, is the figure who symbolizes the passing of the old regime and the dawn of a new order. Everything about his still poorly known reign stirs the imagination and piques our curiosity. It can truly be said, both in a historical and a cultural sense, that Khasekhemui's mysterious reign was transitional and that it is fraught with problems of interpretation that daunt the most stout-hearted scholar. For example: (1) Authorities disagree on whether or not the two names Khasekhemui and Khasekhem represent the same or two different kings. (2) Khasekhemui was interred in a tomb of large and unique proportions on the Umm el-Qa'ab at Abydos. (3) Khasekhemui's reign was apparently marked by fighting and, perhaps, by revolution. (4) The official name cartouche of Khasekhemui depicts *both* Horus and Set, suggesting a departure from First Dynasty preeminence of Horus in royal titularies and reflecting an earlier Second Dynasty attempt by Peribsen to associate the god Set with royal honors. (5) Khasekhemui was clearly the last king of his dynasty and his passing marks a watershed in Egyptian history. (6) Khasekhemui constructed a huge fort at Hierakonpolis, traditional seat of Menes, which was similar to the so-called valley temples of the First Dynasty kings at Abydos.

Walter Emery, who, as we have already seen, was fond of offering alternate explanations not espoused by the majority of his colleagues, long maintained that the two spellings of Khasekhemui and Khasekhem represented two separate monarchs. While this may be true, the linguistic evidence is heavily against it as the Egyptologist Werner Kaiser has pointed out. It is true we do not know why the different spellings existed, but the difference is not serious, especially considering the state of our knowledge of Archaic Egyptian epigraphy, and by admitting that both names denote only one individual we logically simplify our understanding of what is admittedly as complex and sticky a problem as was ever encountered in the annals of Egyptology and archaeology.

Next, the uniqueness of Khasekhemui's tomb is immediately apparent to anyone who compares its plan with the other Archaic royal graves at Abydos, including the Second Dynasty sepulcher of Peribsen. Emery even went so far as to call the structure "a fantastic construction" and we must surely agree.

It measures 68.97 metres in length, with a varying width of between 17.6 and 10.4 metres. It consists of three parts; at the north is a door leading to three rows of thirty-three magazines for offerings and funerary equipment; then comes a stone-built burial chamber flanked

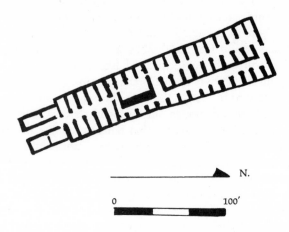

N.

0   100'

83   The Tomb of Khasekhemui at Abydos (drawn by author after Petrie 1901)

by four rooms on either side, and then a further ten magazines, five on each side of a corridor leading to the south door, which is flanked by four more rooms.

The burial chamber was at one time believed to be the oldest example of stone masonry in existence, but excavation at Saqqara and Helwan has shown that building in stone was known in the First Dynasty. A curious feature of Khasekhemui's tomb is its irregularity and faulty planning and, impressive as it is in size, it is difficult to believe that only a few years separate it from the magnificent Step Pyramid of Zoser at Saqqara. *(Emery 1961: 101-102)*

Although one might explain the large size and shoddy planning of this tomb as the result of an attempt to combine the three known principles of mortuary temple, grave, and solar(?) boat in one funerary complex, and thus see the monument as a forerunner of Djoser's Saqqara complex, the fact remains that the tomb is atypical at best and bizarre at worst and definitely in an architectural limbo.

As proof that his reign was characterized by war, conquest, and possibly civil disturbance, Emery has cited the consistent association of the name Khasekhem with records of large-scale fighting and "national disturbance" (Emery 1961: 99), and has ingeniously interpreted some fragmentary inscriptions to show that this king ". . . was a ruler of the Thinite family of Upper Egypt who restored the unity of the Nile Valley after the religious wars between the followers of Horus and Set which had probably divided the country since the reign of Peribsen" (Emery 1961: 100).

The question of the real versus the symbolic nature of the Egyptian myth of the struggle between Horus and Set has long been debated and is, as we have seen, largely unanswerable. For the time being it will be sufficient to know that both gods were held to be in active rivalry for the kingship of Osiris with Horus usually representing good, and Set discord. The kings of the First Dynasty are termed the Followers of Horus by the Palermo Stone and indeed they wrote one of their official names (later called the Horus name) in cartouches surmounted by the Horus falcon and were fond of depicting themselves fighting under the aegis of Horus while waging the wars of unification. What Emery takes to be a literal representation of a deeper ethnic power struggle between followers of Horus and Set during the Second Dynasty stems from the apparently sudden appearance of Set on top of the royal cartouche of Peribsen, in place of Horus. On a later seal of Khasekhemui, both gods bestride the royal cartouche, indicating to Emery that the factions had been reconciled in the person of the king. Once more, however, most Egyptologists feel that Emery interprets his evidence too literally, pointing out that the Egyptians themselves were far from consistent in their hostility to Set and that he often appears linked to the kingship in later periods. At this point, all that seems safe to say is that the appearance of Set as a royally patronized god during the late Second Dynasty probably had both purely symbolic and real political implications and betokens some kind of change in the concept of kingship.

One of the few facts agreed on by most scholars and scientists is that Khasekhemui was clearly the last ruler of his dynasty and that whether his progeny succeeded him or whether a new family altogether took possession of the kingship, there was a change in the nature of royal power as well as in art and burial custom at this time. Emery has suggested that, in order to reunite the Two Lands, Khasekhemui consolidated his conquests by wedding a northern queen, Nemathap, who mothered the future founder of the Third Dynasty. Although essentially guesswork, based on her title as "King-bearing mother" and later tradition that she was the ancestress of the Third Dynasty, this explanation seems in line with the periodic importance of women in transmitting legitimacy or cementing important political alliances—precedents already set by Neith-hotep and Meryet-nit in the early First Dynasty and continued in later years by strong women like Tetisheri and Hapshepsawe of the Eighteenth Dynasty. It is likely that such periodic reemergences of powerful women throughout Egyptian history reflect not only occasionally strong and opportunistic personalities, but the existence of certain underlying social rules or alternatives such as matrilineal descent, which provided a convenient sanction for the explicit political prominence of women in ancient Egypt.

The last enigma associated with Khasekhemui is a large mud-brick monument he built in the desert at Hierakonpolis. The man who first described this so-called fort was Somers Clarke. In the late 1890's he worked with J. E. Quibell and F. W. Green at Hierakonpolis and directly across the Nile at the great Dynastic site of El Kab. He became so fond of the area that he built his retirement home near El Kab on the east bank. Perched high above the valley floor, the castlelike house reflects accurately the mercurial and idiosyncratic personality of its builder, who spent the last two decades of his long life living there in splendid isolation, regaling his occasional visitors with tales of the incompetence of many of his former colleagues. Today the castle of this archaeological Old Man of the Mountain affords comfortable accommodations for the Belgian archaeological mission to El Kab, and from its heights one can still look out across the Nile and barely discern the forbidding walls of Khasekhemui's fort.

> This building lies on the desert edge, but very little removed from the cultivated ground, and at the mouth of a valley which runs into the western desert. In plan, it is rectangular, with the entrance toward the cultivated land. An outer wall has been built 2.34 m. thick, standing in advance of the inner and chief wall, which is 4.87 m. thick. There is a space of 2.23 m. between the walls. The outer wall was lower than the inner.
>
> The entrance is formed in a sort of bastion, or tower-like projection, and is sufficiently circuitous to make it possible for any body of persons to rush through quickly. . . .
>
> If there were walls of ascent to the wall top, and we cannot suppose

84   Khasekhemui's "fort" at Hierakonpolis

there were not, these must have been of wood, and placed in the slits on either side of the entrance. All traces of them have now vanished . . .

Whilst the surface of the outer wall was plain, that of the inner wall, facing into the narrow space of 2.23 m., was built in panels. The walls are entirely of crude brick, and were plastered and whitened. . . .

The south west wall remains unbroken, and stands to a height of some 8.0 or 9.0 m. above the plain. The walls near the gateway are also of about the same height, and it is probable that they have not lost more than 1.0 m. *(Clarke, in Quibell and Green 1902: 19-20)*

Clarke and Quibell grasped immediately the similarity between Khasekhemui's fort and the Shunet ez Zebib at Abydos (see Chapter 18). At that time the walled Shunet was also thought to be a fort although most archaeologists now believe it was a valley temple for a First or Second Dynasty royal tomb. Such a revision of our thinking has necessarily affected the interpretation of Khasekhemui's building at Hierakonpolis, since that structure bears such close resemblance to its larger antecedent at Abydos. Many archaeologists now suspect that the fort was actually some kind of mortuary monument for Khasekhemui. Sadly, we will probably never know its original purpose since the archaeological clearance conducted within its walls by Quibell, Green, and Clarke between 1897 and 1899 and a later effort by John Garstang in 1905 concentrated mainly on salvaging the earlier Predynastic graves that lie underneath and ignored the internal architecture of the building itself. Although to a modern archaeologist it is irksome in the extreme to know that Garstang never adequately recorded or published his findings, in his day he believed he was doing the right thing. Of the ground surrounding the fort he writes:

The whole of this necropolis had been excavated or plundered so that nothing remained; but, within the fortress, except for the uncovering of several walls in the interior, there seemed to have been no systematic excavation [and this six years after Quibell, Green, and Clarke had worked there!]. It seemed to us that such an excavation was essential for determining at any rate the date of the fortress, especially as the tombs of the early dynasties crept up to its outer walls.

After clearing away, therefore, all the sand accumulated against the southerly wall of the fortress in the interior (a very considerable labour), we came upon an entirely undisturbed portion of the original necropolis at an average depth of about 1.50 m. below the real surface. This depth had of course been much increased by the blown sands. In all we excavated 188 of these primitive graves. The position of these graves in relation to the walls of the fortress . . . was of very great interest. They seemed to belong for the most part to about the middle of the predynastic scale, and to be earlier in date than the earliest historical monuments; they would also seem to have been covered with blown sands and forgotten before the fortress was constructed. *(Garstang 1907: 136-137)*

The importance of Garstang's findings was that he demonstrated a very real stratigraphic relationship between an Archaic monument and its prehistoric predecessors—a relationship that, thanks to more recent work in the vicinity, can be extended back through the Predynastic era well into Palaeolithic times. When Khasekhemui built his fort or his cenotaph or his tomb at Hierakonpolis, the earlier Predynastic graves and villages on the desert had lain abandoned for five centuries and Egypt had undergone a great transformation. Half a millennium before Khasekhemui, the country had been unified by a local ruler from this very spot (Menes) and in the centuries immediately preceding his conquests the inhabitants had abandoned their desert villages and hamlets along the banks of the fort or Great Wadi for a larger, more compact settlement on the flood-plain—the town they called Nekhen and which the Greeks later dubbed Hierakonpolis, city of the hawk. Sand drifted over and eroded their old dwellings and covered their graves. What apparently attracted Khasekhemui to this spot was the presence of the thriving town of Nekhen and the great historical associations of the site. Whatever manifest function his walled enclosure performed, whether it was a military precaution to secure a strategically or ceremonially vital town, or an act of pious propaganda, it was latently a political gesture. The area, hallowed by tradition, had become a symbol of Upper Egypt and of the unity of the pharaonic order. For 2,000 years later kings would raise temples on the site of Menes's capital long after it had fallen into ruins. If Emery is right about the political importance of Khasekhemui, then the king's building at Hierakonpolis was probably a key part of his policy, whether that policy involved outright pacification or spiritual revitalization. The building, like the ruler, bestrode two worlds: the prehistoric past and the Dynastic future. Its location on the geographical border of the red land of the desert and the black land of the valley interposed it, probably intentionally, between the desert hinterlands with their hills crowned by Palaeolithic campsites and their greatest water course and terraces dotted with Predynastic hamlets, towns, and cemeteries, and the alluvial bottomland with its sacred city of the hawk. Because of its situation, to walk past the fort in any direction is to move forward or backward from Khasekhemui in time, duplicating an intellectual journey I have undertaken in this book in visiting isolated Palaeolithic campsites, rich Predynastic cemeteries, and sprawling towns to explain and appreciate the great cultural transformations that link Egypt's prehistoric past to the better-known worlds of Menes, Khufu, and Tutankhamon.

BIBLIOGRAPHY
INDEX

ABBREVIATIONS

AJA	*American Journal of Archaeology*
AJPA	*American Journal of Physical Anthropology*
ASAÉ	*Annales du Service des Antiquits de l'Égypte*
BIÉ	*Bulletin de l'Institut d'Égypte*
BIFAO	*Bulletin de l'Institut Français d'Archéologie Orientale*
BSGÉ	*Bulletin de la Société de Géographie d'Égypte*
BSPF	*Bulletin de la Société Préhistorique Française*
CÉ	*Chronique d'Égypte*
EES	Egypt Exploration Society
ERA	Egypt Research Account
GJ	*Geographical Journal*
JARCE	*Journal of the American Research Center in Egypt*
JEA	*Journal of Egyptian Archaeology*
JNES	*Journal of Near Eastern Studies*
JRAI	*Journal of the Royal Anthropological Institute of Great Britain and Ireland*
MDAIK	*Mitteilungen des deutschen archäologischen Institut, Abteilung Kairo*
OIP	Oriental Institute Publications
OIR	Oriental Institute Reports
PPS	*Proceedings of the Prehistoric Society*
ZÄS	*Zeitschrift für ägyptische Sprache und Altertumskunde*
ZDMG	*Zeitschrift der deutschen Morgenländischen Gesellschaft*
ZE	*Zeitschrift für Etnologie*

BIBLIOGRAPHY

ADAMS, BARBARA
1974   *Ancient Hierakonpolis (and Supplement)*. Aris and Phillips, Ltd., Warminster, England.

ADAMS, ROBERT MC CORMICK
1965   *Land Behind Baghdad: A History of Settlement on the Diyala Plains*. University of Chicago Press, Chicago.
1966   *The Evolution of Urban Society*. Aldine Publishing Co., Chicago.

ADAMS, WILLIAM Y.
1967   "Continuity and Change in Nubian Culture History," *Sudan Notes and Records*, 48: 1-32.
1977   *Nubia: Corridor to Africa*. Princeton University Press, Princeton, New Jersey.

ALDRED, CYRIL
1965   *Egypt to the End of the Old Kingdom*. Thames and Hudson, London.

ALIMEN, H.
1975   *Préhistoire de l'Afrique*. Boubée, Paris.

ALMASY, L. E. DE
1936   *Récentes explorations dans le Désert Libyque (1932–1936)*. Sociététe Royale de Géographie d'Égypte, Cairo.
1940   *Unbekannte Sahara: mit flugzeug und auto in der Libischen Wuste*. F. U. Brockhaus, Leipzig.

ALTENMULLER, HARTWIG
1976   *Grab und Totenreich der alten Ägypter*. Hamburg Museum, Hamburg.

AMÉLINEAU, ÉMILE
1899   *Les nouvelles fouilles d'Abydos, 1, 1985–1896*. Ed. Leroux, Paris.

AMER, MOUSTAFA
1933   "Annual Report of the Maadi Excavations, 1930–32," *Bulletin, Faculty of Arts*, Egyptian University, I: 322-324.
1935   "Annual Report of the Maadi Excavations, 1935," *Bulletin, Faculty of Arts*, Egyptian University, II: 176–178.
1936   "Annual Report of the Maadi Excavations, 1935," *CE*, XI: 54–57.

AMER, MOUSTAFA, AND S. A. HUZAYYIN
1952   "Some Physiographic Problems Related to the Pre-dynastic Site at Ma'adi," *Proceedings of the First Pan-African Congress on Prehistory, Nairobi, 1947*, Oxford.

ANDERSON, J. E.

1968 "Late Paleolithic Skeletal Remains from Nubia," in *The Prehistory of Nubia*, Vol. II, ed. by Fred Wendorf: 996–1040.

ARCELIN, A.; E. T. HAMY, AND F. LENORMANT

1869 *L'Industrie Primitive en Égypte; Age de Pierre*. Recueil de Matériaux pour l'Histoire Primitive et Naturelle de l'Homme.

1869–1870 *L'Age de Pierre en Égypte*. Recueil de Matériaux pour l'Histoire Primitive et Naturelle de l'Homme.

ARKELL, A. J.

1949a *Early Khartoum*. Oxford University Press, London.

1949b *The Old Stone Age in the Anglo-Egyptian Sudan*. Sudan Antiquities Service, Occasional Papers, No. 1, Khartoum.

1953 *Shaheinab: An Account of the Excavation of a Neolithic Occupation Site*. Oxford University Press, London.

1955 *A History of the Sudan from the Earliest Times to 1821*. Athlone Press, London.

1959 "Preliminary Results of the British Ennedi Expedition, 1957," *Kush*, VII: 15–26.

1962 "The Distribution in Central Africa of One Early Neolithic Ware (Dotted Wavy Line Pottery) and its Possible Connections with the Beginning of Pottery," *Actes du IVe Congrès panafricain de préhistoire et de l'étude du Quaternaire, Léopoldville, Congo, 1959, section 3, Pré- et Protohistoire*, ed. by G. Mortelmans and J. Nenquin, Tervuren, Belgium: 283–287.

1975 *The Prehistory of the Nile Valley*. Handbuch der Orientalistik, 1, E. J. Brill, Leiden.

ARKELL, A. J., AND P. J. UCKO

1965 "Review of Predynastic Development in the Nile Valley," *Current Anthropology*, VI: 145–166.

ARMELAGOS, G.; G. H. EWING; D. L. GREENE, AND M. L. PAPWORTH

1965 "The Physical Anthropology of the Nile Valley," paper presented at the Symposium on Nile Valley Prehistory, International Assoc. for Quaternary Research, Boulder, Colorado.

ASSELBERGH, HENRI

1961 *Chaos en Beheering: Documenten uit aneolithisch Egypte*. E. J. Brill, Leiden.

AYRTON, E. R., AND W. L. S. LOAT

1911 *Pre-dynastic Cemetery at El-Mahasna*. EES, XXXI, London.

AYRTON, E. R.; C. T. CURRELLY, AND A. E. P. WEIGALL

1904 *Abydos, Part III, 1904*. EES, 25, London.

BADAWY, A.

1948 *La dessin architectural chez les anciens Égyptians*. Cairo.

1954 *A History of Egyptian Architecture, Vol. I*. Cairo.

1959 "Orthogonal and Axial Town Planning in Egypt," *ZAS*, 85: 1–12.

1966 *Architecture in Ancient Egypt and the Near East*. The MIT Press, Cambridge, Massachusetts.

BACHATLY, C.

1942 *Bibliographie de la préhistoire égyptienne (1869–1938)*. Société royale de Géographie, Cairo.

BAER, KLAUS

1960 *Rank and Title in the Old Kingdom: The Structure of the Egyptian Administration in the 5th and 6th Dynasties*. University of Chicago Press, Chicago.

1962 "The Low Price of Land in Ancient Egypt," *JARCE*, 1: 25–42.

BAGNOLD, R. A.

1931 "Journeys in the Libyan Desert, 1929 and 1930," *GJ*, 78: 13–39.

1933 "A Further Journey through the Libyan Desert," *GJ*, 82: 103–129, 211-235.

1941   *The Physics of Blown Sand and Desert Dunes.* Methuen, London.

BAGNOLD, R. A.; R. F. PEEL; O. H. MYERS, AND H. A. WINKLER

1939   "An Expedition to the Gilf Kebir and Uweinat, 1938," *GJ*, 93: 281-313.

BAILLOUD, G.

1960   "Les peintres rupestres archaïques de l'Ennedi," *L'Anthropologie*, 64: 3-4, 211-234.

BALOUT, L.

1955   *Préhistoire de l'Afrique du Nord. Essaï de chronologie.* Arts de Métiers Graphiques, Paris.

BAUMGARTEL, ELISE J.

1947   *The Cultures of Prehistoric Egypt, I.* Oxford University Press, London (rev. ed., 1955).

1960   *The Cultures of Prehistoric Egypt, II.* Oxford University Press, London.

1965   "Predynastic Egypt," Vol. I, Chapter IXa, *Cambridge Ancient History*, Cambridge University Press, London (rev. ed., 1970).

1970   *Petrie's Naqada Excavation: A Supplement.* Quaritch, London.

BELL, BARBARA

1970   "The Oldest Records of the Nile Floods," *GJ*, 136: 569-573.

BERMANN, R. A.

1934   "Historic Problems of the Libyan Desert," *GJ*, 83.

BIBBY, GEOFFREY

1956   *The Testimony of the Spade.* Alfred A. Knopf, New York.

BISHOP, W. W., AND J. D. CLARK (EDS.)

1967   *Background to Evolution in Africa.* University of Chicago Press, Chicago.

BLANCKENHORN, M. L. P.

1902   "Die Geschichte des Nil-Stroms . . . sowie des paläolithischen Menschen in Ägypten," *Zeitschrift der Gesellschaft für Erdkunde zu Berlin*, XXXVII: 694-922, 753-762.

1921   "Die Steinzeit Palästina-Syriens und Nordafrikas," *Land d. Bible, III*, Leipzig.

BOSERUP, ESTER

1965   *The Conditions of Agricultural Growth: The Economics of Agrarian Change Under Population Pressure.* Aldine Publishing Co., Chicago.

BOVIER-LAPIERRE, PAUL

1925   "Le Paléolithique stratifié des environs du Caire," *L'Anthropologie*, XXXV: 37–46.

1926a   "Les gisements paléolithiques de la plaine de l'Abassieh," *BIE*, VIII: 257–272.

1926b   "Une nouvelle station néolithique (El Omari) au nord d'Hélouan (Égypte)," Compte rendu, Congrès International de Géographie, 1925, IV, Cairo.

1926c   "Stations préhistoriques des environs du Caire," Compte rendu, Congrès International de Géographie, 1925, IV, Cairo.

1929   "Les explorations de S.A.S. le Prince Kemal el Din Hussein: Contribution à la préhistoire due désert libyque," *BIE*, X: 33-44.

1930   "Récentes explorations de S.A.S. le Prince Kemal el Din Hussein dans le désert libyque: Contributions à la préhistoire," *BIE*, XI.

1932   "L'Égypte préhistorique," *Précis de l'histoire d'Égypte*, Vol. I, Cairo.

BREASTED, JAMES HENRY

1906–1907   *Records of Ancient Egypt.* 6 Vols., University of Chicago Press, Chicago.

1928   "Foreword" in *First Report of the Prehistoric Survey Expedition* by K. S. Sandford and W. J. Arkell, Oriental Institute Communications, No. 3, University of Chicago Press, Chicago.

1933   *The Dawn of Conscience.* Charles Scribner's Sons, New York.

BREUIL, ABBÉ H.

1930–1931   *L'Afrique préhistorique.* Cahiers d'Art, Paris.

BRODRICK, MARY
1945 *A Concise Dictionary of Egyptian Archaeology.* Methuen, London.

BROTHWELL, D. R., AND B. A. CHIARELLI (EDS.)
1973 *Population Biology of the Ancient Egyptians.* Academic Press, London.

BRUNTON, GUY
1932 "The Predynastic Town-site Hierakonpolis," in *Studies Presented to F. Ll. Griffiths,* London: 272-276.
1937 *Mostagedda and the Tasian Culture.* Quaritch, London.
1948 *Matmar.* Quaritch, London.

BRUNTON, GUY, AND GERTRUDE CATON-THOMPSON
1928 *The Badarian Civilisation and Prehistoric Remains near Badari.* Quaritch, London.

BRUNTON, GUY.; E. W. GARDNER, AND W. M. F. PETRIE
1927 *Qau and Badari, I.* British School of Archaeology in Egypt, No. 44, Quaritch, London.
1928 *Qau and Badari, II.* British School of Archaeology in Egypt, No. 45, Quaritch, London.
1930 *Qau and Badari, III.* British School of Archaeology in Egypt, No. 50, Quaritch, London.

BUDGE, E. W.
1959 *Egyptian Ideas of the Future Life; Egyptian Religion.* University Books, New York.

BUTZER, KARL W.
1957a "Late Glacial and Postglacial Climatic Variation in the Near East," *Erdkunde,* XI: 21-35.
1957b "Mediterranean Pluvials and the General Circulation of the Pleistocene," *Geografiska Annaler* (Stockholm), XXXIX: 48-53.
1958a *Quaternary Stratigraphy and Climate in the Near East.* Bonner Geographische Abhandlungen, Heft 24, Bonn.
1958b *Studien zum vor- und fruhgeschichtlichen Landschaftswandel der Sahara,* Akademie der Wissenschaften und der Literatur in Mainz, Abhandlungen der Mathematisch-Naturwissenschaftlichen Klasse, 1: 1–49.
1959a "Contributions to the Pleistocene Geology of the Nile Valley," *Erdkunde,* XIII: 46-67.
1959b "Environment and Human Ecology in Egypt during Predynastic and Early Dynastic Times," *BSGE,* XXXII: 43-87.
1959c "A Minute Predynastic Flake Industry from Hierakonpolis," *Archivo Internazionale di Etnografia e Preistoria,* II: 1617-1624.
1959d *Die Naturlandschaft Ägyptens wahrend der Vorgeschichte und der dynastischen Zeit.* Abhandlungen der Akademie der Wissenschaften, Mainz, Math-Naturwissen. Kl., 2.
1959e "Some Recent Geological Deposits in the Egyptian Nile Valley," *GJ,* CXXV: 75-79.
1960 "Archaeology and Geology in Ancient Egypt," *Science,* 132: 1617-1624.
1961 "Archaeologische Fundstellen Ober- und Mittelaegyptens in ihrer geologischen Landschaft," *MDAIK,* 17: 54-68.
1962 "Pleistocene Stratigraphy and Prehistory in Egypt," *Quaternaria,* VI: 456-465.
1966 *Environment and Archeology.* Aldine Publishing Co., New York.
1975 "Patterns of Environmental Change in the Near East during Late Pleistocene and Early Holocene Times," in *Problems in Prehistory: North Africa and the Levant,* ed. by Fred Wendorf and Anthony Marks, SMU Press, Dallas: 389-410.
1976 *Early Hydraulic Civilization in Egypt: A Study in Cultural Ecology.* University of Chicago Press, Chicago.

BUTZER, KARL, AND C. L. HANSEN

1967 "Upper Pleistocene Stratigraphy in Southern Egypt," in *Background to Evolution in Africa*, ed. by W. W. Bishop and J. D. Clark, University of Chicago Press, Chicago.

1968 *Desert and River in Nubia: Geomorphology and Prehistoric Environments at the Aswan Reservoir*. University of Wisconsin Press, Madison, Wisconsin.

CAMPS, GABRIEL

1969 *Amekni: Néolithique ancien du Hoggar*. Mémoire Centre Recherches Anthropologie, Préhistoire, Ethnographie, 10, Paris.

1975 "The Prehistoric Cultures of North Africa," in *Problems in Prehistory: North Africa and the Levant*, ed. by Fred Wendorf and Anthony Marks, SMU Press, Dallas: 181-192.

CAPART, JEAN

1923 *Egyptian Art, Introductory Studies*. Allen and Unwin, London.

DI CAPORIACCO, L.

1933 "Le pitture prehistoriche di Ain Doua (Auenat)," Firenze, *Archivo per l'Antropologia e le Etnologia*, 63: 275-282.

DI CAPORIACCO, L., AND P. GRAZIOSI

1934 *Le pitture rupestri di Ain Doua*. Edit. Centro. de Studi Colonali e Instit. Geogr. Milit., Florence.

CARLTON, E.

1977 *Ideology and Social Order*. Routledge and Kegan Paul, International Library of Sociology, London.

CARNEIRO, R. L.

1972 "From Autonomous Village to the State: A Numerical Estimation," in *Population Growth: Anthropological Implications*, ed. by Brian Spooner, MIT Press, Cambridge, Massachusetts.

CATON-THOMPSON, GERTRUDE

1926 "The Neolithic Industry of the Northern Fayum Desert," *JRAI*, LVI: 309-323.

1928 "Recent Excavations in the Fayum," *Man*, XXVIII: 109-113.

1934 *The Desert Fayum*. Royal Anthropological Institute, London.

1946a "The Levalloisean Industries of Egypt," *PPS*, 92: 57-120.

1946b "The Aterian Industry: Its Place and Significance in the Palaeolithic World," *JRAI*, LXXVI: 87-130.

1952 *Kharga Oasis in Prehistory*. University of London, The Athlone Press, London.

CATON-THOMPSON, GERTRUDE, AND E. H. WHITTLE

1975 "Thermoluminescence Dating of the Badarian," *Antiquity*, 49: 89-97.

ČERNY, JAROSLAV

1952 *Ancient Egyptian Religion*. Hutchinson's University Library, London and New York.

DI CESNOLA, A. P.

1960 "L'Industria Litica della Statione de Abka," *Kush* 8: 182-236.

CHAVAILLON, JEAN, AND JEAN LALEY CHAVAILLON

1966 "Une industrie sur Galet de la Vallée de Nil (Soudan)," *BSPF*, 63: 65-70.

CHILDE, V. GORDON

1953 *New Light on the Most Ancient East*, 4th ed. Praeger, New York.

CHMIELEWSKI, W.

1965 "Archaeological Research on Pleistocene and Lower Holocene Sites in Northern Sudan," in *Contributions to the Prehistory of Nubia*, ed. by Fred Wendorf, Fort Bergwin Research Center and SMU Press, Dallas.

1968 "Early and Middle Palaeolithic Sites near Arkin, Sudan," in *The Prehistory of Nubia*, Vol. I, ed. by Fred Wendorf.

CHRISTALLER, WALTER

1966 *Central Places in Southern Germany*. Prentice-Hall, Englewood, New Jersey.

CHURCHER, C. S.

1972 *Late Pleistocene Vertebrates from Archeological Sites in the Plain of Kom Ombo.* Life Sciences Contributions, Royal Ontario Museum, 82: 1-172.

CLARK J. D.

1967 *Atlas of African Prehistory.* University of Chicago Press, Chicago.

1971 "A Re-examination of the Evidence for Agricultural Origins in the Nile Valley," *PPS*, 37: 34-79.

CLARKE, S.

1921 "El Kab and the Great Wall," *JEA*, VII: 54-79.

COHEN, MARK N.

1977 *The Food Crisis in Prehistory: Overpopulation and the Origins of Agriculture.* Yale University Press, New Haven.

COHEN, R., AND E. R. SERVICE

1978 *The Origins of the State: The Anthropology of Political Evolution.* Ishi Publ., Philadelphia.

COLE, SONIA

1954 *The Prehistory of East Africa.* Pelican Books, A316, Harmondsworth, England.

COTTEVIELLE-GIRAUDET, R.

1933 "L'Égypte avant l'histoire. Paléolithique-Néolithique-Âges du Cuivre," *BIFAO*, XXXIII.

CROW, WALTER L.

1942 *The Climate of Egypt.* The California Institute of Technology, Meteorology Department.

DARBY, W. J.; P. GHALIOUNGUI, AND L. GRIVETTI

1977 *Food: The Gift of Osiris, Vol. I.* Academic Press, London and New York.

1978 *Food: The Gift of Osiris, Vol. II.* Academic Press, London and New York.

DAWSON, WARREN

1951 *Who Was Who in Egyptology.* EES, London.

DEBONO, F.

1945 "Hélouan-El Omari: Fouilles du Service des Antiquities, 1943–1945," *CE*, XXI: 50-54.

1948 "El Omari (près d'Hélouan), exposé sommaire sur les campagnes des fouilles 1943–1944 et 1948," *ASAE*, 48: 561-569.

1951 "Expédition archéologique royale au désert oriental (Keft-Kosseir): Rapport préliminaire sur la campagne 1949," *ASAE*, LI: 59–110.

1956 "La civilisation prédynastique d'El Omari (nord d'Hélouan)," *BIE*, 37: 329–339.

DERRICOURT, R. M.

1971 "Radiocarbon Chronology for Egypt and North Africa," *JNES*, 30: 271-292.

DERRY, D. E.

1956 "The Dynastic Race in Egypt," *JEA*, 42: 80-85.

EL DIN, PRINCE KEMAL

1928 "L'exploration du désert Libyque," *La Géographie*, 50: 171-183, 320-336.

EL DIN, PRINCE KEMAL, AND H. BREUIL

1928 "Les gravures rupestres du Djebel Ouenat," *Revue Scientifique*, 66: 105-117.

DIOP, CHEIKH ANTA

1974 *The African Origin of Civilization.* Lawrence Hill, New York.

DIXON, D. M.

1969 "A Note on Cereals in Ancient Egypt," in *The Domestication and Exploitation of Plants and Animals*, ed. by P. J. Ucko and G. W. Dimbleby, Duckworth, London: 131-142.

DRIOTON, E., AND J. VANDIER

1962 *Les Peuples de l'Orient méditerranéen, II: L'Égypte*, 4th ed. Les Presses Univ. de France, Paris.

DUNBAR, J. H.

1941 *The Rock Pictures of Lower Nubia.* Service des Antiquits de l'Égypte, Cairo.

EDWARDS, I. E. S.
1964 "The Early Dynastic Period in Egypt," rev. ed. of *Cambridge Ancient History*, Vol. I, Chapter XI, Cambridge University Press, Cambridge, England.
1972 *The Pyramids of Egypt*, 3rd ed. Viking Press, New York.

EMERY, WALTER B.
1938 *Excavations at Saqqara: The Tomb of Hemaka*. Government Press, Cairo.
1939 *Excavations at Saqqara, 1937-1938: Hor-Aha*. Government Press, Cairo.
1949 *Great Tombs of the First Dynasty, I*. Government Press, Cairo.
1954 *Great Tombs of the First Dynasty, II*. EES, London.
1958 *Great Tombs of the First Dynasty, III*. EES, London.
1961 *Archaic Egypt*. Harmondsworth, England.
1965 *Egypt in Nubia*. Hutchinson, London.

EPSTEIN, H.
1971 *The Origins of the Domestic Animals of Africa*. 2 vols. Africana Publ. Co., New York.

ERMAN, ADOLF
1927 *The Literature of the Ancient Egyptians . . . from the Third and the Second Millennia B.C.* B. Blom, New York.

EVANS-PRITCHARD, E. E.
1962 *Social Anthropology and Other Essays*. The Free Press of Glencoe, New York.

FAGAN, BRIAN
1977 *The Rape of the Nile*. Charles Scribner's Sons, New York.

FAIRMAN, H. W.
1949 "Town Planning in Pharaonic Egypt," *Town Planning Review*, 20: 33-51 .

FAIRSERVIS, WALTER A.
1962 *The Ancient Kingdoms of the Nile*. A Mentor Book, New York.
1972 "Preliminary Report on the First Two Seasons at Hierakonpolis," *JARCE*, 9: 7-27, 67-99.

FAKHRY, AHMED
1973a *The Oases of Egypt, I: Siwa Oasis*. American University in Cairo Press, Cairo.
1973b "Bahrija," *Lex. Ägyptol.*, 1: 601-604.
1974a "Charga," *Lex. Ägyptol.*, 1: 907-910.
1974b "Dachel," *Lex. Ägyptol.*, 1: 976-979.

FAULKNER, R. O.
1953 "Egyptian Military Organization," *JEA*, 39: 32-47.

FAZZINI, R.
1975 *Images for Eternity: Egyptian Art from Berkeley and Brooklyn*. Fine Arts Museum of San Francisco, New York.

FERRING, C. REID
1975 "The Aterian in North African Prehistory," in *Problems in Prehistory: North Africa and the Levant*, ed. by Fred Wendorf and Anthony Marks, SMU Press: 113-126.

FIRTH, C. M.
1927 *The Archaeological Survey of Nubia: Report for 1910–1911*. Government Press, Cairo.

FISCHER, H. G.
1969 *Dendera in the Third Millennium B.C. Down to the Theban Dominion*. J. J. Augustin, Locust Valley, New York.

FORDE-JOHNSTON, J. L.
1959 *Neolithic Cultures of North Africa*. Liverpool University Monographs in Archaeology and Oriental Studies, Liverpool, England.

FORTES, MYER, AND E. E. EVANS-PRITCHARD (EDS.)
1940 *African Political Systems*. Oxford University Press, London.

FRANKFORT, HENRI

1948a *Ancient Egyptian Religion: An Interpretation.* Columbia University Press, New York.

1948b *Kingship and the Gods.* University of Chicago Press, Chicago.

1951 *The Birth of Civilization in the Near East.* Indiana University Press, Bloomington, Indiana.

GARDINER, A. H.

1935 *The Attitude of the Ancient Egyptians to Death and the Dead.* Cambridge University Press, Cambridge.

1961 *Egypt of the Pharaohs.* Oxford University Press, London.

GARSTANG, JOHN

1903 *Mahasna and Bet Khallaf.* ERA, VII, London.

1907 "Excavations at Hierakonpolis, at Esna and in Nubia," *ASAE,* VII: 132-148.

GAUTHIER, H.

1975 *Dictionnaire des noms géographiques contenus dans les texts hiéroglyphiques.* Paris (7 Vols., orig. publ. 1925-1931).

GRINSELL, L. V.

1975 *Barrow, Pyramid and Tomb: Ancient Burial Customs in Egypt, the Mediterranean and the British Isles.* Thames and Hudson, London.

GUICHARD, JEAN AND GENEVIEVE

1968 "Contributions to the Study of the Early and Middle Paleolithic of Nubia," in *The Prehistory of Nubia, I,* ed. by Fred Wendorf, pp. 148-193.

HALL, EDITH

1921 *The Sheikh of Araby.*

HAMDAN, G.

1961 "Evolution of Irrigation Agriculture in Egypt," *Arid Zone Research,* 17: 119-142.

HAMMETT, IAN

1975 *Chieftainship and Legitimacy.* London.

HASSAN, FEKRI

1972 "Note on Sebilian Sites from Dishna Plain," *CE,* 47: 11-16.

1973a "Determinants of the Size, Density and Growth Rate of Hunting-Gathering Populations," IXth International Congress of Anthropological and Ethnological Sciences, Chicago.

1973b "On Mechanisms of Population Growth During the Neolithic," *Current Anthropology,* 14: 535-540.

1973c "The Sebilian of the Nile Valley: Some New Concepts," IXth International Congress of Anthropological and Ethnological Sciences, Chicago.

1974a *The Archaeology of the Dishna Plain.* Papers of the Geological Survey of Egypt, 59.

1974b "Population Growth and Cultural Evolution: A Review Essay of Population Growth: Anthropological Implications, ed. by Brian Spooner," in *Reviews in Anthropology,* ed. by Pelto and Pelto: 205-212.

1976 "Heavy Minerals and the Evolution of the Modern Nile," *Quaternary Research* 6: 425-444.

HASSAN, FEKRI, AND FRED WENDORF

1974 "A Sebilian Assemblage from El Kilh (Upper Egypt)," *CE,* 49: 211-221.

HASSANEIN BEY, A. M.

1924a "Crossing the Untraversed Libyan Desert," *National Geographic Magazine,* 46: 233-278.

1924b "Through Kufra to Darfur," *GJ,* 64: 273-291, 353-366.

1925 *The Lost Oases.* Century Co., New York.

HAYES, WILLIAM C.

1964 "Chronology: Egypt to the End of the Twentieth Dynasty," rev. ed. of *Cam-*

bridge Ancient History, Vol. I, Chapter VI. Cambridge University Press, New York.

1965 *Most Ancient Egypt* (ed. by Keith Seele). University of Chicago Press, Chicago.

HAYNES,

1882 "Discovery of Palaeolithic Flint Implements in Upper Egypt," *Memoirs of the American Academy of Arts and Sciences,* I: 357-361.

HAYS, T. R.

1975 "Neolithic Settlement of the Sahara as it Relates to the Nile Valley," in *Problems in Prehistory: North Africa and the Levant,* ed. by Fred Wendorf and Anthony Marks, SMU Press, Dallas: 193-201.

DE HEINZELIN, J.

1968 "Geological History of the Nile Valley in Nubia," in *The Prehistory of Nubia,* ed. by Fred Wendorf, Fort Burgwin and SMU Press, Vol. I: 19-35.

DE HEINZELIN, J.; P. HAESAERTS, AND F. VAN NOTEN

1969 "Géologie récente et préhistoire au Jebel Uweinat," *Africa-Tervuren,* 15: 120-125.

HEIZER, ROBERT F. (ED.)

1959 *The Archaeologist at Work.* Harper & Brothers, New York.

HELCK, W.

1971 *Die Beziehungen Ägyptens zu Vorderasien im 3. und 2. Jahrtausend v. Chr.,* 2nd ed., Ägyptologische Abhandlungen.

HESTER, T. R.; R. F. HEIZER, AND J. A. GRAHAM

1970 *Prehistoric Settlement Patterns in the Libyan Desert.* University of Utah Papers in Anthropology, no. 92, Nubia Series 4, University of Utah Press, Salt Lake City.

HESTER, T. R., R. F. HEIZER, AND J. A. GRAHAM

1975 *Field Methods in Archaeology,* 6th ed. Mayfield Publishing Co., Palo Alto, California.

HOEBEL, E. A.

1972 *Anthropology, The Study of Man.* McGraw-Hill, New York.

HOEBLER, P., AND J. HESTER

1969 "Prehistory and Environment in the Libyan Desert," *South African Archaeological Bulletin,* 33: 120-130.

HOFFMAN, MICHAEL A.

1970 *Culture History and Cultural Ecology at Hierakonpolis from Palaeolithic Times to the Old Kingdom.* Doctoral dissertation, University of Wisconsin, Madison.

1972a "Occupational Features at the Kom el Ahmar," *JARCE,* 9: 35-47.

1972b "Excavations at Locality 14," *JARCE,* 9: 49-74.

1974 "The Social Context of Trash Disposal in the Early Dynastic Egyptian Town," *American Antiquity,* 39: 35-50.

1976 "City of the Hawk—Seat of Egypt's Ancient Civilization," *Expedition,* 18: 32-41.

HORNEMANN, BODIL

1951–1969 *Types of Ancient Egyptian Sculpture,* 7 Vols. Munksgaard, Copenhagen.

HUOT, JEAN-LOUIS

1965 *Persia Volume One: From the Origins to the Achaemenids.* English translation by H. S. B. Harrison. World Publishing Company, Cleveland and New York.

HUZAYYIN, S. A.

1941 *The Place of Egypt in Prehistory: A Correlated Study of Climate and Cultures in the Old World.* MIE, Vol. XLIII, Cairo.

1952 "New Light on the Upper Palaeolithic of Egypt," *Proceedings of the Pan-African Congress on Prehistory, 1947,* Oxford: 202-204.

HUZAYYIN, S. A. (*continued*)

1953   "Recent Studies on the Technological Evolution of the Upper Palaeolithic of Egypt," Congrès International des Sciences Préhistoriques et Protohistoriques, Actes de la III° Session, Zürich, 1950. Zürich: 174-176.

ISSAWI, BAHAY

1976   "An Introduction to the Physiography of the Nile Valley," in *Prehistory of the Nile Valley*, ed. by Fred Wendorf and R. Schild, Academic Press, New York: 3-25.

IVERSON, ERIK

1955   *Canon and Proportions in Egyptian Art*. Sidgewick and Jackson, London.

JAGUTTIS-EMDEN, MARTIN

1977   *Zur Präzision archäologischer Datierung: Ein Experiment mit C 14-Daten des westlichen Mittelmeerraumes am Übergang Spätpleistozän/Holozän*. Verlag Archaeologica Venatoria, Institut für Urgeschichte der Universität Tübingen, Tübingen.

JUNKER, HERMANN

1928   "Bericht über die von der Akadamie der Wissenschaften in Wien nach dem Westdelta entsendete Expedition (20. Dezember 1927 bis 25. Februar 1928)," *Denkschrift Akadamie Wissenschaft Philosophische-historische Klasse*, 3: 14-24.

1929–   Vorläufiger Bericht über die Grabung der Akadamie der Wissenschaften in
1940   Wien auf der neolithischen Siedlung von Merimde-Benisalame (Westdelta)," *Anzeiger der Akadamie der Wissenschaften in Wien, Philosophische-historische Klasse*: 1929, XVI-XVIII: 156-250; 1930, V-XIII: 21-83; 1932, I-IV: 36-97; 1933, XVI-XXVII: 54-97; 1934, X: 118-132; 1940, I-V: 3-25.

1940   "Geisthaltung der Ägypter," *Anzeiger der Akadamie der Wissenschaften in Wien, Philosophische-historische Klasse*, I-V: 55-56.

KAISER, WERNER

1955   *Studien Zur Vorgeschichte Ägyptens*. Inaugral-Dissertation zur Erlangung der Doktorwürde der Philosophischen Fakultät der Ludwig-Maximilians-Universität zu München.

1956   "Stand und Problem der ägyptischen Vorgeschichtsforschung," *ZÄS*, LXXXI: 87-109.

1957   "Zur inneren Chronologie der Naqadakultur," *Archaeologia Geographica*, VI: 69-77.

1961   "Bericht über eine archäologisch-geologische Felduntersuchung in Ober- und Mittelägypten," *MDAIK*, 17: 1-53.

1963   "Einige Bemerkungen zur ägyptischen Frühzeit," *ZÄS*, 91: 86-125.

1974   *Studien zur Vorgeschichte Ägyptens: I, Die Naqadakultur*. Augustin, Gluckstadt.

KANAWATI, N.

1977   *The Egyptian Administration in the Old Kingdom*. London.

KANTOR, H.

1944   "The Final Phase of Predynastic Culture, Gerzean or Srmainean?" *JNES*, III: 110-136.

1947   "Review of Baumgartel (1947)," *AJA*, LIII: 76-79.

1952   "Further Evidence for Early Mesopotamian Relations with Egypt," *JNES*, XI: 239-250.

1965   "The Relative Chronology of Egypt and Its Foreign Correlations Before the Late Bronze Age," in *Chronologies in Old World Archaeology*, ed. by R. Ehrich, University of Chicago Press, Chicago.

KAPLAN, J.

1959   "The Connections of the Palestinian Chalcolithic Culture with Prehistoric Egypt," *Israel Exploration Journal*, IX: 134-136.

KAPLONY, P.

1963–1964 *Die Inschriften der ägyptischen Frühzeit*, 3 Vols. and supplement.

1964 Ägyptologische Abhandlungen.

KEES, HERMANN

1961 *Ancient Egypt: A Cultural Topography*. T. G. H. James, ed. Faber and Faber, London.

KEMP, BARRY

1968 "Merimda and the Theory of House Burial in Prehistoric Egypt," *CE*, 43: 22-33.

1966 "Abydos and the Royal Tombs of the First Dynasty," *JEA*, 52: 13-22.

1972 "Temple and Town in Ancient Egypt," in *Man, Settlement and Urbanism*, ed. by Ucko, Tringham, and Dimbleby, Duckworth, London: 657-680.

KLEINDIENST, M. R.

1967 "Brief Observations on Some Stone Age Sites Recorded by the Yale University Prehistoric Expedition to Nubia, 1964-1965," Congrès Panafricain de Préhistoire, Dakar: 111-112.

KRAELING, C., AND R. MCC. ADAMS (EDS.)

1960 *City Invincible: An Oriental Institute Symposium*. University of Chicago Press, Chicago.

LANSING, AMBROSIA

1935 "The Egyptian Expedition (at Hierakonpolis) 1934–1935," *Bulletin of the Metropolitan Museum of Art*, section II, November: 37-45.

LARSEN, HJALMAR

1958 "Eine eigenartige Tongefass-scherbe aus Merimde," *Orientalia Suecana*, 6: 3-8.

1959 "Verzierte Tomgefass-scherben aus Merimde Benisalame in der ägyptischen Abteilung des Mittelmeermuseums in Stockholm," *Orientalia Suecana*, 7: 3-53.

1960 "Knochengerate aus Merimde in der ägyptischen Abteilung der Mittelmeermuseums," *Orientalia Suecana*, 9: 28.

1962 "Die Merimdekeramik im Mittelmeermuseums Stockholm," *Orientalia Suecana*, 11: 3.

LAUER, J.-P.

1976 *Saqqara, The Royal Cemetery of Memphis*. Thames and Hudson, London.

LEAKEY, LOUIS S. B.

1936 *Stone Age of Africa*. Cambridge University Press, London.

LEAKEY, MARY

1971 *Olduvai Gorge III*.

LICHTHEIM, M.

1973 *Ancient Egyptian Literature, Vol. I, The Old and Middle Kingdoms*. University of California Press, Berkeley, California.

LUBELL, D.

1971 *The Fakhurian: A Late Paleolithic Industry from Upper Egypt and its Place in Nilotic Prehistory*. Doctoral dissertation, Columbia University, New York.

LUCAS, ALFRED, AND J. R. HARRIS

1962 *Ancient Egyptian Materials and Industries*, 4th ed. E. Arnold, London.

LYONS, H. S.

1910 "Introduction" in *The Archaeological Survey of Nubia, Report for 1907–1908*, Vol. I, by G. A. Reisner, pp. iii-v.

MACE, ARTHUR C.

1909 *The Early Dynastic Cemeteries at Naqa-ed-Der*, Part II. J. C. Hinrichs, Leipzig.

MACRAMALLAH, R.

1940 *Un Cimitière archaïque de la classe moyenne du peuple à Saqqarah*. Cairo.

MAITRE, J. P.

1971   *Contribution à la préhistoire de l'Ahaggar: I, Tédéfest centrale.* Mémoire Centre Recherches Anthropologie, Préhistoire, Etnographie, 17.

MARKS, ANTHONY E.

1968a   "The Halfan Industry," in *The Prehistory of Nubia*, Vol. I, ed. by Fred Wendorf, Fort Bergwin Research Center and SMU Press, Dallas: 393-460.

1968b   "The Khormusan: An Upper Pleistocene Industry in Sudanese Nubia," in *The Prehistory of Nubia*, Vol. I, ed. by Fred Wendorf: 315-391.

1968c   "The Mousterian Industries of Nubia," in *The Prehistory of Nubia*, Vol. I, ed. by Fred Wendorf: 194-314.

1968d   "The Sebilian Industry of the Second Cataract," in *The Prehistory of Nubia*, Vol. I, ed. by Fred Wendorf, Fort Bergwin Research Center and SMU Press, Dallas: 461-531.

1968e   "Survey and Excavations in the Dongola Reach," *Current Anthropology*, 9: 319-323.

MARKS, ANTHONY E.; J. L. SHINER; F. SERVELLO, AND F. MUNDAY

1970   "Preceramic Sites," in *The Scandinavian Joint Expedition to Sudanese Nubia*, Vol. 2, ed. by T. Säve-Söderbergh, Scandinavian University Books, Helsinki.

MASPERO, GASTON

1952   *Art in Egypt.* Scribner's, New York.

MASSOULARD, ÉMILE

1949   *Préhistoire et protohistoire de l'Égypte.* Travaux et mémoires de l'Institut d'ethnologie, Université de Paris, LIII, Paris.

MAUNY, R.

1966   "L'Afrique et les origines de la domestication," in *Background to Evolution in Africa*, ed. by W. W. Bishop and J. D. Clark, University of Chicago Press, Chicago.

MAUSS, MARCEL

1967   *The Gift.* Trans. by I. Cunnison, W. W. Norton, New York.

MCBURNEY, C. B. M.

1960   *The Stone Age of Northern Africa.* A Pelican Book, Harmondsworth, England.

1967   *The Haua Feah (Cyrenaica) and the Stone Age of the Southeast Mediterranean.* Cambridge University Press, Cambridge.

MCHUGH, WILLIAM P.

1971   *Late Prehistoric Cultural Adaptation in the Southeastern Libyan Desert.* Doctoral dissertation, University of Wisconsin, Madison, Wisconsin.

1974   "Late Prehistoric Cultural Adaptation in Southwest Egypt and the Problem of the Nilotic Origins of Saharan Cattle Pastoralism," *JARCE*, XI: 2-29.

1975   "Some Archaeological Results of the Bagnold-Mond Expedition to the Gilf Kebir and Gebel Uweinat, Southern Libyan Desert," *JNES*, 34: 31-62.

MEEK, CHARLES K.

1931   *A Sudanese Kingdom: An Ethnological Study of the Jukun-speaking People of Nigeria.* 2 Vols., Kegan Paul, London.

1949   *Land Law and Custom in the Colonies*, 2nd ed. Oxford University Press, London.

MENGHIN, OSWALD

1931   "Die Grabung der Universität Kairo bei Maadi," *MDAIK*, II: 143-147.

1932   "Die Grabung der Universität Kairo bei Maadi," *MDAIK*, III: 150-154.

1934a   "Die Grabung der Universität Kairo bei Maadi," *MDAIK*, V: 111-118.

1934b   "The Stone Ages of North Africa with Special Reference to Egypt," *BSGE*, XVIII.

1936   *Excavations of the Egyptian University in the Neolithic Site at Maadi, Second Preliminary Report (Season of 1932)*, Cairo.

1942   "El origen del pueblo del antiguo Egipto," *Ampurias*, IV: 25-41.

MENGHIN, OSWALD, AND MOUSTAFA AMER

1932 *Excavations of the Egyptian University in the Neolithic Site at Maadi, First Preliminary Report (Season of 1930–31),* Cairo.

METCALF, PETER, AND W. R. HUNTINGTON

1979 *Celebrations of Death.* Cambridge University Press, New York.

MIXONNE, X., AND F. VAN NOTEN

1969 "De rotsgraveringen en schilderingen van Uweinat," *Africa-Tervuren,* 14: 126-130.

MOND, SIR ROBERT, AND OLIVER H. MYERS

1937 *Cemeteries of Armant I.* 2 Vols., EES, Oxford University Press, London.

MONTET, A. M.

1957 "Les industries levalloisiennes d'Héliopolis et d'Abou Suweir (Égypte)," *BSPF,* LIV: 329-339.

MONTET, PIERRE

1957 *Géographie de l'Égypte ancienne, I: La Basse Egypte.* Impr. Nationale, Paris.

1961 *Géographie de l'Égypte ancienne, II: La Haute Egypte.* Libraire C. Klincksieck, Paris.

MORET, ALEXANDRE, AND G. DAVY

1926 *From Tribe to Empire: Social Organization Among Primitives and in the Ancient Near East.* Alfred A. Knopf, New York.

DE MORGAN, JACQUES

1896 *Recherches sur les origines de l'Égypte, I.* Leroux, Paris.

1897 *Recherches sur les origines de l'Égypte, II.* Leroux, Paris.

1906 *Les Recherches archéologique.* Paris.

MORIER, ALEXANDRE

1927 *The Nile and Egyptian Civilization.* Alfred A. Knopf, New York.

MURRAY, G. W.

1939 "An Archaic Hut in Wadi Umm Sidrah," *JEA,* XXIV.

1951 "The Egyptian Climate: An Historical Outline," *GJ,* CXVII: 422-434.

1955 "Water from the Desert: Some Ancient Egyptian Achievements," *GJ,* CXXI: 171-187.

MURRAY, M. A.

1920 "The First Mace-head of Hierakonpolis," *Ancient Egypt.* 15-17.

MYERS, OLIVER H.

1958 "Abka Re-excavated," *Kush,* 6: 131-141.

1960 "Abka Again," *Kush,* 8: 174-181.

NEWBOLD, D.

1928 "Rock-pictures and Archaeology in the Libyan Desert," *Antiquity,* 2: 261-291.

OBERMAIER, H.

1924 "Ägypten, A. Paläolithikum, 2," in *Realexikon der Vorgeschichte,* ed. by M. Ebert, I: 49-50.

O'CONNOR, DAVID

1927a "The Geography of Settlement in Ancient Egypt," in *Man, Settlement and Urbanism,* ed. by Ucko, Tringham, and Dimbleby, Duckworth, London: 681-698.

1972b "A Regional Population in Egypt to circa 600 B.C.," in *Population Growth: Anthropological Implications,* ed. by Brian Spooner, MIT Press, Cambridge, Massachusetts.

1974 "Political Systems and Archaeological Data in Egypt 2600-1700 B.C." *World Archaeology,* 6: 15-38.

O'CONNOR, DAVID, AND D. REDFORD (EDS.)

1977 *Ancient Egypt: Problems of History, Sources and Methods.* Aris and Phillips, Warminster, England.

PEEL, R. F.
1939 "Rock-paintings from the Libyan Desert," *Antiquity*, 13: 389-402.
PEET, T. ERIC
1914 *The Cemeteries of Abydos, Part II, 1911–1912.* EES, 34, London.
PEET, T. ERIC, AND W. L. S. LOAT
1913 *The Cemeteries of Abydos, Part III, 1912–1913.* EES, 35, London.
PENDLEBURY, J. D. S.
1930 *Aegyptiaca: A Catalogue of Egyptian Objects in the Aegean Area.* Cambridge University Press, Cambridge.
PERRY, WILLIAM J.
1923 *The Children of the Sun.* Methuen and Co., London.
1937 *The Growth of Civilisation.* Penguin Books, Harmondsworth, England.
PETRIE, SIR WILLIAM MATTHEWS FLINDERS
1891 *Ten Years Digging in Egypt, 1881–1891.*
1900 *The Royal Tombs of the First Dynasty, Part I.* Kegan Paul, Trench, Trübner and Co., London.
1901 *The Royal Tombs of the Earliest Dynasties, Part II.* Kegan Paul, Trench, Trübner and Co., London.
1902 *Abydos, Part I, 1902.* Kegan Paul, Trench, Trübner and Co. EES, 22, London.
1903 *Abydos, Part II, 1903.* Kegan Paul, Trench, Trübner and Co. EES, 24, London.
1920 *Prehistoric Egypt.* British School of Archaeology and Egyptian Research Account, Publ. no. 31, London.
1921 *Corpus of Prehistoric Pottery and Palettes.* British School of Archaeology, London.
1926 "Observations on 'The Recent Geology and Neolithic Industry of the Northern Fayum Desert' by Miss E. W. Gardner, M.A., F.R.G.S." *JRAI*, LVI: 325-327.
1932 *Seventy Years in Archaeology.* H. Holt & Co., New York.
1953 *Ceremonial Slate Palettes and Corpus of Protodynastic Pottery.* Quaritch, London.
PETRIE, SIR WILLIAM MATTHEWS FLINDERS, AND A. C. MACE
1901 *Diospolis Parva. The Cemeteries of Abadiyeh and Hu, 1898–1899.* Kegan Paul, Trench, Trübner and Co. EES, XX, London.
PETRIE, SIR WILLIAM MATTHEW FLINDERS, AND J. E. QUIBELL
1896 *Naqada and Ballas.* Quaritch, London.
PETRIE, W.M.F., G. A. WAINWRIGHT, AND E. MACKAY
1912 *The Labyrinth, Gerzeh and Mazguneh.* Quaritch, London.
PFEIFFER, JOHN
1976 *The Emergence of Society.* Harper & Row, New York.
PHILLIPS, JAMES L.
1970 "Ouevre récente sur L'Épipaléolithique de la Vallée du Nil: Rapport préliminaire," *L'Anthropologie*, 74: 573–581.
1972 "North Africa, the Nile Valley and the Problem of the Late Paleolithic," *Current Anthropology*, 13: 587–590.
1973 *Two Final Paleolithic Sites in the Nile Valley and their External Relations,* Papers of the Geological Survey of Egypt, 57, Cairo.
1975 "Iberomaurusian Related Sites in the Nile Valley," in *Problems in Prehistory: North Africa and the Levant,* ed. by Fred Wendorf and Anthony Marks, SMU Press, Dallas: 171–180.
PHILLIPS, JAMES L., AND KARL BUTZER
1973 "A 'Silsilian' Occupation Site (GS-2B-II) of the Kom Ombo Plain, Upper Egypt: Geology, Archeology and Paleo-Ecology," *Quaternaria*, XVII: 343-386.
PITT-RIVERS, AUGUSTUS
1882 "On the Discovery of Chert Implements in Stratified Gravel in the Nile Valley near Thebes," *JRAI*, XII: 382-400.

QUIBELL, J. E.
1900 *Hierakonpolis I.* ERA, IV, London.

QUIBELL, J. E., AND F. W. GREEN
1902 *Hierakonpolis II.* ERA, V, London.

RANDALL-MACIVER, D., AND A. C. MACE
1902 *El Amrah and Abydos, 1899–1901.* EES, XXIII, London.

RAWLINSON, GEORGE (TRANS.)
1932 *The History of Herodotus.* Tudor Pub., New York.

REDFIELD, ROBERT
1953 *The Primitive World and Its Transformation.* Cornell University Press, Ithaca, New York.

REILLY, FRANK E.
1964 *Guidebook to the Geology and Archaeology of Egypt.* Petroleum Exploration Society of Libya, Sixth Annual Field Conference.

REISNER, GEORGE ANDREW
1910 *The Archaeological Survey of Nubia, Report for 1907–1908.* 2 Vols. National Printing Department, Cairo.
1923 *Excavations at Kerma.* Vol. 5, Part 3, reprinted 1959 in *The Archaeologist at Work*, ed. by Robert F. Heizer. Harper & Brothers, New York.
1936 *The Development of the Egyptian Tomb Down to the Accession of Cheops.* Harvard University Press, Cambridge, Massachusetts.
1942 *A History of the Giza Necropolis, I.* Harvard University Press, Cambridge, Massachusetts.

REISNER, G. A.; G. E. SMITH, AND D. E. DERRY
1909 *The Archaeological Survey of Nubia, Bulletin 2.* National Printing Department, Cairo. "Preface" in *The Early Dynastic Cemeteries at Naqa-ed-Der*, Part II, by Arthur C. Mace. J. C. Hinrichs, Leipzig.

RENFREW, COLIN
1972 *The Emergence of Civilisation: The Cyclades and the Aegean in the Third Millennium B.C.* Methuen and Co., London.

RESCH, W. F. E.
1967 *Die Felsbilder Nubiens.* Akademische Druck- und Verlaganstalt, Graz.

RHOTERT, H.
1952 *Libysche Felsbilder.* Ergebnisse der XI und XII Deutschen Inner Afrikanischen Forschungs-Expedition (DIAFE) 1933/1934/1935, Wittich Verlag.

RIZKANA, I.
1952 "Centres of Settlement in Prehistoric Egypt in the Area between Helwan and Heliopolis," *Bulletin de l'Institut Fouad Ier du Désert*, II: 117-130.

ROSCOE, JOHN
1911 *The Baganda: An Account of Their Native Customs and Beliefs.* Macmillan, New York.

RUFFER, SIR MARK A.
1921 *Studies in the Paleopathology of Egypt.* Ed. by Roy Moodie, University of Chicago Press, Chicago.

SAAD, ZAKI Y.
1941–1945 *The Royal Excavations at Saqqara and Helwan.* Cairo.
1945–1947 *The Royal Excavations at Helwan.* Cairo.
1969 *The Excavations at Helwan: Art and Civilization in the First and Second Egyptian Dynasties.* University of Oklahoma Press, Norman, Oklahoma.

SAID, RUSHDI
1962 *The Geology of Egypt.* Elsevier Publ., Amsterdam and New York.
1975 "The Geological Evolution of the River Nile," in *Problems in Prehistory:*

SAID, RUSHDI (*continued*)
North Africa and the Levant, ed. by Fred Wendorf and Anthony Marks, SMU Press, Dallas: 7-44.

SAID, RUSHDI, AND F. YOUSRI
1968   "Origin and Pleistocene History of River Nile near Cairo, Egypt," *Bull. Inst. Egypte*, 45: 1-30.

SAID, RUSHDI; FRED WENDORF, AND R. SCHILD
1970   "The Geology and Prehistory of the Nile Valley in Upper Egypt," *Archaeologia Polona*, 12: 43-60.

SAID, RUSHDI; C. C. ALBRITTON; F. WENDORF; R. SCHILD, AND M. KOBUSIEWICZ
1972   "Remarks on the Holocene Geology and Archaeology of Northern Fayum Desert," *Archaeologia Polona*, 13: 7-22.

SANDFORD, K. S.
1933   "Past Climate and Early Man in the Southern Libyan Desert," *GJ*, 82: 219-222.
1934   *Prehistoric Survey of Egypt and Western Asia, Upper Egypt and Middle Egypt*. OIP, XVIII, University of Chicago Press, Chicago.

SANDFORD, K. S., AND W. J. ARKELL
1928   *First Report of the Prehistoric Survey Expedition*. OIR, no. 3, University of Chicago Press, Chicago.
1929   *Prehistoric Survey of Egypt and Western Asia, Palaeolithic Man and the Nile-Fayum Divide*. OIP, X, University of Chicago Press, Chicago.
1933   *Prehistoric Survey of Egypt and Western Asia, Palaeolithic Man and the Nile Valley in Nubia and Upper Egypt*. OIP, XVII, University of Chicago Press, Chicago.
1939   *Prehistoric Survey of Egypt and Western Asia, Lower Egypt*. OIP, XLVI, University of Chicago Press, Chicago.

SÄVE-SÖDERBERGH, TORGNY
1961   "Preliminary Report of the Scandinavian Joint Expedition: Archaeological Survey between Faras and Gamai," *Kush*, X: 84-85.
1970   *The Scandinavian Joint Expedition to Sudanese Nubia*. Scandinavian University Books, Helsinki.

SCHARFF, ALEXANDER
1926   *Das vorgeschichte Gräberfeld von Abusir-Meleg*. Leipzig.
1927   "Grundzüge der aegyptischen Vorgeschichte," *Morgenland*, 12, Leipzig.
1931   "Die Altertümer der Vor- und Fruhzeit Ägyptens," *Mitteilungen aus der ägyptischen Sammlung*, IV, 1, Staatliche Museen zu Berlin.
1944–1946   "Das Grab als Wohnhaus in der ägyptischen Frühzeit," *Sitzungsber. Bay. Akad. d. Wissensch., Phil.-hist. Klasse, Jahrgang 1944/46*, Heft 6.

SCHILD, ROMUALD, AND FRED WENDORF
1975   "New Explorations in the Egyptian Sahara," in *Problems in Prehistory: North Africa and the Levant*, ed. by Fred Wendorf and Anthony Marks, SMU Press, Dallas: 65-112.

SCHILD, ROMUALD; M. CHMIELEWSKI, AND H. WIECKOWSKA
1968   "The Arkinian and Sharmarkian Industries," in *The Prehistory of Nubia*, Vol. II, ed. by Fred Wendorf, Fort Bergwin Research Center and SMU Press, Dallas: 651-767.

SCHWEINFURTH, GEORG
1886   "Reise in das Depressiongebiet im Umkreise der Fayum," *Zeitschrift der Gesellschaft für Erdkunde zu Berlin*, XXI.
1902   "Kissel-Artefacte in der diluvialen Schutter-Terrasse und auf den Plateau-Höhen von Theban," *ZE*, XXXIV: 293-310.
1903   "Steinzeitliche Forschungen in Ober Aegypten," *ZE*, XXXV: 799-822.
1904   "Steinzeitliche Forschungen in Ober Aegypten," *ZE*, XXXVI: 766-830.
1905   "Recherches sur l'age de la pierre dans la Haute-Égypte," *ASAE*, V.

1909 "Uber Altpalaeolithische Manufakte aus dem Sandsteingebiet von Ober Aegypten," *ZE*, XLI: 735.

1912 "Steinzeitliche Forschungen in Ober Aegypten," *ZE*, XLIV: 627-658.

SELIGMAN, CHARLES G.

1921 "The Older Palaeolithic Age in Egypt," *JRAI*, LI: 115-153.

1934 *Egypt and Negro Africa: A Study in Divine Kingship.* Routledge & Kegan Paul, London.

SHAW, W. B. K.

1936a "An Expedition in the Southern Libyan Desert," *GJ*, 87: 193-221.

1936b "Rock Paintings in the Libyan Desert," *Antiquity*, 10: 175-178.

SHINER, J. L.

1968a "The Cataract Tradition," in *The Prehistory of Nubia*, II, ed. by Fred Wendorf, Fort Bergwin Research Center and SMU Press, Dallas: 535-629.

1968b "The Khartoum Variant Industry," in *The Prehistory of Nubia*, II, ed. by Fred Wendorf, Fort Bergwin Research Center and SMU Press, Dallas: 768-790.

SIIRIANEN, ARI

1965 "The Wadi Halfa Region (Northern Sudan) in the Stone Age," *Studia Orientalia*, 30: 3-34.

SMITH, GRAFTON ELLIOT

1931 "The Influence of Ancient Egyptian Civilisation in the East and in America," in *The Making of Man*, ed. by V. F. Calverton, The Modern Library, New York: 393-420.

SMITH, GRAFTON ELLIOT, AND WARREN R. DAWSON

1924 *Egyptian Mummies.* G. Allen & Unwin, London.

SMITH, H. S.

1964 "Egypt and C-14 Dating," *Antiquity*, XXXVIII: 32-37 .

1971 "Walter Brian Emery," *JEA*, 57: 190-201.

1972 "Society and Settlement in Ancient Egypt," in *Man, Settlement and Urbanism*, ed. by Ucko, Tringham, and Dimbleby, Duckworth, London: 705-720.

SMITH, P. E. L.

1964a "Expedition to Kom Ombo," *Archaeology*, 17: 209-210.

1964b "Radiocarbon Dating of a Late Paleolithic Culture from Egypt," *Science*, 145: 811.

1966 "The Late Paleolithic of Northeast Africa in the Light of Recent Research," in *Recent Studies of Paleoanthropology*, American Anthropologist, Special Publication, 68,2,2: 326-355.

1967 "New Investigations in the Late Pleistocene Archaeology of the Kom Ombo Plain (Upper Egypt)," *Quaternaria*, 9: 141-152.

1968 *A Revised View of the Later Paleolithic of Egypt.* Éditions du Centre National de la Recherche Scientifique, Paris.

SMITH, WILLIAM S.

1952 *Ancient Egypt as Represented in the Museum of Fine Arts, Boston.* 3rd ed. Museum of Fine Arts, Boston.

1958 *The Art and Architecture of Ancient Egypt.* Penguin Books, Harmondsworth, England.

SPOONER, BRIAN (ED.)

1972 *Population Growth: Anthropological Implications.* MIT Press, Cambridge, Massachusetts.

STERNS, F. H.

1917 "The Paleoliths of the Eastern Desert," *Harvard African Studies*, I: 48-82.

STEWARD, JULIAN

1955 *Theory of Culture Change: The Methodology of Multilinear Evolution.* University of Illinois Press, Urbana, Illinois.

STEWART H. M.

1978   *Egyptian Stelae, Reliefs and Paintings in the Petrie Collection Part II: Archaic to Second Intermediate Period.* London.

TIXIER, J.

1963   *Typologie de l'épipaléolithique du Maghreb.* Mémoires du Centre de Recherches Anthropologiques, Préhistoriques et Ethnologiques Alger, Paris.

TOUSSOUN, OMAR

1932   "Note sur les déserts de l'Égypte," *BIE*, 8-10: 14, 189, 202.

TRIGGER, BRUCE G.

1965   *History and Settlement in Lower Nubia.* Yale University Publications in Anthropology, 69, New Haven.

1976   *Nubia Under the Pharaohs.* Westview Press, Boulder, Colorado.

1977   "Egypt and the Comparative Study of Early Civilizations," in *Ancient Egypt: Problems of History, Sources and Methods,* ed. by O'Connor and Redford.

UCKO, P. J.; R. TRINGHAM, AND G. W. DIMBLEBY (EDS.)

1972   *Man, Settlement and Urbanism.* Duckworth and Co., London.

VAN DER MEER, P. E.

1947   *The Ancient Chronology of Western Asia and Egypt.* E. J. Brill, Leiden.

VANDIER, J.

1952   *Manuel d'archéologie égyptienne I,* A. Jean Piccard, Paris.

VERMEERSCH, P.

1969a   "Een Epipaleolithische Industrie te Elkab (Opper Egypte)," *Bull. Soc. Roy. Belge. Anthrop. Prehist.,* 80: 227-241.

1969b   "Les Fouilles d'Elkab," *ZDMG,* XVII: 32-38.

1970   "L'Elkabien: Une nouvelle industrie épipaléolithique Elkab en Haute Égypte: sa stratigraphie, sa typologie," *CE,* XLV, 89: 45-68.

1974   "Three New Epipaleolithic Sites at Elkab (Upper Egypt): A Preliminary Report," mimeographed report, courtesy of the author.

VIGNARD, E.

1921a   "Une station aurignacienne à Nag-Hamadi (Haute Égypte): Station du Champ du Bagasse," *BIFAO,* XVIII: 1-20.

1921b   "Les stations paléolithiques d'Abou del Nour a Nag-Hamadi," *BIFAO,* XIX.

1922   "Stations paléolithiques de la carrière d'Abou el-Nour pres Nag-Hamadi (Haute Égypte)," *BIFAO,* XX: 89-109.

1923   "Une nouvelle industrie lithique: le 'Sébilien'," *BIFAO,* XXII: 1-76.

1928   "Une nouvelle industrie lithique: le 'Sébilien'," *BSPF,* XXV: 200-220.

1929   "Station aurignacienne de Champ de Bagasse a Nag-Hamadi (Haute Égypte)," *BSPF,* XXVI: 199-306.

1934a   "Les microburins Tardenoisiens du Sébilien: fabrication; emplois; origine du microburin," Extrait du Congrès préhistorique de France, X^e session: 66-106.

1934b   *Le Paléolithique en Égypte.* Mémoires de L'Institut Francais d'Archaéologie Orientale, 66: 165-175.

1935   "Le Microburin est-il Sébilien?" *BSPF,* 32.

1935–1938   "Le paléolithique en Égypte," *BIFAO,* LXVI (Mélanges Maspero I): 165–175.

1947   "Une station sébilien III, a Reggen Taourirt, dans le Tanzerouft, Sahara Central," *BSPF,* 44: 293-313.

1955a   "Menchia, une station aurignacienne dans le nord de la plaine de Kom Ombo (Haute Égypte)," Congrès Préhistorique de France, XIVe session: 634-653, Strasbourg.

1955b   "Un Kjoekkenmodding sur la rive droit du Wadi-Shait dans le nord de la plaine de Kom Ombo (Haute Égypte)," *BSPF,* 52: 703-708.

1955c   "Le Levalloisien du Guebel-Silsile . . . ," *BSPF,* LII: 214-218.

1955d "Les stations et industries sébiliennes du Burg el Makkazin, Region de Kom Ombo (Haute Égypte)," *BSPF*, 52: 436-452.

1956 "Les stations de taile de la plaine nord-est de Kom Ombo (Haute Égypte)," *BSPF*, 53: 588-598.

1957 "Pointe de vue nouveau sur l'industrie du Champ de Bagasse de Nag Hamadi (Haute Égypte)," *BSPF*, 54: 298-313.

WADDELL, W. G.

1948 *Manetho*. Heinemann, London.

WEIL, RAYMOND

1961 *Recherches sur la Iʳᵉ dynastie et les temps Prépharaoniques*. 2 Vols., Institut Français d'Archéologie Orientale, Cairo.

WENDORF, FRED (ED.)

1965 *Contributions to the Prehistory of Nubia*. Fort Bergwin Research Center and SMU Press, Dallas.

1968 *The Prehistory of Nubia* (2 vols. and atlas), Fort Bergwin Research Center and SMU Press, Dallas.

WENDORF, FRED, AND ANTHONY MARKS (EDS.)

1975 *Problems in Prehistory: North Africa and the Levant*, Southern Methodist University Press, Dallas.

WENDORF, FRED, AND RUSHDI SAID

1967 "Paleolithic Remains in Upper Egypt," *Nature*, 215: 244-247.

WENDORF, FRED, AND ROMUALD SCHILD

1973 "The Use of Ground Grain during the Late Paleolithic of the Lower Nile Valley, Egypt," IXth International Congress of Anthropological and Ethnological Sciences, Chicago.

1975 "The Paleolithic of the Lower Nile Valley," in *Problems in Prehistory: North Africa and the Levant*, ed. by Fred Wendorf and Anthony Marks, SMU Press, Dallas: 127-170.

1976a "Archaeology and Pleistocene Stratigraphy of the Northern Fayum Depression," in *Prehistory of the Nile Valley*, ed. by Fred Wendorf and Romuald Schild, Academic Press, New York: 155-226.

1976b *Prehistory of the Nile Valley*. Academic Press, New York.

1977 "The Middle Paleolithic of the Lower Nile Valley and the Adjacent Desert," in *Papers of the IX Congrès International des Sciences Préhistoriques et Protohistoriques*, ed. by H. de Lumley, Nice.

WENDORF, FRED *et al.*

1976 "The Prehistory of the Egyptian Sahara," *Science*, 193: 103-114.

1977 "Late Pleistocene and Recent Climatic Changes in the Egyptian Sahara," *GJ*, 143: 211-234.

WENDORF, FRED; R. SAID, AND R. SCHILD

1970 "Egyptian Prehistory: Some New Concepts," *Science* 169: 1161-1171.

WENDT, E.

1966 "Two Prehistoric Archaeological Sites in Egyptian Nubia," *Postilla*, 102: 1-46.

WHEATLEY, PAUL

1971 *Pivot of the Four Quarters*. Aldine Publishing Co., Chicago.

1972 "The Concept of Urbanism," in *Man, Settlement and Urbanism*, ed. by Ucko, Tringham, and Dimbleby, Duckworth, London.

WILSON, JOHN A.

1951 *The Burden of Egypt* (republished as *The Culture of Ancient Egypt*). University of Chicago Press, Chicago.

1955 "Buto and Hierakonpolis in the Geography of Egypt," *JNES*, XIV: 209-236.

1960 "Civilization Without Cities," in *City Invincible*, ed. by C. Kraeling and R. McC. Adams, University of Chicago Press, Chicago.

WILSON, JOHN A. (*continued*)

1964 *Signs and Wonders Upon Pharaoh: A History of American Egyptology.* University of Chicago Press, Chicago.

1971 *The Culture of Ancient Egypt.* University of Chicago Press, Chicago (first publ. as *The Burden of Egypt,* 1951).

1972 *Thousands of Years.* Scribner's, New York.

WINKLER, H. A.

1938 *Rock-Drawings of Southern Upper Egypt, I.* EES, London.

1939 *Rock-Drawings of Southern Upper Egypt, II (including 'Uweinat).* EES, London.

WITTFOGEL, KARL

1938 "Die Theorie der Orientalischen Gesellschaft," *Zeitschrift für Socialforschung,* 7: 90-122.

1957 *Oriental Despotism: A Comparative Study of Total Power.* Yale University Press, New Haven, Connecticut.

WORTHAM, JOHN DAVID

1971 *The Genesis of British Egyptology.* University of Oklahoma Press, Norman, Oklahoma.

YEIVIN, S.

1960 "Early Contacts between Canaan and Egypt," *Israel Exploration Journal,* X: 193-203.

1963 "Further Evidence for Narmer at 'Gat,'" *Oriens Antiquus,* II: 205-213.

ZIEGLER, ALAN C.

1975 "Recovery and Significance of Unmodified Faunal Remains," in *Field Methods in Archaeology* by T. R. Hester *et al.* Mayfield Publishing Co., Palo Alto, California.

INDEX

Abadiyeh, 109, 148
Abbassia Pluvial, 57–8
Abkan sites, 242
Abu Simbel, 48
Abydos
  prehistoric graves, 150–4
  royal tombs, 124, 267–75; Amélineau and Petrie, 267–9, 298; burial trenches, 274–5; cenotaph controversy, 284–7, 335–6; human sacrifice, 275–9; inscriptions and labels, 270–2, 287, 290, 292, 294–8; Khasekhemui's tomb, 274, 349; table, 270; valley temples, 274–5, 279, 287, 349, 353
Acheulean period
  Dungul Oasis sites—dating of, 58
  hand axes, 48, 56
Adams, Barbara, 301–2
Adams, William Y., 253
Aegyptopithecus, 182
Afghanistan, trade with, 293–4
Africa
  British and French colonialism, 36; cultural lag question, 65–6; Olduvai findings and earliest man, 49–52; trade with Old Kingdom Egypt, 283; see also East Africa; North Africa, Nubia
Agriculture, see Farming and herding societies; Food and diet; Grains and grasses
Aha, King, 296, 298, 317
Ain Doua paintings, 237
Alabaster bowls and discs, 203, 274, 282
Alluvium, 24, 27, 131
Amélineau, E., 284, 299

excavation methods, 125, 268–9, 276, 282; and museum collections, 252, 301
Amer, Mustafa, 200, 202, 210–11
American Museum of Natural History Expedition to Hierakonpolis, 4, 130–1
Amratian period (Naqada I), Upper Egypt
  chronology, 16–17, 121; copper tools, 207; pottery, 120–59
Amulets, 110, 143, 154
Animals, see Cattle pastoralism; Donkeys; Faunal remains; Hunting and gathering societies
Archaeological industries, definition of, 70; see also names of sites
Archaic Egypt (Emery), 298
Archaic period (Early Dynastic) (ca. 3100–2700 B.C.)
  agriculture and distribution, 317–19; cenotaph controversy, 280, 284–7; centralization of power, 152, 279, 289–305; chronology, table, 15, 15n; environmental changes, 311–12; and human sacrifice, 272, 275–9; and Khasekhemui, 348–54; language and symbols, 290–8; population concentration, 306–10; powerfacts, 316–17; royal patronage, 321; royal tombs, Abydos and Saqqara, 268–83; technological changes, 312–16; trade, 338–40
Architecture, 17
  Archaic, Khasekhemui's tomb, 348–50; cattle corrals, nomads, 205–6; fortlike mortuary temples, 275, 351–3; Hierakonpolis, 131–2,

A NOTE
ABOUT THE AUTHOR

Professor Michael A. Hoffman has followed a career in
archaeology and anthropology since his earliest years as an
undergraduate. He received his B.A. in anthropology from the
University of Kentucky in 1966, and earned his Ph.D. from the
University of Wisconsin in 1970. He has participated in
archaeological excavations in Egypt, Turkey, Afghanistan, Norway,
Germany, Pakistan, Cyprus, Virginia, and Kentucky. In 1978 he
returned to Egypt as project prehistorian of the Hierakonpolis
Expedition, where he unearthed the oldest substantial architecture
yet found there and began the first careful mapping and
excavation of that Predynastic town.

Professor Hoffman is the director of an innovative study
of the prehistoric and historic remains of the Shenandoah
National Park in the Blue Ridge Mountains of Virginia on behalf
of the U.S. National Park Service. He has taught in the school of
Architecture of the University of Virginia and resides in
Colonial Beach, Virginia.

A NOTE
ABOUT THE TYPE

The text of this book was set in Palatino, a typeface designed
by the noted German typographer Herman Zapf. Named after
Giovambattista Palatino, a writing master of Renaissance Italy,
Palatino was the first of Zapf's typefaces to be introduced
to America. The first designs for the face were made in 1948,
and the fonts for the complete face were issued between
1950 and 1952. Like all Zapf-designed typefaces, Palatino is
beautifully balanced and exceedingly readable.